First published in Great Britain 1993 by Cavendish Publishing Limited, 23A Countess Road, London NW5 2XH.

Telephone: 071-485 0303   Facsimile: 071-485 0304

British Library Cataloguing in Publication Data

Smith, Raymond
Conflict of Laws
I Title
340.9

ISBN 1-874241-85-6

Printed and bound in Great Britain

PREFACE

In the momentous transformation of English law from common law rule to regulation, the Conflict of Laws has, until the last few years, remained as one of the few areas of law largely untouched by the tide. No longer. The last half-dozen years have witnessed dramatic changes: the entry into force of the Jurisdiction Conventions; the implementation of the Rome Convention on contracts; the Hague Convention on trusts. Torts, too, may soon be put onto a statutory basis, and, possibly, the law of domicile as well.

The increasing pressure from within the E.C. for the harmonisation of laws will have an increasing impact on private litigation as Brussels planners shift from the regulation of sausage meat and the designation of fruit to the control of substantive private rights. Not without struggle will irksome idiosyncrasies of national laws give way to the planners' straight lines and, while those differences remain, there will be a need for conflict resolution even within the Single Market. In the wider world, the increasing expansion of trade and travel will continue to supply English courts with cases which involve connections with foreign legal systems.

This book aims to introduce the subject of Conflict of Laws to those who are new to it and to reintroduce it to those who have not kept up with the changes that the last few years have brought. Inevitably with a subject in transition the treatment will be influenced by the old and the new and the mix may not suit everyone. Inevitably too, in a small compass, some things are treated in more detail than others and some matters are mentioned only that their existence should be known.

I have attempted to include the main areas of undergraduate and other courses but at the expense of some important areas which are barely touched upon or altogether ignored – maritime matters, negotiable instruments and issues of corporate law and insurance are the main victims of the coat cutting.

I have tried to state things as they stand on 1st June 1993.

Raymond Smith
The Law School
The University of Hull

i

CONTENTS

TABLE OF STATUTES

TABLE OF CASES

CHAPTER 1

INTRODUCTION

1 THE TASK OF THE CONFLICT OF LAWS

This book is about the problems which arise when one legal system **1-01**
has to deal with the legal rules of another, in matters of private rights.
More particularly, because the ultimate test of the recognition of foreign
law is what courts do about it. The book is concerned with how a court
sitting in one country treats a case of private litigation in which the
parties, the events or the circumstances demonstrate connections with
one or more legal systems foreign to the court. The issue can arise in
multifarious ways. An ordinary, apparently purely domestic, case may be
found to have a significant connection with a foreign legal system. A
case with obvious contacts with one country may happen to be litigated
in another because the plaintiff finds some advantage in bringing an
action there or the defendant cannot be made subject to the jurisdiction
of the country with which the case is, legally, most closely connected. A
case may be so genuinely international that it would be a foreign case in
any court.

This book is about the English conflict of laws in the sense that it **1-02**
looks specifically at English law's responses to the problems raised. Just as
the conflict of laws exists because there are differences in systems of
municipal law, so there are differences in the approaches that legal
systems take to solving problems in the conflict of laws. The English
conflict of laws is, thus, as distinctive as any other area of English law.
Even among societies with a common legal tradition, differences in
domestic law are mirrored in different approaches to conflict
adjudication. As between societies with very different legal traditions, the
differences both in domestic law and in conflict law are more marked.
Thus, while the *raison d'être* of the conflict of laws is the differences in
municipal legal systems, the solution of conflict problems is, itself,
reflective of those differences.

There are several possible responses which a court can make when **1-03**
faced with a case having foreign contacts. Firstly, and most primitively, it
can treat the case as a purely domestic one and apply its own law to its
resolution regardless of the foreign element. There are more and less
sophisticated versions of this approach. The less sophisticated version
merely turns a blind eye to the foreign aspects of the case and treats it in

all respects as a domestic one even to the extent of applying local technical rules which can have no possible relevance to the foreign aspects of the case. The more sophisticated version would recognise that there are special aspects to the case which make the application of technical rules of domestic regulation inappropriate and would, therefore, not apply them, but would make no further concessions to the foreign dimension of the litigation. The injustice that such an approach can produce is easily demonstrated. A plaintiff who has no ground of complaint by any law connected with the defendant's actions can create a right for himself by selecting a forum which applies a law which gives him one. The process of forum shopping will be considered later,[1] but an illustration of it now will make the point. In *Machado v. Fontes*[2] the English court allowed a plaintiff's claim for libel although the document complained of was written in Portuguese and published solely in Brazil whose law provided no civil remedy in such cases.

Secondly, a court could take the view that its processes are inappropriate for a case with foreign contacts and refuse to adjudicate upon it. There are more and less sophisticated versions of this approach as well. The less sophisticated version would simply have the court close its doors to the alien case on the assumption that there was a foreign court somewhere where the case could find a home. The "sorting office" concept of conflict resolution is false because it presupposes that every dispute has a natural home to go to where the local courts can dispose of it by the application of domestic law. In reality, of course, the more significant conflict problems will transcend national boundaries, will be truly multi–contact, and will have no "natural home" in any legal system anywhere in the world. The more sophisticated version would recognise this truth but would seek to ensure that national courts took jurisdiction only when they were, in their own eyes, the appropriate forum or, at least, not an inappropriate one. The doctrines of *forum conveniens* and *forum non-conveniens* have received much attention in recent years and constitute a retreat from the traditional open forum policy of English courts.[3]

The remaining possibility, and the one with which this book is concerned, is that the court recognises that cases with foreign contacts cannot simply be turned away, and that they are special in the sense that they pose particular problems which demand serious treatment. The basic principle of justice – that like cases should be treated alike and different cases differently – precludes the unreflective application of domestic law to

---

1   See below para 8-25.
2   [1897] 2 QB 231.
3   See below para 3-08.

a case which is manifestly not domestic. To what extent these differences should be recognised and how far a court should go in the accommodation of foreign interests is a subject of considerable contention.

2 WHY BOTHER?

Why should the forum not simply apply its own law to the determination of the case before it, without regard to the foreign connections it might have, and have done with it? After all it will dispose of most cases, even those with international connections where the foreign legal contact is not pleaded or not proved, by the application of its own domestic rules, so why make exceptions? There are several answers to this question at various levels of philosophical generality and practical convenience.

1-04

Starting from a mundane proposition, it would clearly be intolerable if a married couple on holiday abroad found that neither their marriage nor their property rights were recognised, as the former had been celebrated and the latter acquired in circumstances which would not have produced these effects according to the domestic law of the country being visited. This is too obvious to require further elaboration but it does not take us to any further proposition about how and on what basis the problem should be resolved.

1-05

If the uncritical application of the court's own law, the *lex fori*, cannot be justified, as it clearly cannot, then a reason which is not purely pragmatic ought to be available, not only to justify the departure from the *lex fori*, for that is inevitable, but to indicate how that ought to be done – but here we have the failure of theory. The attempts which have been made to justify departure are not very convincing largely because they start from the wrong place. There is no theoretical basis for preferring the *lex domicilii* or the law of the habitual residence to the *lex patriae* as the determinant of personal status though there is a heap of practical ones. Equally there are no theoretical reasons for particular choice of law rules save that some are seen as better fitted than others for the task at hand.

As we shall see in Chapter Two there is only a limited number of possible connections which a jurisdiction-selecting approach can utilise in identifying the *lex causae*, and the choice among them depends on their practical use in getting to the legal system which appears to be the most suitable for the particular issue in hand.

For the moment, then, it can be said that English law engages in the conflict process because it would be unjust to treat an international case as a domestic one and apply to it the rules of domestic law in disregard of other legal systems which are clearly connected to the case and may have

1-06

a proper interest in its solution. It would be wrong to treat parties, who have acted under one legal system, as if they had acted under another and to make their rights and status depend on the accident of the forum.

1-07   It would be comfortable to suggest that the object of the conflict enterprise was to produce uniformity; to ensure that wherever a case was brought the same result would follow. Certainly, such an aspiration has been influential in the development of conflict rules. But although the subject is sometimes called Private International Law, it remains centred on domestic legal systems whose differences prevent uniform results. It may be harsh that a right under one system is not accepted under another, or that a remedy, available in one system, is not available or, if available, is worth less, under another, or that there are "limping marriages" where the parties are regarded as married by one system of law but not by another. But, without uniformity in domestic systems, such results are inevitable. The task of the conflict of laws is to minimise such discrepancies and to ensure that, where they cannot be avoided, there is some rational basis for the result.

3   THE MECHANICS

1-08   A legal system which decides to take cases with foreign connections seriously has several jobs to do. Cheshire described these as the consecutive stages in an action involving the conflict of laws but made the point that they are not adverted to in every case nor are they dealt with in the logical order he set out. They are,

- *jurisdiction*
- *classification*
- *choice of law*
- *application of law.*

    Each of these will be examined briefly here and developed later.

    We need to add a further task; that is the establishment of rules for the recognition and, if necessary, the enforcement of foreign judgments and other legal acts.

Jurisdiction[4]

1-09   Legal systems have rules governing the ways in which their courts can be used. The rules deal with the manner in which proceedings can be

---

[4]   See below Chapter 3.

brought and also with such questions as "Can the plaintiff invoke the assistance of the court?", "Has the court authority over the defendant?", "Has the court the power to determine the issue?", "Must the court exercise the power or may it decline to do so?". These rules will, generally, have been formulated with the domestic case in mind and it will be necessary to consider how far the same facilities and obstacles should apply to cases that are not entirely domestic. For example, a country may have very lax rules over personal jurisdiction and may, as does English law, allow jurisdiction to be invoked in an ordinary action for breach of obligation by the mere service of process on the defendant or on his agent in England.[5] If a defendant may be made subject to a jurisdiction simply by being there, with no requirement of any other connection with the county and possibly with no assets there, it may be found that plaintiffs, who also have no connection with the county, are bringing actions there simply because of the ease of process. Now the practice of forum-shopping,[6] as it is known, is not necessarily objectionable, but it may be. Thus every domestic system must decide how far its rules should be amended, if at all, to restrict the availability of its processes. Similarly, a court system has to decide whether or not its processes should be open to all or restricted in some way with regard to the identity of those who can invoke it and of those against whom it can be invoked. English law does not restrict plaintiffs on personal grounds, save for those who have been declared vexatious litigants or who are "alien enemies", but it does restrict those against whom actions can be brought in the recognition, for example, of diplomatic immunities[7] and international conventions.[8]

Another issue here relates to the types of actions which may be brought. Should a court permit a case to be brought before it where the plaintiff seeks to enforce an exotic right unknown to the domestic law? Should a defence be allowed only if it would be allowable in a domestic case? Are there some types of cases which, though perfectly acceptable in domestic litigation, should not be entertained if they involve foreigners or foreign property? How far should the court go in asserting its own national policy? Let us take a few examples from English law; an English court will not currently allow an action based on a tort committed abroad to be litigated here unless the wrong complained of would have constituted a tort by domestic English law.[9] English courts will not

---

[5] See below para 3-05.

[6] See below para 8-25.

[7] See below para 3-12.

[8] Notably the Brussels and Lugano Conventions see below Chapter 3.

[9] See below para 4-108.

generally entertain actions involving rights to foreign immovable property.[10] While it is obvious that an English court will not allow a claim which fundamentally offends English morality it is not so clear when an English court should apply other aspects of domestic policy to exclude claims founded upon foreign law.[11]

Classification[12]

1-10   Legal systems work on the basis of categories. It is necessary for many purposes to put an issue into a particular box. In many instances the categorisation will be so obvious as to be automatic. A buyer's claim against the seller that the thing he bought does not work as it is supposed to, is so obviously a contractual issue that any court or lawyer dealing with it would not even advert to the classification process before turning to the law of contract to seek the solution. But if the malfunction causes injury or damages property, or if the complainant is not the buyer of the product but the user of it, either the initial classification has to be amended in some way or the situation seen as something else entirely – a tort perhaps or the subject of a statutory action.

To take other examples: whether the worker injured in the course of his employment sues his employer in tort or brings an action on the implied terms of his contract of employment (that the employer will take reasonable care to provide him with a safe system of work) may be no more than a conventional practice which has little to do with the nature of the relationship and much to do with traditional views of the proper scope of the conceptual categories of the domestic legal system. Is the deserted wife's claim to an interest in the matrimonial home a matrimonial right against the husband or a property right against all the world or both of these?

1-11   In the conflict of laws it is necessary to review the domestic categories to assess their suitability for dealing with foreign ideas and institutions. To take a simple example, every society has a concept of marriage for its own domestic purposes. That concept may be very technical and specific including, for example, rules about the age at which parties can marry, listing the prohibited degrees of marriage, providing detailed regulations for the conduct of marriage ceremonies and the like. Now it is obvious that different societies are going to have different attitudes to these questions and, unless it is intended to exclude foreign marriages altogether, some accommodation must be found for foreign ways of

---

[10] See below para 5-09.
[11] See below para 7-05.
[12] See below para 8-10.

doing things. At the same time, however, a domestic system will not want to give up all controls and will be reluctant to take a completely *laissez-faire* attitude and simply say "whatever goes for marriage in Ruritania will be accepted here". Between restricting marriages entirely to the domestic concept and the "anything goes" policy there is a position which will preserve the fundamental interests of the recognising system and yet show proper respect for foreign institutions. There is a need for answers to questions such as: will a monogamous society accept a foreign institution of polygamy and for what purposes? Is there an age below which it would be intolerable to accept that a party can be allowed to enter into marriage? Is a foreign prohibition on marriage between people of different races, castes or religions to be accepted?

The extension of the domestic categories which every system of conflict adjudication demands, requires a solution of these fundamental political issues (political in the sense of involving policy decisions) and the concept which emerges from the process will be determinative of many matters. To take a simple example, if one society, being monogamous itself, insists on framing its concept of marriage for conflict purposes to exclude polygamy, then it is defining as outside its recognition all polygamous relationships whatever any other system of law has to say about them, and whatever hardship such a characterisation will inflict on the polygamously married.

One final example here of the classification issue in both domestic and conflict law and the matter can be left for further consideration later.[13] Suppose a long standing cohabitational relationship between a man and a woman is terminated by disagreement. What, if any, are the rights of the parties? The first question one would have to ask is - are the parties married? If they are then we can point to the law, English or foreign, to govern the termination of their status and to assess their mutual rights and obligations if they cannot agree on the allocation of what may have been, up to their parting, common resources. If they are not married, and assuming they had not made a formal contract, we must seek the law governing the precise identification of property rights or seek to find some overall contractual relationship. The task is the same, the manner of doing it, both in domestic and conflict law, is different.

Choice of Law

Once a court has decided that it has jurisdiction and, by its process of classification, has decided what the issue is about, it comes to the main purpose of the conflict of laws, that is to determine what significance is to

1-12

---

[13] See below para 8-10.

be attributed to the foreign aspect of the case. Of course it is not every foreign contact which introduces a relevant element to the situation or transaction. One would hardly suppose that a visiting Frenchman buying a tube ticket in London could argue that French law should have a role to play in that contract or that a U.S. citizen could expect that his liability for, or right to recover in, an accident which occurs in England between himself and an Englishman should be determined by the law of some U.S. state. However, which contacts have a relevance and which have not is not always apparent and were our Frenchman to marry in England or our U.S. citizen to die in England owning property in England the case might appear to be, and would be, different. In practice, of course, a foreign contact will only be raised in English litigation if it is relevant on the basis of existing conflict rules, or if it has a colourable case to be considered so, to warrant the trouble and expense of setting it up. However, some areas of law are not clearly settled and the choice rules are open to argument.

1-13   It is for English law to determine which contacts are relevant and which are not and we will examine some of the choice rules later.

As will be seen, English courts have sought to deal with choice of law by a series of automatic rules following the classification. For example, there is a rule that the formal validity of a marriage which has been celebrated abroad shall be determined by the law of the country in which the marriage was celebrated. So, if a petitioner comes before the English court seeking a decree declaring her foreign marriage void on the ground of informality the court would, if it had jurisdiction and agreed that the matter was one of formal validity, refer to the law of the place where the marriage was celebrated to discover whether or not the formalities required there had been observed. Of course, there is no actual contact with the foreign legal system; no messengers are sent there to make the enquiry. What happens is that the petitioner asserts, and seeks to prove by expert witnesses, the foreign rule that she alleges was not complied with. If the English court is satisfied that the foreign formalities were not observed, and that their non–observance made the marriage a nullity by that law, the English court will grant relief.

In some cases it will not be possible to refer the case to a system of law in quite such a mechanical way either because the issue is not susceptible to a simple formulation or because the English court has no set rule to apply. For example, whether an act which is alleged to constitute a breach of contract has the effect of discharging the other party from his obligation is not an issue which is susceptible to a simple location test. In some areas, tort cases generally but many other more detailed situations as well, English law has not established a satisfactory conflict rule as the issues with which it has to deal raise fundamental political questions which have not been resolved.

There are two sorts of dispute about choice of law rules. In some situations the English courts are still developing the rule to apply, so that what stands for the present may be amended or replaced and arguments can be raised at a high level of generality about the appropriate weighting to be given to the foreign contact. In others the courts have established firm rules, or been provided with them by legislation, in which case the arguments take a different line and relate either to the manner in which any discretion that the rule allows should be exercised or whether the case actually falls within the ambit of the rule.

1-14

Choice of law rules may take a variety of forms. A single localising rule, e.g. that the formal validity of marriage is governed by the law of the place of celebration, represents the simplest model. Slightly more complex are the rules which are multi-reference, in which a number of alternatives are presented, any one of which will do - the most dramatic example of this type of rule is the test for the formal validity of wills[14] where no fewer than seven legal systems may be relevant. While it should not be assumed that factual locating rules are always applicable in a straightforward fashion, there are some rules e.g. those involving references to the personal law[15] which go beyond a factual test and require evaluations to be made. Finally there are rules which require a wide judgmental input, for example the cases under the Rome Convention where the court is required to determine the system of law with which the contract is most closely connected.[16]

1-15

Application of Law

English courts never apply foreign law as such; what they seek to do is to formulate their judgments in the light of the content of a foreign legal system. When conflict lawyers speak of "a foreign law governing" or "applying foreign law" they are simply employing a convenient shorthand for "the court, having received evidence about the content of the rules of a foreign legal system, has formulated its judgment in a way which takes account of those facts". Foreign law is always a question of fact and English judges do not have knowledge of foreign law.

1-16

Even where the relevant foreign law has been established to the satisfaction of the court, there is still room for intervention by the forum. Public policy or the forum's morality may intervene to prevent the application of the foreign law or it may be regarded as not applicable by

1-17

---

[14] See below para 5-58.
[15] See below para 2-03.
[16] See below para 4-33.

the forum.[17] One clear example of this is the distinction between substance and procedure. Every forum governs its own procedure, i.e. decides on its own process. The manner of bringing actions, the mode of proof, the order of business at trial, and the like, are obviously matters which the forum needs to control. It would be intolerable if an English court, dealing with a Ruritanian case, was expected to abandon its proof by cross-examined witnesses in favour of some exotic method of proof used by Ruritanian courts. English courts are not going to return to trial by battle if that happens to be the mode of proof in some country whose law happens to impinge upon a trial going on in England. So an English court never applies foreign procedural law. It is not, however, always easy to distinguish substance from procedure.[18]

1-18   Once it has been decided which law is to apply to the determination of the case, English remedies, English damages and English methods of enforcement will apply[19].

Foreign Judgments

1-19   There will be situations in which parties to foreign proceedings may want their effect to be recognised in England. A successful plaintiff before a foreign court may want to have his judgment recognised in England so that he can enforce it against the defendant's assets in England. A successful defendant abroad may want the foreign judgment recognised in England to stop the plaintiff commencing another action. A person whose marriage has been dissolved by a foreign court may want to rely on that decree in order to be able to remarry in England. A conflicts system has to establish rules to determine how and in what circumstances foreign judgments and other legal acts will be recognised and enforced.[20]

Proof of Foreign Law

1-20   Foreign law is a matter of fact before English courts and has to be proved by appropriate evidence like any other fact in dispute. It is, however, a special sort of fact and the evidence can only be presented by witnesses who are expert in the foreign law. These experts, like any others, are subjected to the processes of examination and cross-examination and any authorities on which they rely are open to the

---

[17] See below Chapter 7.
[18] See below para 7-15.
[19] See below para 7-17.
[20] See below para 3-61.

court's scrutiny. Generally the witnesses will be judges or practitioners in the legal system which is being considered but this is not mandatory.[21] Although the finding on the foreign law is a finding of fact it needs to be established only to the satisfaction of the judge; it is not a matter for the jury in those rare cases where jury trial is still available.[22]

It follows, therefore, that English courts do not take judicial notice of foreign law though in one famous case[23] the court took notice of the notorious fact that gaming was not illegal in Monte Carlo.

Foreign law may however be proved by reference to a previous case in which there is a clear and pertinent finding; indeed such a finding will be proof of the foreign law unless the contrary is shown.[24]

It should be noted, however, that although Scotland and Northern Ireland are separate countries for conflict purposes, so that their laws have to be proved before English courts in the same way as the laws of France or of Japan, when the House of Lords is sitting as the ultimate appellate tribunal on a Scottish or Northern Ireland appeal it does take judicial notice of the law of the relevant country.

If the parties fail to plead foreign law, or fail to prove it, the case **1-21** proceeds on the basis that English law applies to all the issues between the parties raised in the litigation. This should not be done woodenly, however, and the court should remain conscious that the case contains international elements which might make particular rules of English law inapplicable to it.

Jurisdiction Selection and Rule Selection

The English conflict of laws operates on the basis of jurisdiction **1-22** selection – that is its choice of law rules are directed at identifying the legal system from which will come the dispositive rule for the case in hand. So, for example, we say that the applicable law of this contract is French or the law to govern the essential validity of this marriage is Japanese. Theoretically, but only theoretically, the choice is made in ignorance of the actual rule that the system indicated will provide. Like a lucky dip in a bran tub, you can choose your bran tub but do not know what you are going to get out of it. The reality is rather different of course. A party in English proceedings who wants to bring in foreign law has to plead and prove it. Very few litigants embark on the costly process

---

21 Civil Evidence Act 1972 s.4(1).
22 Supreme Court Act 1981 s.69(5).
23 *Saxby v. Fulton* [1909] 2 KB 208.
24 Civil Evidence Act 1972 s.4(2).

of litigation with the Micawberish expectation that something of advantage will turn up. For them the selection of a foreign legal system is incidental to the rule which assists their case. If I argue that French law is the legal system most closely connected to the contract I do so, not for the metaphysics, but because there is a rule of French law, say, excusing the non-performance of the obligation, which is not available to me in any other legal system connected to the contract. If I want Japanese law applied to my marriage it is because that law, rather than any other connected law, contains a rule which produces the result I want. All obvious enough and all those involved in the process know or ought to know what is happening. When the court decides upon the choice of law it does so in the knowledge of the consequence of its choice for the disposition of the case and it would be very naïve to believe that this knowledge never influences the choice of the governing legal system.

This way of doing things is neither inevitable nor always efficient. Instead of searching for the *jurisdiction*, (meaning here the whole legal system), to govern the case, the court could concentrate its attention on the rules that the connected legal systems contain on the matter in dispute, and then select the rule which seems the most appropriate to determine the issue.

True and False Conflicts

1-23   A true conflict occurs where a choice has to be made between the different laws of two or more legal systems which are potentially applicable to the case in hand and which would produce different overall results. If all the connected legal systems have the same rule on the matter in question then, although the conflict exercise may still be gone through, nothing will turn on it. But the choice of law rules which any country adopts may have the effect of creating a problem which has no real existence in the laws of any country. Suppose the question before the English court is the validity of a marriage which took place abroad of a couple who immediately thereafter made their matrimonial home in England. Suppose that the issue is not raised as a matrimonial cause, (the couple are perfectly happy in their marriage), but arises in a succession case where money has been paid over on the assumption, which is now being contested, that the marriage is valid. The conflict rules of English law could point to one of the parties' premarital domiciliary laws to discover that the couple were related to each other in a manner which by that law, but not by English law, prevented marriage between them. If the English court stops, as it characteristically does, at the domestic law of the chosen system it must hold the marriage to be void. Had it gone on to examine the conflict rules of the chosen system it might have discovered that the prohibition would not actually have been applicable on the facts of this case as the conflict rules of the chosen system would have referred, say, to the law of the matrimonial home - English law - where the marriage is valid. The story cannot logically be left at the point I have abandoned it and there may be no satisfactory way out of this particular dilemma. The point is that the rules a system has for resolving conflicts may actually create them.

A good example of a false conflict, one created by the rules on choice of law, is the New York case of *Babcock v. Jackson*.[25] A New York couple took a friend, another New Yorker, with them on a weekend trip to Canada. While in the province of Ontario an accident occurred, in which the friend was injured, due to the negligence of the driver. On their return to New York the friend sued the driver for compensation. It may be thought that this was not a particularly friendly thing to do until it is remembered that the suit would effectively be against the driver's insurer rather than against the driver himself. At the time of this litigation the conflict law of New York was still wedded to the *lex loci delicti*, the law of the place of the commission of the tort, for the resolution of tort cases, and the *lex loci* was Ontario. The law of Ontario contained a special provision known as a "guest statute" which barred actions by gratuitous passengers against their host drivers for personal injuries caused by negligence. Whatever the merits of such a provision in general, and most of the common law world has managed to get by without one, it is not immediately apparent why it should apply in this case at all. Certainly the accident happened in Ontario but there was nothing Ontarian about it; it could just as easily have occurred during the long drive up New York state or on the return journey. Most people would think that the New York law, whatever its content, would be the appropriate law from which to discover the dispositive law for this particular case. Ontarian law came into play simply because the conflict rules of New York made the governing law the *lex loci*. Had the New York court persisted with its habitual rule the plaintiff would have lost her case. In the event the court changed its choice of law rule to one which enabled the court to apply the most closely connected law and to assess the purpose of the Ontarian law to discover that there was no Ontarian interest which the plaintiff's success in the New York court would have infringed.

For the present the point needs to be taken that mechanical choice of law rules, whatever their advantages in terms of certainty and predictability and their benefits in avoiding litigation, can create unsatisfactory results.

---

[25] (1963) 12 NY 2d 473; [1963] 2 Lloyds Rep 286.

4   CHANGING NATURE OF THE SUBJECT

1-25   Until recently the focus of academic interest in the conflict of laws related to the choice of law process itself and within that area the main attention was on the law of obligations and on the law of torts in particular. Courts, too, devoted a lot of intellectual energy to the same concerns, though more time was spent on jurisdictional issues which involved micro rather than macro characterisations.

The English conflict of laws was entirely judge made and, in the terms of the common law, its history was relatively short. The earliest recognisable decisions were made in the middle of the eighteenth century[26] but the period of the late nineteenth century onwards was the time of greatest development. As usual, English courts approached the matters pragmatically. No grand theory informed their decisions, the motivation was their desire to establish a workable system.

1-26   With the passing of the Contracts (Applicable Law) Act 1990 and the imminent reform of choice of law in tort, the problem of producing choice of law rules will have virtually gone from the area of obligations and the courts can no longer invent new choice of law rules in these areas nor respond directly to the inadequacies of the codes that they will be obliged to apply. Certainty, or some measure of it, has replaced uncertainty but at the cost of preventing common law development.

Litigants, unless both very rich and very reckless could not be expected to share the academic fascination with the potential development of the elusive, satisfactory choice of law rule; their concerns are with winning or losing their disputes not with the intellectual appeal of a process which might, who was to know, turn out to their disadvantage.

Certainty is the friend of commerce, and international business wants to know where it stands legally if things go wrong or when things have gone wrong. In some cases a quick and clear negative answer may be of more use than protracted and expensive litigation which promises, and might actually deliver, a positive one.

1-27   If choice rules are more certain, the focus of attention will shift to their interpretation and the ambit of their operation. The subject will be increasingly characterised by statutory or Convention interpretation. The transition from rule to regulation is simply an example of the general trend of English law which, coupled with the increasing pressure for European harmonisation, is producing fundamental changes to traditional attitudes.

---

26   See e.g. *Pipon v. Pipon* (1744) Amb 25 (succession); *Scrimshire v. Scrimshire* (1752) 2 Hag Con 395 (marriage); *Robinson v. Bland* (1760) 1 Wm Bl 234 (contract); *Mostyn v. Fabrigas* (1774) 1 Cowp 161 (tort).

"Heavy litigation", where the issue might be relatively simple but an   **1-28**
awful lot of money rides on the result, has especially affected the
development of conflict law and will continue to do so, but it will take a
different form. If the choice of law rules which might apply are relatively
clear, attention will be directed to issues of jurisdiction or classification
and the whole matter will ride upon them.

5   GLOSSARY OF TERMS

Conflict lawyers use some Latin terms which have been adopted or   **1-29**
derived from continental jurists, although the influence of continental
thinking has not been significant in the modern English law:

lex causae: the law which the court has determined as the governing law of the issue.

lex domicilii: the law of the country where a person is domiciled.

lex fori: the law of the court dealing with the issue. Where an English court decides to apply its own law regardless of the conflict issue it applies English law as *lex fori*; where, however it determines upon the application of English law as a result of operating its choice of law rules, it applies English law as *lex causae*.

lex loci actus: the law of the place where an act was done.

lex loci celebrationis: the law of the place where a marriage was celebrated.

lex loci contractus: the law of the place where a contract was made

lex loci delicti: the law of the place where the wrongful act (tort) was committed.

lex loci solutionis: the law of the place where the contract is to be performed.

lex patriae: the law of the nationality.

lex propria causae: the proper law (see below).

lex propria delicti: the proper law of the tort (see below).

lex situs: the law of the place where a thing is situated, particularly but not exclusively, a piece of land.

locus regit actum: the law of the place governs the deed. An old maxim that finds its modern expression in the *lex loci* rules listed above.

mobilia sequuntur personam: movables follow the person, in modern law this is shown by the rule that succession to movables is governed by the personal law of the deceased.

Some other terms which are in general use among conflict lawyers should also be noted:

applicable law	sometimes used generally to mean the governing law, this term is used specifically to mean the *lex causae* in the Conventions governing contracts and trusts.
choice of jurisdiction:	the selection, often by the parties to a contract, of the national court before which any dispute is to be heard.
choice of law:	the process or the result of discovering the law to apply to the cause.
country:	any area or law district which has its own legal system e.g. Scotland, Ontario, New York.
governing law:	the *lex causae*.
jurisdiction selection:	the process of choice of law by reference to the law of a country as a whole, theoretically without regard to the content of that law.
proper law:	the law which has the closest connection with the issues under consideration usually on the basis of preponderant groupings.
rule selection:	the process of choice of law by reference to the specific rules of the competing legal systems.
State:	used in this book to indicate the international unit only. Sometimes the terms State and country can be used interchangeably – where the State has a unitary legal system e.g. France, Italy, Japan – in other cases they cannot e.g. U.K., U.S.A., Australia.

CHAPTER 2

THE POSSIBILITIES FOR CHOICE OF LAW

1 INTRODUCTION

Assuming that a legal system, faced with a case which it recognises has contacts with laws other than its own, is prepared to attempt to accommodate the foreign aspects of the case, how can it proceed? It has to find some way to link the facts to the foreign legal system but there are only a limited number of connections which can be made. The choice of law process involves the attribution of significance to the foreign contacts – turning factual contacts into legally relevant ones. This is done by choice of law rules which embody factual connections e.g. the formal validity of marriage is governed by the law of the place where the marriage was celebrated – the *lex loci celebrationis*. We will examine some of the connections later, but they only provide the *means* of choice, they cannot determine that choice directly; for example if a Frenchman buys goods from an Englishman in England for delivery on the spot there is little, if any, obvious significance in the French connection; whereas if the Frenchman marries an Englishwoman in England the potential significance of the French contact appears much greater. Why should this be so? The connections are in each case the same so the difference between their apparent significance must depend on the nature of the transactions to which they relate. To decide what weight to accord to a particular connection depends, then, on two elements: the issue which is raised and the connection which is offered. Suppose the French buyer, dissatisfied with the goods, claims that the seller was in breach of contract by French law. One might rule out the objection on the grounds that the contract was made in England or that the controlling law must be English, as it would be impossible for the English seller to know about the personal laws of his casual customers and intolerable that identical contracts should be valid or not, or performed or not, according to diverse legal systems which could not be known in advance and which would produce different results. Could the same be said if the contract in England took place between two Frenchmen?

In the case of the marriage, should the French element play a part in any assessment of the validity of the marriage, and would it matter if a defect in the marriage – in the eyes of French law – related to the form of its celebration or the capacity of one or other of the parties to enter it?

Again, might the intention of the parties to make their matrimonial home in England or in France or somewhere else be significant?

These are relatively soft cases; take a harder one. A contract is made in New York between a French company and an English company whereby the English company is to manufacture goods which are to be delivered to the French company's U.S. branch. The contract is written in English and the goods are to be paid for in $U.S. There are several different contacts here with three different legal systems and more could be added. The choice of law process needs to provide answers to the various disputes which might arise out of the contract including, for example, a claim that the contract is formally invalid, that the contract price has not been paid, that the goods are defective or that they were delivered late as a result of industrial action by New York stevedores.

2-02 Before we look at the choice of law rules in some of the substantive areas, a brief examination of the available connections which can be used for this purpose will be made. These are sometimes called "connecting factors"; they have no independent significance from the choice of law rules which incorporate them. Whilst it is possible to say that a party's capacity to marry is governed by the personal law, and then to qualify this statement by the assertion that for most purposes of the English conflict of laws the personal law is the law of the domicile, in all other cases there is no distinction between the formulation of the rule and the connection. The formal validity of a marriage is governed by the *lex loci celebrationis* – the law of the place where the marriage is celebrated. The connecting factor is clearly the place of celebration but it is an integral part of the rule itself. I do not mean by this that there is no element of choice; there are always alternatives.

The possible connections will now be explored. It needs to be noted however that while the connections are limited in number they can be taken in various combinations.

2 THE PERSONAL LAW

2-03 One way of dealing with conflict problems is to recognise that everybody comes from *somewhere*, and to seek to discover the "home law" on the assumption that, like language, people carry their law around with them when they travel. Thus we could say: "Here is a Frenchman" and deal with his legal problems by reference to French law. There are two obvious problems with this approach. What do we mean by "Frenchman" and what happens when the legal issue involves another who cannot be characterised in the same way? To address the first of these: the attribution of a personal law can be done in several ways by reference to the national, domestic or religious law of the person.

The National Law

While some systems of conflict law rely heavily on nationality the **2-04** problems with it are obvious: there are persons of dual nationality and those who are Stateless. Further, every legal system constitutes a separate entity for the purpose of the conflict of laws irrespective of whether or not it constitutes a separate State in the international sense. So in this context one cannot speak of British law or of American law because each of these international States comprises more than one legal system. For Britain there are three major legal systems, those of England and Wales, Scotland, and Northern Ireland, each with important differences despite many similarities; while the United States of America comprises fifty different legal systems despite their many common features. Any attempt to apply the national law to a person from a federal or composite State requires localising rules to identify the smaller unit[1] and thus, to a considerable extent, undermines the test. Although the problems of using the *lex patriae*, the law of the nationality, in a unitary State such as Italy are much reduced, there remains the major difficulty that, whatever organic relationship is perceived between the citizen and the State, as to which historical and cultural matters play a significant part, it by no means follows that the law of the nationality reflects the society in which the particular individual lives. People who settle abroad often do not change their nationalities with the consequence that the application of the *lex patriae* may well result in determining their legal status by a law with which they have had no connection for many years - if at all.

English law flirted with the possibility of using nationality in the nineteenth century but rejected it in favour of the domicile and a more recent reconsideration came to the same conclusion.[2] Some legal systems are, however, wedded to the concept so that, in attempts to arrive at international agreements, English law has had to accept the concept as one of a package of multi-reference connections in a limited number of situations. So, for example, nationality is one of the tests for the formal validity of wills[3] and one of the connections for the recognition of overseas divorces, annulments and legal separations.[4]

---

[1]   See e.g. the difficulties encountered in *Re O'Keefe* [1940] Ch 124.
[2]   See Law Com 168 (1987).
[3]   Wills Act 1963 s.1 and see below para 5-58.
[4]   Family Law Act 1986 s.46 and see below para 6-66.

The Domestic Law

2-05   Here the concept is one of relationship with a legal system by being in the country itself. There are obviously many degrees of connection and these will be explored.

Presence

2-06   This is, obviously, the weakest connection as it involves no more than a temporary location in the country without any family, work, political or emotional commitment to the place. For this reason it cannot possibly suffice, of itself, as the determinant of the personal law. That is not to say, of course, that mere presence is not of significance in the conflict of laws and we shall consider later some of the localising rules which depend, or at least operate upon, the mere presence of the parties within a particular jurisdiction, as, for example, the rule that the formal validity of marriage is referable to the law of the place of celebration,[5] however transient the parties' relationship with that place may be. But those rules do not purport to be making a personal link, they are only making a factual link. Also, it should be noted that, at common law, the mere presence of the defendant in England is sufficient to enable process to be served on him and thus to make him subject to the English courts' jurisdiction.[6]

Residence

2-07   Residence connotes more than mere presence in that it carries with it a notion of time. Of itself, however, it does not convey any particular duration so it would not be a misuse of English to say that someone was resident in an hotel for one night. A period of residence, however short, does suggest that someone was living in a particular place and it is this idea of living there which makes the concept of residence a potential candidate for the personal law. The main weakness of nationality lies in the fact that there is no necessary connection between the State of which one is a national and the country in which one lives. This defect is entirely overcome by the concept of *residence* provided that a satisfactory degree of attachment can be established. How may this be done? There are two basic solutions here: duration and intention. Where a person has lived for a long time in the same place it would not be unreasonable to characterise that place as his home and to regard the law of that place as his personal law. However, suppose that the long period of residence has not been a voluntary one but has been imposed by forces beyond the control of the

---

[5]   See below para 6-21.
[6]   See below para 3-05.

individual or, contrary-wise, suppose that a desired residence has been interrupted by factors beyond the individual's control. Would we still wish in the one case to impose a personal law on the basis of the protracted, though undesired, residence and, in the other case, to deny the desired connection on the basis of lack of duration? The expatriate working abroad because there is unemployment at home, the soldier or diplomat on a long tour of duty, the prisoner incarcerated in a foreign gaol, the invalid seeking a better climate, the fugitive from political or racial persecution or, most dramatically, the long term political hostage, may all have a long period of residence but we may be reluctant to draw the inference from it that they have their home in the alien country and, by the same token, have lost all connection with their former homes.

Intention cannot by itself determine residence as there are those who, while living in one country, desire above all else to be living in another and those who, without any desire to be in any particular country, passionately wish to leave the place where they currently live. We can add here the person who, although perfectly happy where he is, has no intention of remaining in the country of his current residence when his immediate purpose, say, his fixed term contract or his course of study, is completed. If such people were asked where they intended to go when they left, many might reply: "Home".   2-08

If we interpret intention, as we do in other areas of the law, not simply in terms of desire or aspiration but in terms of realistic purpose or the objective of bringing about a result, we have a basis for marrying intention and residence into a coherent concept of "home' which would satisfy the requirements of a test for the personal law. What still has to be determined, however, is the necessary quality of intention and residence which will suffice. "Residence"[7], "Ordinary Residence",[8] "Habitual Residence",[9] are all tests which English law applies to deal with conflict problems. Currently it is the concept of habitual residence which is most significant in the English conflict of laws, though not for deciding the personal law - that is a matter for domicile as we shall see later - so it is worth exploring it in more detail.

Habitual residence

Habitual residence first appeared in the English conflict of laws as a result of international efforts to get some limited agreement on choice of law rules. It arrived as a compromise between those States which insisted   2-09

---

[7] See e.g. the recognition of foreign judgments below para 3-67.
[8] See e.g. Domestic Proceedings and Magistrates' Courts Act 1978 Part I.
[9] Wills Act 1963 s.1 Domicile and Matrimonial Proceedings Act 1973 s.5.

on the *lex patriae* as the test of the personal law and those countries which, like England, relied on domicile for that purpose - not, it should be noted, that the domicile countries had a unified concept to offer. The compromise did not lead to the replacement of the national law or of the domiciliary law by habitual residence, it was agreed merely as an alternative rule of reference. So, for example, the formal validity of a will may be tested by the law of the nationality, the law of the domicile or the law of the habitual residence.[10] An English court will recognise an overseas divorce if one of the parties to the marriage was habitually resident in the country where the divorce was obtained[11], and an English court will take jurisdiction in matrimonial causes if either of the parties to the marriage has been habitually resident in England for twelve months immediately preceding the presentation of the petition.[12] The first thing to notice about the English concept of habitual residence is that the concentration is upon the quality of the residence rather than its duration, so that a future petitioner to the English court for matrimonial relief will satisfy the jurisdictional requirement of one year's habitual residence even if he or she has been in this country for only one year, provided that the quality of residence is sufficient. Clearly one has to start somewhere and habitual residence for one year presupposes that the necessary quality to make the residence habitual could exist from day one. What is this necessary quality? In *Cruse v. Chittum*[13] the English court had to decide whether a court in Mississippi was competent to grant a divorce to an Englishwoman. The issue turned on whether she was habitually resident in Mississippi at the start of the proceedings. In deciding that she was, the court considered the necessary quality of residence and determined that it must be actual and *bona fide*, not temporary or secondary, involving a regular physical presence which endures for some time. Habitual residence has been equated with the more familiar concept in English law of "ordinary residence".[14] It does not involve continuous residence and is capable of surviving protracted periods of absence where, for example, the party maintained a home in England ready for immediate occupation,[15] but it would seem to require the residence to be lawful, not, for example, in breach of immigration laws.[16]

---

[10] Wills Act 1963 s.1.

[11] Family Law Act 1986 s.46.

[12] Domicile and Matrimonial Proceedings Act 1973 s.5.

[13] [1974] 2 All ER 940.

[14] *Kapur v. Kapur* [1984] FLR 920; *Shah v. Barnet London Borough* [1983] 2 AC 309, [1983] 1 All ER 226.

[15] See *Stransky v. Stransky* [1954] P 428, [1954] 2 All ER 536.

[16] *Shah v. Barnet London Borough* [1983] 2 AC 309, [1983] 1 All ER 226.

"*ordinary* residence refers to a man's abode in a particular place or country which he has adopted voluntarily and for settled purposes as part of the regular order of his life for the time being, whether of short or long duration"[17]

It can apply therefore even if the purpose of the residence is limited in duration e.g. to attend a course of education.[18] It could also apply to the expatriate worker who might clearly be regarded as habitually resident in the country of employment.

Habitual residence is not without its difficulties – it is possible, for example, to be habitually resident in more than one place.[19] What happens when at the operative time a person has abandoned his habitual residence but has not yet acquired another? Nevertheless the concept is a very useful one and many take the view that its freedom from over-definition and over-refinement make it a better test for the personal law than the current test used by English law – domicile.[20]

2-10

Domicile

Domicile in its present form is a concept whose time is past. In the nineteenth century when English courts were trying to decide between nationality and domicile, the concept of domicile which then obtained was much more like the concept of habitual residence than the highly technical concept which we must now consider. In the event domicile won the day and the English courts spent the rest of the century and the early part of this one in refining the concept. The concept of domicile, which had initially meant little more than permanent home,[21] took on an increasingly legalistic dimension with all sorts of unfortunate consequences which remain with us today.

2-11

There are three varieties of domicile known to English law:- the domicile of choice, the domicile of origin, and the domicile of dependence. The three varieties work together to provide an overall and all-embracing concept of the personal law.

2-12

---

17 *Per* Lord Scarman *ibid* at pp 343; 235 respectively.
18 See *Shah* (school in England). *Kapur*, (to take the Bar exams).
19 See *IRC v. Lysaght* [1928] AC 234.
20 Though the Law Commission does not think so. Law Com 168 (1987).
21 See *Whicker v. Hume* (1858) 7 HLC 124 at 160.

(1) Domicile of choice

2-13   Every person in the world who is over the age of sixteen[22] and is not mentally incapable is regarded, by English law, as able to acquire a domicile of choice by residing in a country with the present intention of making it his permanent home. There are thus two requirements - fact and intention.

In most cases it will be quite straightforward to decide where someone is domiciled but the considerable bulk of case law in the area demonstrates that where the issue is contested there can be great scope for argument. There can be no question, unlike the case of habitual residence, of a person having two operative domiciles simultaneously or, as we shall see, having none at all, but these benefits may be bought at too high a price.

2-14   Long residence in a country will raise the inference that a person intended to remain there and this may be so strong as to be almost impossible to rebut. By the same token, a short period of residence may make it difficult to assert that a domicile has been established.

2-15   The abandonment of a domicile requires the same two elements, the physical removal from the country and the intention not to return to it - leaving *animus non revertendi*. There must be a coincidence of non-residence and intention not to reside. So a long period of absence does not destroy a domicile of choice and may not do so even if there is indecision about a possible return. In *Re Lloyd Evans*[23] a Belgian domiciliary who had fled to England died before he had decided whether to return to Belgium or emigrate to Australia. He was held to be domiciled in Belgium. In contrast, all the desire in the world to be somewhere else will not destroy a domicile unless it is accompanied by removal from the country. So an intention to leave England coupled with a mere visit to the intended new home is not enough to destroy the existing domicile.[24]

2-16   Like habitual residence, there must be a relationship between fact and intent but the requirement for domicile is more exacting. A brief examination of some of the leading cases will show the relationship. In *Winans v. Att-Gen*[25] the issue was the domicile of the deceased at the time of his death for, if he had died domiciled in England, his estate would have been subject to English estate duty. Winans had lived a remarkable life in the manner of the heroes of the Victorian age. Born in Baltimore,

---

[22]   Domicile and Matrimonial Proceedings Act 1973 s.3 (1).

[23]   [1947] Ch 695; c/f *Re Flynn* [1968] 1 All ER 49.

[24]   See *IRC v. Duchess of Portland* [1982] Ch 314, [1982] 1 All ER 784; *In bonis Raffenel* (1863) 2 Sw & Tr 49.

[25]   [1910] AC 27.

he spent much of his life in Europe and lived in England for the last thirty-seven years of his life. He built railways in Russia and helped that country against England in the Crimean war by making gunboats. He had an obsession to develop his Baltimore property into a sea-port, equip it with ships of his own special design and capture the world's carrying trade for the United States, at the same time putting an end to the Rule Britannia. His hatred of Britain eventually convinced the House of Lords that, despite his long residence here, he lacked the intention to acquire a domicile in England.

In *Ramsay v. Liverpool Royal Infirmary*[26] the question was, again, the country of domicile of the deceased at the time of his death. The issue was the formal validity of his will. At that time the formal validity of wills was a matter for the personal law.[27] Ramsay was a Scotsman who had lived in England for the last thirty-six years of his life. His will was in holograph form, that is it was signed but the signature was not attested; such a will is valid by Scots law but not by English law. If the will was upheld the residue of his property would have been shared among four charities, of which the L.R.I. was one; if invalid, the residue would pass to those entitled upon his intestacy. In the event the court, (following the precedent of *Winans*) decided that, despite his long stay in England, Ramsay had not acquired a domicile here as he would have moved from England if those members of his family on whom he was living had removed. The two cases are extremely unsatisfactory as they put too much emphasis on the desires, however unrealistic, of the person in question rather than on what he proposed to do. Certainly both Ramsay and Winans could properly be said to be habitually resident in England and that may be taken to show the superiority of that test for the personal law. In defence of the Ramsay decision it should be noted that the court may well have been motivated by a desire to save his will and that there was no other way of achieving that. **2-17**

These cases can be contrasted with a decision of a court in West Virginia which was faced with the opposite problem of very short residence. In *White v. Tennant*[28] a family were moving house and this involved crossing a state-line. It must be remembered that each state in the United States represents a separate country for the purposes of the conflict of laws. Having put their belongings in the new house the family returned to their old state to spend the night with family as the new house was not yet ready to inhabit. When the father died during the night the court decided that he died domiciled in his new state not his old one. **2-18**

---

[26] [1930] AC 588.

[27] See now Wills Act 1963 s.1, below, para 5-58.

[28] (1888) 31 W Va 790 see also *Bell v. Kennedy* (1868) LR 1 Sc & Div 307.

This conclusion is important if domicile has to be established shortly after an individual has arrived in a new country in which he intends to live permanently. Suppose, for example, a couple intend to marry and set up their home in a country whose law would regard that marriage as valid, whereas one or both of them have a prenuptial domicile which does not allow marriage between them because, say, they are within the prohibited degrees. If they are regarded as domiciled in the new country at the time of the marriage, the marriage will be regarded as valid by the English conflict of laws; if not, it will not.

2-19   If it can be established that the intention to make the country of residence the permanent home exists, the fact that the residence was not freely chosen and could be ended by compulsory relocation is irrelevant; so servicemen who had no control over where they were stationed have been held capable of acquiring domiciles.[29] But lots of intention will not, apparently, help someone whose residence is not only precarious but illegal, at least in England,[30] though authorised residence is not a prerequisite.

2-20   Where residence is contingent the intention to remain permanently will not be negated on the basis that the individual would leave the country if a vague and unlikely event were to happen,[31] such as the making of an improbable fortune,[32] but a husband's intention to return home to his country of origin if his wife predeceased him was enough to prevent the acquisition of a domicile in England.[33]

2-21   What happens when a person abandons one domicile without acquiring another? England and the U.S. have come up with different solutions. Within U.S. jurisdictions the practise is to regard the abandoned domicile as continuing until a new domicile has been acquired.[34] One can over-exaggerate the evils of this by setting up a model of a refugee fleeing persecution in his own country who, before he finds a new home, will be regarded as having a personal law related to the country he has struggled to leave. The solution is artificial, although the English Law Commission is recommending its adoption into English law.[35] The English solution is to allow the old domicile to be abandoned but to fill the gap with a special construct - the domicile of origin.[36]

---

[29] *Donaldson v. Donaldson* [1949] P 363 (in the country where he was stationed); *Stone v. Stone* [1959] 1 All ER 194 (in another country).

[30] *Puttick v. AG* [1980] Fam 1, [1979] 3 All ER 463.

[31] *Re Fuld's Estate (No 3)* [1968] P 675, [1965] 3 All ER 776.

[32] *Doucet v. Geoghegan* (1876) 9 Ch D 441.

[33] *IRC v. Bullock* [1976] 3 All ER 353.

[34] See e.g. *Re Jones's Estate* (1921) 192 Iowa 78.

[35] Law Com 168 (1987).

[36] See *Udny v. Udny* (1869) LR 1 Sc & Div 441.

(2) Domicile of origin

Every child at birth is accorded a domicile by English law. Of course 2-22
the gift is a notional one until a matter arises to make the issue live. This
attributed domicile is indelible and remains with the person throughout
his life even if for much of the time or, indeed, always, it is overlaid by
another sort of domicile. The domicile of origin of a legitimate child is
the domicile, of whatever sort, his father has at the time of the child's
birth. An illegitimate child[37] or a posthumous child takes its domicile of
origin from its mother's domicile at the time of its birth, but this is
somewhat artificial as the issue of legitimate status may itself depend on
domicile.[38] The domicile of origin acts as a fall-back; whenever there is
no other domicile,[39] it comes to fill the gap. It avoids assuming the
continuation of an abandoned domicile.

The only alternative to the revival of the domicile of origin is the 2-23
continuation of the existing domicile of choice. This can have
unfortunate results. In one U.S. case[40] a Welshman who had acquired a
domicile of choice in Iowa decided to leave Iowa for good and to return
to Wales. He was killed on the transatlantic voyage when the *Lusitania*
was torpedoed. The Iowa court held that at the time of his death he was
domiciled in Iowa.

English law avoids this but only by creating another type of
artificiality. Suppose, for example, that Mary is born at a time when her
father is domiciled in Jamaica, her parents having come to England
intending to return home after having made some money. Shortly after
Mary's birth they decide to settle in England. For all her childhood and
early adult life Mary knows only England. Later she marries an Italian and
goes to live in Italy and remains there for the duration of her marriage.
On the death of her husband she decides to return "home" to England
but on the way she is killed in a motor accident. Suppose she has not left
a will so that her property will pass to those who are entitled to it
according to the intestacy laws of her domicile. If we trace Mary's
domiciliary history we will find that her domicile of origin is Jamaican.
During her childhood she will have a domicile dependent on her father
(see next section) which on the facts will be English as her parents settled
in England shortly after her birth. The facts suggest that she abandoned
that English domicile when she set up her home with her husband in
Italy and acquired a domicile in her new country. When she left Italy

---

[37] *Udny v. Udny* (1869) LR 1 Sc & Div 441.
[38] See *Re Bischoffscheim* [1948] Ch 79, [1947] 2 All ER 630 and below para 6-90.
[39] See *Bell v. Kennedy* (1868) LR 1 Sc & Div 307.
[40] *Re Jones's Estate* (1921) 192 Iowa 78.

after her husband's death she abandoned her Italian domicile but died before she could establish a new domicile of choice. In the absence of a domicile of choice her domicile of origin revives to fill the gap. Her intestacy will, therefore, be governed by Jamaican law - the law of a country which she may never have visited.

One can think of even more unsatisfactory Solomon Grundy scenarios, but the point is that although the domicile of origin ensures that everyone has one domicile and *only* one domicile, of some sort, at all times, the artificiality means that sometimes it is not worth having. How, though, should Mary's case be resolved? Would Italian law have been a better solution albeit that she had left Italy for ever? It is not easy to see how one could apply English law for, while England may have been Mary's actual home for many years in the past and may have continued to be her spiritual home throughout her life, England has not been her actual home, perhaps, for decades. There seems no satisfactory solution to this problem, though it is clear that Jamaican law is by far the worst result possible. The English Law Commission[41] has suggested the abolition of the domicile of origin and, if their views prevail, Mary would have Italian law applied to her intestacy.

It is worth noting here that a concept of habitual residence would lead to the same result. It would be necessary to continue an abandoned habitual residence until a new one was established in order to avoid a gap in the personal law which could not otherwise be filled.

(3) Domicile of dependence

2-24   A child who reaches the age of sixteen or who marries below that age (which clearly does not apply to English domiciled children) is capable of acquiring his own domicile.[42] Until that time a legitimate child's domicile depends on, and changes with, the domicile of his father unless, both parents being alive, the child has his home with his mother and no home with his father.[43] An illegitimate child, or a legitimate child whose parents are both living but who lives wholly with his mother, has a dependent domicile coincident with his mother's current domicile. A child whose father is dead takes his domicile from his mother but, oddly, here, it seems that, unless he has his home with her, his domicile of dependence does not automatically change with hers.[44] A child whose parents are dead should be domiciled where the person on whom he is dependent is

---

[41]   Law Com 168 (1987).

[42]   Domicile and Matrimonial Proceedings Act 1973 s.3(1).

[43]   *ibid* s.4.

[44]   See *Re Beaumont* (1893) 3 Ch 490.

domiciled but there is no authority for this and it has been assumed that such a child's domicile of dependence cannot be altered from his pre-orphan days.

The domicile of origin will be overlaid by the domicile of dependence. **2-25** So, at birth, the child actually receives two domiciles, *origin* and *dependence*, which are initially, in the vast majority of cases, the same. While the domicile of origin remains constant throughout life, the domicile of dependency changes with the domicile of the person on whom the child is domiciliarily dependent. The idea is that, as far as possible, there should be unity of domicile between the child and its parents.

Traditionally this family domicile notion was taken further and a wife **2-26** acquired upon marriage the domicile of her husband as a domicile of dependency. This, one of the last examples of formal legal inequality of women, was removed by statute,[45] but any existing domicile of dependence continued until a new domicile was acquired.[46]

The abolition of the wife's dependent domicile necessitated the statutory changes to the law of the child's dependent domicile and the complexity of the current law. It needs to be remembered, however, that there are few occasions when the child's domiciliary law is a matter of any significance. We will need to know it if, for example, we are faced with a foreign marriage involving a child below the age of sixteen and a question is raised of the child's capacity to enter a marriage at that age, or if we have to deal with succession to property of a child who dies under the age of sixteen. The incidence of such cases is likely to be tiny.

Reform of the law of domicile

The technicalities of the current law of domicile make it an unsuitable **2-27** test for the personal law in modern times. In contested cases the task of establishing the domicile can be an expensive and protracted business as there is nothing in the individual's life which cannot be grist to the judicial mill.

The Law Commission[47] considered replacing domicile with **2-28** nationality, not a serious contender, or habitual residence, which was. Habitual residence was rejected as the connection was felt to be too weak for the task to be performed. There was concern, particularly from U.S. business people working in England, that a less stringent test of connection would make them liable to U.K. taxation and, on the other hand, worry about expatriate workers who might lose their status

---

[45] Domicile and Matrimonial Proceedings Act 1973 s.1(1).

[46] *ibid* s.1(2).

[47] Law Com 168 (1987).

connection with England and have it replaced by, for example, Saudi Arabian law. In the event the Law Commission went for a substantial reform of the domicile concept.

2-29   In place of the threefold division into domiciles of origin, choice, and dependency the Commission proposes a simple distinction between the domiciles of adults and those of children. The main impact of the proposals is the abolition of the concept of the domicile of origin. No longer would it be necessary to ascribe a domicile by operation of law to a child at birth based on his status, or to encounter the high evidentiary hurdle of establishing that a domicile of origin has been displaced by a domicile of choice. Most importantly, the removal of the doctrine of the revival of the domicile of origin means that an existing domicile will continue until it is replaced by an alternative choice.

(1) Domicile of children

2-30   Under the proposals a child under sixteen, whether married or single, and whether or not himself a parent, will be domiciled in the country with which he is, for the time being, most closely connected. If the child has his home with one of his parents, the most closely connected country will rebuttably be presumed to be the country where both his parents are domiciled. If the parents are domiciled in different countries the child's domicile will be rebuttably presumed to be that of the parent with whom he has his home.

It needs to be noted here that while the country of closest connection would appear to be the country of closest factual connection, the rebuttable presumptions do not necessarily work on factual connections at all. It is possible that the child spends his childhood with a parent who is not domiciled in the country of residence so that while he lives with that parent his domicile may be in a country with which he himself has no connection; whereas if he leaves the parent's home and goes to live permanently with his grandparents, say, his domicile will become that of the country of his habitual residence.

The childhood domicile continues after the age of sixteen until it is changed by acquiring another domicile.

(2) Domicile of adults

2-31   An adult, anyone over the age of sixteen for this purpose, will be domiciled in the country in which he is present, (no special quality of residence is required), and in which it can be established, on the ordinary civil proof of the balance of probabilities, that he intends to settle for an indefinite period. The Commission toyed with the idea of seven years' residence as setting up a presumption of domicile but abandoned the idea in the face of concerns about the difficulty of having to rebut it in the case of long term temporary residence.

To deal with the problem of composite States, where the individual has clearly settled, say, in the U.K. or Canada but has not the intention of indefinite settlement in any one part, it is proposed that he should be regarded as domiciled in that part with which he is, for the time being, most closely connected.   2-32

An adult who is mentally incapable of forming the requisite intention of indefinite settlement will be domiciled in the country with which he is, for the time being, most closely connected. If he regains capacity his existing domicile continues until he acquires another one.   2-33

An ordinary adult domicile can never be abandoned, it can only be replaced by another, so, even if the adult has left his former country for good, his domicile in that country will persist until a new one is acquired. The artificiality of this has already been considered.[48] Though the solution is not ideal it is less cumbersome than the common law rules about the revival of the domicile of origin and no more likely to produce unjust results.   2-34

The reform proposals have been on the table for six years and the prospect of legislation does not seem good. It may be that the way forward would be to recognise that a single test of domicile is inappropriate for purposes as diverse as personal status and liability to taxation and that entirely different codes should apply to these matters. There is a clear precedent for this in the separate code of domicile introduced for the purposes of the Jurisdiction Conventions.[49]   2-35

The Religious Law

Many societies incorporate a religious tradition into the rules of their domestic legal systems. This is merely one, albeit a major one, of the cultural influences which go to make domestic legal systems distinct and thus to create the need for a system of conflict of laws in the first place. Thus the marriage laws of England are founded on the Christian tradition.[50] This does not mean that there has to be a religious element in marriage but it does mean that those wishing to marry in England can do so only on the basis of a broad compliance with the Christian model. No marriage taking place in England can be polygamous.[51] Obviously there   2-36

---

[48] See above para 2-23.
[49] See below para 3-23.
[50] See below para 6-04.
[51] See *Cheni v. Cheni* [1909] P 67; *Maher v. Maher* [1951] P 342, [1951] 2 All ER 37.

will be mismatches between the dictates of religion and those of the civil law, thus, for example, a civil ceremony of marriage will not be recognised for religious purposes among the Roman Catholic, Muslim or Jewish communities in Britain, any more than an English divorce will be accepted by those communities as terminating a marriage between their members. There is no institutional frame-work in English law for the accommodation of religious groupings as such; they must conduct their activities within the legal system which is common to all.

Other societies take a different view and their legal systems may recognise directly, or incorporate, personal religious law – characteristically in the areas of marriage, family and succession rights. Where a society does make specific provision for the cultural religious laws of a particular group, that has to be recognised whichever of the other personal laws has been adopted by the conflict system of another country. So English law, though wedded to the concept of domicile, must recognise that the decision that a person is domiciled in, say, Sri Lanka, will not supply a complete answer to the question of his personal law and that it will be necessary to probe further to discover the religious group to which he belongs.

2-37   Could the personal religious law be used as the general determinant of the personal law for all purposes? The answer must be negative. Not only are there those without a religious grouping and those whose religion is not accorded any special status in the society to which they indubitably belong, but also religious codes do not cover in precise form every aspect of life in a modern complex society. While a faith may well have moral prescriptions about, for example, keeping promises or basic duties of honesty, it is unlikely to give more than a moral guide on breaches of contract or duties of disclosure. In any case it is not clear how far one can realistically speak about universal Jewry or Christianity or a pan-Islamic law. Few societies are fundamentalist in this way, most have put a gloss upon the basic religious dictats in tune with their own needs and aspirations as societies.

2-38   The religious law will be significant for the purposes of the English conflict of laws only when the English test for the personal law – domicile – attaches the individual to a country which has, as part of its internal law, special regimes for particular religious groupings. In such cases account will have to be taken of these special rules in order to determine the status of the individual. So, for example, if the question is whether or not X has capacity to marry polygamously, reference to the law of his domicile may involve a further reference to the rules relating to the particular religious group to which he belongs. This applies, of course, only to the extent that the *lex domicilii* itself recognises such groups for this purpose.

Conclusion

Although the attribution of a personal law may appear to be a more   **2-39**
real and general association than, say, locating a tort or finding where a
will was made, it is worth emphasising that the quest for the personal law
in the English conflict of laws is always a means to an end and not an end
in itself. Obvious enough, but the purpose of the enquiry may well
influence its results and not improperly so. Cases on domicile in particular
can be influenced in this way, for, although there is basically a single
conceptual approach, there may well be a greater desire to find a
particular domicile to validate a will or a marriage than to make the
individual subject to UK taxation.

The possibilities of connecting a person with a territorial system of
law by means of applying a personal law to him is a very old idea and one
which has considerable merit. It is not without its difficulties in cases of
dispute and, whatever test is adopted, there are bound to be artificialities.

It must be noted that, lacking international agreement on the law to   **2-40**
be identified as the personal law, it is possible for different conflict systems
to treat the same case in very different ways, which makes a consistent
attitude to the issue raised impossible to attain. To take an example which
is not too far-fetched:-

Simon is a Nigerian national who has lived in England for many years
and who regards England as his home. For the last two years he has been
working for his English employer in Malaysia and expects to continue in
his job there for several more years. He has no family in England but has
a house in London and he comes to England for some of his leaves. On
these facts a court, applying a conflict system which used nationality,
would find that Simon's personal law was Nigerian, one using the
concept of domicile, that it was English, and one using the concept of
habitual residence that it was Malaysian. If these three legal systems all
applied the personal law to the issue of succession to the property of a
person dying intestate (suppose Simon has just died) then all would
depend on the court before which any dispute regarding Simon's
property arose - likely to be the country where the bulk of it was
situated. There is no way out of this dilemma saving the unification of all
countries' conflict systems, a prospect which is very distant.[52]

The response of English law is straightforward - we use our own test,   **2-41**
currently domicile, we interpret it in our own way[53] and we stand by the
results so obtained regardless of any other country's attitude. If the
application of English law's test of domicile results in the finding that X is

---

[52] But see the Rome Convention below para 4-07.
[53] See *Re Annesley* [1926] Ch 692.

domiciled in Maryland then that is conclusive and it matters not that a court in Maryland would find X domiciled elsewhere or, indeed, that it would use an entirely different test for the personal law.

2-42   There are two major departures from the English concept of domicile applied by English law. For the recognition of foreign divorces, annulments and legal separations a domiciliary connection may be established either in the English sense or in the sense of domicile used in family law matters in the country concerned.[54] More importantly, for the purpose of jurisdictional links under the Brussels and Lugano Conventions a special concept of domicile, one much nearer to the idea of habitual residence, has been introduced into English law.[55]

2-43   It should also be noted that both Australia and Canada have introduced a concept of domicile which applies in matrimonial cases and enables a person to be domiciled in the composite State whereas for other purposes domicile in a particular province or state is required.

What can the Personal Law be Used For?

2-44   It can hardly be assumed that the personal law can be applied in all situations. It cannot be that personal liability to others depends entirely on one's own law - for what of the personal law of the other party? Similarly it would not be expected that liability upon a contract was entirely a matter for the personal law or, for example, that whether a transfer of property had the effect of securing the transferee against all the world should depend on the personal law of one of the parties to that transfer.

There are some matters, however, which seem to be ideally suited to the governance of the personal law. Questions of personal status - whether one has the power to marry or make a will or enter into a contract would seen fit matters to refer to it. For while these issues also affect those with whom one deals, they relate essentially to the individual himself.

2-45   Different societies place differing emphases on the issue of status; generally speaking the common law world is less status conscious in this context than the civil law world. Common lawyers tend to be more transaction oriented than their civilian colleagues. As we shall see, English law confines the personal law within fairly narrow grounds; within those grounds, however, it is given full scope.

---

[54] Family Law Act 1986 s.46(5). See below paras 6-66, 6-67.

[55] Civil Jurisdiction and Judgments Act 1982 s.41. See below para 3-23.

3   THE LAW OF THE PLACE

Like the personal law, the law of the place provides a fairly **2-46**
straightforward test and one which, unlike the personal law, can be applied
automatically. The law of the place where something was done or
something happened also seems perfectly sensible. Two parties come
together and make an agreement or perhaps, more violently, collide, there
is one obvious common factor – they are both in the same place. Why
should not the law of that place be used to deal with any dispute that may
arise between them? Things are, as may be supposed, not quite so simple.
Firstly, it is not possible to encapsulate a complex legal relation into a
simple factual issue in every case; one would not, for example, regard it as
sensible to refer the whole of a contractual dispute solely to the law of the
place where the agreement happened to be signed. Secondly, the place
where an act was done may be entirely incidental if not fortuitous. For
example, after protracted negotiations taking many months an international
contract is signed in a particular country with all due formality. It may be
that the place of signing was chosen for reasons of convenience, ease of
travel, or because it is picturesque and not for any reason connected with
the substance of the agreement. Accidents, by their very nature, are
unplanned and while the place of accident may be the only common
factor, it does not follow that the law of the place has any real connection
with the parties or the occurrence. Thirdly, the law of the place may not
involve a simple factual enquiry but may give rise to a difficult legal
analysis. Suppose that the plaintiff has been injured by a dangerous product
which was made in country A, bought in country B, used in country C,
and which gave rise to injuries the effect of which was felt in country D.
Suppose that the product liability laws of the four countries differ
materially. Now, quite apart from the artificiality of attempting to see this
problem as a single event, there is the problem of deciding the legal
significance of each of the acts in the various countries of action.

However, the old maxim *locus regit actum* – the law of the place
governs the deed has, despite the difficulties mentioned above, some real
merit and has informed the English conflict of laws to a significant extent.
Some examples of its operation will be considered.

Lex loci celebrationis

One of the best established rules of the English conflict of laws is that **2-47**
the formal validity of a marriage is determined by the law of the place
where the marriage was celebrated.[56] Indeed, at one time the whole

---

[56] *Scrimshire v. Scrimshire* (1752) 2 Hag Con 395.

question of the validity of marriage was referred to that law on the basis of the unity of Christendom. The remnant of this general rule makes sense in that the majority of marriages take a deal of arrangement and the place of their celebration is unlikely to be casual or fortuitous. All but the most primitive societies have formal requirements for marriage, as the social consequences of the relationship, as well as the more mundane book-keeping matters, require a degree of public involvement. So those who choose to marry in country X. are expected, both by country X. and by the English conflict of laws, to follow the formal requirements of that law. In the vast majority of cases this will produce no hardship for the parties concerned and, in most countries. the matter is so carefully regulated that there is little likelihood that the requirements are unknown to, or incapable of being observed by, the parties.

2-48   One area of potential difficulty is the religious marriage which satisfies the needs of the faith but fails to satisfy the formal requirements of the local law. Such marriages are formally void in the eyes of the English conflict of laws however much the parties to them consider themselves to be married. We looked earlier at the possibilities of using the religious law to determine issues of personal status and the validity of religious marriages would be a prime area for that law. But unless the country of the celebration of the marriage makes special provision for religious marriages, in which case there is no problem anyway, their recognition by another country but not by the country where they were celebrated would create what is known as a limping marriage – one which is valid in one country but not in another – a situation which, while it cannot be avoided altogether, is something which should be minimised as much as possible.

Lex loci contractus

2-49   The law of the place where a contract is made may, more obviously than the place where a marriage is celebrated, be casual or fortuitous. I have already alluded to the disadvantages and artificialities of applying that law as the general law to govern international contracts. Insofar as the country where the contract is made has formal requirements for contracts of that type, for example that they should be in writing, there is no great objection to expecting that requirement to be carried out, though the chance of inadvertent mistake is greater than in the case of marriages because of the lack of public participation. More difficult is the problem that arises when the law of the place of contracting takes a view not merely about the form of the contract but about the substance of the obligation itself. It might declare that certain types of contract may not be made at all or might seek to include mandatory terms in any contract made within its territory irrespective of the place of performance of the contract or of any other connections - these problems will be considered later.[57]

Lex loci solutionis

The law of the place where a contract is to be performed has had an important position in the English conflict of laws. Like the other localising rules it seems an obvious choice to make. The performance of a contract is, obviously, the whole point of the contractual relationship and its completion the final act of that relationship. Unlike the *lex loci celebrationis* and the *lex loci contractus*, however, the influence of the *lex loci solutionis* has not centred on formalities - though if the law of the place of performance imposed formal requirements on the act of performance there would be a strong case for requiring compliance with them. The *lex solutionis* has been used by English courts as a major connection in the search for the governing law of the contract as a whole in those cases where the parties have failed to select a law to govern their dealings.

     2-50

The major weakness of the *lex loci solutionis* as a localising rule is that it does not necessarily identify a single system of law. An international contract may have several places where acts of performance have to be performed and it may not always be possible to single out one place, and hence one legal system, as more important than the rest.

Like all localising rules it is open to the possibility that the connections it makes have only limited relevance to the wider relations between the parties. So, while the place of the performance of a contract is unlikely to be casual or fortuitous, the legal system of that place may have no interest in, or any other connection with, the contractual relations between the parties. The local law must have the final say on the legality of the acts done within its boundaries, though the effects of the illegality rather than the facts of it may well, as we shall see, fall to be determined by some other law.

Lex loci delicti commissi

Of all the localising rules which conflict systems have developed, the law of the place of the commission of the tortious act has been the most troublesome. This rule of reference, widely used in continental Europe and, until thirty years ago, the basis for ascertaining the governing law in the states of the U.S., and which forms part of the current rule of English

     2-51

---

[57] See below para 4-18.

law, relates entirely to substance. It supposes that tortious liability is the creation of the law where the tort was committed and governs the plaintiff's ability to recover and the defendants liability to pay compensation wherever the case happens to be brought. The concept is one of "vested rights",[58] that is, that the commission of a tort creates, according to the law of the place of its commission, a right of action which the injured party can implement wherever he wishes. It does not matter, according to this theory, whether the personal law of the plaintiff would regard him as having such a right or whether the defendant's personal law would recognise such a right or, indeed, whether the parties come from the same foreign country in which the right given by the local law is unknown. This model of tortious liability is very similar to the notion of criminality, with which the conflict of laws is not directly concerned, where liability is usually a purely territorial matter. In taking this line the concept of tort is artificially narrowed. Of course, there are some torts which have a very close affinity to crimes, not surprising in view of their common origin, but there are many that have no such affinity. Deliberate and violent interferences with person or property are both crimes and torts but they represent only a tiny part of tortious litigation. More characteristic of the modern law of torts are the accident cases where the issue of fault is not about guilt but about liability to pay compensation. Quite apart from the problem, already alluded to, of fixing the *locus delicti* in a complex case, one can question the whole concept of a crude localising rule. The place where an accident occurs is always fortuitous and the application of the local law may appear capricious. In the leading Scots case of *M'Elroy v. M'Allister*[59] the pursuer was the widow of a Scotsman who had been killed in England as a result of negligence for which his employer was liable. The firm was Scots, the workers were Scots and the only thing to link the case with England was that the accident happened south of the Scottish boarder. The remedies of Scots law and those of English law for wrongful death are not identical and, because the Scots court looked for the common element in the two systems, the widow recovered only the funeral expenses. The particular rule of the Scots conflict of laws does not concern us here, the point is that English law was relevant to the case solely because the accident occurred in England. As no English persons or property were damaged there was nothing to concern English law about the case and the intrusion of English law into this Scots tragedy was purely the result of the rules of the conflict of laws.[60]

---

[58] See below para 8-37.

[59] [1949] SC 110.

[60] See *Babcock v. Jackson* above para 1-24.

Where a set of relations pre-exists the particular tortious act, the   **2-52**
concentration on the *locus delicti* becomes even less justifiable, its
artificiality even more pronounced. Some of the leading cases which have
so troubled English courts and which will be examined later[61] are false
problems in the sense that they result from the rules of the conflict of laws
themselves rather than from any real dispute between legal systems. A
crude localising rule in the case of tort, while it undoubtedly has a place
in the resolution of some issues for which there is no alternative, will not
suffice as a general dispositive rule for torts in the conflict of laws.

Lex situs

The *lex situs*, the law of the place where something is situated, has a   **2-53**
long history in conflict adjudication. Unlike the other examples of *locus
regit actum*, the concept of *situs* may be entirely passive in that it does not
pre-suppose the doing of anything within the *situs*; it may come into play
by reason of an act done elsewhere which has implications for the object
that is within the *situs*. Characteristically English law has resorted to the
law of the *situs* to deal with cases involving property, as control of the
property is in the hands of those who are empowered by the local law to
deal with it. Where property is land, or some other immovable interest, it
obviously follows that only the officials of the territorial system of law can
effectively deal with it. English courts have recognised this in two ways.
Firstly, English courts will not generally accept jurisdiction in cases
involving disputes about foreign immovable property.[62] Secondly, even
where the dispute is about movable property, English law generally defers
to the law of the current *situs*.

The acquisition of property rights may be made in several ways; if we   **2-54**
ignore finding, making and the other more uncommon ways, we will
concentrate on those transactions which most of us experience as the
means of getting property, namely - *sale* and *gift*. Now the problem with
these is that there are two dimensions - the relationship between the
parties themselves and the relations between the new owner and the rest
of the world. As between each other, the seller and buyer, donor and
recipient stand in a transaction relationship so that questions like - "Have
I got what I paid for?", or "Can I have my present back?" are referable to
the law, whatever it is, which governs that particular transaction: the law
of contract or the law of gift. The major issue here is not that between
the parties themselves but the recognition by others of the owner's rights

---

[61] See below para 4-106.
[62] See below para 5-09.

in the country where the goods happen to be. Clearly a theft does not become a legitimate form of transfer simply because the thief takes the goods across a border, but if the new country fails to recognise the former owner's interest the result might be very much the same. In short the attitude of the *lex situs* is crucial to the issue of property, at least while the goods remain in the *situs* and the conflict of laws cannot ignore its significance. Where the property is immovable the significance of the *lex situs* is obvious.

Conclusion

2-55   The law of the place has a strong claim in certain areas to govern the form of a transaction. Whether it has claims beyond this depends on whether it is possible to subsume a complex issue into a single question referable to a single fact location. Unless this can be done without too much distortion the danger is that a complex, interconnected legal problem will be resolved by the resort to a single connection which is no better than any other. Also, it must be remembered that fact/place links can be entirely fortuitous.

4   THE TRANSACTIONAL LAW

2-56   Instead of trying to encapsulate a complex legal issue into a single factual question, as the local laws and personal laws would have us do, why not try to make an analysis of the relationship as a whole and try to find the legal system which, overall, appears to have the greatest connection with, or the greatest interest in, that relationship? So, in a contract we could look at the personal laws of the parties, the laws of the places where the contract was made and where it was to be performed, the *lex situs* of any physical property which formed its subject matter and any other connections there might be. We could then decide, on balance, with which legal system the contract was predominantly connected and apply that law either to all issues or at least to those which did not admit of a single fact contact. The same approach could be adopted with marriage, in this case reference being made to the pre-marital and, possibly, post-marital personal laws of the parties, the place of celebration of the marriage and so on. Again with torts and property transactions we could collect together all the relevant information and make a judgement about the appropriate law to apply. Such an apparently simple idea does not come without its difficulties; the major ones being what connections are relevant and what are not, and how the weighing is to be carried out.

What Connections are Relevant?

Suppose we are dealing with a running down case in tort, what significance, if any, is to be given to the personal laws of the parties? Suppose they come from the same country which happens not to be the place of the accident. It might be argued here that if there is no damage to persons or property of the country where the accident occurs, there is no case for referring to the place of injury at all. Suppose, however, that they have different personal laws, what is to be made of this? One would hardly argue that a plaintiff who came from California was entitled to higher damages by reason of the fact that personal injury awards were higher in his home country. To be sure, his expectations might well be inflated by his personal law but what about the expectations of the defendant who, let us suppose, comes from a country in which personal injury awards are low?

The same conflict of expectations is equally applicable to the issue of liability as well as to its consequences. The rights which one personal law gives may not be mirrored in others, an act which is tortious by one system may be innocent by another.

In more complex tort cases, e.g. actions by employees against their employers or by passengers against their carriers, there may be a contractual dimension to add to the personal law and the law of the place.

If we take the example of a marriage, it is not fanciful to imagine four systems of law which might have an interest in the matter. The personal laws of the parties before the marriage, the law of the place where the marriage took place and the law of the new country where the couple set up home might all be seen as having claims for consideration if the validity of the marriage is questioned. Are all these claims equal or can some be ruled out either completely or depending on the particular issue raised? If we accept that the *lex loci celebrationis* has the right to a say in matters of the formal validity of the marriage is it to have the last word? Does it have any contribution to make to questions about the essential validity of the marriage or is it to be confined to matters of form only?

In cases of succession we may need to consider the personal laws of the deceased and of the beneficiaries, the laws which might be relevant to any will, and the laws of the countries in which any parts of the estate are situated. Each of these laws may have an interest in particular parts of the whole but which is to have the dominant position when they are in conflict?

In commercial contracts it might be thought that the personal laws of the human parties have little relevance but the law of the places of business of the corporate parties might well be pertinent. The law of the places where the contract was made or was to be performed, the legal systems indicated by the language of the contract and its form, the location

2-57

2-58

2-59

2-60

or legal connections of the subject matter of the contract and, above all, the system of law which the parties have indicated as their chosen governing law, all have potential relevance as significant connections.

2-61   Every conflict situation involves connections with at least two legal systems; many with more. The relevance of particular connections to any case depends not only on the issue in dispute but on the way the connections cluster around particular legal systems. The examples I have used have all included connections which have some claim to consideration, on some matters at least, in current English conflict law.

Do only Factual Connections Count?

2-62   Suppose that one visitor to a country runs down another visitor as a result of careless driving. Assume that they are the only people involved. We have potentially three systems of law to consider – the plaintiff's personal law, the defendant's personal law and the law of the place of accident. If there are, in fact, only two systems of law involved because the plaintiff and defendant have the same personal law, there is a strong case for ignoring the *lex loci delecti* and applying the rules of the common personal law to the dispute. If, however, the plaintiff and defendant have different personal laws there would seem to be no common element beyond the place of accident and the case for applying the *lex loci delecti* would be a strong one.

Suppose, however, that although the parties come from different countries their personal laws have the same rules on the issue in dispute. Does this provide a case for the displacement of the *lex loci delecti* in favour of the application of either of the personal laws? The answer would seem to be that it does not.

The English conflict of laws has been built around the jurisdiction selecting rule. The connection is made with the whole of the jurisdiction – French law, Nigerian law and the like, – theoretically without regard to the content of the legal system so identified, at least at the time of initial selection. On this basis, then, an English court would not concern itself with the common quality of the laws if the parties were from different countries. Indeed, in such a case it would not take the issue beyond the preliminary stage – recognising that the parties were from different legal systems.

2-63   Likewise, the attempt to find the appropriate law to govern the contract in default of choice would be based on the factual rather than the legal connections. Suppose the contract is found to have ten points of significant connection: three with one country, three with another and four with a third. On a simple point count the law of the third legal system would be applied and its rule would provide the dispositive rule for the case. This would be so even if the two other legal systems were to have identical rules on the issue in question, as the court has no method to make this sort of evaluation.

How are the Contacts to be Weighed?

It is obvious from the previous example that the mere counting of contacts without regard to their individual significance would be a very crude way of establishing the seat of the relationship. A mere point count could have the majority of trivial contacts outweigh the smaller number of more significant ones. On the other hand, to predicate which contacts must always enjoy superiority would remove the flexibility from the system and return it to a localising rule of the simple factual type. So, for example, to make the law of the place of *performance* of the contract always superior to the law of the place of *contracting*, while in the majority of cases a sensible thing to do, would not always fit the bill. The problem here is an obvious one, the court, seeking to do justice in the individual case wants to retain the maximum discretion, the businessman wants a clear rule to enable him to predict which way the court is likely to go - additionally he may well be prepared to sacrifice a better result in favour of a quicker one. Too rigid a weighting arrangement leads us back to the single fact/law connection of the localising rules, too much free law finding leads to unpredictable results and to needless and expensive litigation.

2-64

The Rome Convention on contractual obligations[63] seeks to steer a way between these polarities by applying, where the parties have not chosen a law to govern their contract, the system of law which is most closely connected to the contract but establishes a series of rebuttable presumptions to establish what that is.

Yet surely the principle is sound? For every set of legal relations there may be assumed to be a system which stands out among the others as having the closest relationship to the dispute taken as a whole.

2-65

There are various ways of characterising the process of looking for the predominant connection - the search for the closest and most real connection, the grouping of contacts, the seat of the relationship and, in the English conflict of laws, the proper law, *lex propria causae*. In the English conflict of laws the proper law concept first appeared in the context of contract and was related to the issue of parties autonomy - which will be considered in the next section. The complex interrelations to which a contract may give rise do not lend themselves to a single factual

---

[63] See below para 4-07.

contact. More recently there have been moves to apply similar techniques to the problem of tort cases as a reaction to the artificiality of the *lex loci delicti* and, it could be argued, the complex issues of marriage provide another field for possible proper law approaches. In the case of marriage, however, the personal law supplies much of the proper law requirement.

5 THE LAW CHOSEN BY THE PARTIES

2-66   At first sight it may seem odd that parties should be allowed to select the legal regime which is to govern their legal position, and it would indeed be odd if one could choose the system of criminal law by which one's behaviour was to be judged or the system of tort law which would determine the liability one had to one's neighbour. However, parties can in many ways control the legal system which is to apply to them, and we will look briefly at some ways here.

2-67   Any concept of the personal law is voluntary in the sense that a person can change his residence, domicile, nationality or religion with varying degrees of difficulty. Similarly a corporation can establish its place of business or manufacture where it chooses. In most cases the prime factor in these matters will be personal or financial, rather than legal, though it should not be supposed that legal effects do not follow or are not sought. To take some well-known examples:- the tax exile who sets up home or business in a new country where the incidence of taxation is lower; the fugitive from justice who goes to a country which has no extradition treaty with the country which wants him; the shipowner who registers his vessel with a country which makes fewer demands on him than the older maritime nations.

2-68   Parties can, by changing the location of themselves or their transactions, effectively choose the law by which their acts are to be judged. For example, the eloping couples who went to Gretna Green to enjoy Scots law's freedom from the requirement of parental consent to marriage; the contracting parties who choose the place of formal entry into the contract in order to get the benefit of that country's rules on formal validity (or to avoid those of some other country); the party who comes to England for a year to get an English divorce are all engaging in law choosing processes. In the examples given, they are choosing the law indirectly by altering the facts in a way which triggers the operation of the law.

2-69   Another way in which parties can indirectly select the law to govern is by choosing where to litigate. Different countries have different rules for the establishment of jurisdiction and some are more rigorous than others. It may be that a litigant can find a number of courts in different countries whose jurisdiction he can invoke. One of the factors influencing his choice will be the law which these different courts will apply to his dispute. He will need to be well advised if he is to make a sensible choice. In a genuinely international case the conflict of laws rules of the court will need to be considered.

In cases where courts apply their own domestic law to particular matters coming before them irrespective of the foreign elements in the case as, for example, in the granting of divorces or in the assessment of damages for personal injury, the choice of forum constitutes a direct choice of the law to be applied. So, for example, the liberal divorce jurisdictions of Nevada and South Dakota made those states places of resort for those seeking a speedy divorce. Similarly victims of the Bhopal disaster in India and the Piper Alpha disaster in the North Sea sought to bring their claims before courts in the U.S. where personal injury and wrongful death awards are much higher, rather than before the Indian courts and the courts in Scotland.

In commercial contracts it is not at all unusual to have what is known as a choice of jurisdiction clause specifying the country where any litigation, or arbitration, is to take place.[64]

    2-70

In those countries, like England, where foreign law has to be pleaded and proved, the parties may agree not to take the foreign law point at all and to let the case be decided according to the forum's own law.

    2-71

So, given a knowledge of the law which a court will apply either to the substance of the dispute or to the assessment of damages, the plaintiff, or, by agreement, both parties, can select that forum which will apply the law, whether its own or that of another country, which is wanted.[65]

    2-72

The aspects of choice looked at so far do not represent choice of law in the strict sense, being either examples of factual arrangements which have legal consequences or examples of choices of jurisdiction where the legal consequences follow from the law which the court applies in its ordinary resolution of such cases including, where appropriate, its conflict rules. What about explicit choices of the governing law of the kind "the law to govern this thing shall be the law of X"? Clearly the scope for this is limited. One party cannot usually stipulate a law in a manner which would adversely affect the other party to the litigation. There are, however, situations where such a stipulation would not have such an adverse effect and where it might seem appropriate to have regard to the wishes of the party. A testator cannot make his otherwise invalid will valid merely by saying so, for all testators, one assumes, have the intention of leaving a valid will and there is a public interest in wills to which a legal system gives effect in its rules on validity. At the same time a valid will is intended to give effect to the wishes of the testator, and that these

    2-73

---

64   See below para 4-88.
65   See below para 8-25.

wishes should be frustrated by a misunderstanding of what he wanted to achieve would benefit no-one, although there would be a wind-fall to the residuary legatees or to those entitled on intestacy. Allowing the testator to specify the law by which his will is to be construed would seem both sensible and workable. The same benefit could be conferred on the maker of any unilateral document. Where the dealing is bilateral or multilateral, the agreement of both or all of those concerned should, likewise, be respected.

2-74 As we shall see, the English conflict of laws has got round to this limited freedom of stipulation by a somewhat roundabout route, led by the autonomy of the parties to a contract to choose or incorporate a law for the transaction, but it is worth exploring in other areas. Self regulation is not a concept incompatible with law; such regulation must fall within the prescribed legal limits, of course, and these limits will be fixed according to the notions of the particular society concerned. But it would be wrong to think that, because in default of other arrangement, the job has to be done by the law, that there must therefore be a public interest in the narrow control of the matter. Parties are, anyway, generally free to settle their legal disputes without resort to the courts or to lawyers and the basis on which they settle is not, generally, a matter of interest to anyone else.

6 MORE SOPHISTICATED APPROACHES

2-75 All the connections that we have looked at so far lead to the identification of a legal system and only indirectly to a legal rule. That is, they are jurisdiction selecting not rule selecting approaches. Critics of the traditional system point to its failures not merely in terms of unfortunate results, to which any system of law can give rise, but in terms of a methodology which creates artificial problems. The weakness of traditional jurisdiction selecting processes, even if the connections are *prima facie* sensible and the rules properly applied, is that they take no account of interests. The rules of a legal system are applied to the determination of the issue irrespective of the views of the system from which the rules come. On occasion the rules may be dragged out of context by the foreign court which is trying to apply them.

2-76 The famous case of *Babcock v. Jackson*[66] provides a suitable object lesson for present purposes. The facts have already been given;[67] they all related to New York except that the place where the accident occurred was

---

[66]   (1963) 12 NY 2D 473; [1963] 2 Lloyds Rep 286.

[67]   Above para 1-24.

Ontario which had a "guest statute" preventing a gratuitous passenger from recovering from a negligent driver. There is an obvious case for applying New York law and none, save for the conflict rules of New York, for applying the law of Ontario. Assume, however, that we have to take account of Ontarian law, either because we have been persuaded to do so by the defendant, or because the conflict rules to be applied require it. It does not follow that Ontarian law should control the outcome. The laws of Ontario and those of New York are the same in all respects for this case save for the "guest statute" - what is that provision intended to do? The attribution of purpose to rules of law is notoriously difficult - it shouldn't be, but it is. The reasons for this are manifold but include: the difference between the original intention and the ultimate effect (the notorious history of the English Statute of Frauds 1677 furnishes a clear instance); the fact that legislation passed by an assembly may have been approved for all sorts of motives by those who voted for it, even directly contradictory ones; the fact that a judge-made rule suitable for one case may produce a different effect in another; the possibility that there was no single purpose that the rule was designed to meet in the first place, and so on. Nevertheless we can look at the Ontarian law and try to decide its purpose. Two possibilities immediately emerge - that the law was intended to prevent ungrateful behaviour by guests or that it was designed to prevent collusive frauds against motor insurers. Taking the first of these: where one person does a favour for another it may be thought most ungrateful if he is then asked to pay compensation for the harm which he happens to do in the process. Most people in most circumstances would never consider bringing an action at all but where the loss to them was severe or where it was known that a third party, in this case the driver's insurers, would actually bear the loss, attitudes might be different. Anyway, the issue here is not whether Ontario is wise in having such a provision, that is a matter for the Ontarians alone as there is clearly nothing in the law itself which makes it repulsive to the civilised conscience and requiring its rejection on moral grounds - as would be, for example, a racially discriminatory law. But what is the proper ambit of such a law?. How widely should it apply? Should it apply to all actions before Ontarian courts - that Ontarian courts will not allow their processes to be used to further the claims of ingrates? Should it apply to Ontarians - that ungrateful Ontarians should not be allowed to benefit anywhere? Should it apply to all accidents in Ontario irrespective of where the parties come from and the degree of relationship with Ontario? Only if the third question received an affirmative answer would there be any case at all for a court in New York to apply the Ontarian rule to deny the plaintiff her compensation. Turning to the second possibility, that the law of Ontario is intended to prevent collusive frauds against insurance companies, a similar sort of analysis may be made. All systems of law have an interest in preventing fraudulent claims but the common way to deal with the problem is on an *ad hoc* basis, to disallow the particular claim when the fraud is discovered rather than to disallow a whole class of actions on the basis that some of them may be fraudulent. The English Statute of Frauds provides an unhappy example of an attempt to deal with the problem of fraud by generic prescription rather than on an individual basis. Again we are not concerned with the sense of such a law but with the ambit of its operation. That Ontarian courts should not lend their processes to this sort of claim is intelligible, also perhaps that no Ontarian should be allowed to make such a claim anywhere might be the aspiration, but neither of these apply to the case in hand. Looked at from another angle, the object of the law may be to protect the funds of insurers from false claims and thus to protect the general body of premium payers from the knock-on costs of such claims. If such were the case it seems unlikely that Ontarian law was concerned with claims against foreign insurers being conducted before foreign tribunals. No Ontarian insurer was involved in this litigation and no direct interest of the law of Ontario was at stake. It is not inconceivable that in such a case a court sitting in the *locus delicti* might hesitate to apply the local law to foreign litigants. Enough has been said to establish the artificiality of the New York court woodenly applying the law of Ontario simply on the basis of a simple factual connection. What is the solution?

2-77   Three possibilities present themselves:- change the jurisdiction selecting rule to avoid the artificial contact having too much significance; weed out inappropriate rules at the law application stage; adopt a methodology that goes directly to the possibly applicable rules.

Solution one - adopting a better choice of law rule, while maintaining jurisdiction selecting approaches, would lead to the acceptance of the law of the transaction as the governing rule. This possibility was considered above and, in its simplest form, would involve the grouping of contacts. On this basis the law of New York would apply because all the contacts are with that law save for the purely fortuitous event of the accident occurring in Ontario.

Solution two - weeding out the inappropriate rule at the law application stage, needs a little more explanation. Every court deciding a case will apply its own procedure and will ensure that its decision is congruent with the general policy of the country in which it sits.[68] It will, thus, not apply a foreign law that results in a decision objectionable to the forum; objectionable in a real sense, of course, not merely something that it does not like. This inherent power may be used to vet the rules of a foreign system in terms of their appropriateness to determine the outcome of the case in hand so that the court in *Babcock v. Jackson* could, on the

---

[68]   See below Chapter 7.

basis of the analysis set out above, simply have declared the rule of Ontario law, though *prima facie* applicable, inappropriate on the facts of the case itself and, there being no other difference between Ontarian and New York law in this case, have applied either to enable the plaintiff to recover.

Solution three requires the court to look at legal rules rather than at legal systems and to engage in direct purposive analysis of competing dispositive rules. It involves adopting an entirely different methodology, one based on rule selection instead of jurisdiction selection. There are several varieties of this approach which have produced a vigorous debate in the U.S.A. over the last thirty years. With the single exception of *Chaplin v. Boys,*[69] these ideas have had no significant influence on the development of English conflict law. As the major battleground has been torts, an area which for English law is likely soon to be put on a statutory basis involving jurisdiction selecting rules, and as English conflict law for contracts is already on a statutory jurisdiction selecting basis, there is even less scope for the American influence to be felt in England. For that reason, and for the pressure of space, I have reluctantly decided not to consider them here. The ideas are attractive, some seductively so, and they demonstrate a fundamental re-thinking of the choice of law process. I list some of the major contributors to the debate below.[70]

7 CONCLUSION

As has been seen there are only a limited number of possibilities open   **2-78**
to a court trying a case with a foreign contact or, increasingly, to a legislature or conference seeking to establish a code for the choice of law in a particular area, and none of them are suitable for all cases. While the number is small, permutations are possible so that a rule could offer either a set of alternatives. For example, the formal validity of a will can be determined by three varieties of the personal law, each within two time frames, or by the law of the place of acting,[71] or apply a combination of connections. For example, the law to govern certain types of consumer contract under the Rome Convention is the law of the consumer's habitual residence but only if certain factual contacts with the contract exist

---

[69] See below para 4-113.

[70] Cavers: *The Choice Of Law Process* (1965); Currie: *Selected Essays in the Conflict of Laws* (1963); Ehrensweig: *Treatise on the Conflict of Laws* (1962); Leflar: *American Conflict Laws* (1966); von Mehren & Trautmann: *The Law of Multistate Problems* (1965). See also *Restatement (Second) Conflict of Laws* (1971) and, for an excellent short account, Morris: *Conflict of Laws 3rd ed.* (1984) pp.312-331.

[71] See below para 5-58.

there.[72] How they may be used in the disposition of disputes in the various areas of law will be a matter for consideration in subsequent chapters.

Before leaving this area, however, it might be worth noting a rather strange example in the Rome Convention of going to Birmingham by way of Beachy Head where a court may be required to determine the characteristic performance of the contract, not with a view to applying the law of the place where that is to happen, but to apply the personal law of the party whose duty it is to carry it out under the contract.[73]

---

[72] See below para 4-50.
[73] See below para 4-36.

CHAPTER 3

JURISDICTION AND JUDGMENTS

1 INTRODUCTION

Jurisdiction concerns the competence of courts and other tribunals to determine disputes with an authority which will make the decision binding and enforceable within their own system, and capable of potential recognition and enforcement by the courts and tribunals of other countries. If a country's jurisdictional rules are too restrictive they may result in a denial of justice as cases which ought to be justiciable before the courts are turned away; if they are lax they may result in "forum shopping"[1] with an influx of cases completely unconnected with the law or country of the "open" forum with the result that the decisions are not respected by other countries.

3-01

The issue of jurisdiction involves a set of related questions: Can the plaintiff invoke the assistance of the court? Has the court authority over the defendant? Has the court the power to determine the issue? Must the court exercise the power or may it decline to do so?

In international cases jurisdictional issues are particularly prominent as the degrees of connection between the plaintiff and the court, the defendant and the court and the factual connections of the legal dispute with the system of law operated by the court may in each case be close, tenuous, remote or even non-existent.

Rules of jurisdiction can be plaintiff oriented, defendant oriented or related to the cause of action invoked, and current English jurisdictional rules show the influence of all three approaches.

Courts can take, or be given, a wide or restricted jurisdictional ambit and can take or be given powers to exercise discretion in the cases they actually accept for trial or they may have no choice in the matter. A wider or narrower view of jurisdiction may be taken in the light of the substance of the dispute between the parties so that a court may have jurisdiction over a contractual dispute between A and B but not over a matrimonial one.

Jurisdictional issues go beyond the competence of the forum within its own system. They extend to the enforcement of decisions and the

3-02

---

[1] See below para 8-25.

recognition and enforcement of foreign judgements. Judgments, for this purpose, include both judicial decisioins in the narrow sense, and those determined by arbitrators and others exercising a judicial role. The attitude to be adopted to those who have stipulated in their dealings the law or the dispute system, or both, which they wish to be applied to any issue arising between them has also to be determined.

3-03   There are three matters, properly within the purview of this chapter, which I have chosen to treat elsewhere in the text. They are: –

1) Jurisdiction in matrimonial causes and the recognition of foreign matrimonial decisions. Always a special case under common law, these matters are not touched (save in the single instance of maintenance) by the Jurisdiction Conventions, and are best left to the chapter on Family Law.[2]

2) Jurisdiction agreements. A jurisdiction agreement is a contract under English law and the matter will be principally considered in the chapter on Obligations.[3]

3) Jurisdiction over foreign immovable property. The decision in *British South Africa Co. v. Companhia de Moçambique*[4] declared the common law position that English courts would not take jurisdiction over any matter concerned with title to, or rights to possession of, foreign immovable property. The *Moçambique* rule is mirrored in the exclusive jurisdiction provisions of the Jurisdiction Conventions.[5] It no longer applies to simple cases of trespass or other torts to foreign land which do not raise issues of title,[6] but it has recently been extended to foreign intellectual property rights.[7] The basis of the rule and the exceptions to it are considered in the chapter on Property.[8]

2 JURISDICTION

Jurisdiction at Common Law

3-04   English law has, traditionally, adopted an "open" forum policy for personal actions with the result that resort is had to English courts by parties who have no connection with this country over subject matters

---

2 See below para 6-53, 6-61.
3 See below para 4-88, but see also 3-52.
4 [1893] A.C. 602.
5 See Brussels Convention Art. 16 (1) (a).
6 See Civil Jurisdiction and Judgments Act 1982 s.30 (1).
7 See *Tyburn Productions Ltd. v. Conan Doyle* [1991] Ch. 75; [1990] 1 All ER 909.
8 See below para 5-09.

which are equally unconnected. This is particularly true in commercial cases where English courts and, indeed, English law, are frequently chosen by those whose dealings are otherwise unconnected with England. Whatever this does for the esteem, self or otherwise, of English courts or for the regard in which English law is held it is certainly good business and contributes to the U.K.'s invisible earnings.

Service of process in England

Common law jurisdiction, at least as far as personal actions are concerned, was, and remains, plaintiff oriented, territorially limited and procedural in essence. The basic rule is that anyone can invoke the jurisdiction of the English court in a personal action by the physical service of the writ or other originating process on a defendant who is physically present in England. Neither plaintiff nor defendant need have any connection with this country, beyond the physical presence of the defendant. There is no requirement, for example, that the defendant should have assets in this country, and there is no need for the substantive dispute to have any English connection.

3-05

From the plaintiff's point of view the advantages of this open forum policy are obvious enough but so are the drawbacks. While the defendant who, with no connection with England, can be made subject to the jurisdiction by serving him with process when he comes to this country to see the races at Ascot[9], or has an overnight stay in a London hotel,[10] a fugitive defendant can escape pursuit simply by staying out of the country. To remedy this problem rules of court permit service of process out of the jurisdiction as of right or by the leave of the court but, unlike the basic rule, service out is only available if there is a connection with England either of the defendant personally, e.g. he is domiciled here, or of the cause of action e.g. the tort was committed in this country or the contract was made here.

That the defendant has no assets in this country, while it will not prevent service either in or out, will be a major factor against the plaintiff taking advantage of the liberal common law rules for he will then have to get his judgment recognised in some country where it can be effectively enforced. The tenuous jurisdictional links with the English court will hardly commend the English judgment to, say, a court of the defendant's country of residence or domicile in which assets might be found.

From the defendant's point of view it must be accepted that the plaintiff has the choice both of piste and of weapons and it is not

---

[9] *Maharanee of Baroda v. Wildenstein* [1972] 2 QB 283; [1972] 2 All ER 689.
[10] *Colt Industries v. Sarlie* [1966] 1 All ER 673.

improper for the plaintiff to select the forum which is most advantageous to him, just as he will choose the cause of action. Where the defendant finds himself hauled before a court in a country with which neither he nor the issue in dispute have any connection we might sympathise with his complaint.

Service out of the jurisdiction

3-06   To back up the physical jurisdiction at common law and to deal with the defendant who could otherwise avoid process by the simple expedient of keeping out of the jurisdiction, there has developed a substantial area of "assumed" jurisdiction under which process can be served on a defendant abroad. "Service out", as it is known, is governed by the Rules of the Supreme Court and in all but a few cases e.g. where the English court has jurisdiction under the Conventions,[11] requires the permission of the court. Permission is no mere formality and the plaintiff has to satisfy the court not only that he has a good arguable case against the absent defendant, meaning one in which he has a good chance of success,[12] but also that England is the appropriate forum for the litigation.[13] Examples of situations where permission to serve process out of the jurisdiction may be granted are :- where the defendant is domiciled (in the sense used for the Conventions[14]) in the U.K.,[15] where the plaintiff is seeking an injunction, positive or negative, concerning a substantive right in the U.K.[16] or where the matter affects a contract which was made in England,[17] has been broken in England,[18] is governed by English law[19] or contains an English jurisdiction clause.[20] Other examples include: torts committed (meaning either that the wrongful act was done or the harm was suffered) in England;[21] some matters affecting land within the jurisdiction;[22] the administration of estates of people who died domiciled in England;[23] and

---

[11] See below para 3-26.

[12] *Seaconsar Far East v. Bank Markazi Jomhouri Islami Iran The Times* Nov 22 1992.

[13] For a consideration of the doctrine of *forum conveniens* and *forum non conveniens* see below para 3-08.

[14] See below para 3-22.

[15] Rules of the Supreme Court Order 11 Rule 1 (1)(a).

[16] *ibid* Rule 1 (1)(b).

[17] Rule 1 (1)(d)(i).

[18] Rule 1 (1)(e).

[19] Rule 1 (1)(d)(ii).

[20] Rule 1 (1)(d)(iv).

[21] Rule 1 (1)(f).

[22] Rule 1 (1)(g) and (h).

[23] Rule 1 (1)(k).

actions to enforce judgments and arbitral awards. As can be seen from these examples the basis of service out generally requires a connection of the subject matter of the dispute with England which is not required when personal service in England is possible. However, the leave of the court is required and such leave is not readily given. A comprehensive statement of the present attitude on leave to serve out can be found in the judgment of Lord Goff in *Spiliada Maritime Corporation v. Cansulex Ltd.*[24]

Submission to the jurisdiction

At common law the court will have jurisdiction over the defendant if he submits to the court by entering an appearance and defending the case on its merits, or he makes a claim himself which is met by a counterclaim. The entry of an appearance to contest the jurisdiction does not count as a submission to the jurisdiction. Clearly when a party has submitted to the jurisdiction in this way he cannot claim that he is a victim of the wide jurisdiction of English law. Where a party has agreed that a dispute shall be submitted to the English courts he will, save in very exceptional circumstances, be held to his bargain.[25] While submission to the jurisdiction might seem an ideal basis upon which to establish jurisdiction it should be noted that this is true only of the open forum view. Where jurisdiction is controlled, as it is under the Jurisdiction Conventions, submission will not be a basis of jurisdiction in cases where a particular forum is indicated by the rules as having exclusive jurisdiction.

3–07

Forum conveniens and forum non conveniens

Although English courts have an inherent power to control their own procedures and have refused to let actions continue where it was felt that the case was frivolous or vexatious or an abuse of process, they have not, until relatively recently, been much concerned with the appropriateness of the forum for the particular dispute in hand.[26] In part this was due to the open forum policy, a policy defended vigorously, for example, by Lord Denning in the Court of Appeal in the *Atlantic Star*,[27] and partly, perhaps, to a rather arrogant attitude to the tribunals of other countries. It is obvious that the links which a case may have with particular jurisdictions can range from the exclusively connected to the wholly unconnected and it is impossible to stipulate in abstract terms which

3–08

---

[24] [1987] 1 A.C. 460; [1986] 3 All E.R. 843.

[25] See below para 4–91.

[26] See for the emergence of the doctrine of *forum non conveniens* in applications for a stay of proceedings *The Atlantic Star* [1974] A.C. 436; [1973] 2 All ER 175; *MacShannon v. Rockware Glass* [1978] A.C. 795 [1978] 1 All ER 625.

[27] [1972] 3 All ER 705 at 709.

contacts, or classes of contacts – parties, facts, evidence, witnesses, lawyers, procedure, substantive law, assets, enforcement procedures and so on – should be dominant in any particular case. Like other matters in the litigation, the parties will see things in different lights and, anyway, the plaintiff has already chosen what to him appears the most appropriate forum by bringing the action or seeking leave so to do. But his view is not a proffered stab at objectivity but a self interested and considered decision; he might prefer, all other things being equal, to sue elsewhere; but all other things are not equal and he has to play the percentage game. Equally so the defendant; his objective is to maximise his own advantage and minimise that of the plaintiff and to counterbalance the advantage that all plaintiffs have of choosing the battleground.

3-09   Where to sue can be as great a consideration in an international case as who to sue or on what grounds to sue. The court is not in the business of advising parties where to litigate. It is however faced with the task of assessing the appropriateness of the forum in two instances:-

1)   where the plaintiff seeks leave to serve process out of the jurisdiction and needs to establish that England is a clearly appropriate forum for the trial of the issue – *forum conveniens*.

2)   where the defendant seeks to stay the English proceedings on the basis that trial in England is not appropriate and that a foreign forum is clearly more suitable – *forum non conveniens*.

Despite the different origins and purposes of the questions and the obvious difference that the initial burden of proof is on the aspiring plaintiff in Order 11 cases and on the original defendant in applications for a stay, the issues are essentially the same: "to identify the forum in which the case can be suitably tried for the interests of all the parties and for the ends of justice".[28] In seeking to answer the question the court may have regard to any matter which it considers pertinent and there will be no presumptions that any single factor or group of factors should ordinarily be decisive. To take an example which featured in the *Spiliada* case and was explored by Lord Goff. Suppose, as was the case there, that the only other forum considered, which was British Columbia, had a stricter limitation period than England so that the plaintiffs were time-barred there. At first sight this might seem a clinching argument, as to stay an action or to refuse leave to serve out would leave the plaintiff without the possibility of a remedy. On reflection, however, it becomes clear that this is not an answer but a call for a question – why was no process begun in the alternative forum? If the answer were to be that the plaintiff had dallied so long that he had missed the local bus, his application for an English taxi

---

[28] Per Ld Goff in *Spiliada Maritime Corporation v. Cansulex Ltd.* [1986] 3 All ER 843 at 858 quoting Ld Kinnear in *Sim v. Robin* (1892) 19 R (Ct of Sess) 665 at 668.

suddenly loses its merit. If, however, the foreign limitation period was so short as to take him unaware of the need to put in a protective writ, some sympathy is regained. In other words the reasonableness of the plaintiff's conduct is a legitimate area of investigation. In *Spiliada* Lord Goff felt that the plaintiff's conduct in not starting proceedings in Canada was not unreasonable and had he been minded to accept the appeal against leave he would have made that conditional on the defendants not taking the time point in the Canadian proceedings. In the same way, the American courts stayed the actions of the Indian plaintiffs against Union Carbide Corporation following the explosion of the chemical factory in Bhopal in India on the condition that they were furnished with the information which the generous process of discovery in the U.S. would have given them beyond that which could be obtained under Indian law.

There is a strong case for granting a stay of proceedings where there is **3-10** multiplicity – where there are proceedings taking place in more than one country. This is especially true where the same parties are suing in the same capacities over the same subject matter. But the mere fact that proceedings have been instituted in more than one forum does not ensure that the plea – *lis alibi pendens* – will produce a stay of English proceedings. What needs to be considered is the appropriateness of the foreign and English forums, the state of the proceedings in each country, whether they are advanced or have not gone further than a protective writ, whether either action is a serious attempt to litigate a dispute, and so on.

In appropriate cases an English court, satisfied that the English action **3-11** should proceed, will allow it to continue and issue an injunction to restrain the foreign proceedings. Such an injunction, of course, is not directed at the foreign court but at the plaintiff and operates, as do all injunctions, on him personally. It would seem that this discretion will be exercised only where the foreign proceedings are oppressive and not merely where the English forum is more appropriate.[29]

Plaintiffs and defendants

The only person unable to invoke the jurisdiction of the English courts **3-12** under the common law rules is the alien enemy – a person who is resident in or carries on business in a territory occupied or controlled by a State with which Britain is at war. There are no other general restrictions on plaintiffs but, as jurisdiction is a procedural matter for the *lex fori* anyone invoking the English jurisdiction must comply with English rules. So, for example, the manner in which an action can be brought in England on behalf of a child plaintiff will apply to a foreign child plaintiff irrespective of the autonomous powers of the child under his personal law or any other.

---

[29] See *Société Nationale Industrielle Aerospatiale v. Lee Kui Jac* [1987] AC 871, [1987] 3 All ER 510.

3-13   Much more important is the restriction of those who can be compelled as defendants before English courts. The central issue here is that of sovereign immunity. The problem is not so much the personal liability of sovereigns, heads of State, and their official representatives for their personal actions but the extent to which the immunity extends to interests of the foreign State and bodies which could be regarded as emanations of the State. The matter is now covered by the State Immunity Act 1978. The Act distinguishes the State as such, meaning the sovereign or head of State, the government of that State and the departments of that government, which are entitled to immunity, from a "separate entity" which is distinct from the executive organs of the government of that State and is capable of suing and being sued, which is not. The Act also qualifies the general principle of the immunity of the foreign State[30]. The immunity will not apply if the State has submitted to the jurisdiction[31] and will not extend to a number of matters connected with the U.K. So, for example, if the State is obligated to perform a contract in the U.K.,[32] or certain employment contracts are made or are to be performed in the U.K.,[33] or the proceedings relate to death or personal injury, loss or damage to property caused by an act or omission in the U.K.,[34] or the matter relates to immovable or intellectual property interests which the State may have in the U.K.,[35] the principle of immunity will not apply. Most importantly, immunity does not apply to any proceedings relating to " a commercial transaction entered into by the State."[36] Commercial transactions as defined by the Act[37] cover contracts for the supply of goods or services, loans and other transactions for the provision of finance, and "any other transaction or activity (whether of a commercial, industrial, financial, professional or other similar character) into which a State enters or in which it engages otherwise than in the exercise of sovereign authority". It should be noted that the issue of State immunity is not confined to cases where the foreign State is the intended defendant in the English proceedings; it arises also in cases where the jurisdiction is properly invoked against a defendant who sets up the immunity of a foreign State. An example of such "indirect impleading" would be where the goods which are the subject matter of the dispute are under the control of a foreign State.

---

[30] S.1.
[31] S.2.
[32] S.3(1)(b).
[33] S.4.
[34] S.5.
[35] Ss.6 & 7.
[36] S.3(1)(a).
[37] S.3(3).

Other legislation deals with the legal position of the representatives of foreign states and other international bodies.

3-14

The Diplomatic Privileges Act 1964 ranks the immunity from jurisdiction according to the status of the representative from diplomatic agents who are immune from civil and criminal jurisdiction for nearly everything, through administrative and technical staff, to the domestic staff whose immunity is limited to civil jurisdiction over acts done in the course of their duties and their freedom from U.K. income tax and National Insurance contributions.

The Consular Relations Act 1968 gives effect to the Vienna Convention of 1963 and provides jurisdictional immunity for the performance of consular functions as defined in the Convention.

The International Organisations Act 1968 enables ranked immunities to be conferred on the different classes of representatives of recognised international organisations. Examples of such organisations include: the United Nations, the International Labour Organisation, the International Court of Justice, the E.C. Commission, EUTELSAT, and, recently, the European Bank for Reconstruction and Development.

The ambit of the common law rules

Although the common law rules can now be described as residual in that they are displaced by the Jurisdiction Conventions, they remain in operation and apply whenever the case falls outside the rules of the Conventions either because it is not within the definition of "civil and commercial matter' or, more importantly, because the defendant is not domiciled within a Contracting State in those cases, and they constitute the bulk, where the application of the Conventions depends on that connection. The common law rules will, therefore, continue to apply to a substantial amount of the international business coming before the Commercial Court.

3-15

Jurisdiction under the Conventions

Introduction

The Brussels Convention of 1968 on Jurisdiction and the Enforcement of Judgments in Civil and Commercial Matters was agreed among the six original member States of the E.C. Its object was to harmonise the rules of jurisdiction in conflict cases within the E.C. in order to facilitate the recognition and enforcement of judgments throughout the Community. The U.K. acceded to the Brussels Convention in 1978 and an amended version of the original Convention,

3-16

and a modified version of it to deal with internal U.K. jurisdictional matters (the Modified Convention), were brought into force by the Civil Jurisdiction and Judgments Act of 1982 on 1st January 1987. The accession of Portugal and Spain to the Brussels Convention in 1989 (the San Sebastian Convention) involved further changes and these came into effect in the U.K. on 1st December 1991.[38] Finally, the Lugano Convention extended the main features of the Brussels Convention to the E.C.'s major trading partners, the EFTA countries, – this "Parallel Convention" was brought into effect by the Civil Jurisdiction and Judgments Act of 1991 on 1st May 1992.

Not all these developments have as yet filtered through the whole system. Space is limited enough as it is and I will assume in what follows that both the San Sebastian and the Lugano Conventions are fully in force throughout their respective areas. Clearly this is not at present true and anyone concerned with jurisdictional matters in international litigation would need to check the latest position in order to determine which regime was applicable in the particular States in which litigation is contemplated.

Unless the contrary is stated the term *Conventions* will be used in this section to mean the Brussels Convention, as amended by the San Sebastian Convention, and the Lugano Convention.

Interpretation of the conventions

3-17   The Court of Justice of the European Communities (E.C.J.) is empowered to give preliminary rulings on the interpretation of the Brussels Convention on matters referred to it by designated national courts.[39] The E.C.J. is not an appeal court for this purpose, its interpretative jurisdiction cannot be invoked by a litigant but only by a national court which considers such a ruling to be necessary to enable it to give judgment in the actual case.[40] Judgments and opinions of the E.C.J. are to be taken into account in the interpretation of the Convention and English courts are required to take judicial notice of them.[41]

National courts are expected to adopt a European rather than a national approach to the interpretation of the Conventions and it is specifically provided[42] that courts in the U.K. may refer to the Reports in the Official Journal of the Communities which accompanied the

---

[38] SI 1990/2591.

[39] Luxembourg Protocol 1971 as amended; Civil Jurisdiction and Judgments Act 1982,. Sch 2.

[40] *ibid* Article 3.

[41] Civil Jurisdiction and Judgments Act 1982 s.3.

[42] *ibid*.

Conventions[43] and decisions of other national courts may be regarded as persuasive authority.

The text of the Conventions is nothing like the attempted precision of a U.K. statute. It invites a purposive rather than a literal approach to its interpretation - one which takes account of the object of the Convention as a whole to inform the interpretation of particular provisions - not an easy task and one which the E.C.J. has not always managed.[44]   **3-18**

Although the writ of the E.C.J. does not run in the E.F.T.A. countries, there are arrangements to seek consistency in the interpretation of the Brussels and Lugano Conventions and it seems unlikely that significant discrepancies will emerge.

The ambit of the conventions

The Conventions apply only to international cases; they do not seek to determine jurisdiction when there is no element foreign to the Contracting State, i.e. they allocate jurisdiction among States in the international sense, they do not attempt to allocate to legal systems as such. For the U.K. with its three principal legal systems, an internal process of allocation has been established by the Modified Convention and special provisions in the Civil Jurisdiction and Judgments Act.[45]   **3-19**

The Conventions apply only -   **3-20**

i)   where the issue in dispute is a *civil or commercial matter* and either

ii)   the defendant has his *domicile in a Contracting State*, i.e. in an E.C.[46] State (Brussels Convention) or an E.F.T.A.[47] State (Lugano Convention) or

iii)   a Contracting State has *exclusive jurisdiction* either by reason of the subject matter in dispute (e.g. real estate within the jurisdiction) or by the prior agreement of the parties.

Where the Conventions apply, the court indicated has no choice but to accept the jurisdiction, it cannot hold itself *forum non conveniens*[48] (unless perhaps the appropriate forum is that of a non-Contracting

---

[43]   For the Brussels Convention, the Jenard Report (OJ 1979 C59/1); for the 1979 Accession Convention, the Schlosser Report (OJ 1979 C59/71), the Lugano Convention, the Jenard-Möller Report (OJ 1990 C189/57).

[44]   See e.g. *Rösler v. Rottwinkel* [1985] 1CMLR 806. Note the addition to Article 16 in the 1989 amendment.

[45]   See below para 3-59.

[46]   The European Community states are: Belgium, France, Germany, Italy, Luxembourg, the Netherlands, Denmark, Ireland, the U.K., Greece, Portugal and Spain.

[47]   The European Free Trade Association states are Austria, Finland, Iceland, Norway, Sweden and Switzerland.

[48]   Civil Jurisdiction and Judgments Act 1982 s.49.

State[49]) and it cannot control service of process out of the jurisdiction. This does not mean that there are no choices of jurisdiction open to the parties for there are some overlaps in the Conventions' provisions. Where these occur and multiple proceedings are instituted, the Conventions provide that if there is identity in the roles of the parties and the cause of action, the second court, in time, must stay its proceedings until the court first seised has established whether or not it has jurisdiction and, if it has, the second court must decline jurisdiction in favour of the first.[50] Unlike the common law rules the Conventions are defendant oriented and the domicile of the defendant is a concept key to both the application of the Conventions themselves and the jurisdictional rules they contain.

The elements listed above need to be explored.

(1) Civil or Commercial matter

3-21   The Conventions do not define what civil or commercial matters are but there are some indications as to what they are not. Article 1 provides that the Conventions shall not extend, in particular, to "revenue, customs or administrative matters" and also provides a list of other issues to which the Conventions shall not apply.

Revenue and customs matters are reasonably clear but "administrative matters" can cause problems particularly for English law where the distinction between public and private law is less well defined than in other countries. Whether or not a public authority is acting in the exercise of its powers, a test laid down by the E.C.J.,[51] is not very helpful when the authority is using private law means, e.g. tort actions, to carry out its public role. In most cases, of course, administration will be local in its effect and will not raise international issues.

Matters excluded from the operation of the Conventions include:-

"*the status or legal capacity of natural persons*[52] *rights in property arising out of a matrimonial relationship, wills and succession*".[53]

These exclusions are fairly clear and comprehend issues of majority status and the capacity of a minor to act in law, marriage and matrimonial causes, legitimacy, testate and intestate succession and family property regimes. Perhaps surprisingly it does not exclude maintenance for which

---

[49]   See *Harrods (Buenos Aires) Ltd. No 2* [1991] 4 All ER 348. The matter is now before the ECJ.

[50]   Article 21 both Conventions.

[51]   In *LTU v. Eurocontrol* [1976] ECR 1541: [1977] 1 CMLR 88.

[52]   Article 1(1); note the same exclusion in the Rome Contracts Convention Art. 1 (2)(a) and see below para 4-84.

[53]   *ibid* and in Rome Convention Art. 1 (2)(b) see below para 4-85.

there is a special provision.[54] It does not exclude matters which are related to but do not expressly raise the excluded issues. So, for example, an international action brought by a disappointed beneficiary against the testator's legal advisor over the negligent drafting of the will, or an action by a wife who has lost her interest in the matrimonial home as a result of a surety agreement which she had entered without warning of the consequences, are not excluded.

"bankruptcy, proceedings relating to the winding up of insolvent companies or other legal persons, judicial arrangements, compositions and analogous proceedings"[55]

"social security"[56]

"arbitration".[57]

Arbitration is excluded from the Conventions and this exclusion extends not only to the process of arbitration and the effect of arbitration awards but to disputes about the appointment of an arbitrator.[58]

(2) Domicile in a Contracting State

Except where the special provisions contained in Articles 16 and 17 apply,[59] the Conventions operate only where the defendant is domiciled in a Contracting State. The plaintiff's connections are relevant to the operation of the Conventions in only two instances (both concerned with Articles 16 and 17) and relevant to the rules of the Conventions only as factual matters under certain of the special, additional, jurisdictional rules.[60]

3-22

(3) Domicile under the Conventions

Individuals The Conventions do not define domicile - a concept of which different States have different conceptions - leaving it to the court which is seised of the case to determine whether the defendant is domiciled in that State by the application of its own domestic law.[61] In

3-23

---

54 Article 5 (2) see later para 3-33.

55 Article 1 (2) c/f Rome Convention Art. 1 (2)(e) below para 4-93.

56 Article 1 (3).

57 Article 1 (4) c/f Rome Convention Art. 1 (2)(d) below para 4-88.

58 See *Marc Rich & Co. v. Società Italiana Impianti P.A.* Case C 190/98 (1991) 16 ELR 529.

59 See below paras 3-41, 3-52.

60 See below paras 3-46, 3-53, 3-33, 3-39.

61 Article 52.

determining whether he is domiciled in another Contracting State the court is required to apply the law of domicile of that other State.[62]

For the U.K. the traditional concept of domicile in English law, based on presence and the present intention of permanent residence,[63] could well have meant that the English court would be forced to decline jurisdiction in favour of a country with which the defendant had a more tenuous connection by reason of a less stringent test of domicile applied there. To deal with this, special rules on domicile were introduced by the 1982 Act.[64] The simplified code of domicile, which applies only for the purposes of the Conventions, enables a person's domicile in the U.K. to be established if it can be shown that:-

a)   he is resident in the U.K. and

b)   "the nature and circumstances of his residence indicate that he has a substantial connection with the U.K."[65]

This second requirement will be rebuttably presumed if the person has been resident in the U.K. for the last three months.[66]

It needs to be noted here that domicile under the Conventions is related to a State, not a country or law district. The object of this exercise of domicile is to link the defendant with the U.K. as a whole; special rules apply to the further localisation required.[67]

If the defendant is not domiciled in the U.K. or in another Contracting State, it must follow that he is domiciled in a non-Contracting State! If, however, it is necessary positively to establish that a person is domiciled in a non-Contracting State, as it is to allow the English courts to take jurisdiction at common law rather than under the Conventions, the same test as for U.K. domicile under the Conventions is applied.[68] But in these cases there is no presumption raised by three month's residence and no attempt either to take account of the non-Contracting State's concept of domicile, if it has one. This special test of domicile for the purpose of the Conventions can have odd results. Suppose an English Court takes jurisdiction at common law having satisfied itself that the defendant is domiciled in State X, a non-Contracting State. When it proceeds to the substantive issues its choice of law rules might involve a reference to the defendant's *lux domicilii*. Now,

---

[62]   *ibid.*

[63]   See above para 2-11.

[64]   Civil Jurisdiction and Judgments Act 1982, s.41

[65]   *ibid* s.41(2) (a) and (b).

[66]   *ibid* s.41(6).

[67]   See below para 3-60.

[68]   Civil Jurisdiction and Judgments Act 1982 s.41(7).

of course, the English court will apply its ordinary test of dimicile for choice of law purposes. This could result in a finding that the defendant was domiciled in State Y. State Y could be either a Contracting or a non-Contracting State.

Companies and associations The domicile of a company or unincorporated association is identified with its seat and it is for the national court seised of the case to determine where that is by the use of its own conflict rules.[69]

3-24

The Civil Jurisdiction and Judgments Act[70] provides that a company or association has its seat and, therefore, its domicile in the U.K. if:-

a) it was incorporated or formed under the law of a part of the U.K. and has its registered office or some other official address in the U.K. or

b) its central management or control is exercised in the U.K.[71]

The same test is applied to establish if such a body is domiciled in a State other than the U.K.[72] If the foreign State indicated by the test is a non-Contracting State the common law rules on jurisdiction will be applied. If, however, the State indicated is a Contracting State, the company or association will only be domiciled there if it is so regarded by the law of that State.[73]

Where the matter concerns the exclusive jurisdiction under Article 16(2) a modified version of these domicile tests is applied.[74]

Trusts The domicile of a trust is left by the Conventions to the conflict rules of the court which is seised of the case.[75] For the U.K. a trust will only be domiciled in the U.K. if it is domiciled in a part of the U.K. It will be domiciled in that part of the U.K. whose legal system has the closest and most real connection with it.[76]

Rules of jurisdiction under the Conventions
General jurisdiction

The Conventions apply whenever the defendant is domiciled in a Convention State and *the basic jurisdictional rule is that a defendant must be sued in the State in which he is domiciled.*[77]

3-25

---

[69] Article 53.
[70] Civil Jurisdiction and Judgments Act 1982 s.42.
[71] S.42(3).
[72] S.42(6).
[73] S.42(7).
[74] S.43.
[75] Article 53.
[76] Civil Jurisdiction and Judgments Act 1982 s.45.
[77] Article 2.

3-26   Special rules apply to cases where there are multiple defendants, third party proceedings or counter-claims[78] in order to avoid multiplicity of proceedings but these do not significantly detract from the basic principle.

Where the defendant is domiciled in a Contracting State the Conventions override the ordinary jurisdictional rules of the national courts, which means, under English law, that the jurisdiction based on presence or permissive service out has no application.[79]

3-27   To the basic jurisdictional rule under the Conventions – that a defendant who is domiciled in a Contracting State must be sued in the courts of his domicile – there are some additions and exceptions. These will be explored in the next two sections but they can be listed here.

- Special jurisdiction. The Conventions provide that certain courts shall have jurisdiction over particular types of cases. In such cases the defendant may be sued either in the courts of his domicile or in the courts which have special jurisdiction.

- Exclusive jurisdiction. The Conventions confer exclusive jurisdiction on some courts for some matters. In these cases litigation must come before the courts so designated and the defendant cannot be sued in the courts of his domicile unless, of course, the two happen to coincide.

- Jurisdiction agreements. A valid jurisdiction agreement may confer jurisdiction on a court which is not the court of the defendant's domicile.

- Submission to the jurisdiction. Except in the cases covered by the exclusive jurisdiction provisions the defendant can empower a court to hear the case by submitting to the jurisdiction of that court.

Special jurisdiction

3-28   The Conventions have a number of special provisions which confer jurisdiction on courts additional to those of the defendant's domicile. Where these apply the plaintiff is free to select the forum he prefers. Where actions between the same parties and over the same subject matter are brought in the courts of different Contracting States it is the policy of the Conventions to give precedence to the court first seised.[80]

3-29   A domiciliary of one Contracting State may be sued in the courts of another Contracting State in the following cases:-

---

[78] Article 6.
[79] See Article 3.
[80] Article 21.

(1) Contracts

In matters relating to a contract, action may be brought before the courts of the place of performance of the contract.[81] Despite the generality of "matters relating to a contract" it would seem that the action must itself be contractual. So an action by a buyer against the manufacturer, rather than the seller, of a defective component has been held not to fall within the provision[82] as has an action for restitution of money paid under a void contract.[83]

3-30

In an international contract the "place of performance" may not, of course, be in a single country, the contract may require acts of performance to be made in several different countries. Where this is the case the plaintiff has a choice but the country chosen must relate to the particular dispute, i.e. he cannot invoke the jurisdiction in a place where the contract has been satisfactorily performed in order to litigate his claim that the contract was not properly performed somewhere else.[84] It should be noted here that although the place of performance has a strong connection with the contract, neither it, nor the law of the defendant's domicile, have particular claims to be the applicable law of the contract under the Rome Convention.[85] It may well be the case, therefore, that a country which has jurisdiction under the Conventions will be required to apply a foreign law under the Rome Convention.

The Conventions make special provision for the identification of the place of performance of an individual employment contract. That will be the place where the employee habitually carries out his work or, if there is no such place, the place of business through which he was engaged. It should be noted here that there is a difference between the Brussels and Lugano Conventions on this matter - under the Lugano Convention both employer and employee can, in default of an habitual workplace, sue in the place of business, but under the amended Brussels Convention only the employee has this additional option. It is worth noting here also that both the law of the country where the employee habitually works, and the default provision, are significant in the worker protection provisions of the Rome Convention.[86]

3-31

If a contractual action also involves rights *in rem* the courts of the *situs* of the immovable will also have jurisdiction.[87]

3-32

---

[81] Article 5(1).

[82] *Jacob Handte GmbH v. Traitements - Mechano - Chimiques des Surfaces* (1992) Case 2691 ECJ.

[83] *Kleinwort Benson v. City of Glasgow D.C.* [1992] 3 WLR 827.

[84] See *De Bloos v. Bouyer* Case 14/76 [1976] ECR 1497; [1977] CMLR 60.

[85] See below para 4-14.

[86] See below para 4-58.

[87] Article 6(4).

(2) Maintenance[88]

3-33   Although the Conventions do not apply to marriages or matrimonial property they do apply to maintenance. Suit may be brought, in addition to the court of the defendant's domicile, in the country of the maintenance creditor's domicile or habitual residence or, if the maintenance is ancillary to status proceedings e.g. if the matter is a maintenance order following a divorce, in the court which, by its own rules has jurisdiction over the status issue provided that the court's jurisdiction was not based on nationality.

(3) Torts[89]

3-34   The courts of the country where the harmful event occurred will have jurisdiction in addition to the court of the defendant's domicile. The decision of the E.C.J. in *Bier BV v. Mines de Potasse D'Alsace S.A.*[90] means that the provision covers both the place where the harmful act was done and the place where the damage was suffered.[91] However, the wording of the article precludes an action in the place of threatened harm e.g. an action to prevent the publication of an alleged defamatory document, and leaves the plaintiff seeking this sort of relief to sue the defendant in the latter's country of domicile.

There may be some differences of approach here between the U.K. and other Contracting States over the interpretation of torts, particularly where there is, under English law, concurrent liability in tort and contract e.g. personal injury in employment or professional negligence.

(4) Compensation orders from criminal courts[92]

3-35   Although the Conventions are confined to "civil or commercial matters", they apply "whatever the nature of the court or tribunal"[93] and extend to criminal courts. The victim of a criminal act can seek compensation or restitution from a criminal court, if it has the power to make such orders under its own internal law, even though the defendant happens to be domiciled in a Contracting State other than the one dealing with his criminal offence.

---

[88] Article 5(2).
[89] Article 5(3).
[90] Case 21/76 [1978] QB 708; [1976] ECR 1735.
[91] See *Shevill v. Presse Alliance* [1992] 1 All ER 409.
[92] Article 5(4).
[93] Article 1.

(5) Disputes arising out of the operation of a branch or agency or other establishment[94]

This is not as wide an extension of jurisdiction as it may appear. Before the courts of the place where the branch etc. is situated can take jurisdiction it has to be shown that there is a fixed permanent place of business, not e.g. a stall at a trade fair, or the mere presence of a sales representative,[95] or even an independent commercial agency if it is not under the direction and control of the "parent" company. It also needs to be established that the dispute arises from the operation of the branch itself e.g. the local engagement of staff or obligations locally entered into on behalf of the parent company which are to be performed locally, or obligations arising from the activities of those operating the branch. It will include e.g. a contract made by a branch etc. or a tort committed by members of that establishment in the course of their employment. The jurisdiction of the courts of the country where the branch or agency is situated may be invoked by either party.

3-36

(6) Trusts[96]

The settlor, trustee or beneficiary of a trust created by the operation of a statute or created by or evidenced in writing, can sue in the Contracting State where the trust is domiciled.

3-37

(7) Salvage[97] and insurance[98]

There are special jurisdictional rules for these matters which are outside the scope of this book.

3-38

(8) Consumer contracts[99]

There is a special scheme for consumer contracts in the Conventions. For this purpose a consumer contract is one which a person enters "for a purpose which can be regarded as being outside his trade or profession" and is

3-39

---

94 Article 5(5).
95 See *Sonafer v. Saar-Ferngas* Case 33/78 [1978] ECR 2183; [1979] 1 CMLR 490.
96 Article 5(6).
97 Article 5(7).
98 Articles 7-12A.
99 Articles 13, 14, 15.

- a contract for the sale of goods on instalment credit terms or
- a contract for a loan repayable by instalments or for any other form of credit made to finance the sale of goods or
- any other contract for the supply of goods or a contract for the supply of services (but not transport)

and

- in the State of the consumer's domicile the conclusion of the contract was preceded by a special invitation addressed to him or by advertising and
- the consumer took in that State the steps necessary for the conclusion of the contract[100]

In such a case, and subject to the branch, agency or other establishment jurisdictional basis, which is specifically preserved by the scheme and which enables a supplier in a non- Contracting State who has a branch etc. in a Contracting State to be deemed to be domiciled there, the consumer can sue the supplier either in the courts of the supplier's domicile or in those of his own, whereas the supplier can sue only in the courts of the consumer's domicile.[101]

3-40   There are limitations on the effects of jurisdiction agreements in the case of those consumer contracts to which the special jurisdiction provisions of the Convensions apply. The agreement will be recognised only if :-

- it was made after the dispute has arisen or
- it allows the consumer to bring proceedings in courts other than those specified in the scheme or
- it is made between parties who are domiciled or habitually resident in the same Contracting State and confers jurisdiction on the courts of that state.

Exclusive jurisdiction, jurisdiction agreements and submission

(1) Exclusive jurisdiction

3-41   Article 16 of the Conventions provides for the exclusive jurisdiction of courts of Contracting States in certain limited cases. These situations are exceptional in two ways

---

100 Article 13 cf the definition of a consumer contract for the purposes of the Rome Convention below para 4-44.

101 Article 14.

a) they derogate from the rule that the defendant always can, and generally must, be sued in the State of his domicile. Where exclusive jurisdiction applies the courts of the defendant's domicile must decline jurisdiction unless, of course, they happen to be the designated courts under this Article.

b) they apply whether or not the defendant is domiciled in a Contracting State.

All other Contracting States must decline jurisdiction on their own motion if another Contracting State has jurisdiction under this Article.

Exclusive jurisdiction is given to courts in the following situations: **3-42**

Rights in rem 16 (1) (a) "in proceedings which have as their object **3-43** rights *in rem* in immovable property or tenancies of immovable property, the courts of the Contracting State in which the property is situated have exclusive jurisdiction".

There can be no quarrel with the general proposition here, English courts have traditionally declined jurisdiction where the dispute involved the question of title to or rights to possession of foreign immovable property. Only the courts of the *situs* can effectively deal with immovables within their territory.

The rationale of the inclusion of tenancies, beyond the obvious factual control of the officials of the *situs*, is that social legislation to protect the weaker members of a society would focus, *inter alia*, on the supply of housing and the protection afforded might be ineffective if disputes about it were to be litigated in foreign courts.

The immovable must be situated in a Contracting State; if it is not **3-44** Article 16 has no application though, of course, some other provision of the Convention might. This could present a problem for English courts. Suppose the defendant, who is domiciled in England, is sued here over immovable property situated in a non-Contracting State. The English courts would have jurisdiction under the Conventions but not under the *Moçambique* rule which is confirmed by statute[102] but made subject to the Conventions.[103] An interesting clash of principles as the Conventions internally override the domiciliary principle in favour of the situs in real estate matters but whether this is "insiders" law remains to be seen. I think that English courts will seek to continue to decline jurisdiction in such cases.

Rights in rem include matters of title or possession and interests in and **3-45** over the immovable, and the tenancy interests will include possession, repossession and damage to the property, but it is not clear whether

---

[102] Civil Jurisdiction and Judgments Act 1982 s.30(1).
[103] *ibid* 30(2).

unpaid rent itself, as opposed to the landlord's rights to the property when the rent is unpaid, falls within the exclusive jurisdiction. An action which is a personal action although related to an immovable will not be subject to the exclusive jurisdiction so, for example, a petition for a decree of specific performance will fall outside the provision, as will one which is based on a resulting trust.[104]

However, a literal interpretation of the provision by the E.C.J. in *Rösler v. Rottwinkel*[105] applied it to a case where two Germans agreed upon a short term let of a holiday villa in Italy. The parties had agreed to refer any disputes to the German courts, but, when the landlord sought to recover contributions from his tenant for his share of the expenses of servicing the let and damages for disappointment over a spoiled holiday (landlord and tenant were both on holiday at the Italian house at the same time), the German court referred the matter to the E.C.J.. That court held that the Italian courts had exclusive jurisdiction over the claim for payment of sums due in relation to the let, but not over the landlord's action for disappointment.

Such a wooden approach, which in no way advanced the purpose of Article 16, was widely felt to be unsatisfactory. The San Sebastian Convention amended the provision, but very grudgingly.

3-46 16 (1) (b) "however, in proceedings which have as their object tenancies of immovable property concluded for temporary private use for a maximum period of six consecutive months, the courts of the Contracting State in which the defendant is domiciled shall also have jurisdiction, provided that the landlord and the tenant are natural persons and are domiciled in the same Contracting State."

The effect of this is that while the court of the *situs* retains jurisdiction, the court of the common domicile of the landlord and tenant, provided that they are both natural persons and the other conditions are met, shall also have jurisdiction. In the event of proceedings being begun in both courts the usual rule of first seisure will apply.[106]

The Lugano Convention has treated the same problem in a rather more liberal way. Following the same limitation to temporary private tenancies, it provides that the courts of the defendant's domicile shall have jurisdiction provided that the tenant is a natural person and that neither party is domiciled in the situs of the immovable property.

Both versions of the amendment to the original Article 16 are clearly influenced by the decision in *Rösler v. Rottwinkel*;[107] neither address the

---

[104] *Webb v. Webb* [1992] 1 All ER 17.
[105] Case 241/83 [1986] QB 33; [1985] 1 CMLR 806.
[106] Article 21.
[107] Case 241/83 [1986] QB 33; [1985] 1 CMLR 806.

wider issues of exclusive jurisdiction. Clearly it is generally to be hoped that a single court and a single piece of litigation will determine the parties' dispute. For the Italian courts to have jurisdiction over one element of the case and the German courts another seems ridiculous, but unless the plaintiff instituted process in Italy on his claim for damages for disappointment, and the defendant submitted to the Italian jurisdiction on that claim, it is difficult to see how the matter could be resolved. The German court could, if it wished, stay the action[108] but only if action on the same claim was pending in the Italian courts. This problem cannot be resolved unless all matters connected with the immovable are subject to the exclusive jurisdiction of the courts of the *situs*, which would make far too much of the exception. On the other hand, too narrow a view of the concept of a right *in rem* would destroy the purpose of the exclusive jurisdiction. The equitable jurisdiction of the English courts[109] goes a long way down the road of undermining the concept, as might a vigorous use of the lease/licence distinction, another English peculiarity.

Before leaving the issue of rights *in rem*, though not concerned with exclusive jurisdiction, it should be remembered that, if a contractual action also involves rights *in rem* the courts of the situs, along with those of the defendant's domicile, will have jurisdiction.[110]   **3–47**

Companies and associations Article 16 (2) "In proceedings which have as their object the validity of the constitution, the nullity or the dissolution of companies or other legal persons or associations of natural or legal persons, or the decisions of their organs, the courts of the Contracting State in which the company, legal person or association has its seat."   **3–48**

For the purposes of this provision the U.K. has adopted a modified version of corporate domicile from that used for other parts of the Convention. The corporation or association has its seat in the U.K. if it was incorporated or formed under the law of part of the U.K. or its central management or control is exercised in the U.K. It is not necessary here, as it is elsewhere, to show that it has its registered office or some other official address in the U.K.[111]

Public registers   Article 16 (3) "In proceedings which have as their object the validity of entries in public registers, the courts of the Contracting State where the register is kept"   **3–49**

Intellectual property   Article 16 (4) "In proceedings concerned with the registration or validity of patents, trade marks, designs, or other similar rights required to de deposited or registered, the courts of the   **3–50**

---

[108] Under Article 23.

[109] See below para 5–51.

[110] Article 6(4)

[111] Civil Jurisdiction and Judgments Act 1982 s.43.

Contracting State in which the deposit or registration has been applied for, has taken place or is under the terms of an international convention deemed to have taken place"

3-51   *Enforcement of judgments*   Article 16 (5) "In proceedings concerned with the enforcement of judgments, the courts of the Contracting State in which the judgment has been or is to be enforced."

(2) Jurisdiction agreements

3-52   Article 17 deals with the situation where the parties have entered into an agreement about which courts are to have jurisdiction over their disputes. Jurisdiction agreements[112] are common in commercial contracts and can generally be regarded as a prudent step for the parties to take. Many such agreements are, however, agreements in the legal sense only; it is the stronger party who stipulates which court is to have jurisdiction, or the jurisdiction provision may be one of the terms of a standard form contract to which one or even both of the parties have given little heed in the making of the contract. The Convention seeks to deal with these problems in two ways: firstly, by stipulating the form of the jurisdiction agreement; secondly, by restricting the ambit of the agreement or making it work only in the interests, supposed interests is perhaps the way to put it, of the party who is assumed to be the weaker. Two of these restrictions relate to insurance contracts[113] and consumer contracts.[114] There is a further one under Article 17 itself which relates to individual employment contracts.

3-53   Article 17 provides[115] that jurisdiction agreements shall have no legal force if they are contrary to the provisions of Articles 12 or 15. Nor will a jurisdiction agreement oust the jurisdiction of a court which has exclusive jurisdiction under Article 16 even if, as can be the case under 16 (1) (b), two courts simultaneously have jurisdiction and the agreement relates to one of them.

In all other cases (except individual employment contracts) a jurisdiction agreement can be effective provided it satisfies the formal requirements set out in the article.[116] The agreement must be

---

[112] See above para 4-88.

[113] Article 12.

[114] Article 15 see above para 3-40.

[115] Third paragraph (the paragraphs in Article 17 are not numbered).

[116] Article 17 para 1.

- in writing or evidenced in writing or

- in a form which accords with practices which the parties have established between themselves or

- in international trade or commerce, in a form which accords with a usage of which the parties are or ought to have been aware and which in such trade or commerce is widely known to, and regularly observed by, parties to contracts of the type involved in the particular trade or commerce concerned.

Where such an agreement is made by parties one of whom is domiciled in a Contracting State, or if a trust instrument has conferred such jurisdiction,[117] the courts of the Contracting State chosen have exclusive jurisdiction over the actions. This means that the courts chosen must accept jurisdiction (there is no basis under the Conventions which allows them to decline it) and that the courts of other Contracting States must refuse jurisdiction.

If a jurisdiction agreement to which Article 17 applies is made between parties none of whom is domiciled in a Contracting State, the courts of other Contracting States shall have no jurisdiction unless the chosen courts decline it.[118]

If the jurisdiction agreement is for the benefit of one party only, that party is free to bring proceedings in any other court which has jurisdiction under the Conventions. To allow the party who has the benefit of the agreement to waive that benefit is clear enough, but the determination of benefit is formal not substantial i.e. it would be shown by a statement that one party could bring proceedings in State X or that proceedings against him must be brought in State X. There will be no attempt antecedently to find out who might be advantaged by litigation in one place even less to determine who would actually benefit in the dispute resolution.

In individual employment contracts a jurisdiction agreement will only have effect if:
    3-54

- it is made after the dispute has arisen or

- the employee invokes it to seise courts other than those specified in Article 5 (1).[119] Although there is a difference between the Brussels and Lugano Conventions on Article 5 (1) they agree on this point that the employee can sue in the place where he habitually works or, if there is no such place, in the place where the business through which he was engaged is located.

---

[117] Article 17 para 2.

[118] *ibid* para 1.

[119] Article 17 para 5.

(3) Submission

3-55   Except where the exclusive jurisdictional rules of Article 16 apply, a court of a Contracting State will have jurisdiction if the defendant submits to the jurisdiction of that court by entering an appearance, unless he does so to contest the jurisdiction.[120] Clearly he must contest the jurisdiction at the outset, he cannot wait to see how things go on the substantive dispute before he makes up his mind. Although the English text of the convention states that the appearance must be entered "solely" to contest the jurisdiction, this will not prevent the defendant from entering an appearance to contest the jurisdiction and to defend the action if his jurisdictional protest is not upheld. It should be noted that it is only the cases of exclusive jurisdiction under Article 16 which cannot be ousted by submission, not those under Article 17 or the special protectionary cases under Articles 12 and 15.

The role of the court under the conventions

3-56   Unlike the position at common law, where the court operates on the basis of the submissions made by the parties, courts under the Conventions are expected to take an active role over jurisdictional issues. At common law, a party who wishes to argue that the English court is not the appropriate forum must appeal against the leave given to serve out of the jurisdiction or apply for a stay of proceedings, as appropriate, and the burden is on him to establish at least a *prima facie* case for a refusal of jurisdiction. Under the Conventions the court itself has to examine its jurisdictional position in a number of situations.

It is provided[121] that a court in the U.K. may stay or dismiss actions on the ground of *forum non conveniens* or otherwise, where to do so is not inconsistent with the Conventions. A court cannot, it seems, decline to take jurisdiction which the Conventions confer on the basis that it regards another court as the more appropriate forum, but whether this applies when the *forum conveniens* is a non–Contracting State is controversial.[122]

3-57   A court seised of a case which is principally concerned with a matter covered by the exclusive jurisdiction provisions of Article 16, unless, of course, it is a court given exclusive jurisdiction under that Article, must declare, of its own motion, that it has no jurisdiction.[123] Similarly, the court of a Contracting State before which the domiciliary of another Contracting State is sued must, unless it has jurisdiction under one of the

---

[120] Article 18.

[121] Civil Jurisdiction and Judgments Act 1982 s.49.

[122] See *Harrods (Buenos Aires) Ltd No 2* [1991] 4 All ER 348. The matter is now before the ECJ.

[123] Article 19.

special jurisdictional rules or the defendant submits to the jurisdiction, declare, of its own motion, that it has no jurisdiction.[124]

Where proceedings have been brought between the same parties and over the same cause of action in different Contracting States, both of which have or may have jurisdiction under the Conventions, the court which regards itself as the court second seized of the issue must, of its own motion, stay the proceedings until the jurisdiction of the court first seized has been established. If and when it is established, all courts in other Contracting States must decline jurisdiction.[125] If both courts have exclusive jurisdiction under Article 16 the second court must defer to the court first seised.[126]   **3-58**

Where actions are not identical but are related, that is so closely connected that "it is expedient to hear and determine them together to avoid the risks of irreconcilable judgments", the court second seised may stay its proceedings and, at the request of one of the parties, decline jurisdiction, if its rules of court permit consolidation of such actions and the court first seized has jurisdiction to determine the whole issue.[127]

Allocation of jurisdiction within the U.K.

The parties to the Conventions are States in the international sense and the jurisdiction is allocated to the courts of international States rather than to individual legal systems. For the U.K., therefore, the Conventions do not distinguish English law, Scots law or the law of Northern Ireland. In some cases, e.g. where the special jurisdictional rules apply, the localising job may have been done incidentally but in other cases, e.g. where jurisdiction is based on the wide concept of domicile used in the Conventions, it will not. To deal with these issues the Modified Convention was introduced. This goes further than was necessary simply to make the Conventions operative within the U.K. and, in effect, produces a code for the general allocation of conflict cases based on the Brussels model.   **3-59**

The Modified Convention applies:-   **3-60**

- to internal U.K. cases which would otherwise be outside the Conventions, but only to matters which are civil or commercial within the meaning of the Conventions
- to situations where the defendant is domiciled in the U.K. in the sense of domicile as used for the Conventions or
- to situations where U.K. courts have exclusive jurisdiction under the Conventions.

---

[124] Article 20.
[125] Article 21.
[126] Article 23.
[127] Article 22.

The code of domicile introduced for the international purposes of the Conventions is adapted to deal with the internal allocation of jurisdiction within the U.K.[128]

Suppose the plaintiff wishes to sue the defendant in England on a matter which is within the scope of the Conventions but to which the U.K., localised to England, has no special or exclusive jurisdiction. It will have to be established that the defendant is domiciled in England or in a non–Contracting State. If the defendant is domiciled in Scotland or France or Switzerland, the English court will not have jurisdiction (under the Modified, Brussels and Lugano Conventions respectively) and the proper forum will be the courts of the defendant's domicile. If, however, the defendant is domiciled in New York or Japan or India the Conventions will have no operation and the English court can take jurisdiction under the common law rules. It must be emembered that it is the special, not the traditional rules of domicile, which will determine whether the defendant is domiciled in England, Scotland, Japan, New York or India but it is the French and Swiss laws of domicile which have to be applied by the English court under the Conventions to determine the defendant's domicile there.

3 RECOGNITION AND ENFORCEMENT OF FOREIGN JUDGMENTS

Introduction

3-61   The powers of courts are territorially limited, their judgments have no effect beyond the jurisdiction in which they are given unless other countries agree to accept them.

3-62   A person who has obtained a judgment from a court of one system may wish that judgment to be recognised or enforced in another. Recognition alone, without any further action to enforce the judgment, may be sought when, for example, a defendant has been found not liable in an action brought by the plaintiff in one jurisdiction and wants to stop the plaintiff trying again in another, or a party may want his divorce or nullity decree granted in one country to be recognised in another so that he can remarry there.

A person will seek to have a foreign judgment recognised and enforced in England if, say, the judgment debt has not been satisfied out

---

[128] Civil Jurisdiction and Judgments Act 1982 ss.41 (3)-(6) (individuals); 42 (4) & (5) (corporations); 43 (3)-(6) (for corporate domicile for Art. 16 (2) and 45 (3) (trusts).

of the foreign assets of the defendant and there are assets in this country against which he wants to proceed.

In this section we will look at the law on recognition and enforcement of judgments *in personam*: recognition of foreign matrimonial judgments are examined in the chapter on Family Law.[129]

There are three systems of recognition and enforcement in operation in England at the moment: **3-63**

The common law rules apply to all cases which are not covered by the statutory or Convention rules - basically all the States in the world except those of the Commonwealth and those of the E.C. and E.F.T.A. blocs. The common law rules, therefore, apply to such major areas of the world as the U.S.A., Japan and China, most countries in the Middle East and in Central and South America and all the states of Russia and Eastern Europe.

The Statutory rules basically apply to judgments of the courts of the Commonwealth.

The Convention rules are those contained in the Brussels and Lugano Conventions and apply to the countries of the E.C. and E.F.T.A.

At Common Law

At common law, a plaintiff who has been successful in foreign **3-64** proceedings and who seeks to enforce the foreign judgment in England has to begin process in England in the usual way by service of the writ on the defendant. Originally he could elect whether to sue on the original obligation or on the judgment; but this first possibility has now been removed where the judgment is enforceable in England.[130] The plaintiff with an enforceable judgment proceeds as he would for an ordinary claim in debt, within the limitation period of six years and with the possible benefit, if he seeks it, of summary judgment under RSC Order 14 procedure on the basis that the defendant has no defence to the claim.

Requirements for recognition and enforcement

Before the judgment of a foreign court can be enforced at common **3-65** law three conditions must be fulfilled:-

- the foreign court must have had jurisdiction
- the judgment must be final and conclusive
- the judgment must be for a fixed sum

These will be examined in turn.

---

[129] See below para 6-61.
[130] Civil Jurisdiction and Judgments Act 1982 s.34.

(1) The jurisdiction of the foreign court

3-66   Whatever basis of jurisdiction the foreign court actually used, the English courts will only regard it as jurisdictionally competent if the requirements set by English conflict rules have been met. There is no mirror image approach here as was once used for international divorce,[131] and the possibility that an English court might have taken jurisdiction in similar circumstances will not be significant.

3-67   The foreign court will only be regarded as competent if the defendant was resident within its jurisdiction when the proceedings were brought or he submitted to the jurisdiction.

The residence requirement is well-established.[132] What quality of residence is involved is not clear but it includes presence at the operative time. Whether presence alone is sufficient is doubtful, there is some support for it[133] but to base jurisdiction on the casual visit of a stranger is hardly likely to be acceptable in the future for, though it remains a basis of English jurisdiction,[134] it is mediated by the increased acceptance of the plea of *forum non conveniens*.[135]

For corporate defendants, it seems to be settled that there must be a fixed place of business operated by the company in the jurisdiction of the foreign court.[136]

3-68   The foreign judgment will not be enforced if the proceedings were brought in defiance of a jurisdiction or arbitration agreement unless the defendant submitted to the jurisdiction.[137]

3-69   Submission is the only other basis for jurisdiction. This may be by a jurisdiction agreement,[138] by contesting the case on its merits or by taking advantage of the foreign court's process as plaintiff or counter-claimant. Where, however, the party appears before the foreign court to contest the jurisdiction or to seek a stay of proceedings on the basis of an arbitration agreement or a jurisdiction agreement, or to protect his property which has been seized or threatened with seizure, he will not be taken to have submitted to the jurisdiction.[139]

---

[131] See *Travers v. Holley* [1953] P.246; [1953] 2 All ER 794.

[132] *Emanuel v. Symon* [1909] 1 KB 302.

[133] See *Carrick v. Hancock* (1895) 12 TLR 59.

[134] See above para 3-05.

[135] See above para 3-08.

[136] See *Adams v. Cape Industries plc* [1990] Ch. 433.

[137] Civil Jurisdiction and Judgments Act 1982 s.32.

[138] *Feyerick v. Hubbard* (1902) 71 LJKB 509.

[139] Civil Jurisdiction and Judgments Act 1982 s.33(1).

(2) The judgment must be final and conclusive

The foreign judgment must be a final and conclusive determination of   **3-70**
the issues in dispute between the parties. If the case can be re-opened in
the same court, or if some issues remain to be dealt with, the case is not
res judicata and recognition will be refused. The possibility of an appeal
will not render the judgment unenforceable but it would normally be
prudent for the English court to stay the proceedings pending the
outcome of the appeal.

(3) The judgment must be for a fixed sum

The plaintiff seeking to enforce the judgment in England is treated as   **3-71**
if his action was based on debt, he can claim only for a fixed sum and
unless the foreign court has finally determined the amount there is
nothing to enforce[140]. It follows from this that foreign judgments which
do not take the form of a fixed monetary sum cannot be enforced at
common law. Injunctions, decrees of specific performance or any
judgment which requires the defendant to do more that pay a certain
amount are not enforceable.

Even where the foreign judgment is for a fixed sum it can only be
enforced if it has been made in favour of an individual. The general
principle that English courts will not act as the policemen of foreign states
nor as their tax gatherers[141] precludes the recognition of judgments for
tax arrears or fines. But a compensation order made by a criminal court
for the benefit of a victim may be enforceable at the suit of that victim,[142]
as may an award of exemplary or aggravated damages even if described as
a penalty.[143] However, legislation prevents the enforcement of the most
notorious of the punitive damage cases – those arising from the multiple
damage awards of the US anti-trust laws.[144]

Defences to recognition and enforcement

There are few defences which the defendant can raise. It will not   **3-72**
influence the English court that the foreign judgment was based on
mistaken facts or that the wrong law was applied, or the right law
wrongly[145]. Such matters are for the internal system which produced the

---

[140] See *Saddler v. Robins* (1808) 1 Camp 253.

[141] See below para 7-10.

[142] See *Raulin v. Fischer* [1911] 2 KB 92.

[143] *Huntington v. Attrill* [1895] AC 150.

[144] Protection of Trading Interests Act 1980 s.5(2).

[145] See *Goddard v. Gray* [1870] LR 6 QB 139.

original judgment. If, however, the court lacked jurisdiction by its own law such as would make its judgment void within its own system, it should follow that the judgment ought not to be recognised. There is some authority to support this view in matrimonial cases,[146] where recognition rules are different, and one contrary dictum.[147]

The principle that English courts will not allow the defendant to attack the foreign judgment on the merits extends to a refusal to allow him to argue a defence to the original claim,[148] at least where that defence was factually and legally available to him at trial or on appeal in the courts which gave the judgment. Even where the defence was not available to him in the foreign proceedings, the general principle of not retrying foreign cases should prevent his raising the matter before the English court unless some fundamental principle of English public policy would be offended. The other side of this coin is that unless the foreign judgment was given on the merits there is nothing for an English court to recognise. So, if a foreign court dismissed the plaintiff's action for want of jurisdiction, or for some other reason unrelated to the merits of the case, the defendant cannot raise the judgment as the basis of an estoppel *per rem judicatam* in subsequent English proceedings. At one time, dismissal of an action as time barred was not regarded as a judgment on the merits by English courts, as time bars, at least when they barred the action without extinguishing the right of action itself, were regarded as procedural - but that position has now been altered by statute.[149]

Despite the principle that an English court will not investigate the substantive judgment of a foreign court, there are some defences open to a party opposing the recognition or enforcement of a judgment in the English court; these concern allegations of fraud, a denial of natural justice or that to recognise or enforce the judgment would be contrary to English public policy.

(4) Fraud

3-73   A fraud going to the jurisdiction or the merits of the case in a manner which materially affected the result may provide a case for the non-recognition of the foreign judgment in circumstances where an English judgment would be sacrosanct. There is authority for the proposition that in such cases it will not matter that the fraud was reasonably discoverable or actually discovered by the complainant at a time before the foreign

---

[146] See *Papadopoulos v. Papadopoulos* [1930] P.55; *Adams v. Adams* [1971] P.188; [1970] 3 All ER 572.

[147] See *Pemberton v. Hughes* [1899] 1 Ch.781 *per* Lindley L.J. at 791.

[148] See *Ellis v. M'Henry* [1871] LR 6 CP 228.

[149] Foreign Limitation Periods Act 1984 s.3.

court gave its judgment, or that he had raised the matter unsuccessfully in the foreign proceedings,[150] or deliberately not raised it.[151] In *Owens Bank Ltd. v. Bracco*[152] the House of Lords held, in a case which was brought under the provisions for statutory recognition but is applicable to common law recognition, that the English court could re-open the case on an allegation of fraud even where the complainant knew about the fraud and had raised it before the foreign court. Lord Bridge, with whom the others concurred, admitted that the vulnerability of a foreign judgment to such allegations contrasted sharply with the finality of an English judgment in such circumstances. He felt, however, that the Administration of Justice Act 1920 had, in incorporating the concept of fraud from the common law, also incorporated its conception of fraud as it stood in 1920 and that, while the House of Lords could alter the conception of fraud at common law, which was not directly in issue in the case, it could not alter the statutory conception. Even if this reasoning is right, which seems unlikely, the result is equally unsatisfactory for the common law and the statutory bases of recognition.

(5) Denial of natural justice

While the refusal to recognise or enforce a foreign judgment inevitably affects the substantive rights of the parties to get what they want, the argument about natural justice goes not to the merits of the case, but to the procedure by which the foreign court arrived at its judgment. It is an allegation that due process was not observed; that the defendant had been given inadequate notice of the proceedings or that he was denied the opportunity to put his case. The fact that a foreign court followed its own rules e.g. for substituted service, will not necessarily defeat this complaint for the rules themselves may be regarded by the English court as unreasonable and a denial of natural justice.

3-74

(6) Enforcement contrary to public policy

While fraud and a denial of natural justice have been taken as separate heads, they are equally capable of being subsumed under this head along with duress, coercion or undue influence[153] or, perhaps, a bizarre mode of trial or an idiosyncratic method of assessing damages.[154]

3-75

---

[150] *Abouloff v. Oppenheimer & Co.* (1882) 10 QBD 295.

[151] *Syal v. Hayward* [1948] 2 All ER 576.

[152] [1992] 2 All ER 193.

[153] See *Israel Discount Bank of New York v. Hadjipateras* [1984] 1 WLR 137.

[154] See *Adams v. Cape Industries plc* [1990] Ch. 433.

By Statute

3-76   While at common law the enforcement of a foreign judgment requires a new action to be begun in England, enforcement under the statutory provisions requires the registration of the judgment in England. If that registration has taken place the party may proceed to the direct enforcement of the judgment. There are two provisions in force:-

The Administration of Justice Act 1920

3-77   A judgment delivered by the superior courts of most Commonwealth countries may, provided that it is for a fixed sum of money[155] and application is made within twelve months of the original judgment,[156] be ordered to be registered on application to the High Court.[157] Registration is not automatic but depends on the discretion of the court which needs to be satisfied that it is just and convenient that the judgment be enforced.[158]

The original court must have had jurisdiction by its own rules[159] and must have international jurisdiction – that the defendant, individual or corporate, was ordinarily resident or carrying on business there or has submitted to the jurisdiction.[160] The basic defences at common law – fraud, denial of natural justice and that to enforce the judgment would be contrary to public policy are given statutory form.[161] A judgment cannot be enforced if an appeal is pending or if the defendant intends to appeal[162]. The foreign judgment will not be recognised if given in an action brought in defiance of a jurisdiction or arbitration agreement unless the defendant submitted to the jurisdiction.[163]

The Act only applies to those States which have established reciprocal arrangements for the recognition of judgments given by courts in the U.K. The list is a long one and includes most Commonwealth countries.[164]

A judgment registered under the Act will be regarded in the recognising State as if it had been made by a court in that State.[165]

---

[155] Administration of Justice Act 1920 s.12.

[156] S.9(1).

[157] ibid.

[158] ibid.

[159] S.9(2)(a).

[160] S.9(2)(b).

[161] S.9(2).

[162] S.9(2)(e).

[163] Civil Jurisdiction and Judgments Act 1982 s.32.

[164] Reciprocal Enforcement of Judgments (Administration of Justice Act 1920 Part II) (Consolidation) Order 1984 (SI 1984/129 as amended SI 1865/1994).

[165] Administration of Justice Act 1920 s.9(3).

Foreign Judgments (Reciprocal Enforcement) Act 1933

The 1933 Act also operates on the basis of reciprocity and applies to **3-78** money judgments of the courts of Australian Capital Territory, Bangladesh, Canada, Guernsey, India, Isle of Man, Israel, Jersey, Norway, Pakistan, Suriname, and Tonga. Application may be made within six years of the original final judgment for registration in the High Court and a registered judgment has the same force as a judgment of the registering State.[166] Unlike the 1920 Act, there is no discretion to refuse registration to a judgment which falls within the terms of the Act.[167]

Though registration cannot be refused it can, on the application of the judgment debtor, be set aside.

The original court must have had international jurisdiction.[168] For actions *in personam* this will be established if the individual defendant was resident within the jurisdiction or the corporate defendant had its principal place of business there.[169] If the defendant, whether individual or corporate, had a place of business in the country of the original court and the dispute related to a transaction effected through that place of business, the court will have jurisdiction on that basis.[170] Submission to the jurisdiction by agreement, by taking advantage of the process there whether as plaintiff or counter-claimant or otherwise voluntarily appearing, will also confer jurisdiction.[171]

The registration must be set aside if the judgment was obtained by fraud,[172] or if the defendant did not receive sufficient notice of the proceedings and did not appear in them,[173] or if the enforcement of the judgment would be contrary to public policy,[174] or the action in the original court was brought in breach of a jurisdiction or arbitration agreement.[175]

The registering court has a discretion to set aside the registration if it is satisfied that there is a previous final and conclusive judgment on the identical dispute by a jurisdictionally competent court.[176]

---

[166] Foreign Judgments (Reciprocal Enforcement) Act 1933 s.2.
[167] *ibid.*
[168] S.4(1)(a)(ii).
[169] S.4(2)(a)(iv).
[170] S.4(2)(a)(v)
[171] S.4(2)(a)(i)(ii)(iii).
[172] S.4(1)(a)(iv).
[173] S.4(1)(a)(iii).
[174] S.4(1)(a)(v).
[175] Civil Jurisdiction and Judgments Act 1982 s.32.
[176] Foreign Judgments (Reciprocal Enforcement) Act 1933 s.4(1)(b).

A judgment which satisfies the requirements of the Act and which could have been registered had it been for a sum of money, will be conclusive of all matters raised in that litigation.[177] The matter is *res judicata* and therefore the successful defendant can rely on it to defend a further attack by the plaintiff on the same cause of action.

Under the Conventions

Introduction

3-79   The initiative which gave rise to the Brussels Convention was not prompted by the varying bases of jurisdiction employed by the original six Member States of the E.C., but by the need to establish Community-wide recognition of the judgments of the individual States. The code of jurisdiction which the Convention has produced, if not a prerequisite to the Judgments Convention, has undoubtedly facilitated the process.

"A judgment given in a Contracting State shall be recognised in the other Contracting States without any special procedure being required"[178]

"A judgment given in a Contracting State and enforceable in that State shall be enforced in another Contracting State when, on the application of any interested party, it has been declared enforceable there".[179]

These broad statements require some, though not much, qualification and some explanation of the mechanisms for recognition and enforcement which the Conventions establish. We will examine these under four heads.

- Judgments covered by the Conventions
- Courts which can make the judgments
- Defences to recognition and enforcement
- Mechanisms and appeals.

Judgments covered by the Conventions

3-80   A very wide definition of judgment is given by Article 25 - "any judgment given by a court or tribunal". Decisions, decrees, orders and declarations are all included provided that they are not made *ex parte*.[180]

---

[177] S.8(1).

[178] Article 26.

[179] Article 31.

[180] See *Denilauler v. SNC Couchet Frères* Case 125/79 [1981] ECR 1553; [1981] 1 CMLR 62; *EMI Records v. Modern Music Karl-Ulrich Walterbach GmbH* [1992] 1 All ER 616.

The Conventions apply to civil and commercial matters and a number of cases e.g. wills and succession, personal status, matrimonial property are excluded from its application.[181]

Where a case falls outside the Conventions any recognition and enforcement of the judgment in England will depend on the common law rules or on the bilateral treaties which the U.K. may have with other Contracting States.[182]

There are other international conventions which are expressly preserved by the Conventions[183] e.g. the one relating to the enforcement of maintenance awards in favour of children although maintenance payments are covered by the Conventions.[184]

A judgment under the Conventions, i.e. one relating to a civil or commercial matter, will be recognised and enforced in other Contracting States irrespective of whether the defendant is domiciled in a Contracting State. So a judgment given against an "outsider", whether or not at the suit of an "insider", and whether or not within the exclusive jurisdiction rule of Article 16 or the jurisdiction agreement provisions of Article 17, is subject to the recognition rules of the Conventions. If, therefore, an English court takes jurisdiction at common law in a contractual action between a New York domiciliary and a Japanese domiciliary, whose only connection with England is that they expressed a choice of English law as the governing law of the contract, the English judgment would be entitled to recognition and enforcement in, say, France. Equally an English court has to recognise and enforce a judgment of a French court which has taken jurisdiction on some "exorbitant" ground of its own provided that the subject matter of the case falls within the Conventions.

3-81

Whether the Conventions apply is a matter which has to be determined both by the original court when it takes jurisdiction over the case and by the recognising court. The recognising court has to be satisfied that the original court was operating under the Conventions for automatic recognition to apply. For, while a court of one Contracting State cannot investigate the jurisdictional basis of the original court's decision[185] except where the special rules on insurance contracts, consumer contracts and exclusive jurisdiction under Article 16 apply,[186] it can certainly refuse Convention recognition to a judgment which is outwith the Conventions. Such situations where courts in different

---

[181] See above para 3-21.
[182] Article 56.
[183] Article 57.
[184] See Maintenance Orders (Reciprocal Enforcement) Act 1972 and paras 3-33, 6-85.
[185] Article 28(3).
[186] Article 28(1).

Contracting States come to different conclusions on the interpretation of the Convention are obviously suitable matters for a reference to the E.C.J. and, indeed, several cases have been referred on this basis.[187]

Courts which can make the judgments

3-82   For the Conventions to apply both the original and the recognising court must be courts of Contracting States. While the original court or tribunal can have any place in the hierarchy of the legal system, the Conventions stipulate the courts which can be approached to recognise judgments. As far as England. is concerned the application must come before the High Court[188] for all matters with the single exception of maintenance judgments which are internally directed to the magistrates court which is local to the defendant.

(1) Judgment laundering

3-83   Suppose a court in a non–Contracting State gives a judgment which is recognised by a court in a Contracting State and comes within the definition of a civil or commercial matter. This recognition, if treated as a judgment, would entitle it to automatic recognition in other Contracting States. Suppose a plaintiff manages to get a money judgment against the defendant in the Cayman Islands. The defendant has not sufficient assets or no assets at all in that State but he has substantial assets in Spain or Switzerland where the Cayman Island's judgment would not be recognised. If the judgment can be recognised in England under the 1920 Act and thus becomes an English judgment it will be enforceable in Spain (Brussels Convention) or in Switzerland (Lugano Convention). It is doubtful whether this method of "judgment laundering" comes within the Conventions.

Defences to recognition and enforcement

(1) Lack of jurisdiction

3-84   Whether the court making the original judgment was exercising jurisdiction under the Conventions or not, the recognising court cannot in most cases question the original court's jurisdiction or apply the public policy defence to recognition on the basis of an objection to the original

---

[187] See e.g. LTU v. Eurocontrol Case 29/76 [1976] ECR 1541; [1977] 1 CMLR 88.
[188] Article 32.

court's jurisdictional processes.[189] It can, of course, as we have seen, question whether the judgment comes within the terms of the Conventions i.e. whether or not it is upon a civil or commercial matter.

The original court's jurisdiction may be questioned, however, if it was taken in defiance of the special jurisdictional rules applicable to insurance or consumer contracts or the exclusive jurisdiction provisions of Article 16, or if jurisdiction was taken contrary to the provisions of another convention protected under Article 59. So, for example, a court of a Contracting State, which was not a court of the situs of the property, which took jurisdiction in a case falling under Article 16 (1) relating to immovable property could not expect its judgment to be recognised or enforced under the Convention. Similarly, an original court which took jurisdiction in an action brought by a supplier against the consumer on the sole basis of Article 5 (1) - place of performance - would be acting outside the Conventions. Even here, however, the recognising court would be bound by any finding of fact made by the original court.[190] The distinction between a finding of fact and a ruling of law in the area of jurisdiction is not an easy distinction to make . Suppose the original court in the consumer case above took jurisdiction under Article 5(1) because it did not regard the contract as a consumer contract. Suppose it decided that the unpaid Cannes hotel bill related to a contract which, while it fulfilled all the other requirements of a consumer contract, was made within the "resting" film actor's trade or profession when he went to the film festival in the hope of being noticed and offered employment. Is this a finding of fact or a ruling of law?

(2) Error of fact or law

Provided that the original judgment is within the ambit of the Conventions it is no bar to recognition or enforcement that the original court made an error of fact or law in making the judgment. The recognising court is expressly forbidden to examine the judgment on its merits.[191]

3-85

(3) Public policy

A judgment will not be recognised or enforced if such action would be contrary to the public policy of the recognising state.[192] As a public

3-86

---

[189] Article 28 para 3.

[190] Article 28 para 2.

[191] Article 29.

[192] Article 27(1).

policy objection to the original court's jurisdictional rules is expressly ruled out[193] and as "under no circumstances may a foreign judgment be reviewed as to its substance"[194] and as denial of natural justice is otherwise catered for,[195] it is difficult to see what content the public policy objection might have or what form it might take. The Jarrard Report suggests that the public policy objection goes to the recognition of the judgment not to the judgment itself! Fraud, an offensive procedure, an extravagant award of damages, Shylock's pound of flesh or the award of damages for the disappointing performance of a contract of prostitution (surely a consumer contract) would all appear to be matters of public policy but all matters going to the decision itself which makes the recognition or enforcement repugnant.

(4) Natural justice

3-87   If the defendant did not appear in the proceedings and judgment was given in default, the question of adequate notice must be considered. The recognising court shall refuse recognition if the defendant was not duly served with process in sufficient time to enable him to arrange for his defence.[196]

(5) Irreconcilable judgments

3-88   The recognising court shall refuse recognition if the judgment of the original court given in a dispute between the same parties is irreconcilable with one of its own[197]. There is no first come first served rule here so the judgments may be in either order or contemporaneous. The *lis pendens* and related actions provisions of the Conventions seek to prevent simultaneous actions which might lead to irreconcilable judgments,[198] but even actions which are neither the same nor related may produce judgments which conflict. It should be noted here that the irreconcilability must be between the original judgment and a judgment of the recognising court - irreconcilability between two judgments of different original courts which the recognising court is asked to recognise, or between two judgments of the same original court, is not addressed by the provision.

---

193 Article 28 para 3.
194 Article 29 see also Article 34 para 3.
195 See Article 27(2).
196 Article 27(2).
197 Article 27(3).
198 Articles 21-23.

If there is an existing judgment by a court of a non–Contracting State   **3-89**
on the same cause of action between the same parties, the recognising
court shall refuse to recognise the judgment of the court of the
Contracting State provided that the non-Contracting State's judgment is
capable of recognition.[199]

Finally, if the original court, in deciding the main issue before it, had   **3-90**
to decide a preliminary issue outside the scope of the Conventions
relating to personal status, matrimonial property rights, wills or succession,
say, whether a marriage was valid, and did so in a manner inconsistent
with the conflicts rules of the recognising court, with the consequence
that it produced a decision different from that which the recognising
court would have made, the recognising court shall refuse recognition.[200]

(6) Defences peculiar to the Lugano Convention

There are some defences to recognition which apply only to cases   **3-91**
falling under the Lugano Convention.[201]

(7) Nothing else

There are no other bases for refusing recognition or enforcement.[202]   **3-92**
The fact that the judgment is subject to appeal is not a reason for refusing
recognition or enforcement. However, the recognising court may stay
the proceedings if an appeal has been lodged in the original court's
system,[203] and the person against whom the judgment is intended to be
enforced may apply for a stay if an appeal has been lodged or the time for
lodging one has not yet elapsed.[204] The recognising court must delay
enforcement measures, other than those of a purely protective nature,
where appeal against enforcement has been made until the appeal has
been determined[205] – but these are merely delays in the process.

The fact that the original court took jurisdiction despite an agreement
to refer the dispute to another court or to arbitration will not be a basis
for refusing to recognise the judgment[206]

---

[199] Article 27(5).
[200] Article 27(4).
[201] See Article 54B para 3; 57(4); Protocol 1(1)(b).
[202] Article 34 para 2.
[203] Article 30.
[204] Article 38.
[205] Article 39.
[206] cf Civil Jurisdiction and Judgments Act 1982 s.32 and note (4)(a).

To be recognised and enforced in the recognising State the judgment must be enforceable in the original State, but this seems merely to be a matter of the effect of appeals in the original State on the enforceability of judgments. It is not a peg on which the recognising state can hang an investigation into the validity of the original judgment.

Mechanisms and appeals

3-93   Recognition is automatic under Article 26. But if an interested party wants to raise the recognition of a judgment as the principal issue in a dispute he may apply to the recognising court for formal recognition and this triggers the same procedure as for enforcement.[207] An application for formal recognition or for enforcement must be made, in England, to the High Court (except for maintenance matters which go to the magistrates)[208] which court shall give its decision without delay[209] and advise the applicant.[210] To this stage only the applicant has been involved in the proceedings and the requirements on him are limited to providing an address for service and the necessary documentation.[211].

3-94   If the application for formal recognition is refused, the applicant may appeal against the refusal to the High Court[212] from which there is one further appeal only, and only on a point of law.[213]

If the application is accepted, the defendant in enforcement proceedings is given a month in which to appeal to the High Court.[214] if the recognising court is the court of his domicile, and two months if it isn't (whether he is domiciled in another Contracting State or in a non-Contracting State). If his appeal is unsuccessful he may have one further appeal but only on a point of law.[215]

In both cases of a single further appeal the court will be the Court o f Appeal unless the leapfrog procedure[216] allows it to go to the House of Lords.

---

[207] Article 26 para 2.
[208] Article 32.
[209] Article 34.
[210] Article 35.
[211] See Articles 46–49
[212] Article 40.
[213] Article 41.
[214] Article 36 and 37.
[215] Article 37(2).
[216] Administration of Justice Act 1969 s.12.

The recognising court may decide on the partial enforcement of a judgment which covers several matters and the applicant may apply for the partial enforcement of a judgment.[217]

Relationship between the Brussels and Lugano Conventions

If both the original court and the court where enforcement is sought **3-95** are in E.C. States then only the Brussels Convention applies. If both are in E.F.T.A. states then only the Lugano Convention applies, but if the original court or the enforcing court are in different blocs the Lugano Convention applies the Lugano Convention[218]

Recognition of Judgments within the U.K.

The legal systems which make up the U.K. are, despite many **3-96** common features, distinct entities. Without special provisions for recognition and enforcement of judgments they would treat each other as foreign countries for this purpose.

A judgment given in one part of the U.K. may be enforced in another part if it falls within the wide terms of s 18 of the Civil Jurisdiction and Judgment Act 1982. There are certain types of judgment which are excluded from the operation of these provisions e.g. those relating to bankruptcy and the winding up of companies and maintenance orders and, to the extent that any judgment deals with the matter, personal status. The scheme includes most of the judgments *in personam* or *in rem* which courts of whatever status would be likely to give and extends to the civil decisions of tribunals and to arbitration awards.

A certificate granted by the court of the original judgment may be registered in the part of the U.K. where it is sought to enforce the judgment. Upon that registration the judgment is treated for purposes of enforcement as if it were a judgment of the court of registration.

A case covered by section 18, where the appropriate procedures for money judgments[219] or non-money judgments[220] have been complied with, does not admit of any discretion in the registering court. That the original court lacked jurisdiction by the conflict rules of the recognising court is irrelevant;[221] and the other bases for attack at common law are ruled out by availability of redress in the original court.

---

[217] Article 42.

[218] Article 54 B (2)(c).

[219] Civil Jurisdiction and Judgments Act 1982 Sch.6.

[220] *ibid* Sch.7.

[221] S.19.

There is one situation where registration must be refused and that is where compliance with a non-money judgment would involve a breach of the law in the part of the U.K. where registration is sought.[222] Otherwise, a court may set aside registration only if it is satisfied that the issue had previously been determined by a court of competent jurisdiction and was, therefore, *res judicata* when the registered judgment was made.[223]

4   ARBITRATION

Introduction

3-97   A common form of dispute resolution in international commercial transactions is arbitration. The advantages of this alternative over judicial trial can be its relative speed and cheapness and the confidence which the parties may feel in getting arbitrators who have expert knowledge of the activity, say, marine insurance or an international commodity trade, from which the dispute arises.

Any attractions which arbitration holds would be significantly reduced if it was merely a stage in a procedure which culminated in a court trial, was subject to interfering supervision by courts, or did not lead to an award which could conveniently be enforced in the courts, not only of the country where the arbitration took place but in other countries as well.

3-98   There are four matters which require brief consideration here:

What law governs the choice of arbitration?

What law governs the arbitration process?

What law governs the substantive issues raised in the arbitration?

How are arbitration awards enforced?

What Law governs the Choice of Arbitration

3-99   Arbitration agreements, along with agreements on the choice of courts are excluded from the operation of the Rome Convention (on the law applicable to contractual obligations).[224] Arbitration is also excluded from the Jurisdiction Conventions.[225]

---

[222] Sch.7 para 5(5).

[223] Sch. 6 para 10(6), Sch.7 para 9(b).

[224] Rome Convention Article 1(2)(d).

[225] Brussels and Lugano Conventions Article 1(4).

The effect of the first exclusion is that the law governing the choice of arbitration may be different from the law which the arbitrators have to apply to the substantive contractual dispute between the parties.[226]

Arbitration agreements

Agreements to refer disputes to arbitration may take the form of a free **3-100** standing contract (submission agreement) which the parties make before or after the dispute arises. More commonly an arbitration agreement will be a term in the main contract itself, often a standard term in a standard form contract. The law governing the main contract will be determined, unless it is a contract excluded from the Rome Convention,[227] by the rules of that Convention, but an English court will have to determine the law governing the arbitration agreement by reference to the common law rules. These rules are beyond the scope of this book but, basically, they would identify the proper law of the contract by reference to the parties express or implied choice or, in default, by reference to the law which is most closely connected to the contract. This last would usually be, for an arbitration agreement, where the arbitration is to take place. It is perfectly possible for the law of the arbitration and the law of the contract to be different.[228] At common law a choice of arbitration clause could be treated as an implied choice of law[229] but there seems to be a strong case for the reverse inference in the new situation brought about by the Rome Convention. Where the parties have expressly chosen the applicable law for the main contract under the Rome Convention and have not stipulated a separate law for the arbitration agreement then the applicable law should govern both. Where the applicable law for the main contract has to be found in defect of choice by reference to the rules of the Rome Convention, that law should also apply to the arbitration agreement unless there is a very strong inference that another law was intended. The law so identified should govern all aspects of the arbitration agreement including whether such an agreement actually exists as well as questions about its validity.

---

[226] See below para 3-102.

[227] See below para 4-83.

[228] See *James Miller & Partners Ltd. v. Whitworth Street Estates (Manchester) Ltd.* [1970] AC 583; [1970] 1 All ER 206.

[229] See *Tzortzis v. Monarch Line A/B* [1968] 1 All ER 949 cf *Compagnie d'Armement Maritime S.A. v. Compagnie Tunisienne de Navigation S.A.* [1971] AC 572; [1970] 3 All ER 71.

What Law governs the Arbitration Process

3-101   The parties are free to choose the law to govern the arbitration process from the procedures to be followed, the freedom of the arbitrators to refer matters to the court, time limits etc. This may be done by reference to an international form of arbitration.

What Law governs the Substantive Issues raised in the Arbitration

3-102   While the Rome Convention excludes arbitration agreements it does not thereby exclude the contracts, they will most commonly be contracts, to which the arbitration relates. So the assumption would be that in England the arbitrators, whatever law governs the arbitration, should apply the Convention to determine the law to govern substantive issues that the contract raises. If they are operating under English law anywhere a similar approach should be adopted. However, it was argued against the implementation of the Rome Convention into English law, at least beyond its application to other Contracting States, that the confidence reposed in English courts and arbitrators, and in the law which they applied, would be seriously undermined.

When the parties have not chosen a law to govern their contract it is not clear to what extent the arbitrators are free to apply rules different from those which the courts would use to determine the applicable law. Indeed, some international arbitration models e.g. the International Chamber of Commerce Rules of Arbitration, leave the arbitrators free to determine which conflict rules they should employ to discover the contract's governing law.

How are Arbitration Awards Enforced

3-103   The Brussels and Lugano Conventions apply only to judgments given by courts and tribunals, they therefore have no relevance to arbitration awards.

There are two methods of enforcement - common law and statute.

Common Law

3-104   A foreign arbitration award can be enforced in England at common law in the same way as a foreign judgment i.e. by instituting proceedings based on the award. In place of the jurisdictional requirement of the foreign court there is the requirement that the parties agreed to the arbitration and that the arbitrators did not exceed their authority. The award, like a judgment, must be fixed in amount.

Fraud, a denial of natural justice, or that recognition or enforcement would be contrary to English public policy, provide the bases for attacks on the foreign arbitration award.

Under the Arbitration Act 1950 a party seeking to enforce an arbitration award, whether a domestic or a foreign one, can apply for leave which, if granted, will enable the award to be enforced as if it were a judgment of the recognising court.[230]

Statute

There are a number of statutory provisions under which foreign arbitration awards may be enforced   **3-105**

(1) The Arbitration Act 1950

An arbitration award made in a country which is a party to the   **3-106** Geneva Convention of 1927, between parties who are subject to the jurisdictions of different Convention states, will be recognised in England as enforceable at common law or, by leave of the court, directly. Section 26 (1) of the Act provides

"An award on an arbitration agreement may, by leave of the High Court or a judge thereof, be enforced in the same manner as a judgment or order to the same effect, and where leave is so given, judgment may be entered in terms of the award."

The usual requirements apply: that the award was in conformity with the agreement that the parties had made for arbitration and that the award was final and valid by the law of the country where it was given. The basic defences, of lack of natural justice or that to recognise the award would be contrary to English public policy apply.

(2) The Arbitration Act 1975

The Act implements the New York Convention of 1958 and, like the   **3-107** 1950 Act, operates on the basis of reciprocity. A foreign award, one made outside the U.K., can be enforced at common law or under s. 26 of the 1950 Act.

An award to which the Act applies, if the arbitration agreement is in writing, will be enforced in England unless one of the defences under the Act is raised or the court refuses recognition on the ground of offence to public policy. Besides a denial of natural justice, and incapacity on the

---

[230] S.26.

part of either party, these defences relate to the arbitration being *ultra vires* or procedurally defective or not validly established or the award not being binding.[231]

An arbitration decision that the defendant has no liability will be recognised as a defence to further action.[232]

(3) Enforcement under foreign judgments legislation

3-108   Both the Administration of Justice Act 1920 and the Foreign Judgments (Reciprocal Enforcement) Act 1933 apply to arbitration awards. In the case of the 1933 Act the award holder is not obliged to proceed by registration, he may seek to enforce the award at common law if he wishes or under s.26 of the 1920 Act.

Protection of Arbitration Agreements

3-109   We have noted before that it is a standard basis for refusing to recognise and enforce a foreign judgment at common law or under statute, though, importantly, not under the Jurisdiction Conventions, that the court took jurisdiction in defiance of a jurisdiction agreement or an arbitration agreement between the parties.

Enforcement within the U.K.

3-110   An arbitration award made in one part of the U.K. can be enforced in another by resort to common law enforcement, under s. 26 of the Arbitration Act 1950 or under s.18 of the Civil Jurisdiction and Judgments Act 1982.

---

[231] Arbitration Act 1975 s.5.

[232] See *Dallal v. Bank Mallott* [1986] QB 441; [1986] 1 All ER 239.

CHAPTER 4

OBLIGATIONS

1 CONTRACTS

Introduction

English conflict law's approach to international contracts was greatly influenced by its largely *laissez-faire* attitude to contracts in domestic law. The model was an agreement freely negotiated between economic equals and the philosophy was that agreements must be kept. Such a simple model is not, of course, the reality of many common contracts and, as a result, English domestic law has had to intervene in order to redress imbalances in bargaining power in, for example, housing, employment and consumer contracts. To suggest that the modern English law of contracts is an area of non-regulation would be false. Nevertheless, the business contract is not closely regulated and that was the model for, and often the reality of, international contracts.

English law leaves business parties largely free to determine the content of their contracts. Wise contracting parties will make provision for as many contingencies as they can foresee in order to minimise the disruption of the operation of the agreement and they can, if they wish, produce their own set of rules to deal with those contingencies and to dispose of any disputes that may arise between them. It would be wrong to pretend that many contracts are self governing in this full sense or that, even if they were, this would obviate the need for a court to try an issue, but the possibilities are there; possibilities which English law positively encourages.

Where a contract is truly international, among the matters which prudent contractors should bear in mind are the location of, and law to be applied in, any litigation. As an ordinary part of the agreement a term can specify where any dispute is to be brought. Such a term, known as a choice of jurisdiction clause,[1] can provide that all disputes shall be litigated in the courts of a particular system and English courts are frequently chosen even by contractors who have no connection with this country. Alternatively, the parties may agree that disputes between them

4-01

4-02

---

[1] See below para 4-88.

will be arbitrated and specify the form and place of arbitration. The parties can also agree the rules to govern any dispute by incorporating into the contract rules of their own invention, rules derived from an existing legal system, or, more succinctly, by identifying the system of law that they wish to be applied. Such a term, known as a choice of law clause, derives its validity from the general contractual agreement but, even if it did not, it would be a contract in its own right by English law as the mutual agreement implies mutual forbearances and, thereby, satisfies the requirement of consideration. As a general proposition, then, the parties to a contract are free to include legal stipulations in precisely the same way as they include any other stipulations which determine what is to be done in the fulfilment of the agreement or what is to happen in the event of its breach or failure.

4-03   Just as many contractors are not astute enough or sufficiently well advised to make detailed contingency plans, many parties to international contracts will not advert to the issues of choice of jurisdiction or choice of law. A conflict system must, therefore, provide rules for the determination of the governing law both for those cases in which the parties have indicated the system of law which they wish to govern their contract and for those cases where they have not.

4-04   The common law conflict rules centred on the proper law of the contract which was the law chosen by the parties or, in default of choice, the legal system with which the contract had the closest and most real connection.

The Contracts (Applicable Law) Act 1990 and the Rome Convention

The Contracts (Applicable Law) Act 1990

4-05   The Act[2] gives the force of law to the Rome Convention of 1980 (on the law applicable to contractual obligations). It came into force on 1-4-91 and affects contracts entered into after that date. It puts the English conflict of laws on contracts onto a statutory basis for the first time, replacing the common law rules. It can be argued that the greatest contribution of English law to the conflict of laws was the development of the concept of the proper law of the contract and that there was no need to alter this area of law. There were fears that foreign litigants might lose confidence in the English Commercial Court's ability to deal with non-E.C. cases if an essentially European model replaced the common

---

2   S.2(1).

law rules. It can be argued, on the other hand, that the Convention adopts many of the principles of the English Conflict of Laws, including the right of contracting parties to select the law to govern their dealings free from any requirement that the chosen law be factually connected with the contract. Initially at least, there is not likely to be any major change in the approach of English courts to the disposition of contract conflict cases except, possibly, in the areas of employment and consumer contracts for which the Convention makes special provision where the common law had none.

As the Convention has no retrospective effect[3] for the next few years there will be some litigation under the former common law rules. Those rules are outside the scope of this book.

Although the Convention does not require its application to internal conflicts within Contracting States[4] the Act applies the Convention to all cases coming before the courts in the U.K.[5] It applies equally, therefore, to cases involving choices of law between countries within the U.K. e.g. English and Scots law, as to cases involving the laws of other countries.

4-06

The Rome Convention

The Rome Convention is a further move towards the harmonisation of the laws of the Member States of the E.C. and ties in with the Brussels Convention on jurisdiction and judgments.[6] By standardising the choice of law rules within the E.C., the Convention seeks to further the aims of the single market and to minimise the advantages of forum shopping[7] in that, wherever the action is brought, the same governing law should be applied.

4-07

It is a "universal" Convention, however, in that its operation is not confined to choice of law problems arising between Contracting States. Courts in the Contracting States must apply the Convention to all cases coming before them. It follows from this that the applicable law under the Convention can be that of any legal system in the world[8] and that it can be applied to parties who are residents, domiciliaries or nationals of any country irrespective of whether those countries are parties to the Convention, members of the E.C. or neither.

Art. 2

---

3   Article 17.
4   Article 19(2).
5   Contracts (Applicable Law) Act 1990 s.2(3).
6   See Chapter 3.
7   See below para 8-25.
8   Article 2..

4-08   The Convention establishes uniform rules for the determination of contract conflicts. Its fundamental principles are:

- that the parties are free to choose the law to govern their contracts,[9]

- that, in default of choice by the parties, the contract should be governed by the legal system with which it is most closely connected,[10]

- that some contracts are characterised by such imbalances of power that the weaker party is in need of special protection and, hence, special provision is made for certain consumer contracts[11] and individual employment contracts.[12]

The scope of the Convention

4-09   The Convention applies to "contractual obligations in any situation involving a choice between the laws of different countries".[13] The choice does not have to be a difficult or nicely balanced one. A contract wholly connected with one country which contains a choice of another country's law is clearly within the Convention.[14] A contract, wholly connected with one country, which contains a choice of jurisdiction clause in favour of another or happens to be litigated in a foreign country should equally attract the application of the Convention.

It is, of course, under English law, for the litigant who seeks to rely upon a foreign law to plead it and prove it as a matter of fact before an English court. This principle equally applies under the Convention so that if a litigant fails to plead foreign law the hearing will proceed on the basis of English law alone; and, if foreign law is pleaded but not proved, the case will proceed on the assumption that the foreign law has the same content as English law.

4-10   The Convention applies only to contracts and, initially, English courts will use their own concept of contract for this purpose. That does not mean that they will apply only their domestic rules, they will apply the concept as it operates in the conflict system. Technical rules govern the recognition of contracts under English domestic law and it would be silly to deny a foreign contract recognition simply because it did not correspond to the English model. A good illustration of the English court going about the matter in the right way is *Re Bonacina*,[15] where an Italian

---

[9] Article 3.

[10] Article 4.

[11] Article 5.

[12] Article 6.

[13] Article 1(1).

[14] See Article 3(3).

[15] [1912] 2 Ch 394.

trading in England, incurred a debt to another Italian who was resident in Italy. When the trader became bankrupt his Italian creditor failed to prove his debt in the bankruptcy as he was ignorant of the proceedings. The debtor subsequently promised to pay the debt and the issue before the English court was the enforceability of this promise. Under domestic English law there was no contractual promise to pay as there was no consideration for the promise, the original debt being statute barred. Under Italian law the promise was enforceable as it had been made by "*privata scritura*" and this formality sufficed - in a manner similar to, but not as formal as an English deed - to make the promise binding by Italian law. At trial, Eve J. dismissed the claim for lack of consideration for the promise. This ruling was reversed on appeal, Cozens-Hardy M.R. showing the right way to deal with such cases:-

> "... according to the law of Italy the English doctrine of consideration being necessary to support a contract has no application, and further that the moral obligation to pay the debt is sufficient to found a legal obligation if a document such as the "*privata scritura*" has been executed. It seems to me, therefore, that the claimant is in precisely the same position in this country as he would have been if there had been an English contract of the same date with a new and valuable consideration."

Despite wide variations in different legal systems' recognition rules for contracts, and very different incidents attending valid contracts, English conflict law has had less trouble with the concept of contract than with most of the concepts upon which the conflict of laws depends.

4-11 Where the plaintiff has a choice of cause of action i.e. where the case can be pleaded in more than one way e.g. a negligently injured employee can decide to sue for breach of contract or in the tort of negligence, a decision to sue in negligence will take the case out of the operation of the Convention, notwithstanding that a contractual action would be within it.

The Convention does not apply to all contractual matters

4-12 The Convention sets out a list of matters to which the uniform rules do not apply.[16] These will continue to be governed as far as English law is concerned, by the common law rules relating to contract, insofar as English law sees them as contractual, or by the choice of law rules applicable to the other classifications into which English law puts them.

I list them here merely to flag them up at this stage. The exceptions have very limited contractual significance for the most part and do not detract from the wide operation of the convention. You will find some

---

[16] Article 1(2).

further explanation of these matters, with references to other sections of the text, at the end of this section.[17]

- Status or legal capacity of natural persons
- Matters relating to wills succession, matrimonial property and family relationships
- Bills of exchange, cheques and negotiable instruments
- Arbitration agreements and agreements on the choice of court
- Corporate and incorporate status
- Agency
- Trusts
- Evidence and procedure
- Contracts of insurance covering risks in the E.C.

In addition, the Rome Convention does not affect the operation of other international conventions which lay down choice of law rules in particular areas[18] nor does it affect E.C. legislation establishing specific choice of law rules in particular situations.[19]

The Convention does not apply, as far as U.K. courts are concerned, to matters relating to the consequences of a contract being void.[20]

Interpretation

4-13   It is intended that the European Court of Justice shall have the same powers of interpretation over the Rome Convention as it has over the Brussels Convention and that designated courts may refer matters of interpretation to that Court.[21] The decisions and opinions of the E.C.J. on the interpretation of the Convention will then have to be applied by U.K. courts in their interpretations of the Convention[22] and judicial notice will have to be taken of them.[23]

The Brussels Protocol and, therefore, the relevant parts of the Contracts (Applicable Law) Act are not yet in force so, for the time being, U.K. courts must make their own interpretations unaided by the E.C.J. on this Convention but, as some of the terminology used is identical to that of the Brussels Convention, E.C.J. decisions on that

---

[17] See below para 4-83.

[18] Article 21.

[19] Article 20.

[20] See below para 4-98.

[21] Contracts (Applicable Law) Act 1990 Sch.3, Brussels Protocol.

[22] S.3(1).

[23] S.3(2).

could be taken into account in interpreting the Rome Convention, but there is no compulsion to do so.

Along with other guides to interpretation which courts would ordinarily use, the Act empowers them to use the Report on the Convention by Professor Mario Guiliano and Professor Paul Lagarde[24] (hereafter the *Report*).

The Convention itself underlines the importance of national courts not taking a parochial view when interpreting the Convention:-

"In the interpretation and application of the ... uniform rules,regard shall be had to their international character and to the desirability of achieving uniformity in their interpretation and application."[25]

Decisions of the courts in other Contracting States will constitute persuasive authority in English courts on the interpretation of the Convention.

The Applicable Law

Under the Convention the term "applicable law" is used both for the legal system which the parties have chosen to govern their contractual relationship and for the law which is identified by the rules of the Convention in default of choice.   **4-14**

In every case the applicable law under the Convention will be the internal law in force in the country indicated, there will be no resort to the doctrine of *renvoi*.[26] In this respect also the Convention accords with the position reached at common law.[27]

Choice of the applicable law

Article 3 of the Convention confirms the position which had been reached by English common law – that the parties should be free to select the law to govern their contract. The leading pre-Convention authority for English law, the decision of the Privy Council in *Vita Food Products Inc. v. Unus Shipping Co. Ltd.*,[28] established that the parties were free to select any governing law they wished, irrespective of any connection with   **4-15**

---

24 1980 OJ C292.
25 Article 18.
26 Article 15.
27 See e.g. *Amin Rasheed Shipping Corp. v. Kuwait Insurance Co.* [1984] AC 50, [1983] 2 All ER 884.
28 [1939] AC 277, [1939] 1 All ER 513.

the contract, provided that the choice was *bona fide*, legal and not contrary to English public policy. There is no reported decision of the English courts in which a choice of law was struck down, though there was one Australian case where the choice of law was held to be not *bona fide*.[29] The conflict laws of the other Contracting States contained similar freedoms, though perhaps not quite the same enthusiasm for unrestricted choice as English law displayed, in particular with regard to the choice of a wholly unconnected law. London's historical place in international commodity exchanges, in shipping, and in marine insurance encouraged the English courts to look positively on choice of law clauses and, indeed, choice of jurisdiction clauses, which selected English law or English courts, or, commonly, both. There remain many standard forms of contract which lead to the choice of English law, English courts or English arbitration as parts of their standard terms and there are important financial benefits to this country in the continuation of this practice.

4-16   Article 3 provides

"1. A contract shall be governed by the law chosen by the parties. The choice must be express or demonstrated with reasonable certainty by the terms of the contract or the circumstances of the case. By their choice the parties can select the law applicable to the whole or a part only of the contract."

If we take the three components of this provision in turn it will be apparent that the freedom established by the Convention is very wide indeed.

(1) The law chosen by the parties

4-17   The common law did not require that the law chosen by the parties had a significant connection with the contract or indeed any connection at all. The parties' freedom extended beyond a selection among the laws, which might have been objectively determined to be the proper law, to a free choice of any legal system they wished to use. The Convention adopts the same philosophy.

The law chosen by the parties will govern the substance of their contractual relationship subject to the mandatory rules of the *lex fori*[30] and to its public policy.[31] There are three situations, however, where the Convention makes the parties' choice of the applicable law subject to the mandatory rules of another connected system, they are:-

---

29   See *Golden Acres Ltd., v. Queensland Estates* [1969] Qd. R. 378.
30   See the discussion of Article 7 below paras 4-68, 4-73.
31   See the discussion of Article 16 below para 4-80.

- contracts wholly connected to a single country[32]
- certain consumer contracts[33]
- individual employment contracts[34]

Every choice of law in a contract which is genuinely international **4-18** inevitably avoids the operation of the laws of other connected systems. Whether that avoidance is material to the validity of the contract itself or significant to the rights and duties of the parties to it, will, obviously, depend on the content of the legal rules of those systems. Where the avoidance is not merely incidental but intentional, i.e. the parties consciously choose one system in order to avoid another, the matter may take on a different complexion. Suppose the applicable law of the contract objectively ascertained could be either English or French law - the connections being so nicely balanced that one would need a court ruling to determine the answer definitively - there is no objection to the parties making up their own minds in advance of any dispute arising. Suppose in the same example, however, the parties select Italian law to govern their contract and thereby avoid provisions of French law and English law which would materially alter the legal view of the contract. There is a slide from inevitable avoidance to deliberate evasion. Should evasion be prevented? Some evasions are controlled by the use of the concept of the mandatory rule. A mandatory rule is a rule of the law of a country which cannot be derogated from by contract. This important concept, which appears in several of the Convention's provisions, will be considered later.[35]

(2) Choice must be express or demonstrated with reasonable certainty by the terms of the contract or the circumstances of the case

Express choice The parties may expressly choose, by a term in their **4-19** contract or a separate agreement, a law to govern their contract. The most obvious way to do this would be by inserting a simple statement that the contract shall be governed by the law of a designated country - "this contract shall be governed by English law " which clearly indicates a territorial legal system, or by using a standard form contract which contains such a provision. A choice will still be express even if it is indirect e.g. in a contract for the sale of a ship, a charterparty or carriage contract "this contract shall be governed by the law of the flag" but difficulties can arise here unless the vessel and its registration are known at the time.[36]

---

[32] See Article 3(3) discussed below para 4-28.
[33] See Article 5 discussed below para 4-44.
[34] See Article 6 discussed below para 4-57.
[35] See below para 4-67.
[36] See _Compagnie d'Armement Maritime S.A. v. Compagnie Tunisienne de Navigation S.A._ [1971] AC 572, [1970] 3 All ER 71.

Unless the choice indicates a distinct territorial system of law there will be problems. Suppose the parties were to agree on "British law" or "American law" it would be necessary to determine whether that choice could be given meaning by further localisation e.g. as between Scots law and English law, though it could be argued that insofar as English law and Scots law were the same on the particular point in issue it didn't really matter which was intended.

4-20 The power of the parties to invent their own rules within the contract or to incorporate sets of rules from any legal system they chose led the late F.A. Mann, a fierce opponent of the introduction of the Rome Convention, to suggest[37] that the parties could avoid the Convention altogether by a properly worded choice of law clause selecting the common law rules. While there may be no reason in principle to oppose the selection of the common law rules, or classical Roman law for that matter, after all a choice of the law of Outer Mongolia is perfectly permissible, such a choice works only within the Convention itself. I think that any attempt to select a legal regime which no longer had an existence or to select a choice of law system which had been replaced would not operate as a choice of applicable law. There is no reason to suppose that it would not be recognised by whatever was the applicable law in default of choice as an incorporation into the contract. But such a choice would not be allowed to reopen the choice of law process or to displace the rules of the Convention on choice of law.

4-21 *Implied choice* Where the parties have not expressly chosen the governing law it is necessary to see whether a choice of law has been implied with reasonable certainty from the terms of the contract or the circumstances of the case. The *Report* instances a previous course of dealings between the same parties where a choice of applicable law was explicit, the use of a standard form contract which relates to a particular legal system (such as a Lloyds policy of marine insurance) or references to specific provisions of a particular legal system as cases where the parties have implied a choice of applicable law. The task of discovering an implied choice will often be difficult as the parties, by the time the matter is addressed by the court, will be in contention over the matter, perhaps suggesting that different systems of law were impliedly chosen, or one alleging an implied choice while the other asserts that there was never any choice at all.

4-22 If the parties are in agreement over the choice of law, although they have failed to make this clear in the contract, there will be no problem as

---

[36] See *Compagnie d'Armement Maritime S.A. v. Compagnie Tunisienne de Navigation S.A.* [1971] AC 572, [1970] 3 All ER 71.

[37] (1991) 107 LQR 353.

the Convention provides for this, and indeed for a change in the chosen law,[38] as we shall see later.

English law, under the regime of the former common law rules, applied the maxim *qui elegit iudicum elegit ius* and interpreted a choice of jurisdiction clause as an implied choice of law,[39] but it is clearly the intention of the Convention that such a clause, while a legitimate part of the evidence, should not be taken as raising a presumption in favour of the law of the chosen jurisdiction.

4-23

A mere preponderance of contacts with a particular country, e.g. that one of the parties is there and it is the *locus contractus* or the *locus solutionis* or the money of account is the currency of that country, will not be enough to create an implication that the law of that country is the chosen applicable law. On the other hand, if virtually all the significant contacts are with one country, and there is nothing in the contract to negative the inference, it may well be that the law of that country will be seen as the chosen applicable law. Under the Convention a choice which is not explicit has to be implicit i.e. it is meant to be a real and genuine choice and not a construct of the court based on what it thinks the parties might or should have chosen.

4-24

(3) The law applicable to the whole or a part only of the contract

The parties are free to select the law to govern the whole of their contract or a part of it only or, indeed, to have a series of choices for different parts. A multi faceted international contract requiring performances in various countries might be one reason for the parties wishing to split up the whole into component parts or the parties might wish to select one law to interpret the contract and another to implement the terms so interpreted. This process of chopping things up into bits and subjecting the separate pieces to different legal systems is known as *dépeçage*; we will look at it later.[40]

4-25

Change of the applicable law

The principle of party autonomy is demonstrated by Article 3(2). This enables the parties at any time to alter the applicable law whether they are revising an earlier choice, have discovered the benefits of choice after the contract is under way, or have decided that they don't wish to be subjected

4-26

---

[38] Article 3(2), and see below para 4-26.

[39] See *Tzortzis v. Monarch Line A/B* [1968] 1 All ER 949, and *Compagnie d'Armement Maritime S.A. v. Compagnie Tunisienne de Navigation S.A.* [1971] AC 572, [1970] 3 All ER 71 and below para 4-89.

[40] See below para 8-21.

to the law which the Convention would impose on them. The new or revised choice may apply to the contract as a whole or to any severable part of it. While the Convention permits changes to be made at any time, the effect of any agreement between the parties which is made after the dispute has come to litigation will depend on the attitude of the forum and its rules about amended pleadings. No change in the applicable law can adversely affect the formal validity of the contract or operate to the prejudice of third party rights acquired under the former applicable law. Where, in consumer contracts and individual employment contracts, the Convention imports mandatory provisions of a law other than the one chosen by the parties[41] this importation is not affected by a change in the applicable law. So, for example, in an individual employment contract the mandatory rules of the law of the country where the employee habitually carries out his work will apply whatever the choice of law and will persist through any change in applicable law which the parties may subsequently agree.

Limitations on freedom of choice

4-27   There are no restrictions on the legal systems which the parties may select to govern their contracts - that choice will be respected however exotic or bizarre it may be. However, there are some limits on the effect of the choice of law as there are circumstances in which some rules of the chosen law may have to give way to the rules of another system. These cases are:-

- single country contracts
- certain consumer contracts[42]
- individual employment contracts[43]
- mandatory rules of connected legal systems[44]
- mandatory rules of the forum[45]
- the forum's public policy[46]

4-28   *Single country contracts* Where all the other elements relevant to the situation at the time of the choice are connected with one country only, a choice between connected a foreign law whether or not accompanied by

---

[41] See below para 4-28.
[42] See below para 4-44.
[43] See below para 4-57.
[44] See below para 4-73.
[45] See below para 4-68.
[46] See below para 4-80.

a foreign jurisdiction clause will not prejudice the application of the mandatory rules of the solely connected system.[47]

The Convention applies only to contracts which involve a choice between the laws of different countries[48] and the situation envisaged here is not such a case as, on the facts, all the connections are with a single country. What brings it within the Convention is the selection by the parties of a governing legal system which is factually unconnected with the contract. The *Report* makes it clear that the U.K. in particular was insistent that the parties' freedom to select the governing law should not be confined to contracts which inherently contained a potential choice between connected laws. There were interests to be protected here as choices, particularly of English law, are often made in contracts which not only have no factual connection with England but are wholly connected to a single foreign system. As the Convention has a universal application, i.e. the countries which adopt it are to apply it to all cases coming before their courts, the omission of this freedom would have been detrimental to the business of English courts. The *quid pro quo* for this concession is that the selection of a governing law in such cases will not avoid the application of the mandatory rules of the system with which the contract is solely connected. There is not much ground given here, for under the common law rules the choice of a proper law had to be *bona fide*, legal and not contrary to public policy.[49] A choice of a law unconnected to the contract which had the effect of evading the mandatory rules of the solely connected system might well be regarded as *prima facie* evidence of bad faith. Article 3(3) avoids any need to look into the minds of the contracting parties by providing that any pertinent rule of the legal system solely connected to the contract which that system regards as obligatory will be inserted into the contract notwithstanding the choice of a foreign applicable law. However it leaves open the question of what "all the other elements relevant to the situation" are. Can, for example, a choice of law avoid the mandatory provisions of the almost solely connected law simply because there is some connection, however slight, with a third legal system?

Although the common law did not establish a doctrine of evasion of law in the area of international contracts beyond the qualifications established in *Vita Food Products Inc. v. Unus Shipping Co. Ltd.* there are statutory provisions which do. Most prominently the Unfair Contract Terms Act 1977 deals with the choice of a foreign law where the contract

4-29

---

[47] Article 3(3).

[48] Article 1(1).

[49] *Vita Food Products Inc. v. Unus Shipping Co. Ltd.* [1939] AC 277, [1939] 1 All ER 513.

has a substantial connection with a U.K. legal system. The Act will apply, notwithstanding the choice of a foreign law, if

> "the term appears to the court, or arbitrator, or arbiter to have been imposed wholly or mainly for the purpose of enabling the party imposing it to evade the operation of this Act"[50] or

> "in the making of the contract one of the parties dealt as consumer, and he was then habitually resident in the United Kingdom, and the essential steps necessary for the making of the contract were taken there whether by him or by others on his behalf."[51]

As there are no reported cases involving the application of the provision, it may be concluded, as with the absence of tigers, either that there was no problem or that the precautionary measures have been effective. It may be useful, however to use this provision as an illustration of the relationship of the Convention with a domestic legal system.

4-30 By way of illustration I want to look firstly at a contract unconnected with the U.K. where the parties have chosen English law and then at a contract connected with England where the parties have chosen a governing law which is not a U.K. legal system.

Where the parties have chosen English law to govern a contract which is wholly unconnected with any part of the U.K., their choice will be the applicable law under the Convention and English law will be applied to determine all matters of substance at issue between them. This does not mean that every rule of English law will be applied. It must always be determined whether a rule of a domestic legal system extends to an international contract. For example, the Unfair Contract Terms Act provides that where the law of any part of the U.K. applies to the contract solely by reason of the parties choice and, but for that choice, the contract would be governed by the law of a country outside the U.K., the protectionary provisions of the Act,[52] which include some rules which are undoubtedly mandatory, have no application. The purpose of this provision is to protect the position of English law as a commonly chosen governing law by parties whose contracts have no connection with England.

No mandatory provisions of any other law will be applicable unless:-

i) the contract is wholly connected to a single foreign country

---

50 Unfair Contract Terms Act 1977 s.27(2)(a).
51 S.27(2)(b).
52 Ss 2 to 7 for English law, ss 17 to 21 for Scots law.
53 See below para 4-44.
54 See below para 4-57.

ii) the contract is a consumer contract as provided for in Article 5[53]

iii) the contract is an individual employment contract which is subject to Article 6[54]

iv) there is a mandatory rule of the forum[55] or a rule of the forum's public policy which is imperative.[56]

v) the case is brought before a non-U.K. forum which applies a mandatory rule of another system under the terms of Article 7(1).[57]

This list looks long but length should not be confused with importance and several of these limitations have themselves very limited effect.

In the second situation, where the contract, connected with England, is **4-31** subjected to a chosen foreign law, there must be a strong connection with a U.K. law against which the choice of a foreign law contrasts. Section 27(2)(b) of the Unfair Contract Terms Act stipulates the connection and section 27(2)(a) assumes it, for one cannot evade that which would not otherwise apply. So we can assume either that the contract is wholly connected with a U.K. legal system or sufficiently connected with one to make it at least more probable than not that the applicable law in default of choice would be the law of some part of the U.K. In such a situation the choice of an applicable law under the Convention will be effective in a U.K. court unless there is a finding that the choice was evasionary or that the contract was a consumer contract with the connections specified in the section. In the event of either of these being established the chosen applicable law will still govern the contract but it will do so subject to the application of the provisions of the Act.

Suppose, however, that the case is brought not before a U.K. court, **4-32** where the provisions of the Statute cannot possibly be ignored, but before a foreign tribunal. If the contract is wholly connected with England the foreign tribunal would be bound by Article 3 (3) to apply the mandatory rules of English law and, as by English law the mandatory rules do not apply automatically but only on the basis of a finding, the foreign court would have to determine whether the case fell within the provisions.

If the facts of the case are not wholly connected with the U.K. the problem becomes more difficult as, by definition, it does not fall within Article 3(3).

The choice of law clause will be effective and wholly exclude the possibility of the application of the provisions of the Unfair Contract Terms Act unless either the case falls within the special consumer[58] or

---

[55] See Article 7(2) discussed below para 4-68.

[56] See Article 16 discussed below para 4-80.

[57] See the discussion of Article 7(1) at para 4-73.

[58] See below para 4-44.

employment[59] categories of the Convention or the foreign court is prepared to invoke Article 7(1)[60] i.e. the case falls under ii) iii) or v) above.

The applicable law in default of choice

4-33   In default of choice of a governing law by the parties, the Convention seeks the law which is most closely connected to the contract.[61]

"the contract shall be governed by the law of the country with which it is most closely connected. Nevertheless, a severable part of the contract which has a closer connection with another country may by way of exception be governed by the law of that other country."

The basic principle here is exactly that of the common law which involved a quest for the system of law with which the contract was most closely connected.

The test here is also an objective one and depends on establishing the "centre of gravity" or "grouping of contacts" of the contract rather than an attempt to discover what the parties would have chosen had they thought about the matter.

4-34   In searching for the proper law under the common law rules the better approach of the English court was to have regard to all the connections e.g.

- the place of contracting
- the place of performance
- the language of the contract
- the money of account
- the personal law of the parties
- all the circumstances surrounding the contract.

This was not done with a view to comparing the lengths of the lists of contacts but to weigh the various connections in order to determine the most significantly connected country. The Convention involves the same approach.

The words "by way of exception" are intended to emphasise that the process of *dépeçage*,[62] by which parts of the contract are referred to different systems of law, is to be confined to very limited circumstances.

---

[59] See below para 4-57.
[60] See below para 4-73.
[61] Article 4(1).
[62] See below para 8-21.

The common law had not developed a set of presumptions to identify the proper law, though there was a marked preference for the *lex loci solutionis*. In contrast, the Convention has three, rebuttable, presumptions.

4-35

(1) The presumptions

Presumption one - characteristic performance Article 4 (2) introduces the concept of "characteristic performance" as an indirect connecting factor:-

4-36

> "it shall be presumed that the contract is most closely connected with the country where the party who is to effect the performance which is characteristic of the contract has, at the time of conclusion of the contract, his habitual residence, or, in the case of a body corporate or unincorporate, its central administration."

If the party who is to effect the characteristic performance is acting in the course of his trade or profession, as will most commonly be the case, the reference to the law of the habitual residence or the law of the central administration is replaced by the reference to the law of the place of business through which the performance is to be made.

At common law the law of the place of performance, the *lex loci solutionis*, featured prominently in the search for the proper law in default of choice but under the presumption that law, as such, is irrelevant. The performance is merely a conduit to the applicable law. Once the party carrying out the characteristic performance has been identified the Convention looks to the law of his habitual residence, central administration or place of business.

The characteristic performance will be the work to be done under the contract rather than the payment for that work so that, in a sale contract, it will be the seller's law (the law of the country of his place of business) rather than the buyer's law which will apply. The *Report* gives other instances: the characteristic performance of an agency contract will relate to the agent, a banking contract to the bank, a service to the provider, a hire contract to the hirer out. The *Report* suggests that the presumption relates the contract to the law of its socio-economic function but that assertion is far from convincing.

4-37

If the characterising performance cannot be found (e.g. in a contract which involves the exchange of goods or reciprocal services) the applicable law will be the law of the country with which the contract is most closely connected.

Even if a characteristic performance can be found the presumption will not apply if the contract is more closely connected with another country. The law of that other country will apply instead.[63]

---

[63] Article 4(5).

Suppose the contract requires the English manufacturer to build a machine and to ship it to his customer in Hong Kong. The characteristic performance is the work to be done in England - obviously. If, however, the contract was made in Hong Kong and payment is to be made there in $HK upon delivery and the contract is written in Chinese. It is open to the court to take a wide or narrow view of this presumption just as it is left to the court to decide whether another law is more closely connected to the contract than the system indicated by the presumption.

4-38   *Presumption two - immovable property*   The second presumption in Article 4 provides that where:

"the subject matter of the contract is a right in immovable property or a right to use immovable property it shall be presumed that the contract is most closely connected with the country where the immovable property is situated."[64]

One of the objectives of the Rome Convention is to link with the Brussels Convention on jurisdiction. The Brussels Convention[65] establishes exclusive jurisdiction, where the issue is the right to immovable property, for the courts of the situs - where the immovable property is situated - and those courts have exclusive, though not sole, jurisdiction over tenancy agreements.[66]

English courts apply the *lex situs* to govern the proprietary effects of real estate contracts so the reference to the *lex situs* as the governing law in default of choice is not surprising.

4-39   The problem here is the ambit of the presumption. It clearly extends to the sale of immovable property and tenancy agreements and other rights over immovable property and clearly does not extend to ordinary personal contracts which merely relate to the immovable - to work on it, design it, repair it or clean it. The inclusion of the words "right to use" seems to take us well beyond rights *in rem* to include arrangements which English law would regard as licences - so short term holiday lets or hotel accommodation are within the terms of the presumption. There is an aspect of overkill here. For example - an English holiday company takes a lease of an hotel in Miami owned by a N.Y. company. Certainly the proprietary effects of the contract should be governed by the law of Florida but there appears no special reason to subject the contract itself to the law of Florida.

Suppose a French holiday maker were to contract with that same English company to stay for a week in the Miami hotel. Unless the

---

[64] Article 4(3).
[65] Article 16(1)(a) see above para 3-43.
[66] Article 16 (1)(b) see above para 3-46.

agreement was a package tour and, thus, came under the special provisions relating to consumer contracts,[67] this contract would also fall to be governed by the law of Florida unless the parties chose otherwise.

This presumption, like the others, will not apply if the contract is more closely connected with another country.[68] The *Report* gives the example of two Belgians agreeing on the holiday rental of property belonging to one of them on Elba and offers the opinion that Belgian law rather than Italian law would govern in such a case, but in the examples I have used there is no such easy rebuttal to the presumption.

Although the formal validity of a contract concerning immovables is subject to the general provisions on formal validity contained in Article 9, insofar as the *lex situs* has formal requirements which it regards as mandatory, irrespective of where the contract was made or what law governs its substance, those formal requirements have to be complied with.[69]

4-40

Presumption three - carriage of goods For carriage of goods contracts, and the provision extends to all modes of carriage, the presumption relating to characteristic performance is expressly excluded and a special set of connections is provided.[70]

4-41

In default of choice the applicable law will be presumed to be the law of the country where the carrier had, at the time the contract was made, his principal place of business, provided that such place is also the place of loading or unloading or the principal place of business of the consignor.

The carrier for this purpose is the party who undertakes the carriage whether he does any carrying himself or arranges for someone else to do it.

The presumption applies only to carriage of goods, not passengers. The likelihood that this would separate the passenger from his baggage (a fairly common experience in fact) in legal terms was felt to be less objectionable than that the passengers on the same journey with the same carrier should be subject to different legal regimes.

If the coincidences are not present the courts must search for the most connected country without further help from the Convention.

The Rome Convention, here as elsewhere, is displaced by other international conventions which Contracting States have entered or may in future enter.[71] So, for example, as far as the U.K. is concerned,

---

[67] See Article 5(4)(b) and 5(5). See below para 4-52.

[68] Article 4(5).

[69] Article 9(6). See below para 4-75.

[70] Article 4(4).

[71] See Article 21.

the international carriage of goods by sea remains subject to the Hague–Visby Rules.[72]

(2) General provision

4-42   If a characteristic performance cannot be found or if another law is more closely connected with the contract than the system indicated by the presumptions, the general provision applies, the presumptions are disregarded and the contract is governed by the most closely connected law.[73]

The provision, which is clearly intended to sweep up cases which fall through the net of the presumptions, is very wide and could be used by the courts to engage in a choice of law process largely uninfluenced by the Convention. An English court could, if it so wished, disregard the Convention, apply the common law rules, and then assert, if the governing law so found coincided with that indicated by the presumptions, that it was following them and, if the governing law was other than that indicated by the presumptions, that it was applying the general provision of the Article.

It remains to be seen how effective the presumptions will be in practice and what effect the rulings of the E.C.J. will have upon their operation when that court is given the interpretative jurisdiction under the Brussels Protocol.

Particular contracts

4-43   While the provisions of the Convention apply to contracts generally, there are two provisions which are directed at particular contracts concerning weak contracting parties for whom special protections were thought to be necessary.

(1) Certain consumer contracts

4-44   The Convention establishes rather a complex regime for the treatment of certain consumer contracts. For this purpose a consumer contract is defined as one

> "the object of which is the supply of goods or services to a person ("the consumer") for a purpose which can be regarded as being outside his trade or profession, or a contract for the provision of credit for that object."[74]

---

[72] Carriage of Goods by Sea Act 1971.

[73] Article 4(5).

[74] Article 5(1).

There is nothing in the Convention to suggest that the supplier must be a business or that he must know or believe that he is dealing with a consumer. It would seem likely that the first of these must be the case and the second probably so; the *Report* assumes both. If a consumer pretended to buy by way of trade, say to obtain a trade discount, he should lose the protection of the special provisions. There is also no definition of what is " outside his trade or profession" and it may be contentious when the goods have a dual function e.g. the doctor's motor car. The *Report* suggests that regard should be had to the primary purpose of the transaction.

The consumer movement has been one of the most effective lobbying groups throughout Europe in recent decades and national responses have not been uniform. The lack of a more precise definition is due to the impossibility of finding an agreed solution and mirrors that in the Brussels Convention. It should be noted that the special rules in Article 5 apply both to contracts for the sale of goods and to those for the provision of services (the *Report* instances insurance) and extend to the supply of credit for both of these but do not extend to the purchase of securities or to unlinked credit transactions.

If the parties have chosen the law to govern the contract (which means in effect if the supplier has stipulated a governing law) the contract will be governed by that law. But the chosen law will apply only to the extent that the consumer does not lose the benefits of the mandatory protection laws of the country of his habitual residence,[75] provided that certain, alternative, connections with that country can be established.

    i)   "in that country the conclusion of the contract was preceded by a specific invitation addressed to him or by advertising, and he had taken in that country all the steps necessary on his part for the conclusion of the contract."

This first connection covers doorstep selling and mail order in the sense of replying to an individual mail shot, clipping a coupon in a newspaper or magazine (though only if the publication was specifically targeted at consumers in the country concerned). It also covers cases where a consumer responds to a general advertisement in any media but, again, only if the advertisement was directed at consumers in that country.

The formulation "all the steps necessary on his part for the conclusion of the contract" is a devise to prevent technical arguments about the actual place of contracting which otherwise might arise from, for example, the peculiar distinction in English law between postal and instantaneous communications - the *lex loci contractus* is not pertinent to the issue of consumer protection.

---

[75] Article 5(2).

4-47   ii)   "or if the other party or his agent received the consumer's order in that country."

This second connection covers cases where the consumer approaches the foreign seller e.g. at an exhibition or trade fair or gets in touch with the seller's branch office in the country of the consumer's habitual residence.

4-48   iii)   "or if the contract is for the sale of goods and the consumer travelled from that country to another country and there gave his order, provided that the consumer's journey was arranged by the seller for the purpose of inducing the consumer to buy."

The third connection applies only to contracts for the sale of goods and attempts to deal with "cross-border excursion selling", where the seller takes or arranges the carriage of the consumer from the country of his habitual residence to another country as part of the inducement to buy. The protection afforded by the Convention would apply whether or not the seller had a place of business in the country of sale and irrespective of whether the chosen law was the law of the country where the sale took place or any other law.

4-49   Of course most consumer transactions will take place in the country of the consumer's habitual residence and most of his consumer purchases will take place in retail shops in that country. In most cases there will not be any foreign element at all and the domestic law of that country will apply. Where a choice of law is made in the context of a transaction wholly connected to a single country the chosen law will apply but subject to all the mandatory provisions of the law of the wholly connected country.[76] So an English supplier in such a case cannot avoid the protectionary provisions of English law simply by stipulating a foreign law to govern the contract.

When a consumer buys directly from a retailer in reliance on the manufacturer's advertisement, the ordinary rules of privity exclude any connection in contract between the manufacturer and the consumer, and the Convention does not alter that position.

4-50   Where the parties to a consumer contract which falls within Article 5 have not made a choice of governing law, the applicable law will be that of the consumer's habitual residence.[77]

So, whenever the special circumstances expressed in the Article apply, the consumer will enjoy the protection of the mandatory rules of the law of his habitual residence. For, in default of choice, that law will be the applicable law under the Convention and, if there is a choice of another

---

[76] Article 3(3) see above para 4-28.
[77] Article 5(3).

law, the effect of the choice will not deprive the consumer of the protection of his "home" law.

Advantage rule   The Convention does not deal with the situation **4-51** where the provisions of the chosen law are more favourable, on the particular issue in dispute, than the mandatory rules of the law of the country of the consumer's habitual residence. It must surely be the case that the consumer can have the benefit of the more favourable provisions. For, although the Convention operates by importing the mandatory rules of the law of the habitual residence into the chosen law, the purpose of the special provisions on consumer contracts is the protection of consumers and this purpose would be defeated if less favourable rules were allowed to replace more favourable ones.

In such a dispute the consumer would plead the chosen law and the supplier would be prevented from setting up the less favourable mandatory rule of the law of the consumer's habitual residence in opposition to the law which he himself has stipulated as the contract's governing law.

Although this means that the consumer can blow hot and cold, using the chosen law when it suits him and relying on the mandatory rules of the law of his habitual residence when they are more favourable, so be it.

Exclusions   The special consumer provisions do not apply to contracts **4-52** of carriage nor to contracts for the supply of services where the services are to be supplied to the consumer exclusively in a country other than that in which he has his habitual residence.[78] So if a consumer makes his own separate foreign travel and accommodation arrangements, his contracts will not come under Article 5. In default of choice or the application of other international conventions, the travel contract will be rebuttably presumed to be governed by the law of the country of the carrier's principal or subsidiary place of business[79] and the accommodation contract will be rebuttably presumed to be governed by the *lex situs*[80]. But a "package tour" arrangement i.e. a contract which, for an inclusive price, provides for a combination of travel and accommodation, is covered by the special provisions if the connections are present.[81]

An E.C. directive on package tours[82] has recently been brought into force in U.K. law[83] and applies to any packages sold or offered for sale in

---

[78]   Article 5(4).

[79]   Article 4(2).

[80]   Article 4(3).

[81]   Article 5(5).

[82]   Council Directive 90/314.

[83]   The Package Travel, Package Holidays and Package Tours Regulations 1992 SI 1992/3288 in force 23.12.92.

the U.K.[84] Any terms which the Regulations imply into the package contract are expressed to be mandatory "it is so implied irrespective of the law which governs the contract".[85]

4-53 Article 5 as a whole seems a rather heavy-handed attempt to protect consumers from certain malpractices rather than to recognise consumer rights. The protection afforded to the consumer extends only to the mandatory rules of the legal system of his country of habitual residence and only where the particular, limited, connections exist. It operates in limited circumstances on fairly uncommon transactions.

Examples of mandatory rules in this area in English law range from the implied terms on title, correspondence with description and fitness for purpose under the Sale of Goods Act 1979, to the narrow regulations aimed at particular types of transaction such as the cooling-off period for timeshare agreements[86] and the unenforceability of one-off doorstep sales of goods or services where the consumer has not been given notice of his right to cancel.[87]

4-54 Consumer contracts which do not fall within the narrow range of Article 5 are governed by the general Convention rules and, thereby lose any special quality as consumer contracts.

4-55 The Convention applies, of course, only to contractual obligations; the English consumer's remedies for personal injury or damage to property under the Consumer Protection Act 1987 or his prospects of a tortious claim in negligence against the manufacturer of a defective product are unaffected by it.

4-56 There is a special rule relating to the formal validity of those consumer contracts covered by Article 5. Their formal validity is governed solely by the law of the country in which the consumer has his habitual residence.[88]

(2) Individual employment contracts

4-57 Unlike the common law rules, which treated employment contracts along with all other contracts despite their rather special circumstances and sometimes with results which are hard to justify,[89] the Convention

---

[84] Reg. 3(1).

[85] Reg. 28.

[86] Timeshare Act 1992 s.5.

[87] Consumer Protection (Cancellation of Contracts Concluded away from Business Premises) Regulations 1987.

[88] Article 9(5). See below para 4-77.

[89] See e.g. *Sayers v. International Drilling Co. N.V.* [1971] 3 All ER 163.

introduces special rules for individual employment contracts[90] which are intended to safeguard the employee under an international contract. While allowing the general freedom of choice enshrined in Article 3, the Convention provides that the exercise of that freedom "shall not have the result of depriving the employee of the protection afforded to him by the mandatory rules of the law which would be applicable ... in the absence of choice."[91]

In default of choice, the applicable law will be "the law of the country in which the employee habitually carries out his work in performance of the contract, even if he is temporarily employed in another country."[92] If there is no place of habitual work the applicable law will be the law of the country in which the place of business through which the employee was engaged is situated. In either event[93] if "it appears from the circumstances as a whole that the contract is more closely connected with another country, the contract shall be governed by the law of that country."[94]

4-58

The Convention does not define the term "employment" and it cannot be assumed that the English distinction between *contracts of service* and *contracts for services* is universally known. Ultimately, when the Court is given that power, reference may be made to the European Court of Justice for definitive rulings on this and there are some rulings of the E.C.J. on the term in the Brussels Convention.[95] For the time being, national courts will apply their own tests to distinguish employees from independent contractors. English courts will continue to apply a purposive approach rather than rely on mechanical tests[96] and it is to be hoped that the E.C.J. will adopt a similar approach.

4-59

Although there is no definition of "habitual" in the Convention there is no reason to suppose that its interpretation will differ from "ordinarily employed" under existing British legislation[97]. It does not prevent occasional or periodic employment elsewhere provided that such employment is "temporary".

4-60

The protection provided by the Convention extends only to the mandatory rules of the identified system; these are defined[98] as rules of a domestic legal system which cannot be derogated from by contract. The

4-61

---

[90] Article 6.
[91] Article 6(1).
[92] Article 6(2)(a).
[93] Article 6(2)(b).
[94] Article 6(2).
[95] See e.g. *Shenavai v. Krieschler* C266/85 [1987] ECR 239.
[96] See e.g. *Young and Woods Ltd. v. West* [1980] IRLR 201.
[97] See Employment Protection (Consolidation) Act 1978.
[98] In Art.3(3).

recognised imbalance between the bargaining power of the individual worker and the employer has caused national States to make special provisions for employment contracts and to establish sets of minimum standards of protection for employees.

Examples of mandatory protection rules under English law include the right to a minimum period of notice,[99] to claim that his dismissal was unfair,[100] to maternity pay,[101] to return to work after pregnancy[102] and to redundancy payments.[103] Although these rights can properly be described as mandatory, as they cannot be abrogated by contract, it does not follow that they are universally applicable. So, for example, there is a qualification period – the employee must have worked continuously for the same employer for two years;[104] there is a spatial limitation – the employee must "ordinarily" work within Great Britain;[105] and a limited power of waiver.[106]

4-62 The Convention, by establishing a special regime for individual employment contracts, seeks to ensure that the employee does not lose the benefit of protection simply by being a party to an international contract.

It would make nonsense of any domestic protection provisions if the employer could circumvent them by adding a choice of law clause to the terms of the contract and this will be countered in the law establishing the rights in order to make them mandatory.[107] When the contract is genuinely international the problems of evasion are joined by those of incidental avoidance if the choice of law process fails to recognise the need to protect.

4-63 While the principle of freedom of choice is preserved by the Convention, the employee will always have the benefit of the mandatory rules of the law applicable in default of choice. The chosen law will be respected with regard to all the conditions of employment which are not subject to the mandatory controls – depending on which system of law is applicable; this might amount to most of it.

---

[99] Employment Protection (Consolidation) Act 1978 s.49.

[100] *ibid* s.54.

[101] Social Security Contributions and Benefits Act 1992 s.164. But see EC Council Directive: Concerning the protection at work of pregnant women or women who have recently given birth.

[102] Employment Protection (Consolidation) Act 1978 s.45.

[103] *ibid* s.81.

[104] e.g. for unfair dismissal – Employment Protection (Consolidation) Act 1978 s.64.

[105] e.g. for unfair dismissal – Employment Protection (Consolidation) Act 1978 s.141(2).

[106] e.g. for unfair dismissal by reason only of the non-renewal of a fixed-term contract – Employment Protection (Consolidation) Act 1978 s.142(1).

[107] See e.g. *ibid* s.140(1) and s.153(5).

Effectively the employer, characteristically the party to stipulate the choice of law in the contract, is prevented from derogating from the employee's protections in two ways. In line with the general restriction, he cannot turn a domestic contract into an international one simply by stipulating a foreign governing law.[108] The choice will be respected but the mandatory provisions of the domestic law will be imported into it. Where the contract is genuinely international, any choice of law will not oust the mandatory provisions of the law which would be the applicable law of the contract if no choice had been made. So in each case of dispute it will be necessary to examine the law applicable in default of choice for, obviously, that will be the governing law if no choice has been made, but also the mandatory provisions of that law will apply even where there has been a choice.

An international company which uses a standard form of employment contract which stipulates the governing law of the contract as the law of the country where the employee works will have no difficulty with the Convention as long as the employee "habitually" works there. A contract, however, which selects the law of the country of the company's headquarters for all its employees world-wide will not achieve standardisation of the terms and conditions of employment if the mandatory laws of the country where any employee habitually works are more favourable, in any particular regard, than the chosen law. Arguments of business efficiency, equality of treatment among employees, or the overall quality of the employment contract will not avail if, in any particular case which an individual employee can raise, the provisions of what would be the applicable law in default of choice under the Convention are more favourable to that particular employee than the terms of his contract.

A typical international employment dispute will involve the employee asserting either a contractual or a non-contractual right which he alleges his employer is infringing. If he asserts a right under the employment contract there will be a dispute about the applicable law only if different potentially applicable laws would interpret the contract differently. Unless the parties have agreed otherwise, the interpretation of the contract will be governed by the applicable law.[109]

The assertion of a right which his employment contract does not give him will always involve the determination of the applicable law. The employee will have to establish his right by reference to a mandatory rule of the legal system which is the applicable law under Article 6. If he can

---

[108] See Article 3(3) and above para 4-28.
[109] Article 10.

do this he has a trump card which will defeat his employer's reliance on the terms of their contract including the term, if there is one, that the contract shall be governed by another system of law.

4-64 *Personal injury* Under English law it is the practice to sue for damages for personal injuries arising out of the employment relationship in tort rather than in contract although an action for the breach of an express or an implied term in the contract is equally available. In all cases where there is a choice of the cause of action it is for the plaintiff to pick which one he wants.[110]

As the Convention is concerned only with contractual obligations, a decision by the employee to sue in tort takes the case outside the Convention and the particular rules for the choice of law in tort will be applied by the forum selected to hear the case. So, an employee injured in the course of his employment may need to consider whether to sue in contract or in tort. The choice in contract may turn upon the content of the chosen governing law or the mandatory rules of the country where he habitually works. The choice in tort may depend upon the *lex loci delicti* (being the actual place of injury or the place where the employer failed to take the steps necessary to protect the safety of his employee). There are more issues here than the governing law and the matter will be considered further later.[111]

4-65 *The advantage rule* It seems reasonable to suppose that the mandatory protection rules can be avoided if the protection afforded by the chosen law is greater. The employer should be estopped from setting up the terms of the Convention against the law which has been stipulated in the employment contract. The purpose of the special rules in the Convention is to protect employees and it would be a meaningless exercise for a court to insist on the letter of the Convention with the result that a less favourable law was applied to the employee. But all this turns upon the particular issue in dispute. Generalities cannot be argued. So, for example, an employer cannot argue that the employee gets a good deal from the contract as a whole e.g. better pay or more generous leaves or greater fringe benefits if, in the specifics of the actual dispute, the employee would be deprived of the basic protection of the mandatory rules of the applicable law.

4-66 *Posted workers* A posted worker is one who is sent by his employer to work abroad on his employer's business, or who is recruited by an employment agency in one country to work in another country, or who is seconded by his multi-national employer for a period of work in a connected company abroad.

---

[110] See *Coupland v. Arabian Gulf Petroleum Co.* [1983] 2 All ER 434.

[111] See below para 8-25.

The Convention provides for the temporary posting of workers abroad only to the extent that such a removal from the habitual workplace provided that it is only "temporary" does not break the link with it.[112] An E.C. draft directive,[113] prompted more by Community aims of free movement of services and fair competition than by employee protection, proposes that a posted worker should have the benefit of the mandatory protection laws of the "host" country while he works there. Such protection laws, relating to hours of work, holidays, minimum pay, health, safety and hygiene, maternity rights and protection from discrimination would apply irrespective of the applicable law under the Convention i.e. they would count as mandatory rules and would be imported into the chosen or found applicable law.

While all this is a matter for the future, it may be worth a brief consideration of the posted worker's position under the Convention as it stands. A posted worker can have the benefit of the superior protections of the "host" country, assuming that another law is the applicable law under the Convention, in only two situations. If he can bring his action before the courts of the "host" country and the forum applies its own mandatory rules[114] or if he sues in a forum (not in the U.K.) which is prepared to apply the mandatory rules of the "host" country.[115]

Mandatory rules

One of the main concepts of the Convention, which we have seen runs through many of its provisions, is the mandatory rule. **4-67**

A mandatory rule is a rule of a domestic legal system which cannot be derogated from by contract. The Convention seeks to preserve applicable mandatory rules against casual avoidance or deliberate evasion. For example, under English domestic law the implied term in a contract of sale that the seller has the right to sell the goods, unless he makes it clear that he is selling a limited interest only,[116] cannot be excluded or limited by any contract term. It is applicable under the Convention, whatever law has been chosen by the parties, if the contract is connected with English law in a manner which triggers the operation of the Convention's rules.

There are three situations where the mandatory rules of a domestic legal system will apply under the Convention irrespective of the choice of law by the parties and two others where mandatory rules may be applied

---

[112] Article 6(2)(a).

[113] Concerning the posting of workers in the framework of provision of services. COM (91) 230.

[114] Under Article 7(2) see below para 4-68.

[115] Under Article 7(1) see below para 4-73.

[116] Sale of Goods Act 1979 s.12.

whether the applicable law is chosen by the parties or determined by the rules of the Convention in default of choice. These are:-

- where the contract is wholly connected with a single country and the parties have chosen a different law as its applicable law[117]
- where there is a consumer contract within the provisions of Article 5[118]
- in the case of an individual employment contract under Article 6[119]
- where there is an applicable mandatory rule of the forum[120]
- where the forum chooses to apply the mandatory rule of a system other than that of the applicable law or of its own law[121]

Where a mandatory rule of a legal system other than the applicable law is applied under the Convention it does not mean that the parties' choice of the applicable law or the law applicable in default of choice is invalidated. That law remains effective for the whole of the parties' substantive relationship except for the matters covered by the mandatory rule. In other words the mandatory rule is incorporated into the contract and trumps any contract term, express or implied, or any legal rule of the applicable law which would have a different effect. To take a simple example: suppose that in an individual employment contract the terms specify a minimum two week period of notice to be given to the employee in the event of his dismissal and that the contract is expressed to be governed by the law of country X which would regard it as entirely valid. If the employee habitually carries out his work in country Y where the minimum period of notice is one month and the provision in country Y cannot, according to the law of Y, be reduced by agreement - it is, in other words, a mandatory provision - any dispute involving the period of notice would be resolved by reference to the law of country Y, any dispute not involving that issue, and indeed the implementation of the four week period, would remain subject to the law of country X - the law chosen by the parties.

Of course the mandatory rule imported into the contract may be crucial in the resolution of the particular dispute - there is no need to import it unless it is to have some effect - but we are not only concerned with litigation. The importation by the Convention of the mandatory rules of connected legal systems enables the parties to be clear about their position well in advance of any dispute between them actually arising. So much is true of the positions under Articles 3, 5 and 6 and these matters

---

[117] See the earlier discussion para 4-28.
[118] See above para 4-44.
[119] See above para 4-57.
[120] Article 7(2).
[121] Article 7 (1).

are more fully discussed elsewhere,[122] but there is far less certainty over the operation of Article 7. The Article envisages two different approaches by the forum and we can look at the more straightforward one first.

Article 7(2)

Article 7(2) provides: **4-68**

"Nothing in this Convention shall restrict the application of the rules of the law of the forum in a situation where they are mandatory irrespective of the law otherwise applicable to the contract."

Under the common law rules there are a number of examples of the application of English law in situations where such application could be seen as based on English law as *lex fori* though the cases are not unequivocal on the point and can equally be seen as examples of the application of the public policy of English law, another forum power which is preserved by the Convention.[123]

In *Boissevain v. Weil* [124] an English national, involuntarily resident in   **4-69**
Monaco during the German occupation, borrowed French currency from a Dutch citizen similarly placed. Under British wartime legislation only authorised dealers or those with specific treasury permission could buy or borrow foreign currency and criminal sanctions were attached to breaches of the provisions. It was argued, therefore, that the loan agreement was unenforceable for illegality by English law. Amidst some confusion of reasoning – that the contract was governed by English law anyway; that the statute had extra-territorial effect; that the imperative nature of the legislation could not make the commission of the offence depend on the contract's proper law – some support can be found for the application of a mandatory rule of the *lex fori* irrespective of the governing law of the contract.

Little more helpful is the decision in *Leroux v. Brown*[125] where an oral   **4-70**
agreement which was made in France and which was to last for more than one year was not evidenced in writing and thus fell foul of section 4 of the Statute of Frauds 1677. Although the contract had been made in France, the court took the view that the legislation which provided that "no action shall be brought" precluded the enforcement of the contract. It is accepted that procedure is a matter for the *lex fori* (though what is substance and what procedure can be a difficult distinction to operate[126])

---

[122] See respectively paras 4-28, 4-44, 4-57.

[123] Article 16 see below para 4-80.

[124] [1950] A C 327, [1950] 1 All ER 728.

[125] (1852) 12 CB 801.

[126] See the discussion at para 7-15.

and it could be argued, weakly, on the facts of this case that the form of the contract was a matter for English law or, more strongly, that English law was the governing law of the contract. One of the problems with the pre-Convention English decisions is that they are equally subsumable under the exercise of the public policy powers of the court.[127]

4-71   If we confine ourselves for the moment to the precise power conferred under Article 7(2) we should expect an application of the mandatory rules of the forum only when;

    i)   the contract, though the applicable law is foreign, has a close connection with England or with English law

    ii)   there is a clear substantive rule of English law which applies irrespective of the foreign governing law i.e. a rule of English law which requires its own application despite the foreign applicable law

    iii) justice demands its application on the facts of the particular case.

This is a minimising view of the provision which suggests that the forum should not apply its own rules to a contract governed by a foreign law unless there is an overwhelming reason for doing so. It recognises that the application of English rules will, on the particular issue in dispute, displace the rules of the applicable law, including its mandatory ones, and, indeed, displace any mandatory rules which are read into the applicable law under the provisions of Articles 3[128], 5[129] and 6[130].

A maximising interpretation of Article 7 (2) would hold the whole of the Convention subject to the forum rules. Taken literally the Article allows the forum to ignore the whole regime under the Convention and apply its own exclusions, choice rules, and any other provision it had a mind to, provided that it regards them as mandatory. The *Report* suggests that this provision was included particularly to take account of concerns which some States felt about their rules relating to cartels, competition and restrictive practices, consumer protection and certain aspects of carriage. The inference is, and the object of the Convention must require, that this aspect of forum power be used sparingly.

4-72   I think that there will be few situations in which an English court will apply its own rules in preference to the rules of the applicable law, but here is one possibility under the Unfair Contract Terms Act 1977. Suppose a foreign supplier agrees to sell to a commercial buyer resident in England a quantity of goods which are to be delivered to the buyer in

---

[127] See below para 4-82.

[128] See above para 4-28.

[129] See above para 4-45.

[130] See above para 4-57.

England. The contract is the supplier's standard form of contract and contains a choice of law clause in favour of an unconnected law which leaves the supplier free to exclude or limit his liability in a manner which would not be effective were English law to be applied. In such a strong case it could be argued that English law has made provision for such a situation and provided that it could be shown that the choice of law appeared to be wholly or mainly for the purpose of evasion,[131] the provisions of English law would override the provisions of the chosen law. A similar result might follow under section 27(2)(b) if the contract was with a consumer habitually resident within the U.K. where he took the steps necessary for the making of the contract but fell outside the provisions of Article 5 because, for example, he made the initial approach to the foreign seller in the latter's own country or answered an advertisement in a foreign magazine which was not directed at the British market.

However important a provision is in the domestic legal system the forum should not apply it to an international contract governed by a foreign law unless it is satisfied that a matter of principle is at stake, and here again we stray into the area of public policy. Suppose the domestic law requires a particular type of contract to be registered in order for it to be enforced e.g. a hire purchase agreement. Whatever the domestic policy in favour of such a requirement, a court should be loath to impose it on a foreign transaction unless satisfied either that there was some deliberate default in the non-compliance or that the issues at stake were so important that the provision should be applied even to those who could not reasonably be expected to know of or fulfil it.

Article 7(1)

Art 7(1) enables a court, in limited circumstances, to apply a mandatory rule which is one neither of the forum, nor of the applicable law, nor one imported into the contract by Articles 3[132], 5[133], or 6[134].   **4-73**

This provision has no application to U.K. courts as its operation has been specifically excluded, under the Reservation provision of the Convention,[135] by the implementing legislation.[136]

---

[131] Unfair Contract Terms Act 1977 s.27(2)(a).

[132] See above para 4-28.

[133] See above para 4-45.

[134] See above para 4-57.

[135] Article 22.

[136] Contracts (Applicable Law) Act 1990 s.32(2).

Nevertheless, the provision could be crucial in foreign litigation and is worth some consideration here. The provision is worded in a very restrictive way -

> "When applying under this Convention the law of a country, effect may be given to the mandatory rules of the law of another country with which the situation has a close connection, if and in so far as, under the law of the latter country, those rules must be applied whatever the law applicable to the contract. In considering whether to give effect to these mandatory rules, regard shall be had to their nature and purpose and to the consequences of their application or non-application."

So, to stand a chance of application, the rule must be part of a closely connected legal system and must be not only mandatory in nature but one which the system which contains it would apply in the particular case in hand. Even then, the forum has a discretion whether to apply it and in the exercise of the discretion should take account of its nature and purpose. Although English courts do not have this power under the Convention, there is some indication that at common law a mandatory rule of the *lex loci contractus* could be applicable whatever the proper law of the contract: "Where a contract is void on the ground of immorality or is contrary to such positive law as would prohibit the making of such a contract at all, then the contract would be void all the world over" per Lord Halsbury L.C. in *Re Missouri SS Co.*[137] but there are no unequivocal decisions in favour of the overriding effect of the *lex loci contractus*. There is more certain authority in favour of a rule of the *lex loci solutionis* having a say but the cases turn on illegality by the *lex loci* and are equally, and more convincingly, explicable in terms of the application of English public policy.[138] Presumably, however, it would have to be something on these lines, or a mandatory rule of one of the contracting parties' "home" countries to trigger the application of the provision.

Returning to the earlier example of the business sale contract, requiring delivery of the goods in England where the chosen law allowed the exclusion of the mandatory rules of the Unfair Contract Terms Act,[139] a foreign forum where Article 7(1) applied would have to decide:-

    i)   whether delivery in England to an English commercial customer was a sufficiently close connection to carry the potential application of a rule of English law - I think the answer to this is yes

---

[137] (1883) 42 Ch.321. See also *The Torni* [1932] P.78.

[138] See *Ralli Bros v. Companhia Naviera* [1920] 2 KB 287; *Regazzoni v. Sethia* [1958] A.C. 301, [1957] 3 All ER 286; *Sharif v. Azad* [1967] 1 QB 605 [1966] 3 All ER 785.

[139] See above para 4-72.

ii) whether the English rule is mandatory - clearly it is

iii) whether the English rule applies to a case with a non-English applicable law - again, clearly, it does, subject to the appearance of evasion

iv) whether in the light of its nature and purpose the court ought to apply it - again, I would be happier arguing for this than against it as it would be difficult, having found evasion, not to apply the remedy prescribed for it.

While the operation of Article 7(1) seems in this case to provide a desirable result, it is questionable whether the potential for complexity and time wasting in such cases does not detract from the general clarity that the Convention seeks to establish. After all, the model I chose was a commercial model and it might be argued that commercial contractors should take care to ascertain their positions before they accept standard terms presented by the other side.

To use the other example looked at earlier, of the consumer contract under the Unfair Contract Terms Act which did not fall within the special rules of Article 5[140], the case is both weaker and stronger. Stronger in that we are dealing with a consumer who may be in need of protection, weaker in that there is a set of special rules for consumer contracts which takes account of the consumer's weaker position and so cases falling outside that protection in the Convention are not worthy of special treatment.

As the U.K. has opted out of this provision, U.K. courts will only take account of the rules of a foreign legal system which is not the applicable law if required to do so under the Convention or in the exercise of their own public policy.

Material Validity

The existence and validity of the contract, or of a term of it, is 4-74 governed by the putative applicable law,[141] that is by the law which would be the applicable law if the contract existed and was valid. At common law, in the absence of clear authority, the better view was that the existence of the contract should be governed by the putative proper law but whether the chosen proper law or the objective proper law was open to contention. There was a general preference for the objective proper law as that would defeat a self-validating choice in the face of objective invalidity. The solution adopted by the Convention is more liberal - the putative applicable law can equally be the chosen law as the

---

[140] See above para 4-72.
[141] Article 8(1).

law found in default of choice. The putative applicable law will determine whether an offer has been accepted, whether the agreement is, if it needs to be, supported by consideration and whether the consent to the contract has been obtained by fraud, duress, misrepresentation or undue influence. These matters relate to the formation of the agreement itself not to its subsequent functioning. Suppose the plaintiff contends that his entry into the contract was induced by a misrepresentation such that, had he known the truth, he would not have entered the contract at all. What remedy he seeks will depend on the position he is in at the time of the discovery of the misrepresentation. He may want to contest the validity of the contract, seek rescission of the contract or obtain damages for the effect of the misrepresentation on his performance of the contract. All these are matters for the applicable law – the putative applicable law if the plea goes to the existence or validity of the contract, the actual applicable law if the complaint goes to the performance of an existing contract.[142]

Similarly, the common law had tended towards the objective putative proper law to determine the issue of the consent of the parties. Again, the solution adopted by the Convention is the putative applicable law, whether chosen or found in default, but with the proviso that a party can also rely on the law of his habitual residence to establish that he did not consent.[143] To take a simple example, suppose the alleged contract resulted from the offeror presuming the offeree's agreement unless he heard to the contrary. Unless it had been previously agreed by the parties that such an inference could be drawn, English law would not allow the offeror to bind the offeree in this way. If the applicable law would infer consent in these circumstances an offeree, habitually resident in England, could use English law to counteract that inference.

Formal Validity

4-75   English law has few requirements for the formal validity of contracts and those there are generally go to the enforceability of the contract rather than to its validity. The specialty contract or deed is an obvious example of a contract which derives its validity from its form, but the requirements relating to surety agreements or contracts for the sale of land survive from procedural restrictions. Procedural matters are, according to the English conflict of laws, wholly within the control of the forum. In the absence of authority the English common law rules would probably have allowed a contract to be formally valid if it satisfied the formal requirements of either the *lex loci contractus* or the proper law.

---

[142] See Article 10 below para 4-78.
[143] Article 8(2).

Other States have more elaborate rules of formal validity and their interest in this matter can be shown by the rules contained in the Convention.

A contract will be formally valid if: **4-76**

- the parties being in the same country when the contract was made, it satisfies the formal requirements of the applicable law or of the law of the place where it is made[144]

- the parties being in different countries when the contract is made, it satisfies the formal requirements of the applicable law or those of either place of presence[145]

An act intended to have legal effect e.g. notice of termination, repudiation or rescission, will be formally valid if it satisfies the formal requirements of the applicable law or of the law of the place where it is done.[146]

There are special rules relating to the formal validity of those consumer contracts which fall under Article 5. Their formal validity is tested by reference to the law of the country of the consumer's habitual residence.[147] **4-77**

Contracts for rights to, or to use, immovable property, while subject to the general rules on formal validity, will have to comply with any formal requirements of the *lex situs* which that law regards as mandatory, irrespective of the applicable law or of the *lex loci contractus*.[148]

Any later change in the applicable law brought about by the parties' agreement will not prejudice the formal validity of the contract.[149]

Scope of the Applicable Law

The law applicable to the contract under the Convention, whether chosen by the parties or found in default of choice and including any mandatory rules imported into it, governs the substance of the obligation between the parties. The interpretation of the contract, its performance, frustration, the ways in which the obligations may be extinguished, prescription and limitation of actions are all matters for the applicable law.[150] Of course under Article 3 the parties are free to subject different **4-78**

---

[144] Article 9(1).
[145] Article 9(2).
[146] Article 9(4).
[147] Article 9(5).
[148] Article 9(6).
[149] Article 3(2).
[150] See Article 10(1)(a), (b) and (d); see also Foreign Limitation Periods Act 1984.

parts of their contract to different governing laws so, for example, they can subject the interpretation of the contract to a separate system of law if they wish.

The Convention's provisions much resemble those which the common law had established. One provision, however, seems peculiar to the English lawyer. The applicable law also governs "within the limits of the powers conferred on the court by its procedural law, the consequences of breach, including the assessment of damages in so far as it is governed by rules of law."[151] This goes beyond the decision that the contract has been broken and that consequently the defendant is to pay damages, to the assessment of those damages. The assessment of damages includes the heads of recoverable damages, whether for example, the plaintiff can recover for disappointment or anguish at the breach of the contract, and the issues of causation and remoteness of damage. It does not, under English law, extend to the quantification of damages which is seen as a matter wholly within the realm of the *lex fori*.

4-79
"In relation to the manner of performance and the steps to be taken in the event of defective performance regard shall be had to the law of the country in which performance takes place ."[152]

It would appear that this reference to the *lex loci solutionis* is intended to be confined to details of performance rather than to the substance of the obligation. So, for example, if delivery has to be made during normal business hours, or notice has to be given within seven working days, the local law's rules on these will be taken into account. It should not follow that the law of the place of performance has any say in the substantial performance of the obligation or that a defence for non performance, which is more than technical, which exists in the local law but not in the applicable law, can be pleaded.[153]

Public Policy[154] – "Ordre Public"

4-80
"The application of a rule of the law of any country specified by the Convention may be refused only if such application is manifestly incompatible with the public policy (ordre public) of the forum."[155]

---

[151] Article 10(1)(c).
[152] Article 10(2).
[153] See *Jacobs v. Credit Lyonnais* (1884) 12 QBD 589.
[154] See below para 7-05.
[155] Article 16.

It needs to be noted at the outset that the public policy exception to the application of a rule of the applicable law is intended to be of very limited scope. Objection cannot be taken to the foreign law itself but only to its application by the forum in the particular case in hand. So an objectionable foreign law which operates, in the particular case, in an acceptable way is not to be ruled out under this provision.

The objection has to be a strong one – manifestly incompatible – much more than the recognition of a difference or a mild distaste for the result, it requires that the forum cannot in conscience give effect to the foreign law without doing great disservice to its own fundamental principles.

Where the applicable law, whether chosen or found, is English, the **4-81** case will, for most purposes, be treated as a domestic one by the English forum. This means, *inter alia*, that English morality and English public policy will be applied as appropriate. Even where the case is governed by a foreign applicable law similar standards of English law will be applied. To take an obvious example – an English court would not enforce a contract of prostitution even if the contract was governed by a foreign law under which such contracts were valid. It is not only in gross cases like this that English law has its say.

In *Regazzoni v. K.C. Sethia (1944) Ltd.*[156] the contract was made in **4-82** Germany between Swiss and English parties. The deal involved the seller delivering jute bags to the buyer in Genoa. The buyer knew that the seller was to obtain the jute from India, the seller knew that the buyer intended to transport the jute to South Africa, both knew that Indian law forbade the direct or indirect export of Indian goods to South Africa. The seller failed to supply and relied on the illegality of the transaction by Indian law as a basis for the contract being unenforceable in the English courts. The contract included a clause choosing English law as the law to govern it but nothing turns upon this, the attitude of the English court would have been exactly the same if the clause had chosen some other system of law. Why? While an obvious case can be made for the non-enforcement in England of a contract which requires the breach of the criminal laws of foreign States,[157] at least where those laws are not themselves repugnant, the better basis for the decision is the public policy of English law, not the illegality by the *lex loci solutionis* as such.[158] In *Regazzoni* illegality by the *lex loci solutionis* was a red herring – a false issue as there was no evidence that the Indian supplier was aware of the ultimate destination of the goods and the main parties to the transaction were not subject to Indian

---

[156] [1958] A.C. 301, [1957] 3 All ER 286. See also *Boissevain v. Weil* [1950] A.C. 327, [1950] 1 All ER 728, see above para 4-69.

[157] See *Ralli Bros v. Companhia Naviera* [1920] 2 KB 287, *Foster v. Driscoll* [1929] 1 KB 470.

[158] See *Howard v. Shirlstar Transport Ltd.* [1990] 3 All ER 366.

jurisdiction. The real issue in the case was how far the English court should go in enforcing, or giving damages for the breach of, a contract which interfered with the good relations of this country with India. An English court trying an ordinary action in contract is clearly not the place for the formulation of foreign policy and it would not be proper for the court to give its view of the rights and wrongs of the dispute between India and South Africa which gave rise to the embargo.

The affront to the sovereignty of a foreign State, the prejudice to the relations with that State which might follow the decision of an English court upholding the contract, or simply the offence to domestic policy in allowing an action on such a basis justifies the refusal. It should be noted, however, that the basis for the English court's policy intervention will be the plea of one of the parties who is seeking, perhaps in a rather dishonourable way, to avoid the consequences of his agreement. In *Regazzoni* both parties knew the score when they made their contract. Had that not been the case the problem might have been resolved without reference to public policy. In cases where one party has been duped by the other, the matter would be referable to the applicable law's misrepresentation rules under which, of course, the contract might be rescindable, unilaterally enforceable or remediable in some other way. If both parties were innocent or if the illegality or other difficulty occurred after the contract was made the applicable law's rules on mistake or frustration would be relevant and the case might be resolved without reference to public policy.

The Convention does not apply to all Contractual Matters

4-83 The matters listed earlier, to which the uniform rules of the Convention do not apply, can now be considered in more detail. As far as English law is concerned those matters which are seen as contractual will be governed by the common law rules of choice of law for contract; those which are not seen as contractual will be governed by the choice of law rules which have been established in the areas to which English law assigns them.

Status or legal capacity of natural persons

4-84 Whether a minor, or anyone else, is capable of entering contracts generally or contracts of a particular description is not a matter which has much troubled the English conflict of laws[159] so uncertainty remains over the choice of law. The personal law, which is referred to for other types

---

[159] But see *Bodley Head Ltd. v. Flegnan* [1972] 1 WLR 680.

of capacity e.g. to marry[160] or to make a will,[161] would not seem to have a strong case in contract especially where the contract is made outside the home country. The *lex loci contractus* - the law of the place where the contract is made- has some support in a very old and uncertain authority[162] and in more modern dicta,[163] but suffers from the lack of any necessary connection with the parties or the substance of the contract. It could be subject to the exploitation of the stronger party in establishing the *locus contractus* in a country where the protection of the party whose capacity is in doubt is weakest. The putative applicable law - that which would be the applicable law of the contract if the capacity issue is determined affirmatively -is, in its chosen form, equally unsatisfactory as it enables the stronger party to stipulate a law which, in effect, removes the protection which the weaker might otherwise enjoy. The putative applicable law in the objective sense - the law which would apply to the contract in default of choice by the parties - is probably the safest bet as it avoids both accident and machination. But it does not, of course, ensure the protection of the weaker party as a reference to his personal law might. As the matter appears to raise few issues in practice there is no need to make heavy weather of it here. There is, however, a special provision in the Convention[164] to the effect that where the parties are in the same country when the contract is made, a party who has capacity by that law can invoke his incapacity by another law only if the other party knew of, or was negligent in not knowing about, the incapacity. In these limited circumstances the party who acts in good faith and without negligence will be protected from a subsequent claim of incapacity by the other party based on his personal law before a court whose conflict of laws rules would look to the domiciliary or national law to determine his capacity. The provision in no way affects the ability of the party with capacity from raising the incapacity of the other party.

I have used the term putative applicable law - that which would be the applicable law if the contract was not affected by the incapacity. Strictly, as the issue of capacity is out with the Convention, it would be more correct to speak of the putative proper law. There are several differences between the proper law and the applicable law under the Convention and it would be possible for the court using the proper law test to identify a law different from that indicated by the Convention. I can see no merit whatsoever in maintaining this distinction for the purpose of contractual capacity.

---

[160] See below para 6-30.

[161] See below para 5-60.

[162] *Male v. Roberts* (1790) 3 Esp.165.

[163] See Ld. Greene M.R. in *Baindail v. Baindail* [1946] P.122.

[164] Article 11.

*Matters relating to wills, succession, matrimonial property and
family relationships*

4-85   The list in the Convention is more expanded[165] "contractual
obligations relating to:
*   wills and succession
*   rights in property arising out of a matrimonial relationship
*   rights and duties arising out of a family relationship, parentage,
    marriage or affinity, including maintenance obligations in respect of
    children who are not legitimate

This grouping, which mirrors the wording in the Brussels jurisdiction
convention,[166] seeks to exclude from the uniform rules matters which are
seen as issues of family law. An agreement between husband and wife for
the division of property on divorce, the agreement between father and
mother for the maintenance of their illegitimate child, an agreement with
respect to the destination of property on death are the types of
arrangement that the provision contemplates. In some of these instances
the parties could have obtained a court order for the financial provision
concerned and it may be that the disappointed party will have a choice
between seeking the enforcement of the agreement or seeking a court
order to establish his claim against the defaulter. The overlap of these
proceedings is the reason for the exclusion.

Most situations covered by the exclusion would not be regarded as
contractual matters under English law, but take the following example –
in *de Nicols v. Curlier*[167] the husband and wife, who were French
domiciliaries, were married in France. They made no specific agreement
about the matrimonial property as they could have done and, therefore
by French law at that time, a community property regime applied
automatically to them. The husband died domiciled in England and his
will sought to dispose of property to which his wife had a claim if the
community property law regime still applied. English law was the *lex
successionis,* the general law governing the succession and would, *prima
facie,* have seen the husband as free to dispose of all the property in the
will unfettered by the wife's claim to community, which was a concept
unknown to English domestic law. The Court of Appeal, however, took
the view that the parties, having failed to reach a specific agreement on
differential allocation of the matrimonial property, must be assumed to
have tacitly agreed to the regime of community. Thus the wife had a

---

[165] Article 1(2)(b).
[166] See above para 3-21.
[167] [1900] A.C. 21.

contractual right to half the matrimonial property which the English court would recognise.[168]

A contract which does not arise from the legal relationships which are **4-86** excluded e.g. an agreement among children for the maintenance of their parents, is governed by the ordinary rules of the Convention.

Bills of exchange, cheques and negotiable instruments

The full text of this exception is "obligations arising under bills of **4-87** exchange, cheques and promissory notes and other negotiable instruments to the extent that the obligations under such other negotiable instruments arise out of their negotiable character;" and the important point is negotiability. Such documents run counter to the ordinary rules of contract under English law in two ways: there is no necessary privity connection between the holder of such a document and the person responsible under it, and a holder in due course who is *bona fide* and who has given consideration is capable of having a better title than his transferor had -an exception, in other words, to the general principle of *nemo dat quod non habet.*

The exclusion relates to the issue of negotiability alone. It does not mean that a contract is outside the convention simply because payment is to be made by cheque or the subject matter of the contract is itself a negotiable instrument.

Arbitration agreements and agreements on the choice of court

Under the common law rules arbitration agreements and agreements **4-88** over choice of jurisdiction, whether contained in the main contract or not, gave rise to no classificatory problems – they were contract terms or separate contracts: the mutual forbearance of the parties from litigating out with the terms of the agreement constituting the consideration for a perfectly bilateral contract.

Just as the parties were free under the common law to select the governing law for their contract, they were free also to decide whether disputes would in the last resort go to court or to arbitration and where that should be. Like choice of law clauses, choice of jurisdiction clauses are frequently contained within standard form contracts. The close connection between choice of jurisdiction and choice of law was marked by the presumption that a choice of jurisdiction clause, in the absence of an effective choice of law clause, could be taken as an implied choice of the legal system under which the court or arbitrator operated – *qui elegit iudicum elegit ius.*

---

[168] For further consideration of the law governing succession, see para 5-53; for a consideration of matrimonial property, see para 5-77.

4-89   In *Tzortzis v. Monarch Line*[169] the sale of a Swedish ship by Swedish shipowners to Greek buyers was held to be governed by English law, notwithstanding that the objective proper law of the contract was Swedish, because the parties had chosen to use an English standard form contract which specified arbitration in England in the event of dispute. This wooden use of the presumption was not followed in *Compagnie d'Armement Maritime S.A. v. Compagnie Tunisienne de Navigation S.A*[170]. where, again, the parties, who had no connection with England, had used a standard English form of charter-party which contained a choice of law clause, in favour of the law of the flag, and a London arbitration clause. At the time of the contract the parties had contemplated that French registered vessels would be used for the carriage. As it turned out, Norwegian, Swedish, Liberian and Belgian ships were also used. In favour of English law it was argued that, the choice of law clause being abortive in failing to identify the law to govern the contract, the inference should be drawn that the parties had chosen English law by reason of the arbitration clause. The House of Lords held that French law should govern the contract either because the parties had intended to choose it or because it was the objective proper law. The choice of law clause, even if it had failed to do its job, was enough to negative the inference which might be drawn from the arbitration provision. A choice of applicable law under the Convention "must be express or demonstrated with reasonable certainty by the terms of the contract or the circumstances of the case"[171], thus now ruling out the inference drawn in *Tzortzis*. Nevertheless the *Report* suggests that a choice of jurisdiction clause will continue to play a part in the overall assessment of the contractual connections, when no choice of law has been made, where the presumptions in Article 4 do not apply or are displaced.

4-90   As English law regards a choice of jurisdiction clause as an integral part of the contract and a separate agreement about jurisdiction as a contract in itself, the governing law is the law of the contract to which it relates whether found by the court or chosen by the parties. It would therefore follow that the law to govern the validity of the choice of jurisdiction clause would, for English courts , be the applicable law under the Convention even though the Convention expressly excludes such agreements from its scope. The counter argument would be that the Convention cannot apply to this aspect of the parties' agreement and that, therefore, the common law rules remain in operation for this aspect of the transaction alone. If, against my judgment, this latter view prevails

---

[169] [1968] 1 WLR 406.
[170] [1970] 3 All ER 71.
[171] Article 3(1).

when would the difference be material? In the vast majority of cases the applicable law under the Convention, whether chosen or found, will be the same system as the common law rules would have identified with the following exceptions:

i) where the common law rules would have found an implied choice of law where the Convention will not. I don't think that there will be much of this but an obvious example would be the *Tzortzis* case considered above, assuming a modern court would follow that decision.

ii) where the presumptions in Article 4 apply and are not overridden by the general exception in paragraph 5 of that Article in favour of the more connected law. Theoretically this category should not exist at all as, by definition, the most closely connected system which the common law rules seek must be more closely connected than any other for the purposes of the Convention. In practice, however, the position might not be so clear cut especially in a situation which would have caused difficulties in the application of the common law rules because of the virtually even balance of the factors to be weighed.[172]

iii) where under Article 5 in default of choice the law of the consumer's habitual residence applies in those contracts which have the special connections specified in the Article. Here it is only the cross border excursion selling cases where the common law rules would be likely to indicate a proper law different from the applicable law under the Convention.

iv) where under Article 6, on individual employment contracts, the applicable law in default of choice indicated by the Convention would not be displaced by the general exception in favour of the more connected law. This is essentially the same issue that we looked at under ii) above.

Three further points have to be noted. First, disputes over the validity of choice of jurisdiction clauses are not common. Second, even if the applicable law and the proper law indicated different systems it would not necessarily, or even often, be the case that the different systems would take different views of the jurisdiction clauses. Finally, there are restrictions on the effect of jurisdiction clauses within the Brussels Convention.[173]

What is the effect in English law of a valid jurisdiction clause? If a party tries to sue in England in defiance of an agreement to litigate before the courts of another country the defendant in the English proceedings

4-91

---

[172] See e.g. *Coast Lines v. Hudig & Veder Chartering N.V.* [1972] 1 All ER 451.
[173] See above para 3-52.

can ask the court to stay the process. Generally English courts will grant the application, they have not always done so,[174] but the general attitude is to make the parties stick to their bargain unless there are overwhelming reasons for not doing so. In *Mackender v. Feldia*[175] a block insurance policy was issued at Lloyds to cover the diamonds of three Belgian merchants. The contract was expressly governed by Belgian law and Belgian courts were given exclusive jurisdiction. When one of the merchants was robbed of £50,000 of jewellery while on a smuggling expedition to Italy, an activity, needless to say, not disclosed at the time of the negotiations, the insurers sought a declaration from the High Court that the policy was void for fraud and leave to serve out of the jurisdiction. In rejecting the application the court took the view that non-disclosure rendered the policy voidable rather than void and that therefore both the choice of law and the choice of jurisdiction clauses remained valid until the proper steps had been taken to avoid the policy. Those steps were a matter for Belgian law and Belgian courts.

English courts, at common law but not under the Conventions,[176] have a general discretion to order a stay of proceedings. Where action is brought in defiance of a jurisdiction agreement the discretion should normally be exercised in favour of a stay unless the plaintiff can show strong cause why the action should be allowed to continue. In *The Eleftheria*[177] Brandon J. made a careful analysis of the authorities and summarised the issues to be taken into account. All the circumstances of the case should be taken into account and in particular the following matters should be considered:-

- the location of the factual evidence and the effect of the location on the relative convenience and expense of trial
- whether the law of the foreign court would be the governing law and whether that law differed from English law in any significant way
- the relative strength of the parties' connections with either country
- whether the defendant really wanted the case tried in the chosen country or was merely seeking procedural advantages
- whether the plaintiff would be prejudiced by having to sue in the foreign court because he would be deprived of security for the claim or be unable to enforce the judgment, be faced with a time bar not applicable to the English proceedings or would be unlikely to get a fair trial as a result of political, racial, religious or other reasons.

---

[174] See *The Fehmam* [1957] 2 All ER 707.
[175] [1966] 3 All ER 347.
[176] See above para 3-08.
[177] [1969] 2 All ER 641.

A properly framed jurisdiction clause will confer exclusive jurisdiction **4-92**
on the chosen court under the operation of Article 17 of the Jurisdiction
Conventions,[178] but jurisdiction clauses are not always a simple selection
of a single court system but may seek to leave the dominant party free to
litigate elsewhere. Suppose an international loan agreement where the
debtor has assets in several countries or has assets which are mobile. In
such a case the lender may wish to protect his interests not only by
nominating his favoured jurisdiction but also by leaving it open to him to
litigate elsewhere.

Such non-exclusive jurisdiction clauses, as they are known, presented
no problems to English courts under the common law rules of
jurisdiction. The English courts would take jurisdiction once the
defendant had been served with process and related, though not identical,
proceedings could be pursued elsewhere. The language of Article 17 of
the Jurisdiction Conventions might have been thought to restrict the
traditional freedom by imposing a stricter notion of exclusive i.e. by
interpreting it as sole. This appears not to be the view of the English
courts. In *Kurtz v. Stella Musical Vermmnstaltungs GmbH*[179] there was an
agreement between two German domiciliaries whereby the plaintiff lent
money to the defendant to help finance a theatrical venture. There was a
non-exclusive jurisdiction clause in favour of English courts. When the
plaintiff tried to recover his share of the proceeds the defendant argued
that he was not bound by the jurisdiction clause as it did not fall within
Article 17. The court held that Article 17 left it possible for more than
one court to have jurisdiction and that where the jurisdiction agreement
under Article 17 operated for the benefit of one party alone there was no
reason to prevent that party from suing elsewhere. The English courts
would have jurisdiction in such a case, as even a choice of non-exclusive
English jurisdiction was still a choice of English jurisdiction.

Corporate and incorporate status

The full text of Article 1(2)(e) runs "questions governed by the law of **4-93**
companies and other bodies corporate or unincorporate such as the
creation, by registration or otherwise, legal capacity, internal organisation
or winding up of companies and other bodies corporate or unincorporate
and the personal liability of officers and members as such for the
obligations of the company or body;"

Whether a corporation or unincorporated body has the capacity to
enter a contract and what effect any such contract may have on the
relations between the members of the corporation or unincorporated

---

[178] See above para 3-52.
[179] [1992] 1 All ER 630. See Fentiman [1992] 51 CLJ 234.

association is not the concern of the Convention. This exception affects only the internal operation of the body; a contract made with a corporation or unincorporated body will be subject to the Convention like any other international contract.

Agency

4-94   Whether and in what circumstances an agent can bind his principal, or the organ of a company can bind that company, to the third party are questions which fall outside the Convention, but that is the extent of the exception. The contractual relationship between the agent and the principal, and the contract between the agent and the third party, are subject to the convention.

Trusts

4-95   Trusts are considered in the chapter on property.[180] The concept involved in this exception is the English concept of the trust. The constitution of trusts and the relations between settlors, trustees and beneficiaries will be governed by the Hague Convention on trusts introduced into English law by the Recognition of Trusts Act 1987.

Evidence and procedure

4-96   Evidence and procedure remain matters for the forum law whatever the applicable law of the contract and are, therefore, excluded from the operation of the Convention. This exclusion is subject, however, to Article 14 on burden of proof which provides for two situations where the applicable law under the Convention will apply to matters of proof which would otherwise appear to fall under the exception. First, where the applicable law under the Convention contains, as part of its law of contract, rules which raise presumptions of law to determine the burden of proof, those presumptions shall have effect. So, for example, under English law and aside from the operation of the Unfair Contract Terms Act 1977, where a person signs a contractual document he will be deemed to know and be bound by its contents unless he establishes some ground e.g. *non est factum*, to afford him relief. The burden of proof falls upon the stronger party in a *prima facie* case of undue influence to negative the inference. Second, a contract or other act intended to have legal effect may be proved by any mode of proof allowed by the forum or by any of the laws identified by Article 9 on formal validity, provided, in the latter

---

[180] See below para 5-85.

case, that the mode of proof can be administered by the forum i.e. is physically possible there and not repugnant to the forum's policy on proof.

Contracts of insurance covering risks in the E.C.

The Convention does not apply to contracts of insurance covering risks within the member states of the E.C. Whether a risk so falls is a matter to be determined by the trial judge using his own internal law. Contracts of insurance covering risks outside the E.C. are subject to the Convention and the identification of the applicable law will be governed by Articles 3 and 4 or by 5 if the insured has taken out the policy in his private capacity in circumstances which attract the special rules on consumer contracts.

4-97

The exception here, which is based on the expectation of a separate Convention on insurance matters applicable within the E.C., is confined to direct insurance; the process of reinsurance, whereby the primary insurer lays off the risk or part of it by contract to others, is covered by the Convention.

Nullity

Article 10, which deals with the scope of the applicable law, includes the consequences of the nullity of the contract among the matters governed by the applicable law.[181] English law does not regard the effects of nullity as a matter of contract law at all but as a matter relating to quasi contract or restitution. The U.K. has exercised its power under the Convention[182] to opt out of the provision.[183]

4-98

2 TORTS

More energy has been expended in the discussion of tort cases in the conflict of laws in the common law world than on any other area of the subject. For English law this would be somewhat surprising, as the number of tort conflict cases coming before the English courts is tiny, were it not for the fact that the current choice of law rule for torts is the least satisfactory part of the conflict system The problems in this area are considerable and the attempts to find solutions to them raise fundamental issues for the conflict process.

4-99

---

[181] Article 10(1)(e).
[182] Article 22
[183] Contracts (Applicable Law) Act 1990 s.2(2).

The Nature of Tortious Liability

4-100   Common lawyers have long abandoned the attempt to produce an overall definition of tortious liability, realising that the subject matter defies any unitary treatment. Not only do torts cover a great variety of wrongs but they also cover a variety of ways of doing wrongs and a wide realm of social purposes. There is very little in common among, say, an unintentional defamation, a deliberate assault, a negligent running down and the incursion into another's air-space – yet all these need to be subsumed under a single dispositive rule if the traditional methodology of the English conflict of laws is preserved.

Policing policies in the area of trespass, the protection of the use and enjoyment of property, the picking up of the legal pieces after a road accident, the protection of the consumer, the control of industrial safety, the security of commercial transactions are all jobs which the tort system is given to do alongside its traditional role as the means for the vindication of civil liberties. With such an heterogeneous collection of aims, methods and techniques it is little wonder that no satisfactory rule has emerged and that courts have been influenced by the particular examples of tortious liability with which they happen to have been faced.

Let us explore some of these examples a little further to show both the complexity of the problems and the likelihood that different societies will adopt different methods of dealing with them. What any society has to work out are the interests which are to be protected and the nature of harms which are to be controlled. The common law, for example, has long protected the person from crude physical aggression but has hesitated over the range of those who can seek compensation for carelessly inflicted emotional distress. The protection of the individual's property rights is also a long-standing area of tort law, but what is to count as a property right and what sort of interference is to give rise to an action? Whether the injured consumer of a product should be expected to seek his remedy from the seller or the manufacturer and on what basis, whether the liability of a driver who has injured another road user should depend on fault or trigger strict liability are matters of contention.

The common origin of tort and crime involves a residual public involvement in the tort system, whether the tort is mirrored by potential criminal liability or is purely a matter for private litigation. Tort law protects the basic personal rights which a citizen has, not only against other persons, but against the State itself. The recognition and enforcement of exotic tortious rights may thus be seen as a more difficult job for a conflict system to do than, say, the recognition of a foreign institution of marriage or the acceptance of foreign rules for the recognition of contracts.

The Possibilities

If tort is seen as a sub-species of crime, as in some cases it can be, there   **4-101**
might be reason to apply the law local to its commission in the same way
as a criminal system is seen as applying only within a defined territory.

The local law, although it may be the only "common" law between
strangers, may fly in the face of a pre-existing relationship, a common
personal law or a concurrence of legal rules. There are some spectacular
cases in which the application of the *lex loci delicti commissi* has led to
bizarre results. In *Walton v. Arabian-American Oil Co*[184] the law of Saudi
Arabia was applied to the personal injury claim of one U.S. citizen against
his employer for a motor accident occurring on the U.S. company's
property in Saudi Arabia; while in *Mackinnon v. Iberia Shipping Co.*[185] the
Court of Session applied the law of the Dominican Republic to the
personal injury claim of a Scottish seaman against a Scottish shipowner
simply because, at the time of the accident, the ship was in the territorial
waters of that country. Nor should it be thought that the adoption of a
crude localising rule necessarily leads to the simple, mechanical,
identification of a single legal system, as arguments for the law of the place
where the wrongful act was done can be matched by those in favour of
the different place where the harm resulted.

The personal law which, if it is common, provides a standard reason   **4-102**
against the application of the local law, is of little help if the parties are
from different countries with different legal rules covering the matter in
dispute. There is no general case for applying the defendant's law rather
than the plaintiff's law to the determination of the issue.

The law of the forum is unacceptable, as the forum is generally a matter   **4-103**
for the plaintiff's choice and may well have no contact with the issue.[186]

One solution to some of the difficulties which arise when all the   **4-104**
material facts relate to one country and it is only the occurrence of the
accident in another which makes the case a conflict case at all, is to apply
the law of the social environment or the law which has the closest and
most real connection with the parties and the issue. This "proper law of
the tort", in various guises, has had considerable influence in the decisions
of U.S. courts and some influence in the current English law and in the
reform proposals of the Law Commissions.

---

[184] (1956) 233 F (2d) 541.
[185] [1955] SC 20.
[186] See *Machado v. Fontes* [1897] 2 QB 231.

Horses for Courses

4-105   It would be possible to devise a system which contained not one but a number of conflict rules for tort, each one directed at a particular manifestation of wrong. So, for example, one might have one rule for consumer/manufacturer cases, another for passenger/carrier cases; one for general road accidents, another for defamation and so on. While such a system would have the obvious advantage of recognising that unlike things are best kept separate, it would not take us very far forward unless we could characterise an action as definitively connected with a particular legal system.

To take what might seem an easy example first - the protection of reputation is covered to a limited degree in English law by the torts of libel and slander. It might be argued that a suitable disposition of the case could be made if a court applied the law of the place where the defamatory matter was disseminated and thus where the injury to the reputation was felt. But the idea of the injury to the reputation, rather than the affront to the dignity of the defamed individual, as the essence of the action, is a common law concept; a civil lawyer might concentrate on the personal affront. In the more complex case of consumer protection, should liability depend on where the defective product was designed, made, marketed, bought, consumed, where the injury was caused by its use or consumption, or where the harm actually manifested itself? And would it make any difference whether the manufacturer targeted his product to the country of buying, using, or harm, or not?

What makes the production of separate rules for different cases even more difficult is the personal law - where the parties come from the same legal system it seems artificial to apply a law which may have no more than an accidental connection with the dispute. The same can be said of the situation where the parties, though from different countries, have in common the rules which would dispose of a purely domestic case.

The English Way

4-106   English law has not managed to establish a satisfactory method of dealing with tort problems in the conflict of laws after over a century of trying. Unlike the United States and most of Continental Europe, English law refused to accept the law of the place where the tort was committed as the basic governing law and preferred instead a mixture of the *lex fori* and the *lex loci delicti*.

The prominence of the forum is explicable in terms of the rights thesis of tort, that is, when the English court provides a remedy for a tort it is acknowledging that a recognised interest of the plaintiff has been invaded and that that right should be vindicated by the award of damages. To recognise an exotic "right" does not fit into this pattern. For example, English law does not recognise a right to privacy as such - insofar as privacy is protected at all the plaintiff must establish the commission of some specific tort, for instance, that his property has been invaded or that his reputation has been injured. Suppose that a plaintiff from a country which gave a right to privacy *per se* were to sue in England for the breach of that right and an English court were to give him damages in compensation, it might be thought that the decision had established a precedent for such a right in a purely domestic case. There is no need for fears of this type. When an English court recognises a foreign law, to the extent of giving a remedy based upon its content, it does not thereby make an extension to the domestic law of England and there are no grounds for seeing tort as an exception to this.

If the application of the law of the forum alone to the disposition of **4-107** tort cases undermines the whole idea of the conflict of laws and the application of the *lex loci* imports adventitious elements, the amalgamation of the two would not appear promising. In fact the English way has been to make the forum law dominant, but to require that the wrong complained of before the English court should have at least some quality of wrongfulness by the law of the place where it was done. The *lex loci delicti* was merely required to indicate that an unjustified act had been done and then it was for English law to deal with the matter in its own way.

The classic statement of the position was made by Willes J. in *Phillips* **4-108** *v. Eyre*[187] which, unfortunately, but such is the accident of litigation, was an atypical tort case. Eyre was governor of Jamaica at a time when there was severe unrest in the colony. In putting down a rebellion he used force which contravened the civil liberties of the plaintiff. The plaintiff brought an action for assault and false imprisonment against him. The case was complicated, however, by the fact that, once the rebellion had been successfully suppressed, the Jamaican legislature retroactively validated the steps taken by the governor. The plaintiff lost his case and it would not have attracted much legal notice had it not been for the attempt of Willes J. to state a general rule. His words have been scrutinised by generations of commentators as if he was legislating for all time and the process continues. This is the major passage which has become known as the rule in *Phillips v. Eyre*:-

> "As a general rule, in order to found a suit in England, for a wrong alleged to have been committed abroad, two conditions must be fulfilled. First the wrong must be of such a character that

---

[187] (1870) LR 6 QB 1.

it would have been actionable if committed in England ...
Secondly, the act must not have been justifiable by the law of the
place where it was done."[188]

4-109   Authority for the first limb of the rule - that the wrong complained of
must be a tort by English domestic law - is provided alone by *The
Halley*.[189] In that case, a complaint by a foreign shipowner of damage
caused by the negligent navigation of a British ship in Belgian territorial
waters was rejected as the ship was, at the time of the collision, under the
control of a compulsory pilot. English law, at that time, differed from
Belgian law, the *lex loci delicti*, in holding that a shipowner was not liable
for the negligence of a compulsory pilot. The decision, chauvinistic and
tinged with not a little of the maritime superiority enjoyed by English
law, has had a disastrous effect on the development of a satisfactory system
of tort conflicts because it prevents any claim in England for any wrong
which does not have its precise counterpart in English domestic law.

4-110   The language used for the second limb of the rule - that the act
must not have been justifiable by the *lex locus delicti* - fits the facts of
Phillips v. Eyre, but the word "justifiable" is an odd one in the context
of most tort actions and its use has caused a great deal of difficulty. It
was clearly intended, quite properly, to cover the situation where the
act was not wrongful by the *locus delicti*, where it was lawfully
authorised, in advance or retrospectively, or where the defendant had
by that law a complete defence to the plaintiff's claim. Whether it was
intended to require actionability in the *locus delicti* is more dubious. In
Machado v. Fontes[190] an action was successfully brought in England for a
libel published in Brazil although, at the time, there was no civil
liability, under Brazilian law, for such defamation. In fitting the case
within the rule in *Phillips v. Eyre* there was no problem over the first
limb of the rule - had the libel been published in England it would have
given rise to a successful action here. With regard to the second, the
fact that there was the possibility of criminal proceedings in Brazil was
regarded as sufficient to make the wrong non-justifiable by that law.

This decision has been very heavily criticised as it makes the whole
substance of the obligation turn upon English law, a legal system which is
involved in the case solely because the plaintiff decided to bring his action
in England.

A Quebec court went one step further than this in allowing a personal
injury claim, brought by a gratuitous passenger against his host driver for an
accident in Ontario although the Ontarian "guest statute" prevented the

---

[188] At p.28.
[189] (1866) LR 2 PC 193.
[190] [1897] 2 QB 231.

passenger's recovery. Though there was no civil liability by the *locus delicti* there was potential criminal liability for careless driving; the Quebec court latched onto this notwithstanding that an Ontarian criminal court had acquitted the driver of the offence![191] The conflict here was a false one. Both parties were domiciled in Quebec and only the fact of the accident happening in Ontario brought that system's law into consideration.[192]

Despite these examples, which give the impression that the rule in **4-111** *Phillips v. Eyre* is plaintiff oriented, the reverse is the case as the plaintiff has to satisfy a double test, the most formidable of which is that of English law as *lex fori*. Nevertheless, although traditional interpretation of *Phillips v. Eyre* reduced the *lex loci delicti* to a very minor role, it would deny the action in a number of situations. Where the defendant could show that his act was justified or not in any way wrongful, (i.e. gave rise to no civil action of any description and could not be made the subject of any criminal process) by the *lex loci delicti* or could establish that he had a complete defence to the action by that law, the second limb of the rule in *Phillips v. Eyre* would not be satisfied. The defendant would also escape liability if he could show that he was not liable in the same capacity under the two legal systems. Only the last of these needs amplification here. The rule in *Phillips v. Eyre* requires that the parties be involved in the same capacities, and that the claim is the same, under both legal systems. An object lesson here, though not actually under the rule in *Phillips v. Eyre* as it is a Scots case, is *M'Elroy v. M'Allister*.[193] The action was brought by the widow of a Scotsman employed by a Scots firm who had been killed in a road accident in England while in the course of his employment. Because of the mismatch between the English and Scots remedies for wrongful death, the widow obtained only that item which was common to both systems – the funeral expenses.

To similar effect is *The Mary Moxham*[194], where damage was done by an English ship to a pier in Spain. The plaintiffs failed in their action in England against the shipowners, as Spanish law did not apply the doctrine of vicarious liability and would regard the proper defendants to be the master and crew.

In every case where the rule in *Phillips v. Eyre* has been used, the **4-112** result has been the application of English domestic law to the substantive issue between the parties. It has been suggested that the rule is not a choice of law rule at all, but a further jurisdictional hurdle which has to be surmounted before English law is applied as *lex fori*. In other words the

---

[191] *McLean v. Pettigrew* [1945] 2 DLR 65.

[192] C/f *Babcock v. Jackson* (1963) 12 NY 2d 473, [1963] 2 Lloyds Rep 286. See above paras 1-24, 2-76.

[193] [1949] SC 110.

[194] (1876) 1 PD 107.

rule in *Phillips v. Eyre* is not a double-barrelled choice of law rule which happens to lead to the application of English law as *lex causae*, but a test which, once completed, leads to the application of English law as *lex fori*. As English law has been applied in every case it could be argued that it really doesn't matter whether it was applied as *lex causae* or as *lex fori*. But the issue is not one of indifference when it comes to possibilities of future development. If the rule in *Phillips v. Eyre* is seen as a jurisdictional rule which leaves open the choice of law it may at least be argued that, once the rule has been satisfied, the court is left with the freedom to determine the appropriate governing law, even if in every case so far it has chosen English law for that role. If, however, the line is taken that the satisfaction of the rule leads inexorably to the application of English law as *lex fori*, there is no such scope for development apart from scrapping the rule altogether and starting again.

The defects in a system which always leads to the application of the forum law, like the wooden application of the *lex loci delicti*, can result in an entirely artificial connection which bears little or no relation to the parties or the facts of the case. It has the additional disadvantage that the plaintiff can, by selecting his jurisdiction, create a right which he did not possess under any other legal system or greatly increase the effect of any right which he did have. The criticisms founded on these difficulties, the artificiality of the *locus delicti*, already considered, the development of other theories, not least that of the law of the social environment developed by the late Professor Morris,[195] and the abandonment of the rigid adherence to the *lex loci* by American courts, (manifested for English lawyers primarily by the decision in *Babcock v. Jackson*,[196]) created a mood for change in English law. The litigation in *Chaplin v. Boys*[197] provided just the opportunity.

Chaplin v. Boys

4-113   In *Chaplin v. Boys*, plaintiff and defendant, English domiciliaries, were British military personnel temporarily serving in Malta. The defendant injured the plaintiff by careless driving. There was no issue on liability, the matter in contention was the amount of damages recoverable. Under Maltese law the plaintiff could recover only "special" damages, his out of pocket expenses which, in view of his position amounted to just £53; under English law he was entitled also to "general" damages for his pain and suffering – in this case £2,250.

---

[195] (1951) 64 Harv LR 881.
[196] (1963) 12 NY 2d 473, [1963] 2 Lloyds Rep 286.
[197] [1971] AC 356, [1969] 2 All ER 1085.

Before looking at the choice of law issue it is necessary to consider the matter of damages. The quantification of damages, that is how much in money terms the plaintiff shall be awarded for his injury, is incontrovertibly, a matter for the *lex fori* - one cannot claim that broken legs are more valuable in California than they are in Bangladesh and that therefore the forum should make the necessary adjustment in the particular case (hence the importance of forum selection).[198] If you sue in England you get the English going rate for the injury you have sustained. But, while quantification is a matter for the *lex fori*, is the question of the heads of damage recoverable similarly a matter for the forum law? With varying degrees of precision, legal systems use separate bases of claims which are then quantified. So, to take the example of a personal injury claim, the allowable heads of damage would include medical and other out of pocket expenses, damages for pain and suffering, for losses of amenity, future earnings and so on. It does not follow that the court in making an overall award of general damages will specify the amount awarded under each of the allowable heads. English judges have resisted the invitation to make their awards specifically itemised as they are very far from dealing with a precise process. But the ability to award at least notionally under the specific heads is part of the nature of the action. If the refusal of Maltese law to award damages for pain and suffering - not in this case specifically, but as a general policy of Maltese law - was seen as a matter of quantification only, there would be no problem as the case was being brought before the English court which allows such awards. If, however, the claim for general damages is seen as part of the substantive right then, according to one view of the rule in *Phillips v. Eyre*, there must be a match between the plaintiff's claim in English law and in the *locus delicti*. If English law does, and Maltese law does not, recognise the claim, then the action must fail. It needs to be emphasised that this is true only on one view of *Phillips v. Eyre*. The view that any unjustifiable act in the *locus delicti* satisfies the second limb of the rule, or even that the second limb requires civil actionability of some sort, would allow the application of English law.

It has generally been supposed, and the better judgments in *Chaplin v. Boys* bear this out, that the proper classification is that the heads of damage are matters of substantive right and not merely matters of quantification. If this is so there is a real conflict between English and Maltese law, and not merely an artificial one.

It may be wondered whether that is indeed the better view. Suppose one society, like Malta in this case, decides not to allow compensation to be awarded for harms of a particular type while another decides to

---

[198] See below para 8-25.

confine such awards within narrow monetary limits. An example of this would be English law's attitude to the, now defunct, action for loss of expectation of life where awards were limited to a conventional, if not token, amount; another would be the practise of some U.S. states of putting a ceiling on personal injury awards. The operation of the rule in *Phillips v. Eyre* would mean that where the *lex loci delicti* has no remedy for the plaintiff's claim there can be no successful claim in England. But if it has a remedy, however conventionalised or token it might be, not only does an action lie in England but it lies to the full extent of English law, that is free from the restrictions of the *locus delicti*, because English law governs the quantification. The distinction, then, between the procedural issue of quantification and the substantive issue of the heads of damage ultimately comes down to the difference between nought and one!

4-114 The obvious point to make about the facts of *Chaplin v. Boys* is that the connection with Maltese law was entirely adventitious; no Maltese persons or Maltese interests were involved and the accident could as easily have occurred in England – the social environment of the tort action was unequivocally English. One of the questions that the court had to decide was whether to apply the proper law of the tort. Such an approach would have led to the application of English law as *lex causae* and would have rendered the debate about substance and procedure otiose. Interest analysis would also have rendered that debate unnecessary as there was no evidence at all that Malta had any interest in having its rule of exclusion applied on the facts of this particular case. The case was, then, a soft one, a false conflict, as all the connections, save only for the application of the rule in *Phillips v. Eyre*, pointed unequivocally to England and English law.

4-115 The decision in *Chaplin v. Boys* is one of the most difficult to analyse in the modern conflict of laws; for, while of the nine judges engaged in the various stages of the case only one opposed the application of English domestic law to its solution, there was very little consistency in the reasoning. It may help briefly to review the various judgments before commenting on the overall result of the case.

At trial[199] Milmo J. felt obliged to follow the decision of the Court of Appeal in *Machado v. Fontes*. It followed from that case, inevitably as there was no law of the *locus delicti* on the matter of civil compensation for libel, that English law governed the heads of damage as well as the quantification of damages awarded under any head. The Court of Appeal,[200] arguably not bound by the decision in *Machado v. Fontes*, could explore the possibilities. Denning M.R., showing his characteristic impatience with old decisions which stood in the way of his view of

---

[199] *Boys v. Chaplin* [1968] 2 QB 1, [1967] 2 All ER 665.
[200] [1968] 2 QB 1, [1968] 1 All ER 283.

justice, was prepared to disregard *Machado v. Fontes* as wrongly decided, and to come out fully in favour of the application of the proper law of the tort, both to the cause of action and to the heads of damage as well, as these were substantive matters.

Lord Upjohn took a very traditional view of the rule in *Phillips v. Eyre* which left the *lex loci delicti* with the very minor role of establishing unjustifiability and made the *lex fori* paramount. He wanted nothing to do with the proper law of the tort which he considered to be totally unsuited to English conditions. Diplock L.J., dissenting, recognised that the question of heads of damage was a matter of substantive law but he took an historical view, not borne out by the authorities, that the *lex causae* was the *lex loci delicti*. As Maltese law was the *lex causae* it followed that the plaintiff had no right before the English courts to any more than the damages allowed by Maltese law, to be quantified, if anything turned on it, by the English court. He rejected the proper law of the tort as being a retrograde step, at least outside passenger/carrier, driver/guest cases.

The case went to the House of Lords[201] with all the options still open and, while their lordships were unanimous that English law should govern the case, the lack of agreement on exactly why it should do so continued. Lord Hodson favoured overruling *Machado v. Fontes*, regarded the issue of heads of damage as matters of substance and rejected the proper law of the tort, as a general dispositive law, as too uncertain. He did adopt a form of reasoning which supporters of the proper law can pray in aid of their arguments. The rule in *Phillips v. Eyre*, he said, was only a general rule, as Willes J. himself had stated, and, therefore, it was subject to exceptions based on public policy and

4-116

> "if controlling effect is given to the law of the jurisdiction which because of its relationship with the occurrence and the parties has the greatest concern with the specific issue raised in the litigation the ends of justice are likely to be achieved".

Lord Guest took the view that the rule in *Phillips v. Eyre* was a rule of double actionability – that the plaintiff had to show that his action, while it would give rise to an action in England had it happened here, would also give rise to civil liability by the *lex loci delicti*, thereby avoiding abuses like *Machado v. Fontes*. As the plaintiff could establish that he had a remedy, albeit a limited one, under Maltese law, that would suffice as, he believed, damages for pain and suffering did not depend on a substantive right but were part and parcel of the right to damages for personal injury and, thus, procedural matters for the *lex fori*. He roundly rejected the suggestion that the court might apply the proper law of the tort.

---

[201] [1971] AC 356, [1969] 2 All ER 1085.

Lord Donovan took an even more traditional line, he was not prepared to go even as far as to interpret the rule in *Phillips v. Eyre* as requiring double actionability, though he did concede that the decision in *Machado v. Fontes* was an abuse. If the word "justifiable" was to be given its ordinary meaning, the plaintiff's case was secure as there was clearly a wrong done him by Maltese law. As the English court was competent to entertain the action under the rule in *Phillips v. Eyre* it was right that it should award its own remedies. His rejection of the proper law was even more vigorous than Lord Guest's.

Lord Wilberforce, on whose judgment most attention has been focused, had no hesitation in condemning the decision in *Machado v. Fontes* which he thought ought to be overruled, *Phillips v. Eyre* involved, he asserted, double actionability. He was not in favour of adopting the proper law of the tort as a general choice of law rule but *Phillips v. Eyre* should be applied with some flexibility, subject to exceptions along the lines of the American Law Institute's Restatement Second on the Conflict of Laws, which would enable the court, in a suitable case, to proceed

> "by segregation of the relevant issue and consideration whether, in relation to that issue, the relevant foreign rule ought, as a matter of policy ... to be applied. For this purpose it is necessary to identify the policy of the rule, to enquire in what situations, with what contacts, it was intended to apply; whether not to apply it, in the circumstances of the instant case, would serve any interest which the rule was devised to meet ... The rule limiting damages is the creation of the law of Malta, a place where both respondent and appellant were temporally stationed ... Nothing suggests that the Maltese state has any interest in applying this rule to persons resident outside it, or in denying the application of the English rule to these parties ... No argument has been suggested why an English court, if free to do so , should renounce its own rule.That rule ought, in my opinion to apply".[202]

The final judgment in the House of Lords was given by Lord Pearson, he regarded the issue of pain and suffering to be a substantive matter but rejected any requirement of double actionability. In his view the rule in *Phillips v. Eyre* applied directly, that is, that the *lex fori* became the *lex causae* once non-justifiability by the *lex loci delicti* had been established. He recognised, however, that there was a problem of forum shopping inherent in the English system, as evidenced by the decision in *Machado v. Fontes*, and that this should be controlled by public policy and by the application of the proper law, at least in the identification of the natural forum.

---

[202] At pp. 391, 1104 respectively.

The outcome of the litigation was that English law was applied to the issue of the heads of damage and the plaintiff got his English award. Only Diplock L.J., in the Court of Appeal had opposed this result, but there was nothing like unanimity on the basis of the adjudication. Indeed it is not easy to find a clear majority in favour of any particular important position. If we do a head-count on the major issues we find the following, sometimes strange, alliances:- **4-117**

1) In favour of the proposition that the heads of damage are matters of substantive law: Denning M.R., Diplock L.J. and Lords Hodson, Wilberforce and Pearson

Against it: Milmo J. and Lords Upjohn, Guest and Donovan.

2) Of the view that *Machado v. Fontes* remained good law: Milmo J. (though that is perhaps unfair as he felt bound by the decision of a higher court) and Lords Upjohn, Donovan and Pearson (though the last supported the principle that led to the decision rather than the decision itself).

Against that view: Denning M.R., Diplock L.J. and Lords Hodson, Wilberforce and Guest but whether their disapproval of the decision amounts to its overruling is a matter of some doubt.

3) Supporting the proposition that the proper law should be the general governing law for tort we have the sole voice of Denning M.R.

Opposing it we have the express statements of all the other judges concerned with the litigation though Lord Pearson did suggest the use of the proper law to prevent forum shopping and Lord Wilberforce did in fact apply, in his use of interest analysis, a rather sophisticated proper law approach.

4) If we look at the place of the rule in *Phillips v. Eyre* after the decision in *Boys v. Chaplin*, we find that Denning M.R., Lords Hodson and Wilberforce would regard it as a general rule only to which there were exceptions; in the case of Denning M.R. the exceptions would be numerous. Taking the traditional view that the rule required the application of English law as *lex fori* we have Lords Upjohn, Donovan and Pearson, while Diplock L.J. alone took the view that the rule required the application of the *lex loci delicti commissi*. Denning M.R., Lords Hodson, Wilberforce and Guest can be assumed to regard the rule as now requiring double actionability.

In only a few subsequent cases has the decision in *Chaplin v. Boys* been considered.[203]

---

[203] See *Church of Scientology of California v. Metropolitan Police Commissioner* (1976) 120 Sol Jo 690; *Coupland v. Arabian Gulf Oil Co* [1983] 3 All ER 226; *Johnson v. Coventry Churchill International Ltd.* [1992] 4 All ER 14.

4-118   The position would now appear to be that the rule in *Phillips v. Eyre* requires double actionability; the particular plaintiff must show that he has a cause of action against the particular defendant under both English law and the *lex loci delicti*. While the wrong must be actionable as a tort by English law it would seem that the cause of action by the *lex loci* does not need to be categorised in the same way provided that it is the same claim against the same defendant in the same capacity. It must be a claim based on the wrongful act of the defendant and not a claim which is merely triggered by it. This can be illustrated by a couple of old cases which came before the Privy Council on appeal from Canada. In *McMillan v. Canadian Northern Railway*[204] an action was brought in Saskatchewan against his employer by a workman who had been injured by a fellow employee in Ontario. By Ontarian law employers were not liable to employees who had been injured by those in common employment with them. While this rule did not apply in Saskatchewan it provided a complete defence by the *lex loci* and thus prevented the satisfaction of the second limb of the rule in *Phillips v. Eyre*. The accident entitled the employee to compensation under a workmen's compensation fund but that was not accepted as satisfying the second limb of the rule as the entitlement under that fund was a statutory right which was not dependent on the fault of the employer. The same would apply if, in the *lex loci*, the right to claim damages in a running down case had been replaced by a state compensation scheme which was available on the basis of injury rather than fault or to the system, under German law covering injured workers.[205]

4-119   As for the flexibility introduced by Lord Wilberforce; it is unclear what ambit it has. It has been used only to apply English law[206] and it is doubtful whether it could be used to apply a foreign law, though in principle this must be possible. It applies only to displace the second limb of the rule in *Phillips v. Eyre* and does not affect the rule in *The Halley*. Where all the other connections are with English law then flexibility provides a suitable escape device from the *lex loci*. Whether it will apply in the event of less significant connections, or whenever the policy of the *lex loci* would suggest that it had no interest in its own rule being applied despite significant connections, may well never be known as reform is on the way and may arrive shortly.

---

[204] [1923] AC 120. See also *Walpole v. Canadian Northern Railway* [1923] AC 120.

[205] See *Johnson v. Coventry Churchill International Ltd.* [1992] 4 All ER 14.

[206] *ibid.*

Reform

The case for reform is overwhelming. Despite the better **4–120** interpretation of the rule in *Phillips v. Eyre* as one of only general application and therefore subject to exceptions, and the improvement brought about by taking the second limb of the rule as requiring civil actionability by the lex loci delicti, the rule is still extremely parochial as the first limb of the rule based on *The Halley*[207] still requires that the action satisfies the test of domestic English tort law.

Even the reformed rule swings the balance too much in favour of the defendant as the plaintiff has to establish his cause of action by both the *lex fori* and by the *lex loci delicti* with the concomitant advantage to the defendant who can defeat the claim by a defence open to him under either. The result is that the plaintiff, if he succeeds at all, achieves the lowest common level of relief.[208] Even though the flexibility introduced by Lord Wilberforce in *Chaplin v. Boys* can avoid some of the greater injustices it is far from clear whether it can result in anything other than the application of English law. Suppose that all the significant contacts are with the *locus delicti* can that law be applied to the exclusion of the *lex fori*? Almost certainly not, as the rule in *The Halley* remains intact. Could both the *lex fori* and the *lex loci delicti* be displaced in favour of the law of some third system? Again, the answer would appear to be "no" for the same reason. Suppose the parties in *Chaplin v. Boys* had been French, could French law have been made the *lex causae*? This is possible, though unlikely. Given actionability by English law, which remains a pre-requisite, flexibility would seem to be limited to the elimination of the influence of the *lex loci delicti* rather than positive reference to some third system. Even if reference to a third system were possible, it could *only* have the effect of reducing the plaintiff's claim below that which was recognised by English domestic law.

The rule in the *Halley* continues to prevent the English courts from entertaining any action unknown to English domestic law however well founded under another legal system.

Lord Wilberforce's willingness to examine the policy of Maltese law **4–121** in *Boys v. Chaplin* and to assess whether Maltese law had any interest in the outcome of the case is to be welcomed in terms of general conflict method as it has the effect of avoiding false conflicts, but it cannot by itself alleviate the general position created by the current English rules which put such emphasis on the *lex fori*.

---

[207] (1868) LR 2 PC 193.
[208] See *M'Elroy v. M'Allister* [1935] SC 20.

Reform Proposals

4-122   The main thrust of the Law Commission's proposals[209] is the replacement of the rule in *Phillips v. Eyre* with a scheme for the applicable law. While the proposals centre on the *lex loci* rather than the proper law model they avoid the technical location of the place of the tort and also provide for the displacement of its localising rules, in appropriate cases, by the application of the proper law model.

Most significantly the proposals would remove the rule in the *Halley* so that, for the first time in the English conflict of laws, the existence of the cause of action will not be dependent on English law as *lex fori*. Of course it will remain for English law to determine what constitutes an action in tort. The initial classification, as always, remains for the lex fori, but that classification is no longer to be confined to the domestic model.[210]

4-123   Given the classification of the matter, by the forum court, as tort, the proposals provide presumptions for the identification of the applicable law. So, in the case of personal injury or death the applicable law will *prima facie* be the law of the country where the injury was sustained.[211] In the case of damage to property the prima facie applicable law will be the law of the country where the property was when it was damaged.[212]

In all other cases the prima facie applicable law will be the law of the country "where the most significant elements of the events constituting the subject matter of the proceedings took place"[213]

While the presumptions relating to personal injury and property damage are directed at the result of the tortious action it is by no means clear whether the residual proposal is to be read in the same way. Where, for example, the fraudulent or negligent statement is made in country A, but the loss is suffered in country B, it would seem that the applicable law would be B rather than A. This would certainly seem to be the case where the plaintiff acted on the statement in country B. Where, however, he acted on the statement in A but the loss occurred in B the position is more doubtful.

The proposals envisage the situation where "the most significant element of the events" test does not identify a country and, in such cases, the test of the "most real and substantial connection " is substituted.[214]

---

[209] Law Com. 193 (1990).
[210] Law Com. Draft Bill Clause 1(4).
[211] *ibid* 2(1).
[212] *ibid* 2(2).
[213] *ibid* 2(3)(a).
[214] *ibid* 2(3)(b).

The law of the country indicated by the presumptions can, in all cases, **4-124** be displaced if, comparatively, the connections with the country indicated by the presumptions and those constituting a real and substantial connection with another country demonstrate that it would be substantially more appropriate for the law of the latter country to be applied.[215]

This rule of displacement would certainly deal with the most spectacular cases where the tyranny of the *lex loci* under the present law creates injustice. There would be no doubt that *Chaplin v. Boys, M'Elroy v.M'Allister*[216] and *Mackinnon v. Iberia Shipping Co,*[217] which under the presumptions would have Maltese, English and the law of the Dominican Republic respectively as their *prima facie* applicable laws, would, under the rule of displacement, have English law, Scots law and Scots law as their respective applicable laws.

The proposal that the displacement of the *prima facie* applicable law should occur only where the court concludes that it is "substantially more appropriate" to apply another law is likely to cause difficulty. It is hard to imagine a case where a court found it more appropriate to apply the law of the country with a real and substantial connection and then declined to do so because it was not significantly more appropriate.

The stranglehold that the forum has under the existing rule makes **4-125** several conflict issues irrelevant. The Law Commissions' proposals address some of these by making it clear, for example, that reference to the applicable law is a reference to its domestic rules only – that the doctrine of *renvoi*[218] shall continue to have no application to torts.[219] The forum's principles of public policy are preserved[220] and the application of foreign "penal, revenue or other public law"[221] is excluded.[222] Savings are also made for U.K. statutes and the forum's procedural rules.[223]

Torts within the U.K.

Under the rule in *Phillips v. Eyre* it was assumed that in cases where the **4-126** tort was committed in England no question of foreign law arose whatever connections the tort might have with foreign laws.[224] The coincidence of

---

[215] *ibid* 2(4).
[216] [1949] SC 110.
[217] [1955] SC 20.
[218] See below para 8-07.
[219] Law Com Draft Bill Clause 2(6).
[220] *ibid* 4(1).
[221] See below para 7-05.
[222] Clause 4(2).
[223] Clause 4(3) and (4).
[224] *Szalatanay-Stacho v. Fink* [1947] KB 1

the *lex fori* and the *lex loci delicti* was thought to leave no room for any other possibility. The Wilberforcean exception in *Chaplin v. Boys* would potentially allow the application of a foreign law where the contact with England was incidental as, for example, an accident between two Maltese temporally serving in England which involved no local interests. The possibility should not be over-stated as English courts have never applied anything other than English law in tort cases and the prospect of them doing so when the tort was committed in England is tiny.

The Law Commissions' proposals would, in their ordinary operation, open up a real possibility of the application of foreign law even when, say, the place of injury was England. In principle there should be no objection to this as the same choice of law rule ought to apply whatever the connections and special rules favouring English law, or, more realistically, English defendants would appear discriminatory. However, suppose the defendant has acted lawfully in England but the consequences of his action are felt in a foreign country which regards them as tortious. To take a couple of examples which exercised the Commissions. An English defendant publishes a statement in England and abroad which is, by English law, non-defamatory but is defamatory according to the law of the foreign country of publication. An English factory, operating within the controls of English law, emits pollution which falls, as acid rain, in a country where such pollution gives rise to a private right of action.

Now, clearly, the English defendant could be held liable in foreign proceedings and, public policy aside, the foreign judgment would be enforceable in England. Nevertheless, it might be thought unacceptable that the defendant should be held liable in English proceedings when his act was not wrongful by English law. To deal with this the proposals reintroduce what is, in effect, the second limb of the rule in *Phillips v. Eyre*, so that where the tort action relates to conduct "the most significant elements of which took place in a part of the United Kingdom" the matter shall be exclusively determined by the law of that part of the U.K.[225] It follows, of course, that a casual, incidental, or, indeed, anything less than the most significant elements' connection with a part of the U.K., will leave the general choice of law rules in operation. This provision is likely to be controversial both ways.

4-127 For defamation, the Commissions propose[226] that, where the alleged defamatory publication was also published in a part of the U.K. (e.g. a broadcast received at home and abroad) or, in the case of separate publications, the alleged defamatory matter had already been, or was simultaneously, published in part of the U.K., it shall be assumed that all

---

[225] Clause 3(1).
[226] Clause 3(2).

the significant elements of the conduct complained of took place in the part of the U.K. where the proceedings are brought. In consequence the law of that part of the U.K. will be the applicable law. The effect of this would appear to be that the defendant can rely, in any proceedings in England, on the non-defamatory quality of his statement by English law, or on any defences open to him under English law if he satisfies English law's technical rules for publication here. This is so even if his main purpose is publication in a foreign country where he knows his statement will be regarded as defamatory and actionable at the suit of the victim.

The Relations between Contract and Tort

As the English conflict of laws is based on the conceptual classifications of English domestic law and as those classifications are too crude to embrace all the types of relation within the domestic law, so its deficiencies are equally apparent in the conflict of laws. To take a couple of obvious examples of the limitations of traditional conceptual classifications. A contract may contain a clause which seeks to limit or exclude liabilities for matters, like personal injury or damage to property, which are not part of the express contractual terms and arise either as implied terms in the contract or by the operation of the general law of tort. If the injured party sues in tort the contractual aspect of his relationship with the defendant must be taken into account. Similarly, the employment relationship does not fit easily into either of the conceptual categories of tort contract. Certainly it is contractual and there are some matters which are exclusively such, for example pay rates and working hours (though, of course both could be controlled by statutory rules as well). Other matters, say about the health and safety of employees, can be seen as implied terms in the contract, statutory obligations which, if broken will give rise to an action for breach of statutory duty or matters redressible by an action in the tort of negligence. For English domestic law the niceties of possible classifications are rarely of much concern but for the conflict of laws they are crucial as the choice of law rules depend on the initial classification of the subject matter. The issue is made more relevant for the English conflict of laws than for some others because it is the practice in England to sue for personal injuries in tort rather than in contract even where the tortious duty relied on can be seen as an implied term in the contract itself.[227] **4-128**

Suppose, as was the case in *Sayers v. International Drilling Co NV*,[228] that an English employee of a foreign company is injured abroad in **4-129**

---

[227] See *Coupland v. Arabian Gulf Petroleum Co* [1983] 3 All ER 226.
[228] [1971] 3 All ER 163.

circumstances which would give rise to a tortious action had they occurred in England. Providing that the English court can take jurisdiction the case satisfies the first limb of the rule in *Phillips v. Eyre* and the court, having classified the claim as tort, and, assuming the wrong is also actionable in the *lex loci delicti commissi*, would proceed to give the appropriate award of damages under English domestic law. Suppose further, however, that the employment contract contains terms which limit or exclude the employee's rights of recovery in the very circumstances of which he complains. How is his employer's defence , which is wholly contractual, to be assessed when the rules for the choice of law in contract indicate another system of law which may be neither English law as the *lex fori* nor the law of the *locus delicti*, as the applicable law for the contract? In *Sayers*, Denning M.R. sought the proper law of the issue in an attempt to discover a single system of law to dispose of the case -an attractive idea which failed in the execution as it resulted in a crude choice between competing systems which would have yielded very different results.

An alternative approach is to incorporate the contractual defence into both stages of the *Phillips v. Eyre* test. When the plaintiff alleges his tortious claim the defendant can plead the contractual defence to prevent recovery first under English law and then under the *lex loci delicti commissi*. At both stages the defendant will have to establish that the defence upon which he relies is both valid contractually, that it satisfies whatever tests for it are used by the contract's applicable law, and is acceptable minimally i.e. not contrary to the law or public policy of the forum and the *locus delicti*. If the defendant succeeds in either of these then he has a defence to the plaintiff's claim which will prevent that claim satisfying the double actionability test.

4-130   If the Law Commissions' proposals are implemented there will no longer be the need for the plaintiff in tort to establish his cause of action by domestic English law, and there will be only a single system, the applicable law under the code, to deal with. A defendant seeking to rely on a contractual defence, will have to establish his right by the law governing the contract which, if it is an international one will be identified by the Rome Convention as the chosen or found applicable law. Unless he can do that he has no defence. If he can, the effect of the defence will be a matter for the applicable law of the tort.

A defence, valid under the contract's applicable law, will not be available, of course, if it offends the public policy of the forum or conflicts with a mandatory rule of the forum which is applicable to the contract under Article 7(2) of the Rome Convention.[229]

---

[229] See above para 4-80, 4-68.

CHAPTER 5

PROPERTY

1 INTRODUCTION

Property rights are at once the most concrete and the most abstract of   **5-01**
legal interests. The most concrete in that their origin is physical and
territorial, the most abstract in that they can exist without the
interpersonal nexus which characterises all other legal relations. At the
same time they can be the most simple rights which every social system
has to acknowledge – some protection for current use – and the most
complex, as when ownership is recognised in something which is
currently neither possessed nor controlled by the owner, and where the
subject matter may not even have a physical existence.

Small wonder then that different legal systems have had very different
ideas about what can be owned, by whom, and on what terms and how
ownership can be exercised, protected, transferred and extinguished.
Equally unsurprising are the very different classifications of property
interests which legal systems have, based on physical form, use, means of
transfer, portability, value and social utility, and the possibilities which
they acknowledge of shared ownership in sequence, in parallel, in extent
and for purpose. English common law and equity established a complex
of rules based primarily on the distinction between realty and personalty,
with real interests centring on land and personal interests extending to
everything else, and with very different rules relating to the transfer of
those interests both in life and on death. To these must be added the
complex of interests which have recently become known as intellectual
property rights and which have yet to find coherence in the domestic
legal system.

In every other area of the conflict of laws, English courts have taken   **5-02**
as their starting point the concepts of the domestic law and have
been content to adapt them for conflict purposes, adopting a more
(e.g. contract, marriage) or less (e.g. torts) international approach. For
property it was realised that the distinctions adopted by the domestic law
could not be adapted to provide a workable basis for the adjudication of
conflict cases, and a universal distinction which made sense for all
systems, whatever their domestic rules might be, was substituted. This
division of property rights for conflicts purposes is between interests in
things which can be moved and interests in those which cannot.

The Distinction between Movables and Immovables

5-03   It is conventional to begin any discussion of the English conflict of laws on property by expounding the distinction between movables and immovables as a universal distinction transcending the divisions of property which different domestic systems may have, and particularly English law's distinction between realty and personalty. While historically the contrast is well taken, in modern law there is little of significance remaining in the English domestic division and, in the conflict of laws, the rôle of the *lex situs*, which is what the distinction between movables and immovables is all about, is important in transfers of property *inter vivos* irrespective of whether that property is movable or immovable. In succession cases the distinction is vital, but only because English conflict law has not caught up with the developments in domestic law where unified succession was introduced by the property legislation of 1925.[1]

5-04   The distinction between movables and immovables was clearly established in *Re Hoyles*[2] where a domiciled Englishman left his residuary estate, which included mortgages over land in Ontario, to charity. Both English and Ontarian law prohibited the testamentary gift of real estate to charity, presumably on the common basis that such gifts interfered with the circulation of land in commerce. It was argued that the respective Statutes of Mortmain had only local application and that both systems, for their domestic purposes, classified mortgages as personalty rather than realty. As succession to personal property was, according to the English conflict of laws, a matter for the personal law of the deceased it followed, therefore, that English law, the law of the testator's last domicile, governed gifts of personalty. As English legislation could not pretend to apply in Ontario, the gift should stand. Farwell J. rejected this argument and held that the first question to be answered was whether the subject matter of the gift was movable or immovable. As he had no hesitation in classifying the mortgages as interests in immovable property, the governing law was Ontarian law as *lex situs* of the immovable property. Under Ontarian law the gift fell foul of the mortmain legislation and therefore failed.

5-05   Once the initial classification has been made and the *lex causa* identified – the *lex situs* for immovables, the personal law for movables – the distinction between movables and immovables gives way to whatever classification the *lex causa* uses.

An illustration of the two-stage process can be found in the decision in *Re Berchtold*[3] Here the dispute concerned the identification of those

---

1   Administration of Estates Act 1925 s.33(1).
2   [1911] 1 Ch 179.
3   [1923] 1 Ch 192.

entitled to succeed the deceased on intestacy. The choice was between English and Hungarian law which, while they had common members on their lists of those entitled to succeed on intestacy, were not identical.

The particular item of property in dispute was some land in England which was held on trust for sale. The intestate had died domiciled in Hungary and there was no dispute that his movable property would, according to the established English conflict rules, devolve according to the scheme of intestacy provided by that law. Any immovable property situated in England, however, would pass according to the English rules for intestate succession. What was the status of the land held on trust for sale? It was argued for the Hungarian beneficiaries that the equitable doctrine of conversion[4] required the land to be treated as money i.e. as if the sale had already taken place; money being movable, the persons identified under Hungarian law would be entitled to it.

This argument was rejected as the real question was seen to be whether the property in the estate was movable or immovable, an issue which preceded any question about whether the property was realty or personalty. As the property was land it was obviously immovable and the succession rights to it were to be determined by its *lex situs* - English law. As English law recognised both the distinction between realty and personalty and the equitable doctrine of conversion, the land would pass to those identified by English law to succeed to the personal property, the next of kin by English law.

The primacy of statutes under English law may involve a departure from the logic of *Re Berchtold*. In *Re Cuttliffe's W/T*[5] English land which was subject to a strict settlement had been sold under the powers given to the tenant for life by the Settled Land Act 1882 and the money invested. The beneficiary under the settlement died intestate in Ontario and it was claimed that the succession should be determined by Ontarian law as the capital money was movable. The statute,[6] however, provided that

> "Capital money arising under this Act while remaining uninvested and securities on which an investment of any such capital money shall be made, shall for all purposes of disposition transition and devolution be regarded as land".

The court felt bound by the clear words of the statute in a way in which it had not felt bound by the equitable doctrine of conversion and treated the capital money as an immovable, thereby choosing English law, the *lex situs*, as the law to govern the succession. As the capital money was

5-06

---

4   See *Fletcher v. Ashburner* (1779) 1 Bro CC 497.
5   [1940] Ch 565, [1940] 2 All ER 297.
6   S.33(5). See now Settled Land Act 1925 s.75(5).

classified by the statute as land it followed, of course, that under English domestic law, the property would go to the heir, as realty, not to the next of kin, as personalty.

5-07   As the object of the initial classification is to give effect to the interests of the *lex situs* it must follow that the law of the *situs* has the say in how the distinction is to be applied to property in its territory.

> "The question in all these cases is not so much what are or ought to be deemed, ex sua natura, movables or not, as what are deemed so by the law of the place where they are situated. If they are there deemed part of the land ... they must be so treated in every place in which any controversy shall arise respecting their nature and character."[7]

The fact that another country would classify the subject matter in dispute in a different way is irrelevant. Suppose we are dealing with a "mobile" home situated in France; we know that under English law the degree of physical connection to the land will determine certain issues of contested ownership, but it is not English law but French law which will determine whether the subject matter is movable or immovable, so evidence of the French law of property would be needed definitively to classify the subject matter.

Features of the English Conflict of Laws on Property

5-08   There are a number of features which affect the English conflict of laws on property which appear, not necessarily evenly and not without conflicting, through this area. A glance at them now may help to inform the remainder of the discussion. They are:-

- Restricted jurisdiction
- Procedural requirements
- Effectiveness
- Contract and conveyance
- Party autonomy
- State interests

Restricted jurisdiction

5-09   We have seen that under the Brussels and Lugano Conventions the courts of the *situs* of the immovable have exclusive jurisdiction over proceedings *in rem* brought in relation to it.[8] At common law the English

---

7 Story *Commentaries on the Conflict of Laws* (1885) s.447.
8 See Article 16(1) and above para 3-43.

courts generally refuse jurisdiction when the matter concerns title to or rights to possession of foreign immovable property - this rule, for convenience known as the *Moçambique* rule, derives from the decision in *British South Africa Co. v. Companhia de Moçambique*[9]. Two reasons can be advanced for restrictions on jurisdiction, firstly, that only courts and officials of the *situs* have the power to deal with immovable property, and secondly, that there may be social policies in the *situs*, e.g. protection of tenants, which require the attention of a court there.

There are three exceptions to the *Moçambique* rule. The English court will not refuse jurisdiction solely on the basis that the case involves rights to, or to the possession of, foreign immovable property when its jurisdiction is founded on the Admiralty jurisdiction *in rem*, the equitable jurisdiction *in personam*, or the administration of estates and trusts. The first of these is outside the scope of this book, the other two are pertinent to this chapter. **5-10**

While the courts of the *situs* will generally have jurisdiction over matters relating to immovables there, it should not be assumed that all disputes will be subject to the rules of the *lex situs*, though, as we shall see, many are.

Procedural requirements

In succession cases the starting point, as far as English law is concerned, is the authorisation of the persons who are responsible for the administration of the estate in England. Such persons can only act in England if they have a grant of representation (probate or letters of administration) from the court. The beneficial distribution of the assets of the estate in accordance with the will or the intestacy rules is the final task of the personal representatives and that task is under the supervision of the court. English law governs the administration of the estate, though of course in the vast majority of cases the actual supervision is nominal. As administration includes distribution and as the estate may have assets abroad which are immovable interests, this produces an exception to the *Moçambique* rule. **5-11**

Effectiveness

To call effectiveness a principle is to elevate it beyond its merits. Every rule of law and every court decision is intended to have effect and decisions or rules which cannot effectively be enforced help no one. But the fact that immovable property is permanently, and movable property **5-12**

---

[9] [1893] A.C. 604 and see also Civil Jurisdiction and Judgments Act 1982 s.30(1); *Hesperedes Hotels v. Muftizade* [1979] AC 508; [1978] 2 All ER 1168.

temporally, under the control of the courts and officials of the *situs* has produced not only the jurisdictional limitations but also the belief that the law of the *situs* cannot be disregarded. Indeed, it is usually seen as the appropriate law to apply, at least in those cases where the courts of the *situs* would apply their own domestic law to the case in hand. A concern for complying with the *lex situs*, or rather of assimilating the English court's decision to that which a court of the *situs* would give, has led to the English doctrine of *renvoi* which we will look at later.[10]

Contract and conveyance

5-13   English lawyers are familiar with the distinction between contract and conveyance in the context of the transfer of land but not in the area of sale of goods, yet, analytically, the same issues are at stake. There is the relationship between buyer and seller (or recipient and donor) which is a purely personal relationship concerning only themselves and which is governed by the law applicable to the contract or gift; and there is the property interest which the buyer or recipient holds against the world at large. Whatever the law governing the personal relationship, that law cannot, thereby, determine the property relations. Suppose S sells property to B in circumstances where S has no title, authority, or power to make a valid transfer. B's remedy against S is clearly contractual, but the remedy of O, the owner, against S or B, or both, does not depend on the law governing the S - B relationship but upon a right which he has under the law of property. The conflict of laws relating to property is concerned entirely with the proprietary aspects of disputes, all other aspects are governed by the law appropriate to the interpersonal relations.

Party autonomy

5-14   One principle of English law here, as elsewhere, is that the parties should be free to run their own affairs, that there should be few restraints on the alienation of property, and that on death the testator should be free to dispose of the whole of his property as he wishes. This last is in contrast with the position of the Civil law systems where the family interests are seen to exist in the estate before the death of the current owner.His testamentary wishes operate on what remains after his family, characteristically his surviving spouse and his children, have automatically inherited their "legitimate portions".

---

[10] See below para 8-07.

State interests

In contrast with the idea of party autonomy, but in keeping with the **5-15** restricted jurisdiction and with the idea of effectiveness, is the recognition that States have powers of appropriation and confiscation over property within their territories as a fact of international life and one to be controlled, if it is to be controlled at all, by the public international legal regime and not by the decisions of individual courts trying private law matters.

2 MOVABLES

Having made the distinction between movable and immovable **5-16** property we now have a category with which the choice system can get to grips. We have not, however, finished, as there are further distinctions which need to be made. The most straightforward is the distinction between transfers of property *inter vivos* and transfers on death, as different rules apply to each. The second distinction is less obvious, that is the distinction between tangible and intangible property. The essential problem here is the extent to which rights in intangible property can or should be treated as if they were rights to physical objects. While it is well recognised that interests in intangibles can be property rights, and are often very important ones, it is unwise to assume that either domestic or conflicts systems can simply force them into a mould created for physical objects. The view taken here is that the special relations created in the most common of these interests, debts, makes them unsuitable for assimilation into the law established for physical things.

The Transfer of Physical Objects

Property rights

Sometimes rather archaically described as the transfer *inter vivos* of **5-17** choses in possession, what we are dealing with here is the transfer of the property interests in physical objects (chattels). Most commonly such transfers are brought about by contract and, where they are, the contractual relationship between the parties which, between themselves, but only between themselves, will subsume the property relations, will be governed by the contract's applicable law. So all aspects of the relations of buyer and seller will be determined by the applicable law of their contract.

While English lawyers are familiar with the distinction between contract and conveyance which is such a feature of our land law, there is a tendency to forget that the same distinction, but not happily its cumbrous operation, applies equally to sales of goods. The failure to mark the distinction is because there is a peculiar rule in English law about the passing of property, in default of contrary agreement between the parties, when the subject is specific goods in a deliverable state – here property passes when the contract is made whether delivery has been made or not.[11] This is not the place to discuss details of English domestic law but it is worth pointing out that this rule – an exception which applies in the most common cases – has not come without difficulties to the English law on sale of goods. The distinction between contract and conveyance must be kept in mind for the purposes of the conflict of laws and it is to the conveyancing aspects of the contract, that is to the proprietary interests in the contract's subject matter, that this section is directed.

5-18 There will rarely, if ever, be any difficulty in distinguishing a property issue from a contractual or any other relation, e.g. a gift, which gives rise to the transfer. Firstly, the parties will be different or at least operating in different capacities from those engaged in the transfer relation. Typically the case will involve either the transferee attempting to assert his interest in the thing against someone other than the transferor, or a third party asserting a property interest over the thing which is the subject of the transfer.

To take a simple illustration of the sort of conflict that might arise here. Suppose a domiciled Englishman, by a contract made in England and expressed to be governed by English law, sells goods which he owns in country X. Suppose that, before the buyer gets control of the goods, the seller is adjudicated bankrupt. Is the buyer protected? By English domestic law, which is the stipulated governing law for the contract, assuming that the goods are specific and in a deliverable state and that the parties have not agreed otherwise, property will have passed to the buyer immediately on the conclusion of the contract. The buyer can rest content in his property rights and the seller's collapse is not his concern. But the goods are situated in country X and country X may require some act to be done,[12] some real or symbolic handing over to take place, before the property is regarded as having been transferred to the buyer. In default of such action, the property remains with the seller, becomes part of his bankrupt's estate, and the buyer is left to take his chance among the unsecured creditors. Which law should resolve this conflict?

[11] Sale of Goods Act 1979 s.18 Rule 1.
[12] See *Inglis v. Robertson* [1898] A.C.616.

The Lex Situs

"I do not think that anyone can doubt that with regard to the transfer of goods the law applicable must be the law of the country where the movable is situated."[13]

5-19

The *lex situs* of the movable at the time of the transaction in question determines any proprietary effects of a transfer.

The old, but still leading, authority is *Cammell v. Sewell*.[14] A cargo of Russian timber was en route from Russia to Hull in a Prussian ship when the vessel was wrecked off the Norwegian coast. The master of the ship had the timber sold by public auction in Norway, and the buyer at the auction shipped the timber to England where he sold it to the defendant. The plaintiffs, who were the insurers of the cargo, had indemnified the original owner for the loss and sought to recover the value of the timber from the defendant. The court found for the defendant accepting that he had good title to the timber as the Norwegian sale had, by that country's law, overridden the title of the former owners and created a good title in the buyer at the auction.

In *Inglis v. Usherwood*[15] an action was brought in conversion by the creditors of a bankrupt English merchant against the master of a ship, chartered by the merchant, who had allowed the Russian supplier of the goods to endorse the bills of lading in favour of himself. The contract was f.o.b. and thus, under English law, delivery of the goods on board the vessel would be delivery to the buyer, and the goods would have been part of the bankrupt's estate and available to satisfy his creditors. The law of Russia, however, where the endorsement took place, allowed such a recapture of the delivered goods and it was to Russian law that the court had regard in holding that the property had revested in the supplier and that the master of the vessel was not liable for conversion.

A more recent illustration of the position can be seen in the decision in *Winkworth v. Christie Manson & Woods*[16] where works of art were stolen from their English owner in England and later offered for sale by auction at Christies. The stolen paintings had been taken to Italy and there sold to a buyer who had bought them in good faith. If title to the paintings was to be decided under English law the buyer would have had to set up one of the *nemo dat* exceptions, which on the facts seems unlikely, but Slade J., following *Cammell v. Sewell*, held that Italian law, as the *lex situs* at the time of the transaction, was to govern and, by that law, the buyer had obtained good title when he bought the pictures in Italy.

---

[13] *Per* Maugham J. in *Re Anziani* [1930] 1 Ch. 407 at 420.
[14] (1860) 5 H & N 728.
[15] (1801) 1 East 515.
[16] [1980] 1 All ER 1121.

5-20   Where there has been a series of transactions relating to the same goods, the search is for the most recent transaction which, according to the *lex situs* where it took place, had the effect of definitively altering the previously existing title to the property. So, for example, where the seller has sold the same object to two different buyers, the order of priority will depend on the *situs* of the object at the time of each sale. If the first sale had, by the *lex situs* of the goods at the time, the effect of transferring title with no residual power in the seller to confer title on anyone else, the first buyer will have priority because the seller has nothing to convey to the second buyer. If the seller retains a power to confer title on another, can, in other words, trigger one of the *nemo dat* exceptions, by the *lex situs* of the second sale, the second buyer's claim will be preferred.

5-21   Where the goods have remained in the same foreign *situs*, or where the current *situs* is also the place where the last operative transaction occurred, it should not necessarily be the case that the domestic law of the *situs* is the law to be applied. As the whole purpose of looking to the *lex situs* in the first place is to recognise the power of the territorial legal system - is, in short, the matter of effectiveness again - then it should logically follow that if, in the particular case, the courts of the *situs* would not apply their own domestic law but the law of another country, then that line should be followed and the English court should apply whatever system of law the foreign *lex situs* would apply. To do otherwise would be to fail to achieve the purpose of the original reference to the *lex situs*. The same reasoning should apply even when the goods are no longer in the place where the transaction occurred and reference is made to the law of their former *situs*. This takes us into the concept of *renvoi* which will be discussed later.[17]

5-22   Even where the English or foreign *lex situs* would apply its own domestic law, it does not follow that every jot and tittle of the domestic law must be applied. The case is, after all, a conflict case, and the international aspects of the case should not be disregarded. It may be that particular rules of the system are intended for purely local consumption and that to apply them to an international case would be inappropriate or officious. In each case the rules of the *lex situs* should be examined to see whether they provide a rule of purely internal order or represent a policy stance applicable generally. Courts do not readily engage in such purposive analysis and do not take too kindly when others do it for them, but an example should serve to demonstrate an enlightened approach to conflict problem solving. In *Dulaney v. Merry & Sons*[18] an assignment was made in Maryland whereby two U.S. citizens assigned all their property, wherever situated, to another U.S. citizen whose task it was to treat with

---

[17]   See below para 8-07.
[18]   [1901] 1 K.B. 536.

their creditors. Some of the property to which the assignment related was in England and it was argued for the English creditors that the attempted assignment of the English property would fail as it had not been registered under the Deeds of Arrangement Act 1887. Channel J. concluded that the Act was not intended to bring within its ambit foreign assignments, notwithstanding that some of the property covered by the assignment happened to be situated in England. It should be noted here that the English creditors were not disadvantaged *vis-à-vis* the U.S. creditors by this decision, though they lost whatever advantage there would have been in the segregation of the English assets.

Change of situs

There would be no point in deferring to the *lex situs* if the legal   5-23
position could be immediately changed by the removal of the property from that jurisdiction. The *lex situs* is not simply a window of law it is the system which determines the legal status of the property transaction which takes place within its territory. If that transaction has the effect of altering property rights, the new rights acquired there will remain in force until a later transaction takes place which, according to its *lex situs*, further alters the position. It thus follows that the rights acquired under the *lex situs* at the time will stand until they are overridden by a new transaction having that effect by the current *lex situs*. They will not be destroyed by the non-recognition of what has been done previously elsewhere simply because the new *situs* has no analogous provision.[19]

In *Todd v. Armour*[20] the plaintiff sought recovery of his horse, which had been stolen in Ireland, from the defendant who had bought it in Scotland. The stolen horse had been sold in Ireland to a buyer in market overt who had taken it to Scotland and sold it to the defendant. By Irish law the sale in market overt passed good title to the buyer; Scots law had no such exception to the *nemo dat* rule. The Court of Session held that the buyer, since he had acquired a good title under Irish law, could lawfully pass that title on to the defendant and the original owner's rights had been entirely superseded, leaving him with whatever personal action he could pursue against the actual thief.

To take a couple of examples from English law. A seller, having sold but not delivered goods to the buyer, retains the power to transfer the property in those goods to a second buyer who acts in good faith and without knowledge of the prior transaction.[21] Similarly, a buyer who has deceived the owner into transferring the property to him, who has, in

---

[19] See *Winkworth v. Christie Manson & Woods* [1980] Ch 495, [1980] 1 All ER 1121.
[20] (1882) 9 Rettie 910.
[21] Sale of Goods Act 1979 s.24.

short, a voidable title, can transfer title to a *bona fide* buyer who is ignorant of the defect in title.[22] If the *lex situs* throughout is English law the second buyer in each case will be protected. If the second sale in each case takes place abroad the effect of the sale will have to be determined by the new *lex situs*. How does the second *lex situs* relate to the English transaction? In each case the authority of the seller should be determined by English law as the *lex situs* of the first transaction and therefore, subject to any special rule of the new *situs*, the second buyer will be in the same position as if the sale had taken place in England. By the same reasoning, if the deceived owner in the voidable title case avoids the contract before the second sale, then the second buyer will not obtain good title unless the sale in the new *situs* would, independently give a good title to the buyer, would, in short, constitute an independent exception to the *nemo dat* rule.

Title retention

5-24   In *Century Credit Corporation v. Richard*[23] a car had been sold under a conditional sale agreement in Quebec. Under the agreement the car remained the property of the owner, here the plaintiff finance company, until the buyer had paid all the instalments due. In breach of the agreement, the buyer took the car to Ontario where he sold it to a third party who resold it to the defendant. Was the defendant who had bought the car in good faith to be protected? There was no doubt that under the law of Quebec, where the original transaction had taken place, the rights of the finance company were protected, in other words there was a valid reservation of title under that law. Under Ontarian law - the *lex situs* of the subsequent sale transaction - a reservation of title was only valid if it was registered and a *bona fide* purchaser from a buyer in possession of goods could, in some circumstances, obtain a good title. As to the first of these points one could hardly expect a Quebec finance company to register its' Quebec transactions in Ontario[24] and, in any case, the fact that a similar unregistered transaction under the law of Ontario would not have reserved the title, had nothing to do with the prior transaction in Quebec. The rights vested by the Quebec transaction were valid and remained effective when the car was taken to Ontario. However, the transaction which took place in Ontario, the new *situs*, had the effect, by Ontarian law, of overriding the prior title and creating a new title in the innocent buyer.

---

[22] *ibid* s.23.

[23] (1962) 34 DLR (2d) 291.

[24] See also *Goetschius v. Brightman* (1927) 245 N.Y. 186.

"If the law of Ontario were to seek to invalidate the respondent's title by refusing to recognise that the transaction which took place in Quebec had the effect of continuing the title in the respondent, this attempt of Ontarian law to invalidate a transaction taking place in Quebec would be bad because the validity of a Quebec transaction must be decided according to the law of Quebec, the *lex situs*; ... However if the laws of Ontario provide that a later transaction which takes place wholly within Ontario has the effect of overriding prior titles then since Ontario does not seek to give its laws any extra-territorial effect the laws of Ontario prevail and the title vested under the law of Ontario displaces the title reserved in the Quebec transaction"[25]

Hire-purchase and conditional sales agreements customarily take place in one country so that there is no problem of identifying the original *situs*. Where, however, an international supplier seeks to retain property in the goods supplied until the customer pays for them, or until existing accounts are settled, or seeks to create some right of security over the goods,[26] more difficult questions arise. Where the goods have to be delivered to the customer in his own country, and as delivery in most systems is necessary to pass the property, the *situs* will usually be the customer's country and the validity of the title retention clause will depend on that law. If the customer has to collect the goods from the supplier, or if the supplier delivers f.o.b., the *situs* will be the supplier's country and, if that law recognises the title retention as a property interest, the retention will be recognised by the new *lex situs*, the law of the customer's country unless it is contrary to its public policy.

5-25

While the goods remain in their original condition the supplier should have the benefit of the title retention if that interest was recognised by the *lex situs* of the original transfer. When, however, the goods are incorporated into the customer's product or processed by him in some way, the effect of that on their ownership must be determined by the law of the new *situs*.[27]

State seizure

The principle of territorial authority, which is enshrined in the reference to the *lex situs* on property transfers, implies that when State authorities in the *situs* transfer property by legislation or decree, even to themselves and without compensation, English courts will recognise the transfer. By the same token, however, attempts by foreign States to seize

5-26

---

[25] Per Kelly J.A. (1962) 34 D.L.R. (2d) 291.

[26] See *Armour v. Thyssen Edelstahlwerke AG* [1991] AC 339, [1990] 3 All ER 481 (Scots law).

[27] See *Zahnrad Fabrik Passau GmbH v. Terex Ltd.* [1986] SLT 84 (Scots law).

property situated outside their territories, even if it is owned by their nationals, will have no effect.[28]

In *Luther v. Sagor*[29] the Soviet government expropriated a sawmill belonging to a Russian company. Timber from the mill was sold to an American company carrying on business in England and brought to this country. The Russian company's petition for a declaration that the timber belonged to it was rejected by the Court of Appeal.

The importance of the decision is not that foreign State authorities can deal with property in their own territories whoever it belongs to – that is a fact of political power – but that the change in ownership will be recognised when the property is brought within the jurisdiction of the English courts. It should not matter whether the property belonged to a national or resident of the expropriating State or to a foreigner.[30] However, a foreign law directed at the property of an individual or class of individual which the English court regarded as discriminatory would probably not be recognised.[31]

The Assignment of Intangible Movables

The interests

5-27   The transfer of intangible movables is one of the least satisfactory areas of the English conflict of laws though the dearth of modern authority may indicate that problems are rare or that they are dealt with in alternative ways.

An initial problem is the diversity of interests which can be classified as intangible movables – everything which is not a direct interest in a physical object or in land may fall within the category. So, debts, whether the repayment of loans or sums due under contracts, shares, patents, copyrights and securities fall within this category whether or not they are characteristically evidenced by official documents like share certificates. In this section the discussion will be confined to debts.

5-28   As with physical objects, a distinction must be drawn between the personal relationship of the transferee and the transferor, on the one hand, and the proprietary effects of the transfer on the other. But there is an

---

[28] See *Banco de Vizcaya v. Don Alfonso de Borbon* [1935] 1 KB 140; *A-G of New Zealand v. Ortiz* [1984] AC 1 (but both these cases involved "penal" legislation); *Bank voor Handel v. Slatford* [1953] 1 QB 248, [1951] 2 All ER 779.

[29] [1921] 3 KB 532 and see *Williams & Humbert Ltd. v. W&H Trade Marks (Jersey) Ltd* [1986] AC 368.

[30] But see contra the doubtful decision in *Anglo-Iranian Oil Co. v. Jaffrate: The Rose Mary* [1953] 1 WLR 246.

[31] But see *Frankfurther v. Exner Ltd.* [1947] Ch 629.

additional distinction. Here the property relationship is not between the transferee and the rest of the world but between the transferee and the person under the original obligation. The obvious example would be a simple debt – there is the original relationship between the debtor and the creditor, the relation between the creditor and the person to whom he assigns the debt and the new relation which that transfer creates between the debtor and the transferee. It is the third of these – the relationship between the debtor and the person to whom the original creditor has transferred his interest – which is our principal concern here.

Choice of law

As well as the diversity of interests which can be classified as intangible movables, another problem or opportunity, in this area, is that the choice of law remains open. While there are few and uncertain authorities there are several potential candidates for the governing law, all of which have some support.   **5-29**

The claims of the *lex domicilii* and the *lex loci actus* (the place where the assignment takes place) cannot be taken seriously nowadays. The weakness of the *lex domicilii* is that it does not identify a single system of law. Debtor, creditor and transferee may have different personal laws and, while it would be possible to select the personal law of the debtor that has an archaic ring about it, hardly appropriate for modern commerce. The *lex loci actus* is unsuitable because even if it is not fortuitous it may have no connection with the property interest and can be fixed by the parties to the assignment without reference to the debtor, who may be harmed in the process. The claims of the *lex situs*, the *lex actus* and the proper law of the debt are more substantial.   **5-30**

(1) The lex situs

One possible solution is to give the intangible a notional *situs* and then treat it as if it were a physical object. Quite apart from the metaphysics of attributing a location to something which has no corporeal existence, the attribution of a *situs* to an intangible, while it may have some utility in cases of involuntary assignments,[32] misses the point about the essential difference between a physical object, or a right over one, and an interest in an intangible. For a physical object has an existence independent of the juridical relations which legal systems may recognise with regard to it – it can be lost, found, accidentally destroyed etc. – whereas an intangible interest exists only in the milieu of juridical relations, it cannot have an   **5-31**

---

[32] *Jabbour v. Custodian of Israeli Absentee Property* [1954] 1 All ER 145; *Swiss Bank Corporation v. Boehmische Industrial Bank* [1923] 1 KB 673.

independent existence outside of them. The interest in an intangible is one which represents an existing set of relations - a debt owed by A to B, A's shares in B's company, A's patent or copyright (but not A's ideas alone, or his reputation or the security of his business dealings or his family relations). Some of these may indeed be protected e.g. by a law of defamation, but they do not thereby automatically become interests which can be regarded as property rights.

5-32 The *lex situs*, for a debt is, characteristically seen as the place where the debt is properly recoverable. A debt is, usually, properly recoverable in the country where the debtor resides.[33] The *lex situs* could be used for the issues which arise here - whether the interest is assignable at all, how the assignment is to be effected and the priority of competing assignments, but its weakness is that it does not provide any continuity - the casual removal of the debtor from one place to another should no more affect legal relations than should the casual removal of a physical object from one place to another. Moreover while the transfer of the physical object is usually a single event, the transfer of an intangible substitutes one set of continuing interpersonal relations for another.

(2) The lex actus

5-33 The *lex actus*, if that is seen in this context as the law which governs the substance of the relationship between the assignor and assignee, is not a good candidate for the law to govern the proprietary aspects of the transfer as it is the law which the parties to the transfer may choose and the protection of the debtor is not a consideration in that relationship. To apply this law is to confuse the contractual, or other basis of the assignment, which regulates the relationship between the assignor and assignee, with the proprietary affects of the transfer, that is the regulation of the relationship between the assignee and the original debtor.

(3) The proper law of the debt

5-34 The proper law of the debt is the law which governs the original relationship between the debtor and creditor and, thereby, controls the creation of the interest which is the subject matter of the assignment. The original relation between debtor and creditor will be governed by whatever law applies to its creation, thus if the debt is a contractual debt it will be governed by the law of that contract. If the contract is an international one it will be governed by the applicable law under the

---

[33] See *Kwok v. Estate Duty Commissioners* [1988] 1 WLR 1035.

Rome Convention. If the debt was created by the gratuitous handing over of the money, the governing law will be the *lex actus* – the law which governs the gift, usually the law of the place where the transaction took place. The proper law of a cause of action will be the *lex fori* of the action,[34] that of a renewable copyright, the law of the system under which the copyright was taken out.[35] The validity of the original relationship is obviously vital to the subject matter of the transfer.

The *lex situs* and the proper law of the debt will often be the same.   **5-35** So, for example, where a customer deposits money in a bank the contract, in default of a choice of a different system, will be governed by the law of the country where the transaction takes place, as all the significant connections, including the characteristic performance, are likely to relate to that country. As the debt created by that contract will be properly recoverable where the account is held, the *lex situs* of the debt will also be the law of that country.

A coincidence of the proper law and the *lex situs*, while common, is by no means inevitable. Suppose an English supplier agrees to deliver goods to a foreign commercial customer. Without agreement to the contrary, the proper law of the debt, (the law governing the contract), will be English law (the law of the place of business through which the characteristic performance of the contract is to be affected). But the *lex situs* of the debt will be the law of the customer's country (the place where the contract debt is properly recoverable). These different laws could well have different provisions on the property aspects of any transfer of the debt by the English supplier to, say, an export factor.

The Rome Convention

The English common law authorities had not always properly   **5-36** distinguished the relationship between the assignor and assignee from the property aspects of the transfer which relate primarily to the assignee/debtor nexus. The Rome Convention makes a clear distinction between the two.

For relations between assignor and assignee, the Convention   **5-37** provides:[36]

"The mutual obligations of assignor and assignee under a voluntary assignment of a right against another person ("the debtor") shall be governed by the law which under the Convention applies to the contract between the assignor and assignee."

---

[34] *Trendex Trading Corp. v. Crédit Suisse* [1982] AC 679, [1981] 3 All ER 520.

[35] *Campbell Connally & Co. v. Noble* [1963] 1 All ER 237.

[36.] Article 12(1).

Where the assignment is contractual the ordinary provisions of the Convention, on choice of law, material and essential validity and form will apply to it. The question of the capacities of the assignor and assignee, which are outside the Convention, should be governed by the general principles applicable to contracts - preferably the putative applicable law - rather than by the old authorities[37] which should now be regarded as obsolete.

A non-contractual assignment will be governed by the law appropriate to that transaction e.g. in the case of a gift by the law of the place where the transfer occurred, just as the *lex actus* governs gifts of physical objects.

5-38   The property affects of the transfer are clearly separated from the personal relations between the assignor and assignee. The Convention provides[38]

"The law governing the right to which the assignment relates shall determine its assignability, the relationship between the assignee and the debtor, the circumstances under which the assignment can be invoked against the debtor and any question whether the debtor's obligations have been discharged."

This provision does not, of course, resolve the issue of whether the proper law of the debt or its *lex situs* should determine the property issues of the assignment.

The governing law

5-39   The questions of whether the debt is assignable at all and, if it is, under what conditions; of what rights the assignee has against the debtor; and of the discharge of the debtor's obligations; are governed by the law governing the debt. Where the original debt arises from a contract which has an international dimension the Rome Convention will apply to that contract as it does to others and there is no need here to reiterate the previous discussion. As the English conflict rules on these matters remain uncertain the following statement must be taken as tentative.

5-40   Whether the debt is capable of assignment is determined by the law governing its creation so, in the case of a contractual debt, the law which governs the relationship between the original parties will determine whether the interest created by the contract can be assigned. In the case of a gratuitous loan the governing law will be the *lex actus* The object of the reference to the law of the original transaction is to ensure that the debtor's liability should not be increased by the assignment and to protect

---

[37]   E.g. *Lee v. Abdy* (1886) 17 QBD 309; *Republica de Guatemala v. Nunez* [1927] 1 KB 669.
[38]   Article 12(2).

the debtor against the consequences which might otherwise arise from the weakness of his position. There may also be public interests of which account needs to be taken.

In *Coleman v. American Sheet and Tinplate Co.*[39] an employee sought to assign future wages. The law governing the employment contract was the law of Indiana, that governing the assignment the law of Illinois. By the law of Illinois assignments of future wages were permissible, by the law of Indiana they were not. The Illinois court applied the law of Indiana as the law governing the contract of employment and refused to give effect to the assignment.

Similarly, the law governing the creation of the original debt is the appropriate law to decide on the order of priorities of competing assignments of the same subject matter. In *Kelly v. Selwyn*[40] a New York domiciliary assigned, in New York, his interest in trust funds administered in London. No notice of the assignment was given to the trustees for twelve years and no such notice was required under the law of New York. In the meantime he assigned the same interest, in England, to the plaintiff and immediate notice of this was given to the trustees. In according priority to the second assignee the court applied English law as the *lex fori* – as the law governing the administration, but it is arguable on the facts that English law would in any event have been the proper law of the debt   **5-41**

As between the claims of the proper law and the *lex situs* of the debt, the better approach in the absence of any clear authority seems to favour the proper law, except, perhaps, in cases of involuntary assignments where the position of the *lex situs* appears established.   **5-42**

Neither the proper law of the debt nor the *lex situs* will necessarily provide a satisfactory answer to all questions. Suppose a country prohibits the assignment of future wages presumably to protect the employee from a status akin to slavery. The most interested, but not the only interested, system will be the employee's personal law. That law will not necessarily coincide with either the proper law of the debt, the applicable law of the contract of employment, nor with the *lex situs*, the employee's place of business.   **5-43**

Suppose the prohibition is part of the employee's personal law but not of the proper law nor of the *lex situs*. The case would present itself as one relating to capacity, i.e. that the employee lacks the capacity to make the assignment. Unless capacity is seen as a matter for the personal law there seems to be no way in which the prohibition of the personal law could be

---

[39]   (1936) Ill App 542.
[40]   [1905] 2 Ch.117.

given effect. If the prohibition was part of the proper law alone, in this case the applicable law of the employment contract, the argument would be that the interest created by the employment contract was not a property interest which could be assigned and that, therefore the assignment, whatever law governed the interpersonal relations of assignee and assignor, had no content. If the prohibition was part of the *lex situs* alone the argument would take the same form though this time it would focus on the debtor - the employer. His argument would be that he could not pay the employee's wages to the assignee as that would not discharge him from his obligation to pay them to his worker and could leave him in the position of paying out twice over.

Involuntary assignments

5-44   Although the view has been taken that the governing law for the property affects of the transfer of an intangible movable should be the proper law governing the creation of the original relationship rather than the *lex situs* of the debt there is clear contrary authority in the case of involuntary assignments.

Where the assignment is non-voluntary i.e. where the interest is transferred by operation of law or by a court order, the governing law will be that of the *situs* of the interest at the time the transfer takes place just as we have seen is the case for physical objects.[41] So, for example, in *Jabbour v. Custodian of Israeli Absentee Property*[42] the plaintiff, a Palestinian Arab who lived in Haifa, then part of the Palestinian Mandated Territory, insured his property against fire and riot with the Yorkshire Insurance Co. through its agency in the Palestine Mandate. The prudence of his action was proved when his property was burned down during a riot, part of the civil disturbance which attended the formation of the State of Israel. Jabbour fled to Egypt and emergency legislation of the new State of Israel appointed a custodian of absentee property. There was no doubt that the insurers were liable under the policy, but whom should they pay? Obviously, if they made the wrong choice, they could find themselves liable twice over, so they paid the money into court and issued an interpleader to let the claimants fight it out. The judgment of Pearson J. was carefully framed and he addressed all the right questions. Firstly he had to decide the nature of the subject matter in dispute. Although an amount had been quantified, and indeed paid into court, he concluded that the subject matter was a claim for unliquidated damages, in other words a chose in action, an intangible movable. Secondly, he held that such claims can be given a notional *situs* which is where they are properly

---

[41]   See above para 5-19.
[42]   [1954] 1 All ER 145.

recoverable, and that they are properly recoverable where the debtor resides. Thirdly, the *situs* of this debt was Haifa where Jabbour could expect to be paid for a claim arising under the insurance contract. Finally, the debt being sited in Haifa, only Israeli law could alter the title to it. Effect would be given to the law of Israel unless there was some overriding principle of English public policy which would prevent its recognition e.g. that its purpose was the confiscation of an individual's private property - he held the legislation not to be confiscatory.

The same reasoning means that an English court will not make a garnishment order - one which allows the judgment creditor to proceed directly against one who owes money to the judgment debtor - unless the debt which is the subject of the order is sited in England,[43] and only then if there is some confidence that the garnishee will be protected against paying twice over.[44]   **5-45**

3 IMMOVABLES

The *Moçambique* rule precludes English courts generally from taking jurisdiction where the subject matter of the dispute is the title to or right to possession of foreign immovable property.[45] This position is reinforced by the Brussels Convention.[46] It is subject to certain established exceptions in favour of the international maritime jurisdiction of English courts, the administration of estates and trusts and the exercise of the equitable jurisdiction *in personam*. We have also seen that the Rome Convention presumes, in default of choice, that a contract involving immovables will be governed by the *lex situs*[47] and may have to conform to the formal requirements of that law.[48] It will come as no surprise, therefore, that the property aspects of a transfer of immovables are governed by the *lex situs*.[49]   **5-46**

> "The incidents to real estate, the right of alienating it, and the course of succession to it, depend entirely on the law of the country where the estate is situated."[50]

---

[43] See *Swiss Bank Corporation v. Boehmische Industrial Bank* [1923] 1 KB 673.

[44] See *Deutsche Schachtbua-und Tiefbohrgesellschaft mbH v. Ras Al Khannah National Oil Co. (Shell Training Co. intervening)* [1988] 2 All ER 833.

[45] Though not to a simple action for trespass, see Civil Jurisdiction and Judgments Act, s.30(1).

[46] Article 16(1)(a).

[47] Article 4(3) see above para 4-38.

[48] Article 9(6) see above para 4-77.

[49] *Nelson v. Bridport* (1840) 8 Beav 547.

[50] *ibid per* Lord Langdale M.R. at p.570.

5-47   Where the *lex situs* is foreign, the same concern with effectiveness which determined the reference to the *lex situs* in the first place, may operate to suggest the application of the English doctrine of *renvoi* – the foreign court theory.[51] The application of the domestic law of the *situs* may not accord with what a court of the *situs* would do if it saw the case as an international one and applied its conflict rules to determine the *lex causa*.

5-48   Where the immovable is situated in England the *lex causa* will be English domestic law.

5-49   Even where the *lex situs* is taken to mean the domestic law of the *situs* it does not follow that every legal rule of that system should be applied. Every court dealing with an international case should scrutinise the provisions of the *lex causa* to determine their appropriateness to apply in the particular instance. A good example of best practice here is the case of *Procter v. Frost*[52] By the law of New Hampshire a wife was incapable of becoming a surety for her husband, but there was no such restriction under the law of Massachusetts. A married woman, who was domiciled in Massachusetts, entered a surety agreement there which involved her mortgaging her land in New Hampshire. The Supreme Court of New Hampshire considered the purpose of its own law – was it concerned with the regulation of conveyances of New Hampshire land or was it to protect New Hampshire women domiciliaries against the importunities of financially embarrassed husbands? The court decided on the latter purpose and upheld the mortgage. Of course if the New Hampshire court had felt that its protectionary policy was so fundamental a matter that it should be applied whatever the domicile of the woman and whatever the attitude of her personal law, the decision would have been the other way.

Procter v. Frost can be seen in a different way – as an issue of classification – i.e. that the New Hampshire law on wife sureties was not a part of the real estate law of New Hampshire but part of its law of matrimonial relations and therefore, irrelevant to a Massachusetts wife. Such an approach, while leading to the same result, would have consequences beyond the non-application of this particular New Hampshire law. It would involve a preparedness to investigate, in transactions involving New Hampshire real estate, the protectionary rules of the domiciliary law, with effect to be given to them unless offensive to the public policy of New Hampshire.

---

[51] See below para 8-07.

[52] [1938] N.H. 304.

While the determination of proprietary rights in immovables, the **5-50**
transferability of the interest, the capacities of the transferor[53] and
transferee, the formalities required to effect the transfer[54] and whether the
proposed transfer falls foul of legislation against perpetuities or
accumulations,[55] or conflicts with restrictions on gifts of real estate to
charity,[56] are exclusively under the control of the *lex situs* (or whatever
system of law the *lex situs* would itself apply), the personal relations
between the parties will, on ordinary principles of conflict law, be treated
as distinct.

> "It is true that the law of other states cannot render valid
> conveyances of property within our borders, which our laws say
> are void, for the plain reason that we have exclusive power over
> the *res*. But the same reason inverted establishes that the *lex loci rei
> sitae* cannot control personal covenants not purporting to be
> conveyances, between persons outside the jurisdiction, although
> concerning a thing within it."[57]

A contract to transfer immovable property which does not effect the
transfer under the *lex situs* does not necessarily fail as a contract. In *Re
Smith*,[58] the court ordered specific performance of the undertaking to
create an effective mortgage over land in the West Indies. However, in
Bank of Africa v. Cohen,[59] where an English domiciled married woman
entered a surety agreement respecting her land in the Transvaal, the *lex
situs* had protectionary legislation the benefit of which had to be expressly
renounced in order to make the transfer valid. She had not done this and
the court held that the surety agreement was invalid. A better decision
would have been that the contractual obligation should be enforced, as
the steps necessary to make the transfer effective were within her power
and she had, implicitly, agreed to take them.

Of course the usual remedy for the breach of a contractual obligation
is an award of damages and the specific enforcement of positive
contractual obligations is rare. In some of the cases e.g. those relating to
sureties, the whole object of the exercise would be defeated if the plaintiff
was left with a personal action. This takes us, as far as English law is
concerned, into the area of equitable jurisdiction and this may be an
appropriate place to examine it.

---

53 See *Duncan v. Lawson* (1889) 41 ChD 394; *Bank of Africa v. Cohen* [1909] 2 Ch 129.
54 *Adams v. Clutterbuck* (1883) 10 QBD 403.
55 See *Freke v. Carbery* (1873) 16 Eq 461; *Re Grassi* [1905] 1 Ch 484.
56 *Re Hoyles* [1911] 1 Ch 179.
57 *Per* Holmes J. in *Polsen v. Stewart* (1897) 167 Mass. 211.
58 [1916] 2 Ch. 206.
59 [1909] 2 Ch. 129.

Equitable Jurisdiction *In Personam*

5-51   "Any inability of the court to enforce the decree in rem is no reason for refusing the plaintiff such rights and means of enforcement as equity can afford him."[60]

If a defendant can be brought before an English court, even if the subject matter of the dispute is foreign immovable property, there is the possibility of obtaining equitable relief. As equity acts *in personam* and not *in rem* there is no attempt by the court to alter the title to foreign immovable property itself, the order of the court is directed to the individual to take such steps as are available to him to effect the transfer in accordance with the rules of the *lex situs*. As the plaintiff does not have to establish that the case is connected in any way with English law, a vigorous use of the equitable jurisdiction could subvert substantial elements of the conflicts process, and the Brussels Convention on jurisdiction.[61] This would leave the English court free to impose its own solution regardless of the connection with any foreign law, provided that compliance with the order is neither physically nor legally impossible. In fact the power has not been used in a way which provides an alternative route to conflict adjudication.

"Courts of Equity have from the time of Lord Hardwick's decision in *Penn v. Baltimore*[62] exercised jurisdiction *in personam* with regard to foreign land against persons locally within the jurisdiction of the English court in cases of contract, fraud and trust, enforcing their jurisdiction by writs of *ne exeat regno* during the hearing and by sequestration, commitment or other personal process after decree."[63]

There must be some special reason for the application of equity, some clear personal obligation, fraud or other unconscionable conduct on the part of the defendant. Most of the standard examples date from the last century or earlier and a few instances will suffice to show the ambit of this potentially wide though in practice narrow jurisdiction.

5-52   The grant of a decree of specific performance to compel the completion of a real estate contract can be illustrated by reference to *Penn v. Baltimore*,[64] a contract to fix the boundaries between Pennsylvania and Maryland; *Archer v. Preston*[65] a contract for the sale of land in Ireland and

---

60 Megarry J. in *Richard West & Partners (Inverness) Ltd. v. Dick* [1969] 1 All ER 289 at 292.

61 See *Webb v. Webb* [1992] 1 All ER 17.

62 (1750) 1 Ves. Sen. 444.

63 Wright J. in *British South Africa Co. v. Companhia de Moçambique* [1893] A.C. 604.

64 (1750) 1 Ves. Sen. 444.

65 Eq. Cas. Abr. (pre 1680).

Richard West & Partners (Inverness) Ltd. v. Dick[66] a contract for the sale of land in Scotland. Other obligations less than outright sale can also be specifically enforced. As we have seen, this could have been done in *Bank of Africa v. Cohen*[67] and was done in *Re Smith*.[68] In *Ex parte Pollard*[69] the mortgagor deposited the title deeds to land in Scotland with the mortgagee and undertook to take any further steps necessary to make good the security. The deposit of title deeds created an equitable mortgage by English law but not by Scots law. When the mortgagor went bankrupt the mortgagee petitioned the English court to have his debt secured on the Scottish land in preference to the general body of creditors. He succeeded, as the court took the view that there was nothing to prevent a valid mortgage being created over the Scottish land and there was a personal obligation on the mortgagor's part to do that.

Fraud or other unconscionable conduct can be illustrated by the case of *Cranstown v. Johnston*[70] where the court gave relief to a debtor whose creditor had taken advantage of the law of St. Christopher to seize the whole of his estate there in satisfaction of the debt. The creditor was ordered to reconvey the estate after deducting what was due to him.

Whether there is an established or a constructive trust the court will have the power to order the trustee to carry out his obligations even if the trust property is land situated abroad and even if the decree requires the transfer of that property.[71]

These indirect ways of altering the title to, or affecting rights over, foreign immovables will only be possible if the *lex situs* permits the action which the plaintiff seeks the decree to order. The court will also only issue a decree where there is a privity of obligation between plaintiff and defendant. So in *Norris v. Chambres*,[72] the buyer's knowledge of a previous contract for the sale of the land did not mean that he took the land subject to a charge in favour of the disappointed purchaser, as Lord Romilly saw no personal obligation between them. However in *Mercantile Investment and General Trust Co. v. River Plate Trust Co.*[73] buyers who had taken the land "subject to the mortgage, lien or charge now existing" were not allowed to argue that no such charge existed under the *lex situs* - they knew of the equitable mortgage in favour of the plaintiffs and were bound by it.

---

66 [1969] 2 Ch 424, [1969] 1 All ER 943.
67 [1909] 2 Ch. 129.
68 [1916] 2 Ch. 206.
69 (1840) Mont & Cl. 239.
70 (1796) 3 Ves. 170.
71 See *Webb v. Webb* [1992] 1 All ER 17.
72 (1861) 29 Beav. 246.
73 [1892] 2 Ch. 303.

4 SUCCESSION

Introduction

5-53   Despite the fact that English domestic law was reformed in 1925 so that the traditional distinction between realty and personalty became irrelevant for most purposes of succession, the English conflict of laws continues to operate on the basis of separate systems for movable and immovable property. The justification, if one can be found, lies in the idea of effectiveness, that only courts and officials of the *situs* can effectively deal with immovable property. While it is true that the *lex situs* of the immovable will have the last word on the succession to it, and may reject the intended beneficiary as lacking the necessary capacity to take the property, or disallow the intended gift as contrary to its rules against perpetuities or accumulations, there is no reason to adopt a divided succession in order to deal with these possible problems. Taken to its logical conclusion such an approach would preclude an English court from dealing with any case of succession, however strongly connected with England, which involved foreign land. This would of course be a nonsense. An established exception to the *Moçambique* rule is where the English court is operating its jurisdiction in the administration of estates. It could be argued that movable property in a foreign country is equally outwith the control of English courts but this has never prevented them from making decisions about movable property situated abroad. One explanation of this apparent illogicallity is that there is a widely accepted view that *mobilia sequuntur personam* – that movable property is governed by the personal law, at least for purposes of succession – which is shared both by common law and by civil law jurisdictions.

The Administration of Estates

5-54   Under English law, no English estate can be administered without the authority of the court. The personal representatives, the executors appointed by the will or the administrators on intestacy, require formal authorisation before they can carry out their tasks of debt administration and beneficial distribution. Probate will be granted, or letters of administration in the case of intestacy, if the deceased left assets in this country. The powers can be granted even if there are no assets in this country but this would rarely be done unless the deceased died domiciled here.[74] Where the deceased had a foreign domicile, grants of probate or

---

[74] Supreme Court Act 1981 s.25(1).

letters of administration will normally be made to those entitled to deal with the estate under the domiciliary law[75] and there are special provisions for Commonwealth countries[76] and for other parts of the U.K.[77]

In every case the administration of so much of the estate as is located in England will be subject to English law as *lex fori* whatever the general *lex successionis* i.e. whatever law governs the beneficial distribution of the estate. The distinction between administration and succession is therefore a crucial one.

Where the deceased died domiciled in England and where, therefore, there is a coincidence in the law governing the administration and the succession to movable property, there will generally be no problems of a conflictual nature, even if some of the deceased's movable property is situated abroad. If the estate includes foreign immovable property, the administration will continue to be governed by English law though the foreign *lex situs* will have the last word on its distribution. **5-55**

Where the deceased is not domiciled in England at the time of death but leaves assets in this country, the rôle of the ancillary administrators acting under the English grant will, as far as the administration itself is concerned, be subject exclusively to the control of English law as *lex fori*. So, for example, those administering the English estate must pay all those debts, but only those debts, whether English or foreign, according to the creditor's entitlement under English law. Any remaining assets can then either be transferred to the principal administrator or distributed beneficially immediately. The alternatives were contrasted sharply in *Re Lorillard*[78] where the testator died domiciled in New York leaving assets and creditors in England and the U.S.A. Administration proceedings were taken in both countries. The American debts exhausted the assets there, but there were funds remaining in the English estate. Eve J. held that the surplus English assets could be distributed beneficially notwithstanding the unpaid American creditors as their debts, though enforceable under the law of New York, were statute barred under English law. **5-56**

Once the debts have been paid, the personal representatives may proceed to the beneficial distribution of the property, according to the will or to the intestacy rules of the *lex successionis*. This is subject to a limitation which is included here as, while on one view it relates to succession, it can be seen as affecting the administration of the estate as governed by the *lex fori*. A valid foreign judgment concerning the distribution of the estate will be recognised in England and given full **5-57**

---

[75] See *In Bonis Hill* (1870) 2 P&D 89.

[76] Colonial Probates Act 1892 as amended.

[77] Administration of Estates Act 1971.

[78] [1922] 2 Ch. 638.

effect with regard to assets of the deceased in England, even if the scheme of devolution is not the same as English law would apply, if the deceased died domiciled in the country where the judgment is given.[79] Secondly, a valid foreign judgment determining the succession to property situated within the jurisdiction of that court will be recognised in England, even if English law is the *lex successionis* and would order the distribution differently. The principle of effectiveness places the court of the *situs* in a specially privileged position not only with regard to real estate but also with regard to movables.

Testate Succession

The formal validity of wills

5-58   The Wills Act 1963, the first international convention on the conflict of laws to find its way into English law, introduced a simple mechanical system for the formal validity of wills. The technique adopted was not to select uniform rules from the various possibilities which individual legal systems had arrived at, but to resort to rules of multiple reference so that different systems could have their own preferred solutions but only at the expense of accepting everyone else's. The result is that for every will there are seven legal systems whose rules on formal validity can be used to render the will formally valid. A will is formally valid if it complies with the requirements of the internal[80] law of any one of the following:

• the law of the country where the will was executed or
• the law of the country where the deceased was domiciled, habitually resident, or a national at the time the will was executed or at the time of his death.[81]

Where the will contains gifts of immovable property, in addition to the above, the will is formally valid if it complies with the domestic law of the *lex situs*.[82]

The operative time in each case is the date of the execution of the will but retrospective changes which validate the will can be taken into account.[83]

---

[79] See *Re Trufort* (1889) 36 Ch. D. 600.
[80] Wills Act 1963 s.6(1).
[81] S.1.
[82] S.2(1)(b).
[83] S.6(3).

Very few wills will fail the formal validity test.

There is really very little that needs to be added here. English law will make the connections i.e. will determine where the will was made, where the deceased was domiciled etc. Requirements relating to the capacity of witnesses or of special procedures to be adopted by testators falling within a special category and the like are defined by the Act[84] as matters relating to formal validity only.

There have been only three cases on the Wills Act and they all turn on issues of fact and not on the interpretation of the legislation.

"International" wills fall into a separate category. They are governed by the Administration of Justice Act 1982[85] which gives the annex to the Washington Convention the force of law in the U.K. A will which satisfies the requirements of the annex[86] will be formally valid irrespective of " the place where it is made, of the location of the assets and of the nationality domicile or residence of the testator"

5-59

Capacity to make a will

Capacity to make a will is governed by the testator's personal law at the time the will was made. This, for English conflict law, will be the testator's domiciliary law.[87] If the testator had personal capacity at the time the will was made - and we are dealing here with testamentary capacity in general terms not with the capacity to make any particular gift in the will - by the law of his domicile at the time, any subsequent loss of capacity whether by reason of infirmity or by a change of domicile to a country with more stringent testamentary requirements, should not make any difference. There is however one exception to this which will be familiar to English lawyers; and that is the rule of law that a will, not being one made in contemplation of marriage, is revoked by the subsequent marriage of its maker. We will return to this issue and to the law applicable to it under the heading of *Revocation of Wills*.[88]

5-60

Where the estate contains immovable property, the distinction between testamentary capacity in general and the power to make particular gifts becomes less sharply defined. In such cases we need to have regard to the *lex situs* to determine both the capacity and the power.[89]

5-61

---

[84] S.3.

[85] S.27.

[86] Set out in Sch. 2 of the Act.

[87] See *In the Estate of Fuld (No 3)* [1968] P 675, [1965] 3 All ER 776.

[88] See below para 5-71.

[89] See *Re Hernando* (1884) 27 ChD 284.

The capacity of legatees

5-62   The significance of the control exercised by the English *lex fori* over the administration of estates is clearly demonstrated when the issue is the competence of a beneficiary to take a gift. The real question is not the status of the beneficiary as such but the security of the executors who need to be protected against the consequences of an unauthorised distribution – unless the will so directs, a receipt from an infant legatee will not be a valid discharge of the personal representatives' duty.

The question, of reduced importance with the assimilation of ages of majority, would be characteristically posed when the beneficiary is of full age and competence under one system of law, but not under another.

There are three possible legal systems to which an English court could refer – the *lex fori* which governs the administration of the will, the general *lex successionis* (the law of the testator's last domicile for movables, the *lex situs* for immovables) or the personal law of the beneficiary.

English courts have played an advantage rule in such cases and have been prepared to allow the beneficiary to take the legacy into immediate possession if he is of full age either by English law or by his personal law.[90]

Where the gift is of immovable property no transfer of the property is effective unless the beneficiary is competent to take it according to the *lex situs*.

Interpretation

5-63   Under the English conflict of laws the concept of a will as an autonomous act means that the testator is free, within very wide limits, to make what provision he wishes. As he can say what he wants, it follows that he can select whatever law he wishes for the interpretation of his will. In the usual absence of any choice, the law to govern the interpretation is the law of his domicile at the time when the will was made. The Wills Act 1963 provides "The construction of a will shall not be altered by reason of any change in the testator's domicile after the execution of the will".[91] It should be emphasised here that the issue of construction is confined to the interpretation of the testator's wishes, not their effectiveness. The quest is for what the testator wanted to achieve and is distinct from the practicability, legality or implications of his desires.

5-64   Though sometimes the distinction is not easy to see, there is a division between construction and identification which needs to be maintained. Suppose the testator uses the terms "wife" or "husband" or "spouse" or

---

[90] See *Re Hellmans Will* (1866) LR 2 Eq 363; *Re Schnapper* [1928] Ch 420.

[91] S.4.

"children"; now it may be obvious that this is merely an alternative for Mary or John or the twins, in other words there can be absolutely no doubt about who was meant, and no one would wish to challenge the distribution. In other circumstances the matter may be more complex and, where there is possible ambiguity, there will be no shortage of persons who want to join the fray. Suppose the testator used the term "wife" but had been married twice and the validity of the second marriage is in doubt, or he has used the word "children" and there are a number of them, some legitimate and some not. Whether the word "children" does or does not include illegitimate children and whether "wife" includes a divorced spouse are matters for the construction of the will. It will, therefore, be for the testator's chosen law, or the law of his domicile, to answer these questions.

Once this interpretation has been made, e.g. that only legitimate children qualify for the inheritance, the issue shifts from the area of construction to the area of status if the next question is – "is this person a legitimate child?" This raises an incidental question which will be considered later.[92]

Giving effect to the testator's wishes

It is a very well established principle of the conflict of laws that *mobilia*   **5-65**
sequuntur personam – movables follow the person. The effect to be given to the testator's wishes with regard to a will of movables will be governed by the domiciliary law at the time of death.[93] That law will determine whether the gifts in the will can be lawfully carried into effect and whether the intended beneficiaries can inherit.

Where the testator has changed his domicile after the will was made,   **5-66**
the domiciliary change can have profound effects. In *Re Groos*[94] the testatrix, a Dutch woman, was domiciled in Holland when she made her will. She left all her property to her husband subject to the legitimate portions to which her children were entitled. Under both Dutch and English law that gift would be interpreted as a bequest of all that she could lawfully dispose of by will, the difference came in the substance of that interpretation. Dutch law, in common with the laws of other countries of continental Europe, provided that a certain proportion of the estate passed on death to certain family members. Significantly here the "legitimate portion" to which her children were entitled under Dutch law amounted to three quarters of the estate. As English law makes no

---

92   See below para 8-17.
93   *Thornton v. Curling* (1824) 8 Sim 310.
94   [1915] 1 Ch 572.

such provision, the testatrix was free by her domiciliary law at the date of her death, English law, to dispose of all her property as she wished. Her wishes were interpreted to be that her husband should receive all that she was free to give him. Her husband therefore inherited the whole estate.

5-67   The law of the last domicile, the general *lex successionis*, governs all matters relating to the substance of the testamentary dispositions concerning movables – whether, for example, the testator has a limited or complete power of testation, whether dependents can challenge the will,[95] whether particular gifts comply with rules about charities, accumulations, perpetuities and the like.

5-68   In the case of wills of immovables, or of gifts of immovable property in mixed wills, the *lex successionis* is the *lex situs*[96] and the validity of the dispositions will have to be tested by that law[97]. The reference to the *lex situs* may involve the doctrine of *renvoi*.[98]

5-69   It remains an open question whether the *lex successionis* is chrystalised at the date of the testator's death or whether subsequent changes in that law can be taken into account.[99] As far as gifts of immovables are concerned, the whole idea of effectiveness must involve the application of the *lex situs* as it stands at the time of the proceedings. For movables there is authority that it is the *lex domicilii* as it exists at the time of death which is to be applied,[100] but the authority is weak as the foreign legislation in that case was both retrospective and confiscatory.

5-70   As with all other applications of the *lex causae*, it is only the substantive rules of that law which apply, matters of procedure are governed by the *lex fori*.[101] What is a substantive rule and what a procedural one is often not as self evident as may be supposed and a case in this area furnishes an excellent example. In *Re Cohn*[102] mother and daughter, German nationals and domiciliaries who had taken refuge in England, were killed in an air raid on London. It was impossible to tell which one had died first. In such cases of comorrientes there was a difference between German law, the *lex successionis* and English law, the *lex fori*. By German law they would be regarded as having died simultaneously with the result that neither could succeed under the other's will; under English law the younger is deemed

---

95   See, for English law, Inheritance (Provision for Family and Dependents) Act 1975 s.1.

96   *Freke v. Carbery* (1873) LR 10 Eq 461.

97   But see the decision in *Re Piercy* [1895] 1 Ch 83.

98   See below para 8-07.

99   See below para 8-23.

100   *Lynch v. Provisional Government of Paraguay* (1871) LR 2 P&D 268.

101   See below para 7-15.

102   [1945] Ch 5.

to have survived the elder[103] and therefore may succeed to the estate. If this issue was a procedural question it would be governed by English law, if a substantive one, the rule of German law would apply. The court held that both the English and the German law were substantive provisions and that therefore the daughter could not succeed to her mother's estate.

Similarly, whenever the court is applying the *lex causa*, whether its own law or a foreign one, it should not be assumed that every rule of the substantive law should be applied. Regard should be had to the purpose of the substantive rule and to the range of its application. A gift which infringes the rule of the *lex successionis* on perpetuities, for example, should be allowed if it is to have effect in some other country, where it is valid, unless to allow it would infringe some serious policy of the *lex successionis* or of the *lex fori*.[104]

Revocation of wills

Under English domestic law a will is said to be ambulatory, that is it **5-71** speaks from death. During the lifetime of the testator it has no legal significance; it is merely a statement of intention which the testator is free to change, literally, at will. There are two exceptions to this which are pertinent here : the first is that a testator who loses testamentary capacity and never regains it is stuck with whatever will he has already made; the second is that under English domestic law, but not necessarily under other systems, a will is revoked by the marriage of the testator unless it was made in contemplation of marriage.

A testator with capacity may, therefore, revoke his will at any time – what law should determine whether the alleged act of revocation was effective to destroy the original will or to replace it? There is little authority on revocation but it would seem that the law of the testator's domicile at the time of the act of revocation is the key, though it must be said that for wills involving gifts of immovable interests the role of the *lex situs* cannot be ignored.

Suppose the testator physically destroys the will. If such an act of destruction is a valid way of revoking his will by his domiciliary law at the time, then the English conflict of laws will accept that the will has been revoked at least as far as gifts of movables are concerned. If the testator has not replaced the will by another, the distribution of his movables will depend on the intestacy rules of his domiciliary law at the time of his death. Similarly if the act of revocation is alleged to be some other statement by the testator less than the physical destruction of the

---

[103] Law of Property Act 1925 s.184.

[104] See *Fordyce v. Bridges* (1848) 2 Ph 479.

will itself e.g. a formal statement of repudiation, then the same rules would appear to apply. There is a case here for determining the issue by reference to the law of the place where the act of revocation was done, but there is no authority to support that suggestion.

A new will which replaces an existing one or operates as a codicil to it will be subjected to the same tests as we have already seen for the establishment of a will with two additions. The first relates to formal validity; the revoking will is regarded as formally valid if it satisfies the standard tests that we have already seen, but also if it satisfied the requirements which were or could have been applied to the original will.[105] The second relates to codicils, to additions to the original will, these too can have a self standing validity or can satisfy the formal requirements of the original will. In addition, as English domestic law regards a codicil as the re-publication of the original will, the whole testamentary set can be validated by the codicil.

5-72   Revocation of a will by marriage can present problems in two ways; firstly, not every legal system takes the same view as English domestic law that the subsequent marriage does revoke the will, and, secondly, it raises an issue of classification. Is the rule that marriage revokes the will, and the provisions in other legal systems to the like or to the opposite effect a rule of the law of succession or a rule of the law of marriage? If it is a rule of succession, the governing laws will be the last domiciliary law for movables and the *lex situs* for immovables, if on the other hand, it is a matter of matrimonial law, the reference should be to the personal law at the time of the marriage. There is no logical answer to this question but there is a practical case for the application of the matrimonial law. It would be harsh if a will, valid despite a supervening marriage because the testator was wholly connected with a legal system which did not regard marriage as a revoking event, were to be revoked by the acquisition of a domicile in, say, England, shortly before the death. This would add an even more bitter twist to the situation, as was seen in *Re Groos*,[106] whereby a subsequent change of domicile had a profound effect on the testamentary dispositions.

The issue arose in *Re Martin*[107] where the testatrix made her will while she was domiciled in France. She subsequently married a French national, in England, where he was domiciled. She died domiciled in France. English law would regard her will as revoked by her marriage: French law would not. If, therefore, the matter was governed by the

---

[105] Wills Act 1963 s.2(1)(c).
[106] [1915] 1 Ch 572. See above para 5-66.
[107] [1900] P 211.

general testamentary law her will would have stood, but the court took the view that it was a matter of matrimonial law. It applied the premarital domiciliary law of her husband, which was English, with the effect that the will was regarded as revoked by the subsequent marriage. We must not confuse the outcome with the methodology here. In 1900 a wife acquired her husband's domicile, as a domicile of dependency by operation of law, upon her marriage. The matrimonial domicile was therefore English. Since 1973 marriage does not impose the husband's domicile upon the wife,[108] and whether a common matrimonial domicile is acquired is a question of fact in each particular case, irrespective of whether you take the dual domicile test or the matrimonial home test.[109] If we put the case into a modern setting the result would have been different, as the starting point (leaving aside the matrimonial home test for the moment) would be the testatrix's premarital domiciliary law which was French and French law did not see the subsequent marriage as a revoking event. It could be argued that the idea of a subsequent marriage revoking a will is not for the benefit of the testator but for the benefit of the spouse. Certainly historically, the rule must have been for the benefit of wives, whose property would be acquired by the husband on marriage, and who therefore would need protection from accidental disinheritance. Today, if the rule serves any purpose at all, it must be to reflect the new relationship to which the marriage gives rise and the claims of the new spouse for consideration in the distribution of the partner's property on death. As it cannot be assumed that there will be a common matrimonial law, then the choice has to be made between the testator's personal law and the spouse's personal law, and I see now no reason to go for the latter. There is certainly no longer a case for preferring the husband's domiciliary law to that of the wife, although, as we shall see, this anachronism may remain in other areas of family property.

Intestate Succession

Those items of the intestate's property which are regarded as movables, **5-73** and, of course, it is the *lex situs* of the particular item which has the last word on its characterisation, will devolve according to the scheme of intestate succession established by the legal system of the country of the intestate's last domicile. This is one of the oldest established rules of the English conflict of laws[110] and accords with the widely accepted principle – *mobilia sequuntur personam*.

---

[108] Domicile and Matrimonial Proceedings Act 1973 s.1.

[109] See above para 6-30.

[110] *Pipon v. Pipon* (1744) Amb 25.

5-74   Immovable property will devolve according to the scheme of devolution prescribed by the *lex situs*[111]. Effectiveness may, however, involve a reference to the conflict rules of the *lex situs* according to the doctrine of total *renvoi* which has been employed by the English courts from time to time in the resolution of cases of succession to foreign immovable property.[112]

Fairly straightforwardly, then, the administrators need only inform themselves of the classes of person entitled to succeed according to the *lex successionis* (the intestate's last domiciliary law or the *lex situs* depending on the nature of the property) and distribute accordingly. However, as we have seen with testate succession,[113] incidental questions may arise relating to the membership of the classes identified by the *lex successionis*. The "surviving spouse" or "children" may raise questions about the validity of marriages or divorces, or issues of legitimacy, and these incidental questions will have to be resolved either according to the *lex causa* or the *lex fori* in the same way as they are resolved in cases of testate succession.[114]

5-75   One peculiarity which follows from the persistence of the English conflict of laws in separating movables from immovables for the purpose of succession is that the surviving spouse may be able to collect a number of statutory legacies. Suppose the intestate dies domiciled in England leaving property of either type here and immovables in other countries. Despite the fact that English domestic law has had unitary succession since 1925, and let us suppose that the other countries concerned have it too, the surviving spouse of the intestate appears to be entitled to the statutory legacy under English law and to any statutory legacies that the other systems may have.[115] Pretend there are three countries involved all with the same rules – that where there are children the surviving spouse is entitled to £75,000 outright – and suppose that each estate is worth £150,000 and that the two foreign estates consist principally of immovables. The deceased dies in domiciled in England. Had all the property been in England, or had all the property been movable, and, therefore subject to English law alone, the surviving spouse would have been entitled to a statutory legacy of £75,000. As things stand he or she is entitled to £225,000.

5-76   It sometimes happens that there are no qualifying persons under the intestacy rules – that the deceased left no heirs or next of kin. The solution here would be to look to the *lex successionis* to determine what is to happen in such cases, what provisions exist to deal with the ownerless estate. In English domestic law the English estate of an intestate without

---

111 *Duncan v. Lawson* (1889) 41 Ch D 394.

112 See below para 8-07.

113 See above para 5-64.

114 See below para 8-17.

115 See *Re Collens* [1986] Ch 505, [1986] 1 All ER 611.

next of kin passes to the Crown as *bona vacantia* – this means in effect that the Crown is seizing ownerless goods under the prerogative power. Suppose the *lex successionis* is a foreign law with a similar response. Will the foreign State or sovereign be able to claim the property in England or will it pass to the Crown on the basis that if there is any confiscation to be done the *lex situs* of the property, whether that property is movable or immovable, should prevail over the *lex successionis*?

In *Re Barnett*[116] the deceased, who died domiciled in Austria, left property in England. There was no one to succeed him and the Austrian State claimed the property in England. The court classified the matter as one of the administration of estates, not as succession, and as administration is a matter for the *lex fori*, the Austrian claim was rejected and the property went to the Crown as *bona vacantia*. In contrast, in *Re Maldonado*[117] on similar facts, though the *lex successionis* was Spanish, the State's claim to succeed as ultimus heres was accepted as a genuine claim of succession and the English court allowed the property to be taken by the Spanish State. Both cases, of course, involved movables. Had the property been immovable the *lex situs*, English law, would govern the succession and any claim of the foreign State would be in vain.

5   FAMILY PROPERTY

Introduction

There are several ways in which a legal system can treat family property. English law deals with it by not having a concept of family property at all, but leaving it to individuals to deal with their property as they wish and to dispose of it on death, largely unfettered. Of course there are family trusts and settlements and the arrangements which are made on divorce; and disappointed family members, and others, can seek to have provision made for them out of the estate if the testator has failed to have regard to them.[118]

5-77

Private family arrangements can have a significance for the ordinary operation of the domestic law and, thereby, affect conflict rules. To take a simple example from English law, while there is no community of property between husband and wife , it is common for the matrimonial home to be legally vested in the joint names of the spouses. This legal joint tenancy brings with it the right of survivorship – the *ius accrescendi*. The interest

---

[116] [1902] 1 Ch. 847.

[117] [1954] P.223, [1953] 2 All ER 300.

[118] Inheritance (Provision for Family and Dependents) Act 1975.

which a spouse has passes to the other on death and does not form part of the deceased's estate for purposes of succession, either testate or intestate.

The example is merely one form that joint ownership can take. The French law of community property shares the couples' property in life and vests half of it on death in the survivor. Most Civil Law systems regard surviving spouses and children as having direct interests in the succession which vest on death and, therefore, those "legitimate portions"[119] do not form part of the deceased's estate.

Whatever form the family property regime of a particular country takes, conflict problems most commonly arise on succession; for transfers *inter vivos* raise problems either between the family members themselves, which are most likely to be determined by local courts, or in sale contracts, where the question might arise of the seller's power to transfer a jointly owned item. This would not, in regard to the buyer, raise an issue any different from the common problem of sellers exceeding authority.

5-78 Where the issue of family property arises because a legal system gives automatic inheritance rights to the surviving spouse or the children, where, in other words, the deceased had power to dispose of property in life but not to leave all of it away from the family on death,[120] the question is properly characterised as one of succession and is covered by the succession rules we have already considered.

5-79 Where, however, the property regime gives rights to the property in life, as with a regime of community of property between husband and wife, although the issue may well present itself as a conflict problem involving succession, it does not follow that its proper classification is succession. English conflict law has taken the question of community property, like the question of whether a subsequent marriage revokes a will, as a matter of matrimonial law.[121]

Choice of Law

5-80 Where the parties have not made a contract to determine their matrimonial property rights, the conflict of laws has to address questions such as: which law is to determine the regime of matrimonial property? Is the initial determination definitive? Can it be altered by act of parties or operation of law?

5-81 If the questions are to be treated as matters of matrimonial law it would be sensible to refer them to the law governing the substance of the marriage rather than its form, but there is a problem of determining what

[119] See, for example, *Re Annesley* [1926] Ch 692; *Re Ross* [1930] 1 Ch 377.
[120] See e.g. *Re Groos* [1915] 1 Ch 572.
[121] *Re Martin* [1900] P 211; *Re Egerton's W/T* [1956] Ch 593, [1956] 2 All ER 817.

that law is. The old cases, and there are no modern ones, applied the law of the husband's premarital domicile, a test which used to be applied for the essential validity of the marriage. Traditionally that law would become the matrimonial domiciliary law by operation of law and, in most cases, would represent the social and economic reality of the marriage. However, the abandonment of that test in favour of the dual domicile test for the essential validity of the marriage, coupled with the liberation of married women from domiciliary dependence on their husbands, must raise doubts about the suitability and, indeed, the acceptability of the law of the husband's domicile.

The attractive alternative, the law of the matrimonial home, is beset with the same difficulties in this regard as it is as a test of the validity of the marriage - what happens if the parties do not immediately, within a reasonable time, or ever, establish a matrimonial home? Suppose they continue to have separate domiciles, what is the fallback or interim position? The reserve position seems to be the established rule - the law of the husband's premarital domicile.

Where the husband and wife have common laws on matrimonial **5-82** property, though they are domiciled in different countries, this common factor might be enough to establish community, or to deny it. Where the parties come from different countries with different regimes there is an increasingly weak case, both in moral and in socio-economic terms, for preferring the husband's law to that of the wife. It may however accord with the way that the community regimes themselves deal with such "mixed" marriages.

Assuming that an appropriate law can be found for this first question, **5-83** that law will determine whether the community regime applies to all property brought to the marriage or only that, or how much of that, acquired after it. What it cannot determine is what is to happen when there is a change of domicile by either of the parties or by both. Community property regimes are not consistent on the effect of a change of domicile but there clearly is a strong case for recognising the rights acquired under the original regime and not to allow, for example, the husband to destroy his wife's community claims by the simple expedient of a change of domicile. However, a change of domicile to a country which, like England, does not have community of property could well be seen as terminating the community arrangement regarding any property acquired after the change. The same reasoning would suggest that a change from a separate property country to a community regime, while not affecting existing property rights, should have the effect of making all subsequent property acquisitions subject to community. This, however, appears not to be the case as it seems that the question is to be asked only at the inception of the marriage.[122]

---

[122] See *Re Egerton's W/T* [1956] Ch 593, [1956] 2 All ER 817.

If the matrimonial property is immovable it would seem, on general principles, that the *lex situs* should determine the question of single or joint ownership[123] though, here as ever, with the possible resort to *renvoi*.[124]

Contracts

5-84   Whether a country has a regime of matrimonial property or not, the couple are free to agree one for themselves or to vary the one which the law implies. An agreement between husband and wife for, say, joint ownership of all property will be tested by the ordinary law of contract. It will be the common law rules which apply not those under the Rome Convention, for that expressly excludes contracts relating to "rights of property arising out of a matrimonial relationship"[125] and, presumably, the exclusion extends to any contractual creation of property rights between the married couple.

The contract will be governed by the law expressly or impliedly chosen[126] by the parties, or by the law with which it is most closely connected,[127] and may itself in appropriate circumstances be implied.[128] The contract may apply to both movables and immovables.[129]

6   TRUSTS

Introduction

5-85   A fairly short section, one might imagine, as the English concept of the trust is the creation of Equity and does not find its counterpart in the laws of countries outside the Common Law tradition. The administration of trusts, along with the administration of the estates of deceased persons is, as we have seen, one of the exceptions to the refusal of jurisdiction in matters of real estate under the *Moçambique* rule. The trusts in these cases are trusts recognised under English law and the law governing their administration is English law as *lex fori*.

---

123 See *Welch v. Tennent* [1891] AC 639.

124 See below para 8-07.

125 Article 1(2)(b).

126 See *Re Bankes* [1902] 2 Ch 333.

127 See *Duke of Marlborough v. A-G* [1945] Ch 78, [1945] 1 All ER 165.

128 *De Nicols v. Curlier* [1900] AC 21. See above para 4-85.

129 *Re De Nicols* [1950] 2 Ch 410.

This does not mean that these are not cases involving reference to **5-86** foreign law: the interpretation of the settlor's intentions may fall to be determined by a foreign law chosen by him or by the law governing the interpretation of the will if the trust is a testamentary one; the status of beneficiaries may raise incidental questions which need to be referred to foreign law and, of course, trust property may be situated abroad.

Although the English trust is commonly used as an example of the problem of classification in the conflict of laws - how can a system classify an institution which does not have its counterpart in the domestic law - there was sufficient interest in the trust to establish a Convention at the Hague Conference on Private International Law in 1984 which has been given the force of law within the U.K. by the Recognition of Trusts Act 1987.

The Convention "on the law applicable to trusts and on their **5-87** recognition" substantially gives codified form to the position reached in the English conflict of laws. It enables countries which do not have this particular concept of a trust to apply "off the peg" choice of law rules and thereby avoid the problems and uncertainty which might otherwise arise when trust property is acquired in a "non-trust" country, and it allows the U.K., which has adopted the Convention for internal conflicts, to retain its own internal rules.

The Convention defines a trust as " the legal relationship created - *inter vivos* or on death - by a person, the settlor, when assets have been placed under the control of a trustee for the benefit of a beneficiary or for a special purpose".[130] It goes on to list the characteristics of a trust - the trust assets constituting a separate fund which is not part of the trustee's estate; the title to the trust assets residing in the trustee or in another on his behalf; and the trustee being under an accountable duty to manage, employ or dispose of the trust assets in accordance with the terms of the trust and the general law. Finally the Convention makes it clear that neither the reservation of rights and powers by the settlor nor the fact that the trustee may have rights as a beneficiary are necessarily inconsistent with the concept. English lawyers should have no problems with this definition and "non-trust" countries should be able to recognise a trust relationship without difficulty.

The Convention applies only to trusts created voluntarily and **5-88** evidenced in writing,[131] but the U.K. has extended its application to "any other trusts of property arising under the law of any part of the U.K. or by virtue of a judicial decision whether in the United Kingdom or elsewhere." So, as far as the U.K. is concerned, "resulting", "statutory" and

---

[130] Article 2.
[131] Article 3.

"constructive" trusts are covered. But for those countries which adopt the bare Convention "statutory" and "constructive" trusts will not be included, as they are not voluntary, but "resulting" trusts will be if they are evidenced in writing. An "automatic" resulting trust (one which arises on the failure of the original trust purpose) is included, insofar as the original trust was voluntary and a "presumed" resulting trust may fall within the Convention unless it is imposed by the court i.e. is seen as a constructive trust.

Choice of Law

5-89   The Convention provides[132] that the applicable law shall be that chosen by the settlor either expressly or by implication. It is open to the settlor to choose different laws for different aspects of the trust - he could, for example, select the legal system of the country where particular trust assets are situated to govern the operation of the trust with regard to those assets; or he could choose one law for the interpretation of the trust and another for its administration.[133] The settler's freedom to select the applicable law does not enable him to validate a prior act concerning the establishment of the trust or the allocation of assets to it so, for example, the settlor cannot use his power under the Convention to give formal or essential validity to the will in which the trust was established.[134] The Convention only applies to trusts which have been set up, whether or not they are valid, it does not relate to earlier acts or transactions, however closely related they are to the establishment of the trust.

5-90   Where the settlor has failed to select the applicable law, the Convention provides[135] that the applicable law will be that of the country with which the trust is most closely connected and, in deciding that issue particular regard shall be made to the designated place of administration, the *situs* of the trust assets, the residence or place of business of the trustee, the objects of the trust and the place where they are to be fulfilled.

For a perfectly sensible reason, though in rather a peculiar way, the Convention self destructs if the applicable law turns out to be the law of a country which doesn't have a domestic law of trusts. It is possible, though rather unlikely, that a court dealing with the case might decide that the applicable law is the law of country X, a country which does not have a law of trusts. Should it do so the Convention ceases to operate[136] and the

---

132 Article 6.
133 Article 9
134 Article 4.
135 Article 7.
136 Article 5.

court is left to whatever other rules that system probably doesn't have to determine the issue. Slightly more probable is the case where the settlor chooses an applicable law which does not have a domestic concept of the trust – in such an event it is provided that the choice fails and the rules for determining the applicable law in default of choice apply.[137]

A legal system may, while not possessing a general law of trusts, recognise particular types of trust e.g. charitable trusts. In that case the chosen or found applicable law will apply if the substance of the trust is in the recognised category. **5-91**

Suppose the settlor were to choose the law of a composite State in conflict terms e.g. U.K. law or U.S. law. The Convention expressly excludes the operation of the doctrine of *renvoi*[138] so reference can be made only to the domestic law of the chosen system. It is arguable whether rules of internal reference within a composite State amount to *renvoi* anyway, and efforts should surely be made to implement the settlor's wishes if at all possible. In the event that localising proves impossible, the choice would have to be disregarded and the rules for the objective discovery of the applicable law applied. **5-92**

Scope of the Applicable Law

Article 8 of the Convention provides an extensive list of the matters which shall be subject to the applicable law, this includes: the validity, construction, effects and administration of the trust; the powers, duties and accountability of trustees, their appointment and removal; perpetuities and accumulations; the variation and termination of the trust and the distribution of the trust assets. **5-93**

The applicable law will also determine whether a change may be made in the law applicable to the whole or part of the trust where, for example, the settlor has empowered the trustees to alter the law governing the trust.[139]

The Recognition of Trusts

Besides the determination of the law applicable to trusts, the Convention's object is to regulate the recognition of trusts particularly in those States which do not have a domestic law of trusts. Article 11 provides that a trust created in accordance with the applicable law shall **5-94**

---

[137] Article 6.
[138] Article 7.
[139] Article 10.

be recognised with the minimum implications that the trust property shall be regarded as a separate fund, that the trustee may sue and be sued in that capacity, and act in that capacity before notaries and other officials. In addition, if the applicable law of the trust so provides, the recognition implies that personal creditors of the trustee shall not have recourse to the trust assets and that trust assets shall not form part of the trustee's estate on insolvency, bankruptcy or death nor of his or his spouse's matrimonial property.

5-95   Where the trustee has mixed trust assets with his own property or otherwise alienated them, the Convention provides that tracing of the trust assets shall not affect third parties beyond what is allowed by the rules of the system indicated by the choice of law rules of the forum. As we have seen,[140] the general rule which English conflict of laws shares with other systems, is that the property effects of a transfer are governed by the *lex situs* of the property at the time the transfer takes place. The sale of trust assets by a trustee in breach of the terms of the trust will generally transfer good title to a purchaser who has no actual or constructive knowledge of the breach of trust. If the trustee's disposal is not by sale but by gift, there might be a difference between "trust" and "non-trust" countries; trust countries, following English law, will not protect the innocent volunteer whereas "non trust" countries may well do so.

If the transferee is aware of the breach of trust the transaction will not confer good title and both the trustee and the receiver of the trust property may be tortiously liable for fraud – though this would depend on the tort law of the *situs* of the transfer.

Whatever the position regarding tracing, the trustee will remain personally liable for his breach of trust – this action is not dependant on any law other than the applicable law of the trust itself.

To safeguard trust funds and to facilitate the acquisition of trust property in "non-trust" states, the Convention provides[141] for the trustee to register trust assets as such in the country where they are situated if this is allowed by the law of that country.

Advantage Rule

5-96   The Convention seeks to establish minimum standards, not to curtail the provisions of more generous and developed trust laws.[142] If the law of the country concerned, say as *lex situs* of trust assets, has a more extensive

---

[140] See above paras 5-19, 5-46.

[141] Article 12.

[142] Article 14.

law on trusts than that provided in the Convention, the recognition of the trust under the Convention rules allows access to those more favourable laws.

Exceptions

Where the choice of law rules of the forum indicate a system of law other than the law applicable to the trust (e.g. the *lex fori* itself, the personal law or the *lex situs*) to govern certain matters, and that law's provisions are mandatory in the sense that they cannot be derogated from by voluntary act, the Convention does not seek to override those laws. Article 15 particularises some of these matters:- **5-97**

- the protection of minors and incapable parties
- the personal and proprietary effects of marriage
- testate and intestate succession rights
- the transfer of title to property and security rights in property
- the protection of creditors on insolvency
- the protection of third parties acting in good faith.

Where these exceptions lead to the application of a law which prevents the recognition of the trust, the Convention provides that " the court shall try to give effect to the objects of the trust by other means."

The overriding public policy of the forum and mandatory laws of the forum which have to be applied to all cases whether domestic or international are preserved by the Convention.[143] **5-98**

The Convention applies to all trusts irrespective of the time they were set up,[144] but the Act[145] makes it clear that the Convention shall not affect the law to be applied in relation to anything done or omitted before the coming into force of the Act.[146] **5-99**

---

[143] Articles 18 & 16.
[144] Article 22.
[145] Section 1(5).
[146] 1st August 1997.

CHAPTER 6

FAMILY LAW

1 INTRODUCTION

Marriage provides an excellent counter example to the notion that classifications can be made on the basis of analytical jurisprudence and comparative law. While it is a universal institution, in that all societies have a concept of marriage, very different cultural traditions have influenced the development of the concept in different countries. So, while the institution can be recognised easily enough, its attendant incidents vary considerably. Even within the Western Christian cultural tradition different rules on capacity and form and different attitudes to the termination of marriage produce important variations from the core of monogamy.

6-01

The task of the conflict of laws on marriage is very much greater than simply to take account of the minor adjustments necessary in order to recognise the validity of established relationships between people from different countries, there are issues about the very nature of the institution itself which require consideration.

6-02

The conceptual approach which English law has adopted in this, as in most other areas of the conflict of laws, requires that a positive approach is taken and one which is sufficiently flexible to accommodate foreign institutions of marriage.

6-03

English law was, for example, slow to come to terms with judicial divorce. Even more difficult was the problem of the institution of polygamy. Monogamy was essential to the Western Christian concept of marriage. Though it was never the case that recognition was confined to Christian marriages,[1] the exclusivity of the relationship was its fundamental characteristic. Yet it could not be denied that polygamous relationships had social significance, legal implications and, often, deep religious importance.

In this chapter we will examine the English conflict rules, nearly all common law rules, on the recognition of valid marriages and then consider the powers of English courts to grant and to recognise matrimonial reliefs and, finally, matters relating to the status of children.

---

[1] See *Isaak Penhas v. Tan Soo Eng* [1953] AC 304 (Jewish/Chinese marriage celebrated by mixed rites in Singapore and held to be a valid marriage by traditional common law).

2 MARRIAGE

The Concept

6-04   Until the Court for Divorce and Matrimonial Causes was established in 1857 the civil courts, insofar as they had to deal indirectly with marriages, had operated upon an ill-defined, though widely assumed, understanding of the Christian marriage. The opening up of the courts' jurisdiction made the need for a firm statement of the concept of marriage as understood in English law more pressing. The issue came to the fore in a case involving a Mormon marriage which had taken place in Utah Territory under a regime which certainly practised, and may have legally sanctioned, polygamy.

6-05   In *Hyde v. Hyde*[2] Lord Penzance sought to define marriage for the purpose of "the remedies the adjudication and the relief of the matrimonial law of England." It was not his object to define marriage for any other purpose but his definition characterises the basic concept of marriage in English law and as a starting point for the conflict of laws.

His definition is a romantic one; marriage, he said, may for this purpose be defined as

"the voluntary union for life of one man and one woman to the exclusion of all others".[3]

If we take this definition apart and examine its components we can see that there are a number of difficulties.

6-06   Perhaps a cautionary word here would not be amiss - we are dealing at the moment with the concept of marriage for the purposes of the English conflict of laws. Once a relationship has been accepted by an English court as falling within the definition, the rules of choice of law on marriage come into play and they may involve reference to a foreign law which takes a different view of the nature of the institution of marriage. The foreign law may require, for instance, that, for a marriage to be valid, the parties must intend at the time of the marriage to establish a genuine matrimonial relationship.[4] Where this is the case it will be for the English court to decide whether account is to be taken of the foreign law and this may well involve issues of English public policy. For the present we are concerned only with the identification of those relationships which will trigger the application of the English conflict of law's rules on marriage.

---

[2]   (1866) LR 1 P&D 130.
[3]   At p.133.
[4]   See *Vervaeke v. Smith* [1983] 1 AC 145, [1982] 2 All ER 144 , note the attitude of Belgian law.

(1) Voluntary

The idea of romantic love, which has been such a boon to the popular **6-07**
music industry, generally displaced arranged marriages in Europe, but they
lingered on in the dynasties and have come to the fore in recent years in
marriages arranged for their children by parents who have immigrated
from the Indian sub-continent. There is little doubt that a shotgun
marriage with real shotguns would not be recognised under English
conflict law; but where the force used to overcome the free will are more
subtle, where it takes the form of appeals to filial duty or to family honour
or cultural tradition, the response is less clear cut.[5] If one of the parties to
the marriage can establish that he or she did not agree to its establishment,
it ought to follow that the relationship should not be recognised as a
marriage. It should be noted here, however, that English domestic law
provides that a marriage shall be voidable for lack of consent whatever the
cause of the failure.[6] Nevertheless, two obvious cases relating to mistake –
where one of the parties fails to understand the nature of the ceremony or
is mistaken about the identity of the other party – ought in principle to
render the marriage void under English domestic and English conflict law.

(2) Union

English law does not require a marriage to be a sexual relationship **6-08**
although it gives relief where the marriage has not been consummated by
sexual intercourse.[7] Such a petition under English domestic law is a claim
that the marriage is voidable not that it is void *ab initio* and, as far as the
English conflict of laws is concerned, a marriage between parties who are
too old or infirm or otherwise incapable of sexual relations remains
capable of being recognised as a marriage. One qualification and one
observation here – although sexual intercourse is not essential for the
validity of a marriage it remains the case that, though the parties need not
wish or be capable of consummating the marriage, they must be male and
female.[8] There is no requirement under English law that the parties
intend to live together as husband and wife or indeed have any serious
intention to make the marriage any sort of relationship – so marriages
entered into for the purpose of conferring nationality or enabling
immigration or preventing the deportation of a prostitute as an
undesirable alien[9] have all been upheld as valid under English law and
would fall within the concept for the purposes of English conflict law.

---

5   See e.g. *Hirani v. Hirani* [1982] 4 FLR 232.
6   Matrimonial Causes Act 1973 s.12(c).
7   *ibid* s.12(a) and (b).
8   S.11(c).
9   See *Vervaeke v. Smith* [1983] 1 AC 145, [1982] 2 All ER 144.

(3) For life

6-09   The introduction of judicial divorce into English law[10] necessarily involved the acceptance that any marriage might be terminated before the death of one of the parties; and this was known to Lord Penzance at the time he formulated his definition. What it could only mean then, and what it clearly means now, is that the relationship must be potentially for life and a "marriage" which is time delimited at its inception cannot be recognised as a marriage for the purposes of the English conflict of laws. If the marriage is potentially for life the ease of its termination is not a relevant consideration.[11]

(4) Of one man and one woman

6-10   This raises three issues. Firstly age. Although Lord Penzance might just as well have said one male and one female, the issue of the age of the parties ought not to be ignored. Different systems have different views on the minimum age of marriage. English law requires the parties to be at least sixteen years old,[12] though the rule at common law was fourteen for boys and twelve for girls. The age of consent to sexual intercourse does not have to be the same as the age for marriage but, in the past at least, it would have been unthinkable for the legislature to have decriminalised unmarried sexual intercourse at an age lower than it permitted marriage. Recognition that marriage below the English age of sexual consent is permitted abroad is evidenced in domestic criminal legislation which assumes an answer to a charge of unlawful sexual intercourse with a girl under the age of thirteen that the defendant was married to the victim and that, therefore, the intercourse was lawful.[13] In cultures where marriages are arranged for infant children it is the practice only to allow them to become physical unions when both parties have reached puberty. It remains to be seen what the lower limit of English public policy will be on marriages where one of the parties is very young.

Secondly, it is clear that under English law a marriage has to be between a man and a woman[14] and a homosexual relationship cannot be accepted for the purposes of the English conflict of laws. Suppose a progressive Scandinavian State introduced a recognised form of relationship between persons of the same sex or extended the concept of

---

10   Matrimonial Causes Act 1857.
11   *Nachimson v. Nachimson* [1930] P 217.
12   Marriage Act 1949 s.2.
13   Sexual Offences Act 1956 s.5; and see *Alhagi Mohammed v. Knott* [1969] 1 QB 1, [1968] 2 All ER 680.
14   Matrimonial Causes Act 1973 s.11(c) and *Corbett v. Corbett* [1971] P 83, [1970] 2 All ER 33.

marriage to them. English law would not recognise such a relationship as falling within its concept of marriage. Whether it would take account of any special rules applicable to it under the foreign law would be a matter of public policy – in principle there is no reason why certain rights should not be acknowledged and given effect to in England just as we recognise foreign companies and partnerships. English law has not faced the palimony litigation[15] which has become prominent in the U.S. in recent years – were it to do so there is, again, no reason why such claims, insofar as they are based on agreements rather than status, and, provided they do not offend English public policy in their detail, should not be accepted as valid contracts.

The third problem which arises here is polygamy. Clearly the institutions of English law were directed at monogamous relationships and so, not only with regard to marriage itself but for all related purposes e.g. legitimacy and succession, the monogamous marriage was the model. The expansion of trade, but more significantly the expansion of Empire, brought English law in touch with vast numbers of peoples who lived under regimes where polygamy, if not the norm, was a legitimate form of relationship. The initial reaction was to deny to these relationships the status of marriage and this rejection of them was often accompanied by vituperative and chauvinistic ignorance,[16] yet throughout the world there were many peoples who accepted the institution and were prepared to defend its social function. When *Hyde v. Hyde* was decided, polygamous marriages could be found not only among Muslims, the most obvious group today, but among Hindus, Jews and those living under African and Chinese customary laws.

Nowadays polygamous marriages, with the exception of capacity, are subjected to the same basic conflict rules as monogamous marriages and English law allows those polygamously married to invoke the matrimonial jurisdiction of English courts.[17]

(5) To the exclusion of all others

Although at the time of the decision in *Hyde v. Hyde* adultery was the main basis for judicial divorce, this part of the definition reinforces the point about polygamy and is not a requirement of sexual continence. The adultery of one party, or indeed of both, never resulted in the invalidity of a marriage but only in grounds which might allow one party to petition for its termination.

6–11

---

[15] See *Windeler v. Whitehall* [1990] 2 FLR 505.

[16] See *Warrender v. Warrender* (1835) 2 Cl & Fin 488.

[17] Since the Matrimonial Proceedings (Polygamous Marriages) Act 1972 see now Matrimonial Causes Act 1973 s.47.

The purpose of the enquiry

6-12   The status of marriage has a wide range of implications under systems of domestic law. Under English law, for example, marriage is significant, *inter alia*, for succession, social security, damages for bereavement, immigration, taxation and legitimacy as well as the more obvious issues of the special relationship between the parties themselves.

For all these purposes the key distinction is between those marriages which are void and those which are not. Whatever defects a marriage might have, unless it is void it counts as valid for all purposes. The only concern about defects in a marriage which is not void arise when it is sought to terminate the marriage - only at that stage when the question is whether to petition for nullity or divorce do they come into play.

6-13   Usually the defects which make marriages void are easily established e.g. formal defects, non-age, prohibited degrees of relationship; though the determination of the status of a former marriage may involve complex conflict problems. The idea that no decree is necessary when a marriage is void and that all the world can treat it as such, needs to be taken carefully.

In some cases of a marriage which is void by English or foreign law there will be triable issues e.g. if lack of consent renders the marriage void by the foreign law, the matter may have to be tested by trial even if, in the result, the marriage is void and no decree would actually have been needed to make it so.

In cases where the marriage is voidable the problem does not arise in the same way because a decree is always necessary to change the status. Such a decree operates prospectively under English law.[18] It would be logical, therefore, to postpone all discussion of defects which render a marriage voidable to the consideration of matrimonial causes for it is only in that context that they have any significance. It is not practical to do so, however, as there are defects which, though English law treats them as matters of voidability, may be regarded by foreign law as defects rendering the marriage void *ab initio* e.g. impotence, lack of consent, mistake of quality. They will, therefore, be treated in this section.

Marriage defects

6-14   Under English law a marriage will be void if the required formalities have not been observed,[19] or the parties are within the prohibited degrees of relationship,[20] or either of them is under the age of sixteen,[21] or

---

[18]   Matrimonial Causes Act 1973 s.16.
[19]   *ibid* s.11(a)(iii).
[20]   S.11(a)(i).
[21]   S.11(a)(ii).

already lawfully married,[22] or they are not respectively male and female.[23] The marriage will also be void if one of the parties is domiciled in England and the marriage is polygamous in character even if it is monogamous in fact.[24]

Under English law a marriage will be voidable and will, therefore, be regarded as valid until one of the parties to it obtains a decree, if it has not been consummated as a result either of impotence or wilful refusal,[25] if either party did not validly consent to it,[26] or was suffering from such mental disorder as to make him or her unfitted for marriage,[27] if the respondent was suffering at the time of the marriage from communicable venereal disease[28] or if the wife was, at the time of the marriage, pregnant by another man. There are bars to the award of a nullity decree for a voidable marriage in all cases.[29] The court will not make the award if the respondent satisfies it that the petitioner knew of the effect of the defect but behaved in such a way as to lead the respondent reasonably to believe that he would not act on it, or that it would be unjust to the respondent to grant the decree.[30] In all cases, except failure to consummate, the proceedings have to be brought within three years of marriage,[31] and in the cases of venereal disease and pregnancy the court must be satisfied that at the time of the marriage the petitioner was ignorant of the facts.[32]

It would be naïve to suppose that foreign systems of law would be likely to have precisely the same taxonomy and although some defects, like lack of age, failure to observe formalities, and prohibited degrees, might be expected to be common, others, like lack of consent or mistake of quality cannot be expected either to have the same content or, even if they have, the same effect. Foreign systems may have additional grounds or may restrict defects to a narrower field. **6-15**

There is more pragmatism than principle in the distinction between void and voidable marriages under English law and, indeed, the whole concept of a marriage being voidable for an initial defect lacks in logic what it gains in practicability. **6-16**

---

22 S.11(b).
23 S.11(c).
24 S.11(d) but see *Radwan v. Radwan (No2)* [1973] Fam 35. [1972] 3 All ER 1026; *Hussain v. Hussain* [1983] Fam 26. [1982] 3 All ER 369.
25 S.12(a) and (b).
26 S.12(c).
27 S.12(d).
28 S.12(e).
29 S.13.
30 S.13(1)(a) and (b).
31 S.13(2).
32 S.13(3).

So when English conflict law is faced with a marriage which is argued to be defective under a foreign law it cannot be assumed that foreign defects have their English counterparts or that, even if they have, they will be categorised in the same way i.e. as having the same effect upon the marriage. Nor should it be assumed that the only classification to be made is that of English law.

6-17   The matter of a foreign marriage may come before the English courts in a number of ways. The question of the validity of a marriage may be raised incidentally in proceedings which are not primarily directed to its validity e.g. in a succession case. In such cases the issue will be whether the marriage was or was not valid at its inception or whether, if valid, it was still subsisting at the time in question or had been validly terminated by a divorce or annulment.

More directly, the English court may be asked to dissolve or annul the marriage or make a declaration of its validity, subsistence, or termination.

In nullity proceedings the English court has only two responses available to it. An invalid marriage can be void *ab initio* or voidable, and the decrees involved are different, one is effective from the date of the void marriage, the other prospective from the date of the decree. When a foreign defect does not match a defect under English law, or operates in a different way, the English court has to decide into which of its two categories the matter falls.

6-18   Which law is to classify the defect? The case for the legal system which imposes the defect to determine what effect it should have was put clearly by Lord Greene in *de Reneville v. de Reneville*[33] The case, which turned upon a jurisdictional issue which is no longer pertinent, involved parties who had made their matrimonial home in France. The wife sought to petition the English court for a decree of nullity on the ground that the marriage had not been consummated. Lord Greene, having observed that impotence and wilful refusal might not be classified in the same way, gave the opinion that it would be for French law to determine the effect of either defect as making the marriage void or voidable "not merely in a verbal sense but in the sense of the words as understood in this country, that is as indicating or not indicating as the case might be, that the marriage would be regarded in France as a nullity without the necessity of a decree annulling it"

6-19   This test presupposes that foreign systems of law operate on the basis that there are some defects so fundamental that their presence renders the purported marriage a total nullity, so that any resort to the courts for a judgment to that effect, is legally unnecessary; and other defects which

---

[33]   [1948] P 100, [1948] 1 All ER 56.

require the court's active involvement. It assumes, in short, that other systems have something akin to the two-fold classification of English domestic law. Such a presupposition may not be well-founded. However, the test does provide a basis for putting foreign defects in context. This will be considered further after the examination of choice of law rules.

Choice of Law

It is well established that questions on the validity of marriage are divided into those regarding the formal validity of the marriage and those concerning the capacity of the parties to marry or the essential validity of the marriage. The distinction between formal matters and the others has always been made by English law as *lex fori*, but it is arguable whether this is always appropriate.[34]

6-20

Formal validity and the lex loci celebrationis

Probably the oldest rule in the book, derived from the general principle - *locus regit actum* - the law of the place rules the deed - is that the formal validity of marriage is governed by the *lex loci celebrationis* - the law of the place of celebration.[35]

6-21

A marriage will be formally valid if the formalities required by the law of the place where it was celebrated have been observed. It does not matter whether these formalities are wholly secular or wholly religious or a mixture of the two; provided whatever is done has the effect under the law of the place of celebration[36] of establishing the relationship as a marriage. If the local law has special rules for certain types of foreigners, compliance with those rules will be required.[37]

Formalities include the licensing, certification and publicity requirements, the form of ceremony, what has to be said, number of witnesses, officials present and whether proxies can be used.[38] Other matters are more controversial, whether a marriage can take place without the parental consents required by the under-aged party's domiciliary law,[39] or whether a party can marry contrary to the ritual required by his domiciliary law[40] may well be viewed differently by

6-22

---

[34] See below para 6-39.

[35] *Scrimshire v. Scrimshire* (1752) 2 Hag Con 395.

[36] See *Berthiaume v. Dastous* [1930] AC 79.

[37] See *Hooper v. Hooper* [1959] 2 All ER 575.

[38] *Apt v. Apt* [1948] P 83. [1947] 2 All ER 677.

[39] See *Ogden v. Ogden* [1909] P 46.

[40] See *Papadopoulos v. Papadopoulos* [1930] P 55 (Greek Orthodox); *Formosa v. Formosa* [1963] P 259 [1962] 3 All ER 419 (Roman Catholic).

different systems; English law has treated them as formal matters and it is quite clear that the initial classification of an alleged defect, as relating to formal or essential validity will be made by English law, as *lex fori*, and not by the foreign law which imposes it.

6-23   The time factor[41] should present no problem here. The formal validity should be tested by the *lex loci celebrationis* at the time the marriage takes place, but there might be a case for accepting retrospective legislation which makes up for a technical defect and repairs it before anyone has acted in reliance on the formal invalidity. The English courts went a lot further than this in the case of *Starkowski v. A-G*,[42] where a Polish couple had married in Austria but had not complied with the formal requirements of the *lex loci*. Austrian legislation allowed such marriages to be validated by registration shortly thereafter and the English court recognised that the registration made the marriage formally valid. This was despite the fact that the couple had acquired a domicile in England and that the effect of the recognition was to deny to the applicant the legitimated status that his mother's marriage to her second husband would otherwise have provided, but it also had the effect of establishing the legitimate status of her first child, born of the original marriage.

6-24   As form is governed by the *lex loci* and parties can marry where they wish, it follows that couples can evade formal requirements of their "home" laws by marrying abroad.

6-25   It would seem obvious that reference should be made to the internal law of the *locus celebrationis* without reference to the conflict rules of that system. *Renvoi*[43] was considered, though it didn't help, in one case,[44] and the Law Commission toyed with the idea in some proposals on choice of law in marriage,[45] but the mischief of rare invalidity in which *renvoi* might be helpful is outweighed by the complexity of the operation of the doctrine, and the proposals were, sensibly, dropped.[46]

(1) Exceptions

6-26   There are some exceptions to the general rule that a marriage will only be formally valid if it complies with the formal requirements of the *lex loci celebrationis*. "Consular" marriages in foreign countries solemnised by a designated "marriage officer" where one of the parties is a U.K. national

---

[41] See below para 8-23.
[42] [1954] AC 155. [1953] 2 All ER 1272.
[43] See below para 8-07.
[44] *Taczanowska v. Taczanowski* [1957] P 301. [1957] 3 All ER 563.
[45] Law Com Working Paper 89 (1985).
[46] Law Com Report 165 (1987).

will be formally valid if they comply with the rules set out in the statutes, as will marriages abroad between parties one of whom is serving with the British forces, provided that it is celebrated by a chaplain serving in those forces and the other requirements of the legislation are complied with.[47]

A particular problem was raised by a large number of religious **6-27** marriages which had taken place at the end of the Second World War in parts of Europe recently liberated from German control between couples who had been displaced by the upheavals of the war. These marriages were formally invalid as there had been a failure or refusal to comply with the German marriage laws. To deal with this problem English courts adapted an old institution, – the common law marriage – the marriage *per verba de praesenti* – in order to give these marriages formal validity by English law, although the marriages, at the time they took place, had not the slightest connection with England. There is little to be said for the reasoning in these cases and much for the good will of the courts in seeking to resolve a serious problem affecting deeply religious people. It is best to regard the cases[48] as a particular response to what one hopes is a one-off problem and it is unlikely that there will be any further development of the concept.

(2) The rôle of the lex loci celebrationis

While the job of the *lex loci celebrationis* is to control the formal validity **6-28** of marriage and, possibly, to determine whether a marriage at its inception is potentially polygamous,[49] it is undoubtedly the case that where marriages are closely regulated by the *lex loci*, that law will police its country's capacity rules. So, for example, parties, whatever their personal laws may permit, will not be able to get the necessary permission to marry in England if they are under age or within the prohibited degrees by English law. Were they to slip through the net and celebrate their marriage in England it is unlikely that the marriage would be upheld. However, this is probably not the case if the *lex loci* is foreign and the parties manage to marry there despite that law's view of their capacity. A reference to the foreign *lex loci* will probably be confined to the question of formal validity only, and its view of the essential validity of the marriage ignored.

---

[47] See Foreign Marriages Acts 1892 and 1947 and the Foreign Marriage (Amendment) Act 1988.

[48] The leading ones are *Taczanowska v. Taczanowski* [1957] P 301, [1957] 2 All ER 563; *Kochanski v. Kochanska* [1958] P 147. [1957] 3 All ER 142; *Merker v. Merker* [1963] P 283, [1962] 3 All ER 928 and *Preston v. Preston* [1963] P 411, [1963] 2 All ER 405.

[49] See below para 6-44.

Capacity, essential validity and the personal law

6-29   Although it might seem logical to distinguish the issues of capacity and essential validity as we do, for example, in the law of contract, the issues are conventionally treated together for two reasons. The choice of law rules are the same, and, more importantly, the issues are harder to separate here than elsewhere. While there are some matters, age, for example, or existing marriage, which quite obviously affect an individual's capacity to marry as such, there are others which relate, not to the individual's personal capacity directly, but to his or her ability to enter a particular marriage. For example, rules of exogamy, consanguinity or affinity, concern the proposed relationship. The two parties, single and of full age and status, may be able to marry whomsoever they wish, except each other, because they stand in a relationship which the system of law will not allow as a marriage. It is equally correct to describe, say, the Portuguese prohibition on the marriage of cousins as a matter of the essential validity of the marriage or as an incapacity on the part of a Portuguese domiciliary to marry a cousin.

Dual domicile and intended matrimonial home

6-30   There is no doubt that the essential validity of marriage is governed by the personal law. While the English conflict of laws retains domicile as the determinant of the personal law, all questions of the capacities of the parties to marry one another will be referred to the *lex domicilii*. The reference is to the internal law of the chosen system not its conflict rules,[50] so no issue of renvoi arises. The Law Commission suggested the incorporation of *renvoi* into the basic rule of reference[51] but did not propose legislative change to this effect.[52]

6-31   There is some controversy, however, on how this reference to the personal law is to be interpreted. Two views characterise the debate. Dicey took the view that the matter should be referred to the law of each of the parties' antenuptial domiciles – the question being in each case not only, has this individual capacity to marry but can this person marry the intended partner? Cheshire took the view that reference should be made to the law of the matrimonial domicile, the search being for the intended matrimonial home with the fallback that, if no matrimonial home could be discovered, reference should be made to the husband's antenuptial domiciliary law.

---

[50] But see *R v. Brentwood Superintendent Registrar of Marriages Ex p. Arias* [1968] 2 QB 956, [1968] 3 All ER 279.

[51] Law Com. Working Paper 89.

[52] Law Com. 165 (1987).

The obvious advantage of the Dicey test is that it puts the parties on   **6-32**
an equal footing and does not prefer the husband's law to that of the
wife. Its disadvantage is that it makes reference to legal systems which
may have no further interest in the future of the individuals or their
marriage. It also tends towards invalidity by subjecting the marriage to
two legal tests, the failure in either making the marriage defective.
Suppose H and W are domiciled in country X where they are regarded
as being within the prohibited degrees of marriage as they are cousins.
They decide that they will make their home in country Y, which has a
less restrictive regime on consanguinity, and they go through the
marriage ceremony there. If a question arises about the validity of their
marriage the court will have to determine whether they had acquired a
domicile in country Y before they married or only subsequently. If
before, their capacity will be determined by the law of Y and their
marriage will be valid. If after, their capacity will be determined by the
law of X and their marriage will be void. The same problem would arise
if their antenuptial domiciles were in different countries, only one of
which regarded them as within the prohibited degrees. It would be easy
enough to advise them to avoid any problems by the simple expedient of
establishing domiciles in Y before getting married, and we may suppose
the acquisition of such a domicile would be a simple and speedy process;
but no advice may be sought, not least because the parties may not be
aware of either the prohibition or, indeed, of their relationship.

Cheshire's intended matrimonial home test would avoid this difficulty
by referring directly to the law of country Y. But this advantage is bought
at a cost which most consider to be too high. There will be circumstances
where the parties have no matrimonial home in mind when they marry,
and other cases where the intention to establish their home in a particular
country is not carried into effect. Clearly the issue cannot be left in the air
for very long and, logically, the validity of a marriage must be capable of
being determined at the time that it takes place. Cheshire suggested that
the premarital intention of making a country the marital domicile would
have to be carried into effect within a reasonable time of the marriage
taking place. The other objection to the Cheshire test is to the provision
it makes where no matrimonial home is established within a reasonable
time of the marriage. In such cases reference is to be made to the law of
the husband's premarital domicile. When Cheshire propounded the test,
the law of domicile still made wives dependant on their husbands - they
acquired their husband's domicile as a domicile of dependency upon the
marriage and had no power to change it while the marriage lasted. There
was, therefore, a unity of domicile between husband and wife and,
therefore, one could speak correctly of a matrimonial domicile even if
there was no matrimonial home. The Domicile and Matrimonial

Proceedings Act 1973[53] liberated married women from domiciliary dependence and, by so doing, put an end to the concept of an automatic matrimonial domicile. Of course the vast majority of cohabiting married couples will share the same domicile, but they share it as a matter of individual autonomy, not as the operation of a legal process. There is no reason for preferring the husband's domicile to that of the wife either in law or in logic, and while it may well be true that where the couple come from different countries it is more common for the matrimonial home to be established in the husband's country than the wife's, this does not help when no such home has been established nor justify such discriminatory treatment.

It might have been thought that the passing of the Domicile and Matrimonial Proceedings Act 1973 (if not the passing of the Marriage (Enabling) Act 1960, which removed the prohibition on marriages between parties related by affinity, after divorce had severed the connection, provided that no such marriage would be valid if either of the parties was, at the time of the marriage, domiciled in a country which did not allow such relationships) would have decided the issue in favour of the Dicey test once and for all. However, although there is no doubt that the dual domicile test is the one most commonly applied and, indeed, the issue normally goes in its favour by default, a few recent cases have chosen to apply the Cheshire test, so, to that extent, the issue remains a live one.

6-33 Space does not permit a consideration of the old authorities on which the arguments for the two tests are based – many of them are equivocal anyway, at least on the facts. Suffice it to say that the standard test for the essential validity of marriage is the application of the law of each party's antenuptial domiciliary law. A few illustrations will demonstrate how the standard dual domicile test applies.

In *Re Paine*[54] the testator, who died in 1884, had left property on trust for his daughter for life, but if she left any children the interest was to go to her estate absolutely. The daughter, who was domiciled in England, had gone through a marriage ceremony in Germany in 1875 with her dead sister's husband, a domiciled German. Such a marriage was permitted by German law but not by English law at that time. The question before the court was whether the children of the marriage were legitimate for only if they were would their mother's interest under the trust have become an absolute interest in accordance with the wishes of the testator.

The legitimacy of the children was assumed to depend on the validity of their parents' marriage, which itself depended on the capacity of the

---

[53] S.1.
[54] [1940] Ch. 46.

parties to enter the union. As English law, the wife's antenuptial domiciliary law, did not allow the marriage of parties within such a degree of affinity, the marriage was void, the children illegitimate and the wife's interest in the trust fund died with her.

Pugh v. Pugh[55] shows the double operation of the dual domicile test. The marriage took place in Austria between a domiciled Englishman and a fifteen year old Hungarian girl. By Austrian law the marriage was formally valid and Austrian law would not have regarded the age of the girl as any impediment; Hungarian law, the girl's premarital domiciliary law, also regarded the marriage as valid. English law, the husband's premarital domiciliary law, prohibits marriages below the age of sixteen[56] and, although the husband was well above that age, the court held that the English statute was not confined to marriages taking place in England or to the age of English domiciliaries. This interpretation is partly correct, there would be little point in establishing a minimum age for marriage if it could be avoided by marrying abroad. But a purposive analysis would suggest that the object of minimum age legislation is to protect people from youthful folly or the importunity of older people, not the protection of adults from the attractions of foreign youngsters who are of marriage age by their personal laws

Although the use of the dual domicile test is standard; as mentioned earlier, there are a couple of recent cases in which the matrimonial home test has been applied and it is necessary to look at these.[57]

6-34

In *Radwan v. Radwan* (No 2),[58] the husband, a domiciled Egyptian who was already married, went through a marriage ceremony in the Egyptian consulate in Paris with the second wife, a domiciled Englishwoman. After the marriage they carried out their premarital intention to make their matrimonial home in Egypt. Subsequently the husband divorced his first wife and came with his second wife to live in England, acquiring a domicile here. He attempted to divorce her by *talak* – Muslim unilateral divorce – presented at the Consulate General of the United Arab Republic in London; but this attempt to terminate the marriage failed, as the court held[59] that the divorce had been obtained in England and did not, therefore, fall within the recognition rules for overseas divorces. On the wife's petition for divorce, the validity of her marriage to the husband was raised.

---

55 [1951] P 482, [1951] 2 All ER 680.

56 Age of Marriage Act 1929 s.1(1).

57 See, in addition, the remarks of Ld. Greene in *de Reneville v. de Reneville* [1948] P 100, [1948] 1 All ER 56; Denning J. in *Kenward v. Kenward* [1951] P 124, [1950] 2 All ER 297; and *Perrini v. Perrini* [1979] Fam 84, [1979] 2 All ER 323.

58 [1973] Fam 35, [1972] 3 All ER 1028.

59 *Radwan v. Radwan* [1973] Fam 24, [1972] 3 All ER 967.

Under English law a marriage is void if

"in the case of a polygamous marriage entered into outside England and Wales that either party was at the time of the marriage domiciled in England and Wales."[60]

Now the marriage in this case was undoubtedly polygamous so the only question was the English legislation. On the face of it the legislation applied directly, as the wife was domiciled in England at the time of the marriage and the ordinary application of the dual domicile test would regard her as prevented by her domiciliary law from entering such a marriage. Cumming-Bruce J. applied a different approach. Relying on the identical predecessor provision to section 14 of the Matrimonial Causes Act 1973 which provides:

"Where, apart from this Act, any matter affecting the validity of a marriage would fall to be determined (in accordance with the rules of Private International Law) by reference to the law of a country outside England and Wales nothing in this Act shall

a) preclude the determination of that matter as aforesaid or

b) require the application to the marriage of the grounds or bars there mentioned except so far as applicable in accordance with those rules",

he decided, in a judgment which he specifically limited to polygamy, that if by the rules of the English conflict of laws capacity to marry is to be determined by the intended matrimonial home, the intended matrimonial home here being Egyptian, the provision precluding English domiciliaries from marrying polygamously would have no effect. The decision has been extensively criticised for obvious reasons as it flies in the face of the clear words of the statute which apply to all English domiciled men and women and come before the application of the conflict rules. Nevertheless the decision is in line with earlier reasoning to the effect that a domiciled Englishwoman ought to be able to enter a polygamous marriage if it was her intention to live with her husband in a country which allowed polygamy.[61]

In *Lawrence v. Lawrence*[62] a Brazilian domiciliary obtained a divorce in Nevada and then married a domiciled Englishman there with whom she came to live in England. The Nevada divorce would not make her a single woman by Brazilian law, so that under the standard dual domicile test the second marriage would be void for bigamy. On the wife's

---

[60] Matrimonial Causes Act 1973 s.11(d).

[61] See Denning J in *Kenward v. Kenward* [1951] P 124, [1950] 2 All ER 297.

[62] [1985] Fam 106, [1985] 1 All ER 506 - decision, though not method, upheld by Court of Appeal.

petition for nullity, the validity of the second marriage was upheld, the trial judge applying the matrimonial home test.[63]

Finally, it is worth noting that in a couple of cases[64] it has been **6-35** suggested that a proper law of the marriage test might be applied so that reference could be made to the system of law with which the marriage is most closely connected. The idea of real and substantial connection which can be found in some obsolete cases on the recognition of foreign decrees[65] clearly has, like the matrimonial home test itself, certain attractions in those cases where the premarital domiciliary law is remote from the marriage but, again like the matrimonial home test, it cannot be applied universally. There will be situations where it is impossible to say with which of two or three legal systems the marriage is most closely connected. If the test is to be developed there will need to be careful consideration of its ambit.

Application of the *Lex Causae*

Where the test for the essential validity of marriage discloses an **6-36** incapacity, the marriage is generally void. So if one of the parties is under age, or already married, or if the parties are within the prohibited degrees of consanguinity or affinity, or not respectively male and female or if the marriage is polygamous and one of the parties is precluded by the personal law from entering a polygamous marriage, the marriage will be regarded as void *ab initio*, without the need for a decree annulling it. These are all defects by English domestic law, but the principle should equally apply where the defect imposed by one of the party's personal laws is unknown to English law. Where the foreign defect is simply a variant of a defect known to English law - a different age for marriage, for example, or a more extensive list of prohibited degrees - there should be little difficulty in its accommodation. Where the defect is altogether unknown to English law its acceptance will depend on the operation of public policy. So, for instance, while the anti-miscegenation laws were operative in South Africa to preclude mixed race marriages, one would have expected an English court, faced with a mixed-race marriage between domiciled South Africans, to refuse to give any effect to the foreign defect on the basis of a public policy against racial discrimination.

The general principles would appear to apply to non-age, prohibited degrees, single sex marriages and foreign defects which by, the law which

---

[63]   See also *Perrini v. Perrini* [1979] Fam 84, [1979] 2 All ER 323.

[64]   See Lord Simon in *Vervaeke v. Smith* [1983] 1 AC 145 at 166; Lincoln J. in *Lawrence v. Lawrence* [1985] Fam 106 at 112-5.

[65]   See *Indyka v. Indyka* [1969] 1 AC 33, [1967] 2 All ER 689.

imposes them, render the marriage void. In the case of foreign defects this should be so irrespective of whether they constitute grounds of voidability by English law (lack of consent would be an obvious example or certain mistakes as to qualities), or are unknown to it as marital defects. However there are a number of exceptions which need to be addressed separately.

Bigamy

6-37   The Western Christian tradition of marriage, which at one time disapproved even of deuterogamy, made bigamy a serious crime. A valid first marriage precludes a subsequent one[66] until the first has been annulled, dissolved or ended by the death of the partner. This applies to all marriages taking place in England even if the first marriage is actually or potentially polygamous.[67] The subsequent marriage will be void though, in the case of a polygamous first marriage, it may not be sufficient to found a prosecution for bigamy.[68]

Where it is alleged that the first marriage has been dissolved or annulled, the status of that divorce or annulment is, obviously, crucial to the validity of the subsequent marriage; but which law is to determine that issue? The separation of the recognition rules for divorce and nullity from those relating to the validity of marriage[69] may lead to inconsistencies in the application of the standard test for the validity of marriage. Both the dual domicile test and the matrimonial home test are capable of recognising two inconsistent valid marriages if the validity of a divorce, say, is recognised in one system but not in another. To keep the example simple, suppose that, at the time of their marriage, H and W are domiciled in the same country X and that the marriage is perfectly valid. H obtains a divorce in country Y and then acquires a domicile in country Z where he marries W2 who is also domiciled there. If country X does not recognise the divorce but country Z does, the standard choice rules for capacity would indicate two valid marriages. How should English law answer a question, say, about the intestate succession to H's immovable property in England?

In *Lawrence v. Lawrence*[70] on the wife's petition for a decree of nullity on the ground of bigamy it was found that her Nevadan divorce would be recognised in England but not in Brazil, so that the operation of the

---

[66] Matrimonial Causes Act 1973 s.11(b).

[67] *Baindail v. Baindail* [1946] P 142, [1946] 1 All ER 342.

[68] See *R. v. Sarwan Singh* [1962] 3 All ER 612 cf *R. v. Sagoo* [1975] QB 885, [1975] 2 All ER 936.

[69] See below para 6-62.

[70] [1985] Fam 106, [1985] 2 All ER 733 see above para 6-34.

dual domicile test (though not on these facts the matrimonial home test) would make the second marriage void. However, the Court of Appeal took the central issue to be the recognition of the divorce and, as the divorce would be recognised in England, it followed that the parties to it were free to marry notwithstanding the non-recognition of the divorce in the wife's premarital domicile. In other words the court answered the incidental question[71] by reference to the *lex fori* not the *lex causae*. This position has now been confirmed by statute,[72] so that whenever a divorce or annulment is recognised by English law, the remarriage of the parties will be recognised wherever it takes place and irrespective of the attitude of any other system of law to it.[73]

Where the first marriage is alleged to be void *ab initio* but there has been no annulment (as there need not be under English conflict law), the incidental question can, again, be resolved by the *lex fori* approach. If the English conflict of laws regards the first marriage as void, the parties to it are free to marry, notwithstanding the validity of the first marriage by the domiciliary laws of the parties to the second.

There is no English authority for the opposite case, where the decree is recognised in the *lex domicilii* but not by English law. Clearly, reference of the incidental question to the *lex fori* would result in the second marriage being void for bigamy. In the Canadian case of *Schwebel v. Unger*[74] the first marriage was "dissolved" by the Jewish *gett* in circumstances not entitling it to recognition by any connected legal system. The parties later became domiciled in Israel, where the *gett* was regarded as having terminated the marriage and, while domiciled there, the wife married her Canadian husband. The Canadian court, applying the dual domicile test, found that the wife was single by her *lex domicilii* at the time of the marriage and did not consider how she acquired that status as a matter of relevance. There is no way out of this dilemma which will maintain consistency, and had the Canadian court declared the marriage void for bigamy, as the divorce was not entitled to recognition in Canada at the time it was made, the effect would have been to assert the continuing validity of the first marriage which by the domiciliary laws of both the parties to it had been validly dissolved. Nevertheless that would have been the better solution.[75]

---

[71] See below para 8–17.

[72] Family Law Act 1986 s.50.

[73] For a remarkable example of the earlier position see *R. v. Brentwood Superintendent Registrar of Marriages ex parte Arias* [1968] 2 QB 956, [1968] 3 All ER 279.

[74] (1964) 45 DLR 2d 644.

[75] See below para 8–19.

Consent to marry

Parental Consents

6-38   With the general reductions in the age of majority, the issue of parental consent has ceased to be a matter of significance to the validity of marriages. It is included here as another example of the workings of the conflict process and to illustrate the need to understand a problem before resolving it.

English domestic law does not take the parental consent necessary to allow a minor to marry as a particularly serious matter. The English conflict of laws established early on that the issue was one of formal validity to be governed by the *lex loci celebrationis*; hence the practice of couples eloping to Gretna Green, just over the border in Scotland, to marry there, after a short period of residence, without hindrance, as Scots law has no requirement of parental consent. Their marriages would be recognised in England as English law would refer to Scots law as the *lex loci celebrationis*. Indeed for a while there was quite an industry in Gretna Green catering for young couples, some of whom had come from farther afield than England, to avoid what they felt were unreasonable restrictions on their autonomy placed on them by their own legal systems.

6-39   We can analyse the issue as a straight conflict between the autonomy of the young persons and parental authority. The Western idea of romantic love would suggest that the parties, once they are of an age to marry, should be able freely to decide whom they wish to marry. The contrary view is that marriage is more socially significant than the decision to have sexual intercourse and that parental guidance, in the interests of the child, is something which should be taken sufficiently seriously to justify a parental veto for the two years, in the case of English law, between the age of sexual consent and the age of majority. A more extreme version of this view would be advocated by the culture of the arranged marriage, where the whole matter is put in charge of the parents and elders whose job it is to arrange a suitable match.

This is not the place for a discussion of the merits of each of these possibilities and it is clearly open to debate which produces the most stable relationships, protects the social significance of the status of marriage or results in the greatest amount of human happiness. It would be reasonable to expect that a society, and therefore its law, ought to have some idea of what it is doing in this area, and for a system of conflict of laws at least to be aware that there is more than one way of doing things.

English conflict law has treated the question as one of formal validity only. A couple of examples on this show that the results of this approach do little credit to our conflict system. In *Simonin v. Mallac*[76] a French

---

[76]   (1868) 2 Sw & Tr 67.

couple came to marry in England in order to avoid the parental consent requirement of French law. The provision in the French Civil Code merely required the youngsters to ask formally for consent on three occasions, failure to achieve it at the third attempt left them free to marry without their parents' blessing. The reference to English law as the *lex loci celebrationis*, therefore did not produce an exceptionable result. In *Ogden v. Ogden*,[77] however, on similar facts, the same result from the English court is much more questionable as there the operative provision of the French Civil Code quite clearly made the issue one of capacity; a French court had granted a decree of nullity in respect of the marriage, and a remarriage had taken place on the strength of it. The result of the English decision was to set at nought, as far as English law was concerned, the French decree, and the remarriage which had followed it, and to affirm the validity of the initial English marriage. If one needed a stark example of the advantage of the test proposed by Lord Greene in de *Reneville v. de Reneville*,[78] *Ogden v. Ogden* provides it. Despite widespread academic criticism of the decision English courts still classify all cases of parental consents as matters of form to be referred to the *lex loci celebrationis* alone.[79]

Consent of Parties

The effect that a lack of consent by one of the parties should have was a matter of some controversy in domestic English law for some time. The arguments are fairly evenly balanced between regarding the marriage as void *ab initio* for the lack of an essential ingredient, and treating it as voidable on the basis that, despite the reluctance of one of the parties to enter into the marriage, the relationship might work out and, therefore, leaving it to one of the parties to bring a petition if it doesn't. The matter was finally resolved in favour of violability by the Nullity of Marriage Act 1971 and the same provision is now contained in the Matrimonial Causes Act 1973, section 12 (c) of which provides that a marriage will be voidable if

6-40

> "either party to the marriage did not validly consent to it, whether in consequence of duress, mistake, unsoundness of mind or otherwise".

Despite the completeness of the provision there are some mistakes – mistake about the nature of the ceremony or mistake about the identity of the other party, which would seem too fundamental to leave to the wait and see principle.

---

[77] [1908] P 46.

[78] See above para 6-18.

[79] See *Lodge v. Lodge* (1963) 107 Sol Jo 437.

6-41   The uncertainty over the position of mistake in domestic law was reflected in the English conflict of laws by uncertainty over the choice of law rule to be applied. Cheshire favoured the *lex loci celebrationis* and there is some authority to support that view.[80] Dicey took the view that consent, like capacity, should be governed by the dual domicile test. The modern authorities, such as they are, are not helpful. English law has been applied to a case involving a mistake going to the nature of the foreign ceremony,[81] and English law, as the *lex loci celebrationis*, to a case of duress,[82] but there is strong support for the Dicey view,[83] although it can be argued that only the non-consenting party's law should be applied and that, if he or she consented by that law, a lack of consent by the other party's law is irrelevant.[84] We might notice here the effect of the ease of divorce on nullity of marriage. Where divorces are difficult to obtain or cannot be got at all e.g. in some of the Catholic countries, the regime of nullity seems to have been extended in order to offer relief from marriages which don't work. So, for example, the concept of mistake may be extended to mistakes about the attributes of the other party which would not be regarded as vitiating consent under English domestic law. That the husband falsely believed that the wife was a virgin at the time of the marriage or that the wife had been misled into believing that the husband was a member of the aristocracy would have no effect under English domestic law, but might be grounds for nullity elsewhere. Again, any petition in England would be subject to English public policy and a trivial ground might well not be recognised. Were a ground unknown to English law to be accepted, then the usual question which has been mooted before recurs -what law is to determine the effect of the defect? The same question arises when a common defect has a different effect in different legal systems. Under Scots Law, for example, a lack of consent renders the marriage void, under English law the same defect renders the marriage voidable. The application of the dual domicile test, in such a case, might reveal that both parties were, say, under an operative mistake by their own premarital domiciliary laws or that only one of them was. Alternatively, it is possible that one of the parties could be found to be under an operative mistake by the other party's law but not by his or her own. Whether we apply both parties' laws to each party's mistake or only the mistaken party's own law to his or her error, there is a case for determining the result by the application of the law which recognises the mistake as a ground of nullity. That law should be allowed to determine

---

80   See *Mehta v. Mehta* [1945] 2 All ER 690; *Parojcic v. Parojcic* [1959] 1 All ER 1.
81   *Mehta v. Mehta* [1945] 2 All ER 690, see also *Kassim v. Kassim* [1962] P 224, [1962] 3 All ER 426.
82   *Parojcic v. Parojcic* [1959] 1 All ER 1.
83   See *Szechter v. Szechter* [1971] P 286, [1970] 3 All ER 905.
84   Cf *Pugh v. Pugh* [1951] P 482, [1951] 2 All ER 680.

whether the mistake makes the marriage void or voidable. In the case of a common operative mistake, where both parties' laws regard the marriage as defective, it would seem appropriate to apply the law which gives the greatest effect to the mistake, i.e. to the law which makes the marriage void rather than to the law which makes it voidable.

Impotence and wilful refusal to consummate

This, the most common ground for nullity petitions in England, presents special problems for the conflict of laws as for domestic law. Firstly it is not one ground but two; but, although the matters can be considered separately, they are commonly pleaded together. Technically they are distinct in that impotence involves the physical or psychological inability to consummate the marriage and is an existing state at the time the marriage takes place, whereas wilful refusal involves the psychological or other dispositional refusal of sexual intercourse with the marriage partner and does not preclude the possibility of sexual intercourse *per se*. Secondly, logically, wilful refusal is a post marital defect and its relation back to the inception of the marriage is a fiction.

6-42

The common merger of impotence and wilful refusal under English law in practice, though they are separate heads of nullity in the statute,[85] does not obviate the need to treat them as distinct when applying a foreign law.[86]

The authorities, such as they are , are inconclusive on choice of law and support can be found for the *lex fori*,[87] the *lex loci celebrationis*[88] and the domiciliary law.[89]

If the issues are separated, there is every reason to apply the dual domicile test, or the matrimonial home test, to impotence as that is a premarital defect. It could be argued with regard to the dual domicile test that one law only should be applied but there seems no reason to prefer the impotent party's law to that of the other. For wilful refusal, however, there is no reason to apply the premarital domiciliary law for what is a post-marital defect which could, equally well, be the basis for an English divorce. Wilful refusal might have been taken out of the nullity category had it not been regarded as socially desirable that those whose religious sensitivities made the divorce option ineligible should retain some way of getting out of an unsatisfactory marriage. Viewed in this light the case for

---

[85] Matrimonial Causes Act 1973 s.12(a) and (b).

[86] As was envisaged by Lord Greene in *de Reneville v. de Reneville* [1948] P 100, [1948] 1 All ER. 56.

[87] *Easterbrook v. Easterbrook* [1944] P 10.

[88] See *Robert v. Robert* [1947] P 164, [1947] 2 All ER. 22.

[89] *de Reneville v. de Reneville* [1948] P 100, [1948] 1 All ER 56; *Ponticelli v. Ponticelli* [1958] P 204, [1958] 1 All ER 357.

the application of a post-marital domiciliary law, the common matrimonial domicile, if there is one, would be the obvious choice, or even for the *lex fori,* becomes more attractive. If the matter is to remain wedded to the issue of impotence then there is reason in using a common choice of law rule though with this distinction. It may be acceptable for a party to plead his own impotence but not his own wilful refusal. That does not, of course, answer the question of whether the refuser's law or the refused's, or both, should be applied.

It need hardly be said that the defect here is a failure to consummate the marriage, not a post consummation failure or refusal of sexual intercourse. No pretence can be made that such a later lack of sexual intercourse is related to the inception of the marriage, and English law would neither give a nullity decree in such circumstances nor recognise a foreign annulment based on such a ground though it could, in appropriate circumstances, both grant or recognise a divorce.

Polygamy

6-43   The normal mode of polygamy involves the husband's power to have more than one wife (polygyny) rather than the wife's power to have more than one husband (polyandry) but the rules should apply equally to both institutions. There has been a general decline in the practice of polygamy world-wide during the last fifty years but the issue has come closer to home with post-war immigration.

6-44   A polygamous marriage entered in a country which permits polygamy between parties whose personal laws allow it and which is formally valid by the law of the place of its celebration will be valid for all purposes in the eyes of English conflict law. However, a marriage in England, or other country which permits only monogamy, will be monogamous, irrespective of the personal laws of the parties.[90]

The main problem arises where a person whose personal law does not permit him or her to marry polygamously marries one whose personal law does allow it, in a country where polygamy is recognised, according to a form suitable to it. We have seen that English law regards a marriage as void if it is polygamous and one of the parties is domiciled in England[91] and that this obstacle was overcome in the decision in *Radwan v. Radwan* (No 2)[92] by the application, albeit in an illogical way, of the matrimonial home test. In that case the marriage was actually polygamous but the English prohibition applies not only to actually polygamous marriages but to potentially polygamous ones also.

---

[90] *Cheni v. Cheni* [1909] P 67; *Maher v. Maher* [1951] P 342, [1951] 2 All ER 37.

[91] Matrimonial Causes Act 1973 s.11(d). See above para 6-14.

[92] [1973] Fam 35, [1972] 3 All ER 1028. See above para 6-34.

Most marriages contracted in countries where polygamy is permitted are actually monogamous. But English law has worked on the basis that the distinction lies not between the actually monogamous and the actually polygamous, which might seem the sensible approach, but between *de jure* monogamous marriages and those not so.

In the past the quality of the marriage, at its inception, was determined by the nature of the ceremony by the *lex loci celebrationis*. If, by that law, the marriage was polygamous in form, even if monogamous in fact, it would be regarded as a polygamous marriage and, if one of the parties' personal laws did not permit that form of marriage, void.[93] However, English law would draw its own conclusions about the status created and not simply take the local law's word for it.[94] However, English law was prepared, in certain situations, to test the matter at the time of the English proceedings and thereby to accept the possibility that the marriage had been converted to legal monogamy.[95] The Law Commission[96] has proposed the treatment of the potentially polygamous marriage as if it were *de jure* monogamous and there seems no reason for not doing so.

In *Hussain v Hussain*[97] the court was faced with a common modern problem. Hussain was domiciled in England, he went to Pakistan to go through a ceremony of marriage with a woman domiciled in Pakistan. The marriage was an arranged marriage, in Muslim form, in a country where polygamy is recognised. By the standard tests the marriage was potentially polygamous and, as the husband was domiciled in England, it fell within the statutory provision.[98] By an interpretation no less ingenious than that adopted in *Radwan v. Radwan (No 2)*[99] the court held that the marriage was a valid monogamous one as Hussain was precluded by his personal law from marrying polygamously and could not lawfully take a second wife while he retained his English domicile. Of course the wife was capable by her domiciliary law of marrying polygamously but that didn't matter, for, as far as she was concerned polygamy was not a power she could use but a potential disability that she was under. The court achieved a satisfactory result in holding the marriage valid but it did so by distorting the application of the standard rules which determine the monogamous or polygamous quality of the marriage by reference to the nature of the ceremony. A better way, and one recommended by the Law

6-45

---

93 See *Re Bethel* (1887) 38 Ch D 220.
94 See *Lee v. Lau* [1967] P 14, [1964] 2 All ER 248.
95 See below para 6-46
96 Law Com 146 (1985).
97 [1983] Fam 26, [1982] 3 All ER 369.
98 Matrimonial Causes Act 1973 s.11(d) see above para 6-14.
99 See above para 6-34.

Commission[100] in the wake of the *Hussain* case, would have been to alter the rules for determining the nature of the marriage and to put less emphasis on the ceremonial (for Islamic marriages in the U.K. do not differ in form from those in countries which allow polygamy, it is merely that their legal effects are different) and more on the personal laws of the parties. Nevertheless the decision produces the right result and allows English domiciled Muslim men to go through Islamic marriages abroad without the fear that the marriage will not be recognised as valid in England – it will, but it will be monogamous.

Despite the obvious sense of the decision it works only in the case of a domiciled Englishman marrying in a country which allows polygamy, not of a domiciled Englishwoman doing the same thing even if she and her new husband intend to make England their permanent home. The man's marriage is valid and the woman's is void because the basis of the Hussain decision is that the marriage is monogamous because the husband is domiciled in England and cannot, therefore, take further wives.[101] The woman, though subject to the same restrictions, cannot claim that she lacks the capacity to take further husbands as she never had this power in the first place, as the institution we are dealing with is polygyny not polyandry, and her Pakistani domiciled husband retains the capacity to take further wives[102] Of course if he acquires a domicile in England the marriage would become monogamous[103] but that is too late for the application of the dual domicile test.

(1) Conversion of the Marriage

6-46   Just as the dissolubility of a marriage can be changed by a change of domicile or habitual residence e.g. a couple domiciled in and marrying in Ireland, where there is no divorce, can change the dissolubility of their marriage by either of them becoming domiciled or habitually resident in England and thus obtaining access to the divorce jurisdiction of the English court, so a marriage, originally polygamous or potentially polygamous, can become monogamous. Before the passing of the Matrimonial Proceedings (Polygamous Marriages) Act 1972[104] there was an incentive to the court to find that a potentially polygamous marriage had been converted into a monogamous one as only then could the parties have recourse to the English matrimonial law. The issue arose also in succession cases and in criminal proceedings for bigamy.

---

[100] Law Com. 146 (1985).
[101] Matrimonial Causes Act 1973 s.11(b).
[102] See *Risk v. Risk* [1951] P 50.
[103] *Ali v. Ali* [1968] P 564, [1966] 1 All ER 664.
[104] See now Matrimonial Causes Act 1973 s.47.

Changes in the content of the domiciliary law,[105] the failure of a precondition set by the religious law,[106] a change of religion,[107] and a change of domicile[108] have all been accepted as converting a potentially polygamous marriage into a monogamous one, and the same should apply to an actually polygamous marriage which has become factually monogamous by the death or divorce of supernumerary wives.

Does it work the other way? Suppose a domiciled Englishman, who is married monogamously, changes his domicile to a country which permits polygamy. Does that convert the marriage to a potentially polygamous one? No, because no system requires polygamy or even its potential. To convert the marriage there would need to be a conversion to a religion such as Islam which permits polygamy. If our domiciled Englishman was already a Muslim then, of course, the simple change of domicile would suffice. The effect of a conversion on the monogamous wife is open to question. If she also converts to Islam and changes her domicile, there is no reason to assume that the marriage should not be totally converted so that she now has the status of first wife in a marriage which is capable of becoming actually polygamous.

If, on the other hand, she retains her English domicile or habitual residence she should have no problem in obtaining a divorce on her husband's taking a second wife, on the basis of his unreasonable behaviour or on the basis of adultery even if she has no other ground of complaint, which seems unlikely. For while a complaint based on adultery is not open to the wife in an actually polygamous marriage, when the intercourse complained of is the marital intercourse with another wife, what we actually have, in the example given, is a monogamous marriage overlaid with a potentially polygamous one, and the monogamous wife cannot be deprived of the protection which her status gives her. There is no English decision on this but there is a clear inference from *A-G for Ceylon v. Reid*[109] that the first wife should be protected. The case involved a conversion to Islam by a Christian man domiciled in Sri Lanka; the court upheld his right to change his religion and exercise the powers that his new faith gave him. The case related to criminal liability for bigamy but the decision is broader than that.

There is a substantial Muslim community in England and a brief consideration of its position may be helpful. If the husband came to this country and settled here with an existing polygamous marriage, his

6-47

---

[105] See *Parkasho v. Singh* [1968] P 233, [1967] 1 All ER 737; *R. v. Sagoo* [1975] QB 885, [1975] 2 All ER 936.

[106] *Cheni v. Cheni* [1965] P 85, [1962] 3 All ER 873.

[107] *Sinha Peerage Claim* [1946] 1 All ER 348; see also *Mehta v. Mehta* [1945] 2 All ER 690.

[108] *Ali v. Ali* [1968] P 564, [1966] 1 All ER 664.

[109] *A.G. for Ceylon v Reid* [1965] AC 720, [1965] 1 All ER 812.

marriage will be fully recognised and he and his wives will have the same resort to the matrimonial relief of English law as their monogamously married neighbours.[110] He cannot, however, take further wives while domiciled here[111] nor resort to Islamic forms of divorce.[112] If he came here married to one wife only, his potentially polygamous marriage became a monogamous one when he acquired an English domicile, and the same applies if the actually polygamous marriage has become actually monogamous by the death or divorce of the other wives.

Children of immigrants may well be in a difficult position culturally as they try to reconcile their traditional Islamic culture with contemporary values in modern British society, but their legal position is clear. While they remain domiciled in England the rule of monogamy prevails and they cannot take advantage of the attitude their religion adopts to polygamy.

The Effect of Defects

6-48   If on the application of the choice of law rules a defect is disclosed, what is to be its effect? If the defect is one imposed by English law either as *lex domicilii* or as *lex loci celebrationis* it will be for English law to determine its effect. If the defect is imposed by a foreign law it can be argued that the effect of that defect should be determined by the law which imposes it. This is the approach propounded by Lord Greene in *de Reneville v. de Reneville*[113] in which the criterion would be whether a decree was or was not necessary. If no decree was necessary, the marriage would be void in the English sense, if one was, the marriage would be voidable in the English sense and, thus, for all purposes, save nullity proceedings, valid. Such an approach puts the foreign defect in its legal context and gives it the weight which the system that English law has chosen to determine the existence of the defect accords it. To carry out such a policy effectively, however, the analysis has to be made before the choice of law, not after it. The criticism of the decision in *Ogden v. Ogden*[114] is that English law, as *lex fori*, determined that parental consent was a matter of formal validity and referred to the *lex loci celebrationis*, rather than a matter of capacity to be referred to the *lex domicilii*. But it was only the *lex domicilii* which regarded it as a matter of capacity not the *lex fori* or the *lex loci celebrationis*. In other words, the initial characterisation as form precluded the enquiry into the effect of the defect.

---

[110] Matrimonial Causes Act 1973 s.47.

[111] *ibid* s.11(b).

[112] Family Law Act 1986 s.46(2)(c).

[113] [1948] P 100, [1948] 1 All ER 56 and see above para 6-18.

[114] [1908] P 46.

The problem is not insuperable. Whenever it is alleged that a marriage is defective the system of law under which the defect is alleged to exist will be identified. It is no hardship for the English court to hear evidence of the effect of the defect under that system. There can never, save possibly in the case of wilful refusal to consummate the marriage, be more than three connected laws in addition to the *lex fori* – the *lex loci celebrationis* and the antenuptial domiciliary laws of the two parties. Having established the identity of the defect, as form or substance, by the law which imposes it, the court can then proceed to apply its choice rules in the usual way and, if it finds an operative defect, applying that system's view of its effect. English public policy would apply, of course, to vet the acceptability of the result produced and to rule out offensive or trivial defects.

The rule in Sottomayer v. de Barros (No 2)

An exception to the dual domicile test which enjoys universal **6-49** disapproval is contained in the decision in *Sottomayer v. de Barros (No2)*.[115] In the first litigation in the *Sottomayer* case[116] the parties were thought to be domiciled in Portugal. They had married in England where they intended to make their home. They were, however, within the prohibited degrees by Portuguese law. The Court of Appeal held the marriage to be void. In the second litigation, however, the case having been referred back to the Divorce Court on an issue of fact, it was found that the husband was domiciled in England at the time of the marriage, with the result that the marriage was upheld. Under this rule, where one of the parties is domiciled in England, and the marriage takes place here, a foreign incapacity which does not have its counterpart in English law will be disregarded, not on the basis of any objectionability to English public policy but simply because of the connection with England. Of course those who support the Cheshire intended matrimonial home theory can take this case as an example of the operation of that theory, and this is the most charitable light in which it can be viewed. The Law Commission favours its abolition.[117]

English public policy

An impediment to marriage imposed by a foreign law should not be **6-50** regarded as contrary to English public policy simply because we do things differently here. The unruly horse of public policy should not be ridden roughshod through foreign concepts of exogamy. Public policy should

---

[115] [1879] 5 PD 94.

[116] (1877) 3 PD 1.

[117] Law Com 165 (1987).

not be invoked unless the recognition of the foreign law would seriously offend our susceptibilities. In *Scott v. A-G*[118] the parties were domiciled in South Africa where the husband obtained a divorce. By South African law, the guilty party (divorce then depending on the commission of a matrimonial offence) could not remarry while the innocent party remained single. The wife, the guilty party, remarried in England while the husband remained unmarried. The court refused to recognise the foreign defect on the basis that it was a penalty which had only local application. A better approach would have been to consider the nature of what was being recognised. The penalty followed a divorce; the object of divorce is to free the parties from the bonds of marriage and thus enable them, if they so wish, to remarry. If English law recognised the divorce then it should recognise the unfettered power of either of the parties to the former marriage to marry again.[119] A short time gap, however, as between decree nisi and decree absolute, is clearly not objectionable.[120]

6-51   Equally a marriage which is valid by the personal laws of the parties and by the *lex loci celebrationis* should not be treated as invalid by English law unless serious issues of public policy are at stake, so, for example, in *Cheni v. Cheni*[121] the validity of a Sephardic Jewish marriage between an uncle and his niece was recognised.

6-52   It is sometimes said that the English conflict of laws will not recognise religious incapacities but this is far too sweeping a statement, for many of the rules about prohibited degrees go far beyond the usual measures to avoid incest in the narrow sense and differ from one religious group to another. There are certainly cases where English courts have refused to uphold petitions based on the rules of exogamy of the Hindu caste system,[122] or where it was contended that the petitioner lacked capacity to marry other than in accordance with the rites of a particular religion.[123] The Maltese marriage cases – *Chapelle v. Chapelle*,[124] *Formosa v. Formosa*,[125] *Lepre v. Lepre*.[126] These cases, which concerned the recognition of foreign nullity decrees, present an interesting issue of classification. Suppose that a domiciled Maltese man marries a domiciled Englishwoman in a register office in England and later petitions for nullity on the ground that he lacked capacity to marry except in accordance with the rites of the

---

[118] (1886) 11 PD 128.
[119] See now Family Law Act 1986 s.50.
[120] *Warter v. Warter* (1890) 15 PD 152.
[121] [1965] P 85, [1962] 3 All ER 873.
[122] *Chetti v. Chetti* [1909] P 67.
[123] *Papadopoulos v. Papadopoulos* [1930] P 55.
[124] [1950] P 134, [1950] 1 All ER 236.
[125] [1963] P 259, [1962] 3 All ER 419.
[126] [1965] P 52, [1963] 2 All ER 49.

Roman Catholic Church. The court could classify the issue as one of marital capacity, apply the dual domicile test, discover the incapacity under Maltese law and then refuse to accept it on the grounds of public policy. Alternatively, it could apply the intended matrimonial home test and, if the couple had intended to make their home in England, apply English law to the capacities of both parties. On the other hand the English court could classify the issue as one of formal validity and apply English law as *lex loci celebrationis*. Finally, if all else were to fail, the court could apply the rule in *Sottomayer v. de Barros (No2)*.[127] In all these cases the marriages would be valid by English law.

3 MATRIMONIAL CAUSES

The Jurisdiction of English Courts

The jurisdictional rules, which are exclusive, are now contained in the **6-53** Domicile and Matrimonial Proceedings Act 1973. The English court will have jurisdiction if at the time of the institution of the proceedings either party to the marriage was domiciled in England or Wales[128] or was habitually resident there and had been so resident for the preceding year.[129] In the case of a void marriage only, if one of the parties to it is dead, jurisdiction can also be based on his or her domicile or one year's habitual residence at the time of death.[130] The jurisdiction is not tested with regard to the petitioner or respondent as such, but by the parties to the marriage. So a petitioner who is neither domiciled nor resident in England or Wales can invoke the jurisdiction on the basis of the respondent's connection and, in the case of a void marriage, any interested party can invoke the jurisdiction based on the life or death connection of either of the parties to the marriage.

The connections of domicile and habitual residence are the ordinary ones employed by English conflict law.[131] As habitual residence is tested, like domicile, at the time of the institution of the proceedings, it follows that if proceedings are begun a year after one of the parties came to England and habitual residence is found to exist, then that party was habitually resident here on day one of the residence. It is clear that the residence does not have to be married residence, pre–marriage residence will count.

---

[127] (1879) 5 PD 94.

[128] Domicile and Matrimonial Proceedings Act 1973 s.5(2)(a) (divorce); s.5(3)(a) (nullity).

[129] *ibid* s.5(2)(b) (divorce); s.5(3)(b) (nullity).

[130] S.5(3)(c).

[131] See above paras 2-09, 2-11.

6-54   Despite the fact that the connections can be used by a person
resorting to English jurisdiction, there is no general power in the court to
refuse jurisdiction, stay an action, or refuse leave to serve process on an
absent respondent for no leave is required. There is a limited duty to stay
English divorce proceedings in favour of proceedings, whether for
divorce or nullity, more properly located in another part of the British
Isles[132] and a power to stay where proceedings respecting the marriage
are taking place in a foreign court.[133]

Choice of Law

Divorce

6-55   This issue can be quickly dealt with: there is no issue of choice of law
in divorce, the English court always applies English law as *lex fori*.

To obtain a divorce in an English court the petitioner must establish
that the marriage has irretrievably broken down according to the criteria
established in the implementation of the legislation.[134] Nothing less than
that will do and, while the petitioner is free to rely on any facts which
support the contention, including those facts which would sustain a foreign
petition based on the concept of the matrimonial offence or on a different
concept of breakdown, the position under any foreign law is irrelevant.

The application of English law as *lex fori* can be rationalised by the
firm statement that what is being sought is an English judgment *in rem*
definitively affecting the status of the parties to a marriage and that,
therefore, it is only right that English law should govern exclusively. Such
a statement is not compelling. Every litigant in an English court is seeking
the exercise of the authority of that court and the proposition could be
extended to the universal application of English law in all cases coming
before the English courts. This would render the whole of the conflict of
laws redundant, at a considerable cost to justice. Certainly the argument
could be extended with pretty well equal force to nullity proceedings
and, indeed, it was thought at one time that there was no choice of law
issue in nullity proceedings. The contrary has been clearly established by
the legislation.[135]

A better explanation is available from the history of the development
of divorce jurisdiction in England. When the Court for Divorce and
Matrimonial Causes was set up in 1857 no provision was made for the

---

[132] Domicile and Matrimonial Proceedings Act 1973 Sch 1 para 8.

[133] *ibid* para 9, and see *de Dumpierre v. de Dumpierre* [1988] AC 92, [1987] 2 All ER 1.

[134] Matrimonial Causes Act 1973 s.1 as amended.

[135] Now Matrimonial Causes Act 1973 s.14(1).

jurisdiction of the court. The court established its own rules for divorce jurisdiction based on the domicile of the parties. At that time, of course, the parties would have the same domicile as it has always been the precondition for granting a divorce that the parties were validly married in the eyes of English law; and valid marriage communicated the husband's current domicile of choice to the wife as a domicile of dependency.[136] Such being the case the Court arrived at a neat and simple proposition that for every marriage there would be one court, and only one court, which was competent to grant a dissolution.[137] This line, could it have been held, would at once have dealt with jurisdiction, choice of law and the recognition of foreign divorce decrees. There would have been one competent court for every marriage, that court could apply its own domestic law, as that would simultaneously be the *lex fori* and the *lex domicilii* and its decrees would have been entitled to universal recognition. But the line could not be held. It became apparent that using domicile as the sole jurisdictional basis was capable of working great hardship particularly to wives who had been deserted by their husbands and who found themselves, by reason of their husband's acquisition of a new domicile abroad, with a domicile of dependency in a country with which they might have no connection. Their only hope of matrimonial relief was to resort to the courts of that country, a resort which for legal or financial reasons was often unrealistic. A series of measures aimed at relieving such hardship put an end to the exclusive jurisdiction of the courts of the domicile. In consequence, the question whether in granting a divorce the English court was applying English law as *lex fori* or as *lex domicilii*, a question which had always existed but was not worth asking before, as it made not the slightest difference one way or the other, became a matter of significance. It was answered in favour of the application of English law as *lex fori* and there the matter has rested,[138] though from 1949[139] until 1973[140] there was a statutory basis, the courts being instructed, whatever the actual jurisdictional base, to behave in the same way as they would if both parties were domiciled in England. The provision precluded a choice of law rather than suggesting that the *lex domicilii* was applicable and then pretending that all parties were domiciled in England.

The exclusive operation of English law as *lex fori* does not mean that there are no conflict problems associated with the grant of English divorces. Clearly the concepts of domicile and habitual residence are

6-56

---

[136] See now Domicile and Matrimonial Proceedings Act 1973 s.1(1).

[137] See *Le Mesurier v. Le Mesurier* [1895] AC 517.

[138] See *Zanelli v. Zanelli* (1948) 64 TLR 556.

[139] Law Reform (Miscellaneous Provisions) Act 1949, s.1(4).

[140] Matrimonial Causes Act 1973.

pertinent, even if they are being applied for purely domestic purposes. It is preconditional to the grant of an English divorce that the parties to the proceedings are validly married – an issue which could take the court into some difficult conflict territory. Questions might arise which involve a decision about the validity of a foreign marriage or of the effect to be given to foreign divorces or annulments.

The concept of irretrievable breakdown, which is the only basis for divorce in England,[141] involves an investigation into the individual marriage and "unreasonable behaviour" is not a standard product. Where the parties come from a social context which is different from the general run, whether they are part of some particular group in Britain or a foreign country, this can certainly be taken into account so far as it is perceived as relevant in the enquiry.

Nullity

6–57   If a marriage is void by English conflict law there is no need for a decree annulling it; the parties and the rest of the world can behave as if the marriage had never taken place (though the status of any children of the marriage may be protected). Nevertheless prudent parties may seek a decree to keep the record straight and there will be some cases where the issue is controversial and an authoritative determination of the question is needed. For example, an allegation that a marriage is void for bigamy may depend on the disputed status of an acknowledged prior marriage. Although the position of a remarriage after a recognised divorce or annulment is now clear,[142] if there has been no annulment of a first marriage claimed to be void there may be difficult questions to answer.

6–58   It was thought for some time that the award of a nullity decree, like a divorce, was a matter of the exclusive authority of the granting court which should apply its own domestic law to the matter. Such a proposition may seem strange as it is a recipe for inconsistency, but inconsistency is sometimes inevitable as the choice of law rules for marriage may be applied for a whole host of reasons unconnected with the award of a nullity decree. Suppose, for example, an English court has jurisdiction over a succession case and it has, incidentally, to decide the validity of a marriage; it cannot avoid making its decision, say that the marriage is void, simply because it lacks the jurisdiction, because neither of the parties to the marriage is habitually resident or domiciled in England, to grant a decree to that effect. This is so, even if the courts which are competent to grant a decree would not see the marriage as defective. Questions about the validity of a marriage may arise in all manner of cases

---

[141] *ibid* s.1 as amended.

[142] Family Law Act 1986 s.50.

from taxation and immigration to legitimacy and damages for bereavement so that a conflict system might have a developed set of choice of law rules even if it never granted a nullity decree to any foreign marriage. However, where the court has nullity jurisdiction, it is obviously preferable that it applies the choice of law rules which it ordinarily uses.

Since 1971[143] it is clear that issues of choice of law are raised by nullity petitions with foreign contacts but there are few clear decisions on choice of law. The older authorities, especially where they lead to the application of the *lex fori*, must now be treated with great caution.

6-59

We have already seen the choice of law rules that English courts have produced to determine the formal and essential validity of a marriage, and it would seem obvious that these rules should be applied to the question of whether a decree of nullity should be granted. Such is the case.

6-60

However, the English courts have only two nullity options to play with -voidness and voidability - and if the foreign defect does not have its analogue in English domestic law, or a convenient category cannot be found for it, there may be problems. English courts could avoid these by classifying foreign defects in a way which prevents difficulties for themselves, as they have with foreign parental consents, or apply public policy to reject defects which do not fit the domestic mould. But suppose they act in the spirit of the legislation. It may happen either that there is an operative defect unknown to English law, or that the foreign law, while it has the same defect as English law, gives it a different effect. The foreign law could treat the defect as rendering the marriage void rather than voidable (lack of consent by one of the parties has this effect under Scots law); or voidable rather than void (non-age could be a candidate here - a foreign law might say that a marriage above a minimum age, but below the age for marriage, would be voidable at the option of the under age party provided that he or she acted within a time limit); or classify a defect, which English law recognises as a matter of nullity, as a matter of divorce (wilful refusal to consummate would be an obvious candidate). In these cases the English courts should give effect to the foreign law, including its limitations or bars to relief, e.g. that a complaint can only be made by one party or must be brought within a certain time, unless to do so would offend public policy. It is clear that the limitations and bars of English law do not have to be applied where the petition is governed by a foreign *lex causae*,[144] and the inference clearly is that the foreign qualifications may be.

The converse case, where English law sees the marriage as defective in some way but the *lex causae* does not, is covered adequately by the legislation,[145] and English courts should not intrude except in those cases,

---

[143] Nullity of Marriage Act 1971 s.4(1), see now Matrimonial Causes Act 1973 s.14(1).

[144] *ibid.*

[145] *ibid.*

e.g. single sex marriages, where English public policy would prevail. If the foreign law regards the alleged defect, say, wilful refusal to consummate the marriage, not as a marriage defect but as a ground of divorce, there would seem to be no justification for the English court to grant a decree of nullity at all. However, it can be argued in this particular case that this defect, as a post marital one, might be referable to a law other than the antenuptial domiciliary law of the petitioner.

A further refinement could be a situation where both English law and the *lex causae* regard the marriage as voidable, but the foreign law would regard a decree for such a marriage as having retrospective effect, whereas English law, since 1971,[146] has given such a decree prospective effect only. There is nothing to stop a foreign court qualifying the recognition of an English decree and giving what effect, if any, to it which it wants; but it is difficult to see how an English court can modify the type of decree it gives to accommodate the *lex causae* in such a case and, anyway, little is likely to turn on the distinction.

Recognition of Foreign Divorces, Annulments and Legal Separations

Introduction

6-61   Recognition is entirely statutory and is exclusively contained in Part II of the Family Law Act 1986.

6-62   As in the case of the recognition of foreign judgments in non-matrimonial cases, the basic issue is the jurisdictional competence of the court whose decision is under consideration. If that court is regarded by English law as competent to make the decision, then the decision will be recognised in England without investigation of its merits, unless there are overwhelming reasons of public policy against doing so.

The statute, however, applies not only to judicial awards but extends to divorces, annulments and legal separations, which are not made by courts at all and may be no more than the individual exercise of power by a party to the marriage. It therefore covers, for example, what are called "bare" *talaks* – Islamic divorces which are not based on any proceedings.

Note: The basic code established by the statute applies equally to divorces, annulments and legal separations. To avoid repetition of a cumbersome expression the word "divorce" will be used to include the other two forms of relief and may be understood to do so unless the contrary is stated.

---

[146] Nullity of Marriage Act 1971 s.5, now Matrimonial Causes Act 1973 s.16.

U.K. divorces

A divorce granted by a court of civil jurisdiction in any part of the **6-63** British Islands will be recognised throughout the U. K.[147] Only divorces which have been obtained in the U.K. by court proceedings are capable of recognition,[148] so unilateral and non judicial divorces obtained here will not have any effect unless obtained before 1.1.74.[149] and recognised by rules of law applicable before that date.

An English court may refuse recognition only if the decree is irreconcilable with an earlier decision of the English court on the subsistence or the validity of the marriage, or with an earlier decision of a foreign court which has been recognised or is capable of recognition, by the English court.[150]

A divorce or legal separation (though not, obviously, an annulment) may be refused recognition by the English court if there was no subsisting marriage between the parties in the eyes of English law, including its conflict rules.[151]

Overseas divorces

For overseas divorces the Act distinguishes between those obtained by **6-64** proceedings and those not.

(1) Proceedings

For this purpose proceedings do not have to be court proceedings, **6-65** though they most commonly will be, they include "other proceedings"[152] and a *talak* pronounced in Pakistan in accordance with the Muslim Family Law Ordinance of 1961 has been held to have been obtained by proceedings.[153] The proceedings do not have to be judicial or quasi-judicial in character to count for this purpose and it would seem that any divorce which requires official involvement in some active way, e.g. formal attempts at reconciliation, would be one obtained by proceedings. Whether a mere process of registration without more would constitute proceedings is more dubious, and it would certainly appear that a simple formal renunciation of the marriage, even before witnesses, will not.

---

[147] Family Law Act 1986 s.44(2).

[148] *ibid* s.44(1).

[149] *ibid* s.52(5)(a).

[150] *ibid* s.51(1).

[151] *ibid* s.51(2).

[152] s.54(1).

[153] See *Quazi v. Quazi* [1980] AC 744; c/f *Chaudhury v. Chaudhury* [1984] 3 All ER 1017 – a bare *talaq*.

(2) Connections

6-66   If the divorce was obtained by proceedings it must be connected to the country where it was obtained by one of the parties to the marriage being habitually resident in that country, domiciled there or a national of that country[154] at the date of the commencement of the proceedings.[155] Nationality and habitual residence are to be determined by English law but the domiciliary connection can be established either by English law or by the law of domicile as used for family law matters by the country concerned.[156]

6-67   Where the divorce is obtained otherwise than by proceedings e.g. a "bare" *talak* or a *khula*, the connections are far less generous. At the time the divorce was obtained[157] both parties to the marriage affected must have been domiciled in that country,[158] or one party must have been domiciled there and the other domiciled in a country where the divorce is recognised as valid.[159] Such a divorce will not be recognised if either party was habitually resident in the U.K. throughout the period of one year immediately preceding the obtaining of the divorce.[160] Again, domicile can be established either by the English concept or by the law of domicile as used for family law matters in the country or countries referred to.[161]

(3) Effectiveness

6-68   Before the divorce can be recognised in England the court must be satisfied that it is effective under the law of the country where it was obtained.[162] In the vast majority of cases this will present no problem either in establishing where the divorce was obtained or whether it was effective by that law. Extra judicial divorces and those obtained in federal states on the basis of the nationality connection present some difficulty. It is necessary to consider where a divorce is obtained and what is meant by the law of a country.

6-69   Where a divorce is obtained from a court there will usually be no difficulty either in establishing where it was granted or whether it was effective under that law, but extra judicial divorces may present problems. Suppose H declares the *talak* to W who is in England, or sends it to her

---

[154] Family Law Act 1986 s.46(1)(b).
[155] S.46(3)(a),; there is a special rule for post mortem nullities in s.46(4).
[156] S.46(5).
[157] S.46(3)
[158] S.46(2)(b)(i).
[159] S.46(2)(b)(ii).
[160] S.46(2)(c).
[161] S.46(5).
[162] S.46(1)(a), 46(2)(a).

from overseas. Where is the divorce obtained? If it is a bare *talak* and if either of the parties has been habitually resident in England for the year preceding its delivery, it cannot be recognised anyhow.[163] If it is obtained in England it cannot be recognised either, as it was not obtained from a court of civil jurisdiction.[164] If, however, it was obtained by proceedings in Pakistan, say, it would be entitled to recognition in England on the basis of the nationality connection even if both parties are domiciled and habitually resident here at the time when it was obtained.

In *Fatima v. Secretary of State for the Home Department*[165] a case under previous legislation, a *talak* was regarded as a divorce obtained by proceedings which partly took place in England, where the words of divorcement were pronounced, and partly in Pakistan where the formal proceedings took place. The "trans-national" divorce was refused recognition as, part of the proceedings have taken place in England, it could not be regarded as an "overseas divorce". Under the different wording of the 1986 Act, which centres on where the divorce was effectively obtained rather than on where the proceedings took place,it may be that a different result would ensue. Should it?

A finding that the *talak* was effectively obtained under the law of Pakistan would entitle it to recognition, whatever view was taken of the location of the proceedings. However, a decision that the pronouncement of the *talak* in England was fatal to its recognition would result in a serious anomaly. On the one hand, a party to a marriage who has every connection with England but who can resort to a foreign court, where a weak sense of domicile gives it international jurisdiction, can obtain a decree which will be recognised in England. On the other hand a Pakistani Muslim, resident and domiciled in England, cannot resort to his religious law in England, but if he goes to Pakistan and there delivers a talak in reliance on his nationality it might make all the difference whether his wife accompanies him or stays at home.

(4) The law of a country

Throughout this book the word "country" has been used to identify a single territorial system of law, a law district as the Americans call it, as opposed to a State which is an internationally recognised political unit. Several States, the U.K. itself is one, have a number of countries within the political unit which have their own law systems. When it comes to applying this distinction to the recognition of foreign divorces there can be problems.

6-70

---

163 S.46(2)(c).
164 S.44(1).
165 [1986] AC 527, [1986] 2 All ER 32.

There is no difficulty where the country is also the political State – France, Japan, Saudi Arabia and, indeed, most States in the world – both the questions of the effectiveness of the divorce and that of the jurisdictional nexus are referable to a single legal system.

The next group are federal states which have separate countries within them for most conflict purposes but which have a unitary law on family matters – Australia and Canada, for example. While for other conflict purposes it is necessary to decide whether a person is domiciled, say, in Queensland or New South Wales, Ontario or Quebec, for the purpose of the recognition of divorces it is possible to be domiciled or habitually resident in Australia or Canada, just as one can, obviously, be a national of those States. So the questions of effectiveness and the jurisdictional nexus are referable to the federal State as a whole.

The third group are the federal states whose separate countries remain distinct for the purpose of all conflict matters. The U.S.A. is the obvious example; one cannot be a domiciliary of the U.S.A. as an entity any more than one can be a national of Texas or Nebraska. The jurisdictional connection, based on domicile, whether the English or local interpretation of that concept is applied, and habitual residence must relate to the individual law district.[166] The connection based on nationality must, of course, relate to the international State but what about effectiveness? It should go without saying that the divorce must be effective in the country where it was granted, for, if it isn't, there is nothing to be recognised. But must it be effective in the eyes of the federal unit? If it must, does that depend on whether the jurisdictional connection is based on domicile or habitual residence or only if it is based on nationality? Where, and only where, the jurisdictional connection is nationality the divorce must be effective not only in the law district where it was obtained but throughout the federal unit.[167] Indeed the wording of the statute would suggest that even if the divorce is not effective in the country where it was obtained it could still be recognised in England if, the jurisdictional connection being nationality, it was recognised by the federal State, though this seems unlikely.

(5) Proof of jurisdictional facts

6-71 The basis of recognition of judicial divorces is the international jurisdictional competence of the court where the divorce was obtained. An English court is concerned neither with the grounds on which the divorce was given nor with the jurisdictional basis on which the foreign

---

[166] S.49(2).
[167] S.49(3).

court itself took jurisdiction. However, insofar as the foreign court made, expressly or by implication, a finding of fact on the basis on which it took jurisdiction, including a finding that either party to the marriage was a national of, or domiciled or habitually resident in the country where the divorce was obtained, such a finding will be conclusive evidence of that fact if both parties took part in the proceedings. If only the petitioner took part in the proceedings, such a funding will be sufficient evidence of that fact i.e. it will stand unless the contrary is shown.[168]

Refusal of recognition

Recognition of a divorce may be refused in England if it is irreconcilable with a previous decision of an English court on the subsistence or validity of the marriage, or with a previous decision of a foreign court which is entitled to recognition in England,[169] or, if, being a divorce or judicial separation (though, obviously not an annulment), in the view of English conflict law there was no subsisting marriage between the parties.[170]   **6-72**

In the case of an overseas divorce (but not one obtained in the British   **6-73** Isles) obtained by proceedings, recognition may be refused if there has been a denial of natural justice, in that the respondent was not given adequate notice of the proceedings or was otherwise not given reasonable opportunity to take part in them.[171] The denial of natural justice or the lack of opportunity to take part in the proceedings applies only where such participation is meaningful and even then there is a discretion. If we take a model of judicial proceedings, a failure to notify the other side of what is happening, or the denial of, or simply the lack of, an opportunity to put his case, strikes at the root of judicial justice. However, it is not the case that such a failure is a fatal flaw[172] even if it is an obvious one. The respondent may not be concerned about taking part in the process, may have no possible defence to put, no property to safeguard or children to consider, and may be happy with the outcome.[173] To deny recognition in such a case because the proceedings were a travesty of a judicial trial because, for example, the respondent did not know that they were going on, would be to take principle to the point of officiousness and to create an avoidable limping marriage for no benefit. It must be remembered that

---

[168] S.48

[169] S.51(1).

[170] S.51(2).

[171] S.51(3).

[172] See *Newmarch v. Newmarch* [1978] Fam 79, [1978] 1 All ER 1; *Hack v. Hack* (1976) 6 Fam Law 177; cf *Joyce v. Joyce* [1979] Fam 93, [1979] 2 All ER 156.

[173] See *Gordon-Findlay v. Gordon-Findlay* [1966] 110 Sol Jo 848.

to be recognised the divorce must be effective under the law of the country where it was obtained and the most blatant cases of the denial of natural justice may prevent the divorce being effective in that country.

6-74   Where the proceedings are extra-judicial, the "respondent" may have no rôle to play in them anyway and so lack of notice or participation, provided that it does not make the divorce ineffective in the country where it was obtained, may well be irrelevant. All the more so where there are no proceedings at all, in such a case the English court does not have a discretion to refuse recognition to the decree on the ground of lack of notice or lack of opportunity to take part, though it could, in an appropriate case, refuse recognition on the basis of public policy even if the facts related to the denial of a right under the governing law to participate in the process.

6-75   If the divorce has been obtained otherwise than by proceedings the English court may refuse recognition if there is no official document, one "issued by a person or body appointed or recognised for the purpose",[174] certifying that the divorce is effective under the law of the country where it was obtained (or valid under the *lex domicilii* of the party who is domiciled elsewhere).[175]

6-76   However the divorce was obtained, the English court can refuse to recognise it if it is manifestly contrary to public policy.[176] In considering such cases the court should be reluctant to apply its own notions of propriety and should resort to public policy only if the recognition of the divorce would deeply offend its sense of justice. A dissolution granted on racial grounds, or as a result of duress,[177] or one which was a travesty of the judicial process (e.g. the petitioner's claim for divorce based on his own adultery with persons unknown) should be refused recognition. Recognition should not be refused simply because the decree was given on grounds unknown to English law e.g. incompatibility of temper. The court should have regard to all the circumstances of the case including the consequences which would follow from the refusal of recognition.[178] Fraud on the other party and on the foreign court[179] would be a suitable basis for refusal.

What of the situation where the court is undoubtedly jurisdictionally competent, procedurally correct and gives a decree on a basis that is

---

[174] Family Law Act 1986 s.51(4).

[175] S.51(3)(b).

[176] S.51(3)(c).

[177] See *Re Meyer* [1971] P 298, [1971] 3 All ER 378.

[178] See *Newmarch v. Newmarch* [1978] Fam 79, [1978] 1 All ER 1.

[179] See *Kendall v. Kendall* [1977] Fam 208, [1977] 3 All ER 471; *Middleton v. Middleton* [1967] P 62, [1966] 1 All ER 168.

intelligible to, though not shared by, English law, yet the decree has serious effects on an English party? For example, a foreign decree declares void a marriage which English law would regard as perfectly valid and would have declared so if asked, and where the consequence of the decree is to render illegitimate a child which English law regards as legitimate. This situation arose in three cases which are collectively known as the Maltese Marriage Cases: *Chapelle v. Chapelle*,[180] *Formosa v. Formosa*,[181] *Lepre v. Lepre*.[182] The basic situation has already been set out.[183] The marriage being valid by English law, the couple would have, at that time, a common domicile - that of the husband. As the husband had retained Maltese domicile, the Maltese court was, therefore, the court of the common domicile and indisputably jurisdictionally competent. Should the decrees be recognised? In *Chapelle v. Chapelle*, the court undermined the jurisdictional base of the Maltese court in an ingenious, if spurious way; but in *Formosa v. Formosa*; and *Lepre v. Lepre* it resorted to the idea of substantial justice. If the decrees were recognised, substantial injustice would be done to the wife and to any children who would be deprived of the status they clearly had in the eyes of English law. Had the nullity decree of the Maltese court been given prospective effect only an alternative way out would have been available. However, there is good reason to give a nullity decree the effect it has under the legal system which granted it. It is open to question whether, in similar circumstances, the English courts would refuse recognition today.

(1) Exclusive basis

While the 1986 Act provides the sole basis for the recognition of internal U.K. and overseas divorces and is retrospective in its operation,[184] there are savings for divorces, but not annulments, which would have been recognised under earlier, more liberal, rules.[185] So, some extra-judicial divorces obtained in Britain before 1974 and some overseas divorces obtained before the 1986 Act and previously recognisable on the basis of recognition by both parties' domiciliary laws (though not obtained in such a country), can still be recognised. It is, of course, not unusual for the matter of recognition to be raised long after a divorce was obtained.[186]

6-77

---

180 [1950] P 134, [1950] 1 All ER 236.

181 [1963] P 259, [1962] 3 All ER 419.

182 [1965] P 52, [1963] 2 All ER 49.

183 See above para 6-52.

184 Family Law Act 1986 s.52(1).

185 *ibid* s.52(4).

186 See e.g. *Hornett v. Hornett* [1971] 1 All ER 98 (45 years).

(2) Savings

6-78   The recognition of a divorce does not affect any property distribution that took place before the date of recognition e.g. if the personal representatives had distributed the property of the deceased on the basis that X was, or was not, married to Y. Similarly, where a matter has been determined by a court in the British Isles, the matter will be treated as *res judicata* in other parts of the U.K. so that a petitioner for the recognition or non recognition of a foreign divorce cannot have another go after the rules have changed.[187]

Declarations of Marital Status

6-79   For a number of purposes, from succession to social security, it may be necessary to determine the validity of a marriage without any desire to change the status of the couple concerned. The Family Law Act 1986 provides a code for such declarations of marital status.

Any person who is regarded as having a sufficient interest,[188] as well as the parties to the marriage, may apply for a declaration that a marriage was at its inception valid or that it subsisted, or did not subsist, at a certain date or that a divorce, annulment or legal separation obtained in a country outside England and Wales is, or is not, entitled to recognition.[189] If a person wants to establish that a marriage was invalid at its inception he cannot proceed by way of declaration[190] but has to petition for a decree of nullity.

The English court will have jurisdiction to make any of these declarations, whoever the particular applicant is, only if one of the parties to the marriage is, or was at the time of death, domiciled in England or habitually resident here for the one year minimum period.[191]

Ancillary Orders

6-80   Orders relating to the financial arrangements between couples, made during the subsistence of the marriage or upon its termination, and orders made respecting children, raise no issues of choice of law. English law as *lex fori* is applied exclusively. But they do raise questions of jurisdiction and of the recognition of foreign orders which require brief treatment here.

---

[187] Family Law Act 1986 s.55(2).

[188] *ibid* s.55(3).

[189] S.55(1).

[190] S.58(5)(a).

[191] S.55(2).

When an English court has jurisdiction to grant a decree of divorce it **6-81** also has jurisdiction to make its full range of financial orders whether the case is or is not a domestic one.[192] Of course there may be situations, where the respondent has no connection with England and no assets here, where it would be pointless to do so.[193]

An English court can make financial orders during the subsistence of **6-82** the marriage if either party is domiciled in England, the applicant has been habitually resident here for the one year period or the respondent is resident here,[194] and Magistrates Courts can make maintenance orders if either party to the marriage is ordinarily resident within the court's area.[195] English courts will have jurisdiction over maintenance applications to which the Brussels and Lugano Conventions apply if either party is domiciled in England[196] (in the special sense of domicile used for the Conventions[197]) or if the "maintenance creditor" is habitually resident here.[198]

Orders in respect of children, both those made under the inherent **6-83** jurisdiction of the English court as *parens patriae* and those under the Children Act 1989 - "section 8 orders" - can be made in the matrimonial proceedings, or if the child is habitually resident in England and Wales, or present here (unless he is habitually resident in another part of the U.K.)[199] and, *in extremis*, without even these connections.

A foreign divorce does not automatically put an end to an English **6-84** order, though the changed circumstances might well be a reason for varying or discharging one, and the recognition of a foreign divorce does not involve the recognition of the foreign court's ancillary orders.[200] English courts have the same powers to make orders following a foreign divorce as they have when making their own.[201] They will have jurisdiction if either party to the marriage was domiciled in England or had been habitually resident for one year in England, either at the time of the institution of the English proceedings or at the time that the foreign divorce became effective, or if either party has a beneficial interest in English property which is or was the matrimonial home[202]

---

[192] Matrimonial Causes Act 1973 s.23-24A (financial orders); Family Law Act 1986 Part I as amended by Children Act 1989.

[193] See *Tullack v. Tullack* [1927] P 211.

[194] Matrimonial Causes Act 1973 s.27.

[195] Domestic Proceedings and Magistrates' Courts Act 1978 Part I.

[196] Both Conventions - Article 2 and 5(2).

[197] See above para 3-23.

[198] Both Conventions - Article 5(2).

[199] Family Law Act 1986 Chap.II.

[200] Family Law Act 1986 s.51(5).

[201] Matrimonial and Family Proceedings Act 1984 Part III.

[202] *ibid* s.15(1).

6-85   A foreign order might constitute a final and conclusive judgment of a jurisdictionally competent court and thus be entitled to recognition at common law or by statute.[203] This will not apply to a maintenance order or an order respecting a child as both of these are subject to variation. Foreign maintenance orders may be recognised and enforced under a number of statutory provisions.[204] Maintenance judgments made by courts in Contracting States under the Brussels and Lugano Conventions are entitled to recognition and enforcement in England.

6-86   Foreign orders respecting children have no special position before English courts as, in general, "the child's welfare shall be the court's paramount consideration."[205] English courts have made orders respecting children brought here in violation of a foreign order[206] or detained here in breach of agreement.[207]

To prevent the removal of children from one jurisdiction to another whether a straight "kidnapping" or in an attempt by one parent to get a favourable order from a new court, the U.K. has ratified two international conventions, one concerned with the return of abducted children, the other with the recognition and enforcement of custody orders.[208] In neither case, of course, is return or enforcement automatic and the English court will not, in dealing with cases under the Act, and seeking to further the purpose of the Conventions, abandon its proper concern with the child's welfare.[209]

4 LEGITIMACY, LEGITIMATION AND ADOPTION

Introduction

6-87   Despite the efforts which have belatedly been made in English domestic law to remove the stigma of illegitimacy and to treat all children equally,[210] it remains the case that it may be necessary for conflict purposes, particularly in cases of succession, to distinguish the legitimate

---

[203] See above paras 3-64, 3-76.

[204] See for orders within the U.K., Maintenance Orders Act 1950; for overseas orders Maintenance Orders (Facilities for Enforcement) Act 1920, Maintenance Orders (Reciprocal Enforcement) Acts 1972; 1992.

[205] Children Act 1989 s.1.

[206] See Re D's Settlement [1940] Ch 54.

[207] See Re A [1970] Ch 665, [1970] 3 All ER 184.

[208] Child Abduction and Custody Act 1985.

[209] See Re A & anor (minors) (abduction acquiescence) (No2) [1993] 1 All ER 272.

[210] See Family Law Reform Act 1987 s.1.

child from the illegitimate one. Even in domestic law, despite the reversal in 1969[211] of the traditional interpretation of words like "children" or "issue" in wills and trusts so that they now include all children, and the further extension of that principle in the Family Law Reform Act 1987, the testator or settlor remains free to distinguish his beneficiaries on the basis of their legitimacy, although now he has to be clear in his rebuttal of the inference of equality.

Historically, the exercise of establishing legitimacy has been the need to connect the child with his father on the basis that motherhood is a fact but fatherhood is never more than a hypothesis, and this historical approach permeates the current law.

Traditionally solely, and still most commonly, legitimacy is determined by the validity of the parental marriage. But there is another basis. Even if a child is illegitimate at birth there is the process of legitimation by which he can become legitimate. And there is also the process of adoption by which the legal links with the natural parents are severed and replaced by a new set of family relations.

The issues to be discussed here are matters of status. The effect to be   **6-88**
given to the status will vary according to the *lex causae* of the issue which gives rise to the enquiry. So, for example, whether illegitimate children or those legitimated or adopted can succeed on intestacy or can share in a testamentary or trust gift to "children" will depend, respectively, on the *lex successionis* of the intestacy; the law governing the interpretation of the will, and the *lex successionis*; and the law governing the interpretation and effect of the trust.

Legitimacy

Parental marriage

A child born or conceived during a marriage is presumed to be a   **6-89**
legitimate child of the marriage[212] but the marriage must be valid by English conflict law. If the marriage is not valid on that basis its validity by another system of law is for this purpose irrelevant.[213] The two propositions are not, however, mutually exclusive. If the parental marriage is not valid by the English conflict of laws the child's legitimacy cannot be based upon it, but that does not mean that the child is illegitimate.

---

[211] Family Law Reform Act 1969 s.15.
[212] See *Re Bozelli's Settlement* [1902] 1 Ch 751.
[213] *Shaw v. Gould* (1868) LR 3 HL 55.

Child's personal law

6-90   In *Re Bischoffsheim*[214] the mother married the brother of her dead husband in New York. The parties were within the prohibited degrees by English law but not by the law of New York. The couple, domiciled in England at the time of the marriage, had acquired a domicile in New York by the time the son was born. Was the son the legitimate child of his mother? The court held that the test should be whether the child was legitimate by the law of his domicile of origin (his parent's domicile at the time of his birth) and as, on such a test, the child was legitimate, the validity of the parental marriage by the English conflict of laws was irrelevant. If the parents have different domiciles it would seem that the one to go for is not the one to which the enquiry relates, i.e. whether the child can succeed through the mother or the father, but the law of the father's domicile alone.[215]

Putative marriage

6-91   Since 1959[216] English domestic law has recognised the legitimacy of a child born of a void marriage provided the father is domiciled in England and that one of the parties reasonably believed the marriage to be valid, this belief is now rebuttably presumed to exist.[217] This, indirectly, supports the *Bischoffsheim* principle for the recognition of foreign legitimacies, bearing in mind, however, that a foreign law might recognise legitimacy beyond the putative marriage concept.

Status

If the better view is that the issue of legitimacy, or rather the removal of the legal stigma of illegitimacy, is a matter of status referable to the child's domiciliary law at the time of birth, it follows that if, by that law, no distinction is made between legitimate and illegitimate children, and all children are treated equally, then no distinction should be taken by any other legal system with regard to them. In short, they should not be stuffed into another legal category by a different legal system on the basis, for example, that their parents were not married. However, a distinction will still remain in so far as a will or settlement stipulates a particular precondition e.g. that benefits are to go to the children of a

---

[214] [1948] Ch 79, [1947] 2 All ER 830; see also *Hashmi v. Hashmi* [1971] 3 All ER 1253.

[215] *Re Grove* (1888) 40 Ch D 216.

[216] Legitimacy Act 1959, see now Legitimacy Act 1976 s.1 as amended by Family Law Reform Act 1987 s.28.

[217] Legitimacy Act 1976 s.1(4) added by Family Law Reform Act 1987 s.28.

particular marriage; but that is no different from any other precondition e.g. that the beneficiaries live in a particular place or follow a stated trade or profession.

A foreign *lex successionis* which provides for intestate inheritance and which identifies the successors by reference to their legitimate descent raises an incidental question[218] which would appear to be resolved in favour of the succession rather than the status.

Legitimation

Although not introduced into English law until 1926,[219] legitimation of a child, born illegitimate, by the subsequent marriage of his parents was recognised by the English conflict of laws long before that date. But the requirements of the common law, based on canon law, are rather cumbersome. For the subsequent marriage to legitimate the child, the father has to be domiciled, both at the time of the child's birth,[220] and at the time of the marriage,[221] in a country, or countries if he had changed domicile in the meantime, which allow this form of legitimation. Under statute,[222] a child born illegitimate will be legitimated by the subsequent marriage of his parents if the father is domiciled in England at the date of the marriage.[223] The same principle applies to foreign legitimations,[224] obviating the need for the father to be domiciled in a country allowing such legitimations at the time of the child's birth. The statute does not, however, abolish the common law rules[225] and there are certain advantages retained by common law legitimation. Whereas the statute applies the legitimation from the date of the marriage, the common law rules legitimate from birth. Common law legitimation alone covers cases other than subsequent marriage. So, for example, if it is sought to establish that a child was legitimated by his father's formal recognition of him, this can be done only at common law and the double rule applies. The father must have been domiciled, both at the time of the child's birth and at the time of recognition, in a country or countries which allow such legitimation.[226]

6-92

---

[218] See below para 8-17.

[219] Legitimacy Act 1926 s.1.

[220] *Re Wright's Trusts* (1856) 2 K & J 595; *Re Goodman's Trusts* (1881) 17 Ch D 266.

[221] *Re Grove* (1887) 40 ChD 216.

[222] See now Legitimacy Act 1976.

[223] S.2.

[224] S.3.

[225] See *Re Hurll* [1952] Ch 722.

[226] *Re Luck's Settlement Trusts* [1940] Ch 864, [1940] 3 All ER 307.

Declarations on Parentage, Legitimacy and Legitimation

6-93   Any person may seek a declaration that any person was or is the applicant's parent, that he himself is the legitimate child of his parents or that he has, or has not, become a legitimated person.[227] As regards legitimation, the declarations extend to those legitimated or recognised as legitimated, or not, under the common law rules as well as under the statutory ones.[228]

Jurisdiction will be taken by the English court if the applicant is domiciled in England or has been habitually resident here for a period of one year. The court cannot make a declaration that the applicant is illegitimate[229] and the failure to declare that he is legitimate does not operate as a definitive statement of his status.

Adoption

English adoptions

6-94   Adoption is the process whereby the child's links with his natural parents are legally destroyed and legal relations with his adoptive parents established in their place In English law the adopter (or if a couple, one of them) must be domiciled in England[230] and the adoption can be achieved only by court order. Although there is no requirement that the child be connected with England, the involvement of welfare agencies in the adoption process makes it likely that he will be.

6-95   Though the child and his natural parents could be nationals of, domiciled in and habitually resident in a foreign country, there is no issue of choice of law in English adoption procedures; English law applies as *lex fori*, though the foreign law may be relevant in the general review of the circumstances of the case.

6-96   There is a Hague Convention on adoption which is implemented by the Adoption Act 1976,[231] but it is of very limited application.[232] Where one party to the adoption is a national of, or habitually resident in, a Convention State, an application for an adoption order made to another Convention State will be made on the basis of a national or habitual residence connection, and the governing law will be that of the adoptee's nationality.

---

[227] Family Law Act 1986 s.56(1) as amended by Family Law Reform Act 1987 s.22.
[228] S.58(4).
[229] S.58(5)(b).
[230] Adoption Act 1976 (as amended by Children Act 1989) s.15(2)(a).
[231] *ibid* s.17.
[232] U.K. Austria and Switzerland.

Recognition of foreign adoptions

All adoptions made in the British Isles are entitled to automatic   **6–97**
recognition in England.[233] A foreign adoption will be recognised in
England provided that the order has been made by a court and the
adopted person is unmarried and under the age of eighteen. Recognition
can only be refused if the foreign tribunal lacked internal authority to
make the order (there are no jurisdictional prerequisites) or the order is
contrary to public policy.

A foreign adoption can also be recognised at common law, the
required nexus being the domicile of the adopter in the granting country
and, possibly, the presence of the adoptee there.

Declarations on adoption

While there is automatic recognition of adoptions within the British   **6–98**
Isles[234] there is no equivalent for overseas adoptions. The court may
declare that the applicant is, or is not, the adopted child of a particular
person[235] whether the adoption depends on the common law or statutory
rules. Jurisdiction depends on domicile or one year's habitual residence.

---

[233] Adoption Act 1976 s.38(1)(c).

[234] *ibid*.

[235] Family Law Act 1986 s.37.

CHAPTER 7

THE RÔLE OF THE FORUM

1 INTRODUCTION

Although a satisfactory system of conflict law should avoid the need **7-01**
for litigation by enabling people to arrange their affairs in a manner
which will avoid disputes, or, at least, to settle any disputes which do
arise on the basis of clear principles, the rôle of the forum remains central
to the operation of the system. Not only is this true when a dispute has
to be litigated but also when the operation of the conflict system has to
be explored.

So much is true of any branch of the law – that the ultimate test in
any private dispute is what the courts will do about it in the last resort.
But there are additional dimensions in conflict adjudication as the court
has to handle foreign law. A short resumé of the job of the English court
faced with a conflict case will indicate the extent of the task and the
opportunities for forum influence.

At the jurisdictional stage, the task of interpreting the jurisdictional **7-02**
rules has the added dimension that a case with significant foreign contacts
may not present itself conveniently within the domestic categories. So
jurisdictional rules based on the concept of contract or marriage must be
interpreted to accommodate foreign institutions of contract or marriage,
or at least some of them. If the Law Commissions' proposals, or anything
like them, on torts are implemented,[1] English courts will have to develop
a concept of tort which goes beyond the limits of the domestic law not
only for choice of law but for jurisdiction also.

Even when no classification is needed for jurisdictional purposes one **7-03**
has to be made for choice of law. The categorisation of the case is a
prerequisite to choice of law and the initial classification, at least, has to
be made by the *lex fori* though not simply according to its domestic laws.[2]

Despite statutory provisions, particularly with regard to contracts, the **7-04**
recognition of foreign divorces and, perhaps soon for torts, the bulk of
the English conflict of laws remains judge made law, created in the
normal common law tradition in the decision of individual cases. It is not

---

1 See above para 4-122.
2 See below para 8-10.

surprising, then, that the influence of English domestic law pervades the attitude to the adjudication of conflict cases and that the concepts, mores and even some of the technicalities of the domestic law spill over into the conflict field. Furthermore, as conflict problems can arise in the most innocuous seeming litigation, there is no chance of separating conflict cases from the generality of litigation. So the law has been developed by judges who may not have much experience of that type of case.

Where a case has significant connections with a foreign legal system so as to raise a potential choice of law, the basic attitude of English courts is that the foreign connection is a matter of fact to be taken into consideration like any other factual matter which might have a bearing on the outcome of the litigation. English judges do not pretend to an expertise in foreign laws, they cannot be taken to know them so they have to rely on the evidence of experts just as they would if the case turned upon a medical or engineering issue. It is up to the party who seeks to rely on foreign law to plead it and to prove it. The fact that a case has significant foreign contacts, then, does not mean that it will be subject to the rules for the choice of law which English courts apply. The parties may be happy to ignore the foreign element of the case and rest content with a decision which domestic English law provides. There will be some cases, of course, where the facts will immediately alert the court to the presence of a significant foreign connection. But, unless English law takes on board the foreign connection automatically, as for example it does in the recognition of foreign divorces, the presence of the exotic element will not trigger the application of conflict rules unless there is an issue made of it by one of the parties. If foreign law is not pleaded, or is pleaded but not proved, the English forum will apply English law to the determination of the issue. In the latter case they will do this on the basis that the content of the foreign law is the same as English law, but nothing turns on this distinction. The obvious foreign connection might, however, have the effect of qualifying the application of a rule of domestic English law if that was seen to have only local application.

Many of these tasks may be done mechanically without reflection on the nature of the exercise, but sometimes they raise issues which require judgment and involve policy.

2 THE POLICY RÔLE OF THE FORUM

7-05   There can be no doubt that the forum controls the cases which come before it and that the forum must have the power to reject suits, both domestic and foreign, which offend some fundamental principle of its operation. The following two statements show the different emphases which can be placed on this undoubted rôle.

"Whenever the courts of this country are called upon to decide as to the rights and liabilities of the parties to a contract the effect on such contract of the public policy of this country must necessarily be a relevant consideration. Every legal decision of our courts consists of the application of our own law to the facts of the case as ascertained by appropriate evidence. One of these facts may be the state of some foreign law, but it is not the foreign law but our own law to which effect is given ... As has often been said Private International Law is really a branch of municipal law and obviously there can be no branch of municipal law in which the general policy of such law can be properly ignored." *per* Ld. Parker in *Dynamit A G v. Rio Tinto Co.*[3]

"A right of action is property. If a foreign statute gives this right, the mere fact that we do not give a like right is no reason for refusing to help the plaintiff in getting what belongs to him. We are not so provincial as to say that every solution of a problem is wrong because we deal with it otherwise at home ... The courts are not free to refuse to enforce a   foreign right at the pleasure of the judges, to suit the individual notion of expediency or fairness. They do not close their doors unless help would violate some fundamental principle of justice, some prevalent conception of good morals, some deep rooted tradition of the common - weal" *per* Cardozo J in *Louks v. Standard Oil Co. of New York.*[4]

Even a country which takes the conflict of laws seriously and is prepared to recognise foreign laws and foreign institutions to the fullest extent must, nevertheless, retain its own fundamental principles and not descend to moral relativism. At the same time it must take care not to make a fortress out of the moral underpinnings of its own domestic rules. The balance is neither easy to find nor maintain. What is clear however is that the English court should not assume that a difference, between the result which would be produced by the application of the foreign law and the result which English domestic law would provide, illustrates a conflict of fundamental principle in which the English court should be an interested combatant.

A distinction can be drawn between those cases, otherwise not substantially connected with England, which simply require the adjudication and enforcement processes of English law, those which, while governed by a foreign *lex causae* have a significant factual connection with this country, and those where the *lex causae* is English.

---

3   [1918] A.C.260 at 292.
4   (1918) 224 NY 99 at 111.

7-06   When the case has no factual connection with England, English
public policy should be applied to prevent the outcome dictated by the
foreign *lex causae*, or to reject the application of a rule of foreign law, only
where to do otherwise would be an affront to fundamental principles of
English law or to its basic morality. So one would not expect an English
court to uphold a foreign contract of prostitution even if it was to be
performed wholly abroad, or to recognise a foreign law prohibiting
marriage between people of different races, creeds or nationalities.
Beyond such easy cases, however, an analysis needs to be made of the
objective of the English rule or principle which is in issue. To take an
example, English law has set the age of marriage at sixteen but it is clear
that English law will recognise foreign marriages of persons below that
age – but how far below? At some stage the point will be reached when
an English court would say that the apparent consent to marriage was not
effective, or that the very youth of the party meant that the marriage
could not be accepted as the relationship was exploitive or that the moral,
physical, or other risks to the child require the non recognition of the
marriage. Similarly, an English court might well say that the duress or
undue influence surrounding the entry into the contract made it
unenforceable even though valid by the applicable law.

Examples of public policy interventions are: the non enforcement of a
contract, valid under French law, whereby a wife promised to repay
money misappropriated by her husband if criminal proceedings were not
taken against him,[5] the non enforcement of a contract obtained by duress
or undue influence[6] and the refusal to enforce a foreign judgment based
on such a contract;[7] a contract of prostitution valid by a foreign law[8] or a
contract gained by the improper use of an intermediary.[9]

7-07   For the second category of cases – those which are governed by a
foreign law but which have a significant connection with England –
lower order policy issues need to be considered. Issues which cannot be
said to be moral fundamentals but which domestic law sees as central to
its operation may come into play. Here one might instance rules against
restraint of trade[10] or those against contingent fee arrangements to finance
litigation.[11] In such cases, whatever the governing law, English law would
have a legitimate say to the extent that the contract was to be performed
in England.

---

5   *Kaufman v. Gerson* [1904] 1 KB 591; cf *Addison v. Brown* [1954] 2 All ER 213 where the
ouster of the jurisdiction of a foreign court was recognised.

6   *Kaufman v. Gerson* [1904] 1 KB 591.

7   *Israel Discount Bank of New York v. Hadjipateras* [1984] 1 WLR 137.

8   See *Robinson v. Bland* (1760) 2 Burr 1077.

9   *Lemenda Trading Co. Ltd. v. African Middle East Petroleum Co. Ltd.* [1988] 1 All ER 513.

10   See *Rousillon v. Rousillon* (1880) 14 Ch D 351.

11   See *Grell v. Levy* (1864) 6 CBNS 73.

There are some provisions of English law which apply irrespective of the *lex causae* and the English court will apply these without any analysis of the policy behind them e.g. where a statute expressly applies to a connection with England irrespective of the applicable law.[12]

The third category – where the case is governed by England law as *lex causae* – extends to the whole range of possible connections. Some cases will be seen as domestic ones for all intents and purposes so that the whole range of domestic policy can properly be applied to them. Others, contracts are an obvious example, may have no factual connections with England at all, English law being applicable solely through the parties' choice. The application of English public policy, like the application of technical rules of English law, should depend on an analysis which takes account both of the importance of the policy or rule and the proper ambit of its operation internationally.   **7-08**

We have already seen some public policy reservations incorporated into the rules for the recognition of foreign judgments,[13] in the mandatory rule of the forum and the *"ordre public"* provisions of the Rome Contracts Convention[14] and in the scheme for the recognition of foreign divorces, annulments and legal separations.[15] In addition to these there are some general categories of exclusion which can be examined briefly here.   **7-09**

Foreign Penal, Revenue and other Public Laws

Although the conflict of laws is concerned with private litigation, there are situations in which the public laws of foreign states can be raised in the proceedings. This may be by way of plea or defence by private litigants or more directly at the suit of the foreign state itself to enforce, or to obtain redress for the breach of, a public law right in a civil action.   **7-10**

It is clear that the English courts will neither act as a police agency for the foreign law nor act as a foreign state's tax gatherer. They "do not sit to collect taxes for another country or to inflict punishment for it."[16] While this prohibition can be seen as an aspect of public policy it can also be seen as the recognition of the territorial limitation of law and the fact that the writ of a foreign sovereign does not run in England.

---

[12]   E.g. Employment Protection (Consolidation) Act 1978 ss.141(2), 158(3); Unfair Contract Terms Act 1977 s.27. See also *Boissevain v. Weil* [1950] AC 327, [1950] 1 All ER 728; *The Hollandia* [1983] 1 AC 565, [1982] 3 All ER 1141.

[13]   See above paras 3-75, 3-86.

[14]   See above paras 4-68, 4-80.

[15]   See above para 6-76.

[16]   *Regazzoni v. K.C. Sethia (1944) Ltd.* [1965] 2 QB 490 at 515, [1956] 2 All ER 487 at 490.

Foreign penal laws

7-11   The English court will not allow the recovery, at the suit of a foreign state, of a penalty imposed by a criminal court of that state or for an ancillary matter like a forfeited bail bond.[17] The prohibition extends to any penalty imposed by the foreign law in favour of the foreign state but not laws, even public laws, which benefit individuals.[18] So, for example, a penalty clause in a contract valid by its applicable law would not be regarded as penal *per se* nor would the prohibition prevent the enforcement in England of a foreign award of exemplary damages,[19] though the multiple damage awards under U.S. anti-trust laws are subject to a specific statutory exclusion.[20] To fall within the prohibition the penalty does not have to be pecuniary, so a prohibition against the remarriage of a divorced person has been held to be within it,[21] though there were better reasons for the decision based on the nature of divorce.

Foreign revenue laws

7-12   The revenue laws of foreign States will not be enforced in English proceedings. This old rule[22] is supported by more modern instances. So, for example, in *Government of India v. Taylor*[23] the Indian Commissioner for Income Tax was not allowed to prove in the winding up of an English registered company for the recovery of the tax due on its trading in India. The prohibition extends both to direct and indirect[24] attempts to enforce foreign revenue laws and, by statute, to the enforcement of foreign tax judgments.[25] It does not prevent the recognition of such laws. So a scheme for their evasion will not be upheld[26] and foreign exchange control regulations have been respected.[27] It is not easy to explain the prohibition, at least when the case before the English court is a civil action for the recovery of a tax debt as there is nothing penal or contrary to public policy *per se* and, one would have thought, good policy reasons for not assisting foreign tax fugitives.

---

17   *United States of America v. Inkley* [1989] QB 255, [1988] 3 All ER 144.
18   See *Huntington v. Attrill* [1893] AC 150.
19   *SA Consortium General Textiles v. Sun and Sound Agencies Ltd.* [1978] QB 279.
20   Protection of Trading Interests Act 1980 s.5.
21   *Scott v. AG* (1886) 11 PD 128.
22   *Holman v. Johnson* (1775) 1 Cowp 341.
23   [1955] AC 491, [1955] 1 All ER 292.
24   See *Rossano v. Manufacturers' Life Insurance Co. Ltd.* [1963] 2 QB 352, [1962] 2 All ER 214.
25   Foreign Judgments (Reciprocal Enforcement) Act 1933 s.1(2)(b).
26   See *Re Emery's Investment Trusts* [1959] Ch 410, [1959] 1 All ER 577.
27   *Sharif v. Azad* [1967] 1 QB 605, [1966] 3 All ER 785.

Other public laws

Even if foreign legislation cannot be characterised as a penal or revenue   **7-13**
law in the senses just outlined, it will not be enforced in England if it has a
public quality and is not confined to, though it impinges on, private rights.
Examples of such public laws are price control legislation, import and
export controls, exchange controls and anti-trust laws even if they give rise
to private actions. As with penal and revenue laws, their non-enforcement
in England does not mean that their existence will not be recognised, so a
contract involving their breach will not be enforced.[28] While the scope of
this exception is unclear, it was used by the Australian courts to refuse
injunctive relief at the suit of the U.K. in the "*Spycatcher*" case.[29]

Foreign expropriation laws

Foreign expropriation laws are often included within the category of   **7-14**
public policy exclusions and they may well fall within the "penal" and
"other public laws" groupings. They all, however, represent instances of
the territorial operation of the *lex situs* and will be recognised, or not, in
England on that basis.[30] Neither a good motive for the expropriation – as
where the Dutch government in exile sought to seize property in
England to help the war effort[31] – nor an evil one – Nazi confiscation of
Jewish property in Austria[32] – affects the basic principle that the *lex situs*
governs, though discriminatory acts directed against individuals or groups
should do so.

3 SUBSTANCE AND PROCEDURE

When an English court, applying its conflict rules, has arrived at a   **7-15**
foreign law and found it potentially applicable and not objectionable on
policy grounds, the task of classification is not necessarily complete. Only
rules of the foreign law which are substantive will be taken into account,
those which are procedural will be disregarded as it is well established that
the *lex fori* exclusively governs procedure. It is obvious that too broad a
view of procedure, easier to take in the common law tradition than in
others perhaps, could subvert the whole conflicts enterprise by
exaggerating the forum rôle, and English courts need to be wary of this.

---

[28] See *United City Merchants v. Royal Bank of Canada* [1983] AC 168, [1982] 2 All ER 720.

[29] *A-G (U.K.) v. Heinemann Publishers Australia Pty Ltd.* (1988) 165 CLR 30.

[30] See above paras 5-15, 5-26, 5-44.

[31] See *Bank voor Handel v. Slatford* [1953] 1 QB 248, [1951] 2 All ER 779.

[32] *Frankfurther v. Exner Ltd.* [1947] Ch 629, but see *Oppenheimer v. Cattermole* [1976] AC 249 at
278, [1975] 1 All ER 538 at 567.

In the vast majority of cases the distinction between substance and procedure will be obvious. The order of process, the manner of the examination of witnesses, the proceedings generally are clearly matters of procedure, whereas rules which directly impose liability or provide a defence on the merits of the case, are clearly substantive. As always, the problems arise with those rules which are in the middle, limitation rules for example which can be viewed either as extinguishing the right or as barring the remedy,[33] or with provisions which appear to be applicable to all cases. In *Leroux v. Brown*[34] a contract made in France and wholly to be performed there and which was obviously governed by French law, fell foul of the Statute of Frauds 1677. The Statute required that contracts which were not to be performed within one year had to be in or evidenced by writing, otherwise, while they remained valid, they were unenforceable. On an action to enforce the contract Maule J. considered himself bound by the plain words of the statute – "no action shall lie". This was a clear prohibition on allowing the action to continue in England irrespective of the contract's total validity by French law. It is worth noting that had the plaintiff obtained a judgment from a French court there was no basis for refusing to enforce that judgment in England.

If the Statute of Frauds established a procedural rule then, clearly, Maule J. was right, but if it was a substantive rule there was no case for its application to defeat the plaintiff's claim, for the contract was neither made in nor to be performed in England. The decision has been much criticised and it does seem remarkably wooden. However, if the purpose of the statute was to avoid the occasion of fraud by making litigation depend on written evidence of the agreement (or an act of part performance) then it was clearly applicable to all litigation including foreign contracts. Such a policy towards the discouragement of fraud, crude, harsh and counter-productive as it was, is a policy matter which is not confined to domestic contracts but would extend to all cases even those involving foreign contracts, as constituting a procedural bar to action. It should not be supposed that procedural rules cannot embody policy considerations just like substantive rules. The decision that such a rule is procedural is defensible. In contrast, the provision under English law that collective labour agreements should be conclusively presumed not to be legally enforceable, unless the agreement clearly states that it is,[35] was correctly classified as a rule of English substantive law not applicable to contracts governed by a foreign *lex causae*.[36]

---

[33] Now declared to be substantive – Foreign Limitation Periods Act 1984.

[34] (1852) 12 CB 801.

[35] Trade Union and Labour Relations Act 1974 s.18 – it is proposed that this rule should be reversed.

[36] *Monterosso Shipping Co. Ltd. v. International Transport Workers' Federation* [1982] 3 All ER 841.

Remedies

As a judgment given in any conflict case is a judgment of the forum, it   **7-16**
follows that only those remedies which the forum has on offer are available
to the successful litigant. Just as he cannot expect, say, a mode of trial
different from that which is used by the forum, so he cannot claim an
exotic remedy. More than that, the remedy he obtains is that which is
appropriate for his case in the view of the forum even if the remedy
available in a court of the *lex causae* is known to English law. So, a
successful litigant in contract will not get an order for specific performance,
though a court of the *lex causae* would give him one, if that remedy is not
available for his case under English law. By the same token, however, he
could obtain an order for specific performance from an English court even
though the *lex causae* would provide him with damages only.

Equitable remedies are, of course, discretionary. So, even if specific
performance or injunctive relief was, in general terms, available both by
the *lex fori* and by the *lex causae*, it would be for the forum to apply its
own principles and to refuse the relief, say, on the basis of the plaintiff's
dirty hands, even if, by the *lex causae*, his hands were clean or not grubby
enough to be taken into account.

As we have seen,[37] matrimonial orders are entirely within the control
of the forum, even when made on the basis of a foreign *lex causae*, and the
petitioner cannot claim for their adaptation on the basis of what a court of
the *lex causae* might do.

Damages

Most commonly the litigant in a conflict case will be seeking damages   **7-17**
for the breach of an obligation owed to him under the *lex causae*. The
obligation, its breach and the consequent losses complained of, will have
to be established by the *lex causae* and that law's rules of remoteness of
damage will determine whether losses are legally attributable to the
breach. But there is a double overlap here; the heads of damage which
can be recovered can be seen either as issues of remoteness of damage,
governed by the *lex causae*, or as part of the quantification of damages –
valuing the recoverable losses – which is undoubtedly a matter for the *lex
fori*. We saw[38] that in *Chaplin v. Boys* one of the major problems was the
classification of Maltese law's refusal to allow recovery of damages for
pain and suffering in personal injury litigation. Did it mean that the
plaintiff had no right to compensation for that loss or merely that Maltese
law would leave it out when calculating the value of the claim?

---

37   See above para 6–80.
38   See above para 4–113.

Similar questions can be asked about economic losses or mental anguish in tort cases, or distress at breaches of contract, or the status of a foreign law's ceiling on personal injury claims. It would appear that these are all matters for the *lex causae*.

Quantification – the calculation of the loss in money terms – is a matter for the *lex fori*. In tort actions, at least in those actions where unliquidated damages are claimed, the damages awarded will be those which would apply in a purely domestic case and one can look up the going rate for personal injuries of a similar type and start from there. It would clearly be unacceptable to value an individual's pain and suffering by reference to the going rate in the courts of the *lex causae* even if the consequence of not doing so is the encouragement of forum shopping.[39]

7-18   Where a liquidated loss was sustained in a foreign currency, English courts used to make a conversion into sterling as at the time of loss, with the consequence that the weakening of sterling in exchange terms reduced the plaintiff's actual recovery at the time of judgment. In *Maliangos v. George Frank (Textiles) Ltd*[40] the plaintiff would have lost getting on for half his award in real terms had the old rule prevailed. The House of Lords decided that judgments could be given in foreign currencies. If the judgment debtor pays in the foreign currency that will suffice, but if the judgment has to be enforced against him, a conversion to sterling will still be necessary. That conversion will be made according to the exchange rate at the time of judgment not at the time of loss.

---

[39] See below paras 8–25.
[40] [1976] AC 443, [1975] 3 All ER 801.

CHAPTER 8

FURTHER CONSIDERATIONS

This chapter deals in a little further detail with some matters which have been raised earlier, which have a bearing on the workings of the English conflict system.

1 THE MEANING OF FOREIGN LAW - *RENVOI*

It is necessary to determine what exactly the meaning and scope of any reference to foreign law is to be. There are two situations.

Firstly, there are cases where all the significant connections are with the same foreign legal system, so that a court of that system would properly regard the case as a domestic one.

Secondly, a case may be truly international so that it might be seen as involving the conflict of laws in any court in which litigation was brought.

In the first situation there can be no objection to the English forum applying the domestic law of the system with which the case is wholly connected. Indeed, in cases like this, the English court may feel that it should refuse jurisdiction as *forum non conveniens*.[1] Where the defendant is content to allow proceedings to continue in England, or there are good reasons for English litigation e.g. that after the issue arose the defendant became domiciled in England, then the application of the foreign law is relatively straightforward and there is a chance that the same law will be applied in England as would have been applied in the "home" country. There are, however, other factors beside the choice of law which stand in the way of decisional uniformity.[2]

Cases which are truly international and which would be seen as conflict cases in any forum, present some difficulties. If the case has no obvious single legal "home" then its governing law must be a matter of contention. As any conflicts system is part of a domestic legal system, it follows that different national courts might apply different choice of law rules to the same issue. The Rome Convention[3] is an attempt to

8-01

8-02

8-03

---

1 See above para 3-08.
2 See below para 8-26.
3 See above para 4-07.

standardise the approaches of the E.C. States to contracts. In non-standardised areas individual legal systems will maintain their own particular approaches.

Suppose an English forum is faced with a question about the capacity to marry of a French national who is domiciled in Italy. It would refer to the Italian domiciliary law.[4] An Italian court, dealing with the same case, would refer to the French national law. If Italian law and French law happen to differ on the particular capacity in dispute, the results would be different. Should it just be accepted as a fact of legal life that the result of a case will depend on the place of litigation and leave lawyers to take it on board when advising their clients - just an international dimension to a fact already known? Should it be left to international efforts to standardise the choice of law rules?[5] Should it be a matter for the forum to consider in its approach to the particular case?

8-04   What are the possibilities open to a court embarrassed by the realisation that a foreign forum would decide the same case differently; more than that, that the courts of the legal system which the English court has selected as the governing law for the case would take such a different view of the matter?

Change of Choice of Law Rule

8-05   If the choice of law rules is judge-made the court may be able to change it. If a choice of law rule regularly produces unsatisfactory results and there is an obvious and preferable alternative there is no reason not to go to it. In the example of capacity to marry, however, the case for the application of the personal law is overwhelming, and, whatever the defects of the current English law of domicile, there is no case for replacing it with nationality.

Changes in choice of law-rules, unless the result of international agreement, are unlikely to advance decisional consistency unless the former rules were out of step with common practice elsewhere. In the formation of choice of law rules a consideration of how other systems tackle the job can provide useful information. But the search must always be for the system of law which most effectively encapsulates the legal relationship which is in question. That, in turn, depends on the view that the forum takes of the nature of the relationship; a view which depends on the legal culture of the forum.

---

4   See above para 6-29.

5   There is a Hague Convention on Celebration and Recognition of the Validity of Marriages (1978) but it has gained little acceptance.

Change of Connection

English law has persisted with the concept of domicile despite the many criticisms of its arcane legalism and over-rigidity. Nationality as a possible alternative was abandoned in the nineteenth century and there is even less of a case for it now.[6] Habitual residence presents a strong case to displace domicile, and perhaps, in time it will, either directly or by the addition of greater flexibility to the traditional view of domicile. A decision to shift from domicile to habitual residence as the determinant of the personal law would not help in our marriage example. Unless the country of habitual residence happened to be France, or a country which happened to have the same legal rules as French law there would still be a discrepancy between the English and Italian courts' solution of the problem. Such a coincidence would be purely fortuitous and not determined by the change in connecting factor - the possibility of domicile and nationality coinciding is just as great.

8-06

Renvoi

Renvoi is an attempt to solve the problem of the scope and application of a foreign *lex causae* by looking not only to the domestic rules of the chosen system but to its conflict rules as well. There are two varieties of the approach. "Single", "simple" or "Continental" *renvoi*, involves a reference to the conflict rules of the chosen system which results in either transmission to another legal system or remission back to the forum's law. "Double", "total" or "English" *renvoi*, sometimes called the "foreign court theory" involves a reference not only to the conflict rules of the chosen system but to its *renvoi* rules as well i.e. to the attitude it takes to a reference back to itself under a single renvoi system. In the foreign court theory the English court seeks to achieve the actual result which a court of the *lex causae* would produce.

8-07

The conflict rules of the *lex causae* may:-

a)   refer the issue to its own law. So if, in our marriage example, the party was an Italian national, English law would refer the question to the law of the domicile, Italy. An Italian court seized of the same case would refer to the Italian national law. Here all roads lead to Rome so there is no doubt that the domestic law of the *lex causae* will be applied. But this is so purely happenstantially, and it cannot be supposed, though it will often be the case, that an individual is domiciled in the country which is also the State of nationality.

---

6   See Law Com No 168 (1987).

b) refer the issue to a third system. This was the case in the original example of the Italian domiciled French national where Italian conflict law would refer to the lex patriae – French law. This is an example of transmission. Now an English court could go along with this if it wished,[7] though the consequences of doing so, while it would produce consistency between the decision of the English court and the Italian court in this case, would not produce any overall consistency, as we would just be substituting one system of conflict law for another. The criticism, that if English law wants to use nationality it should do so itself and not through the medium of Italian law, is pertinent. While the practical objections have great force, there is a logical objection which has at least equal weight – why stop there? If the process itself has any logical basis, that logic cannot artificially terminate the enquiry at the first reference. Why not see what the French conflict rules have to say about the question of capacity to marry? Suppose French conflict law would look to the law of the habitual residence and suppose that law to be German. Should we then look to German conflict law and see what a German court would do if it had been seized of the case?

Given both different choice of law rules and different connecting factors, and also different interpretations of common connecting factors, it would be possible to construct a scenario where references went on and on with no logical stopping place, or sooner or later became caught up in a reciprocal or circular motion which would have no end beyond the patience of the forum.

c) refer the issue to the legal system which happens to be the forum. This is known as remission. So, again amending our example, if the party is a British national living in England but domiciled in Italy, Italian conflict law would refer the matter to English law. In such a case the English court could:

i) accept the reference and apply English law rather than Italian law; that is accept the *renvoi*. The effect of this would be that English law would be applying, indirectly, the law of the nationality to a question which its own rules refer to the domicile.[8] The simple answer to this is that if English law wants to use nationality in place of domicile it should do so directly and cut out the middle man.

---

[7] See *R. v. Brentwood Superintendent Registrar of Marriages Ex parte Arias* [1968] 2 QB 956, [1968] 3 All ER 279.
[8] *ibid.*

ii) reject the reference back, that is reject the *renvoi,* and stay with its initial identification of the *lex causae.* If it is going to do this it might as well not have engaged in an examination of Italian conflicts rules in the first place. There is no point in going to Birmingham by way of Beachy Head, but the court made this detour in *Re Annesley.*[9]

iii) follow what an Italian court would do if its reference to English law was met by a reference back to Italian law. This is the doctrine of English, double, or total *renvoi* - the foreign court theory - nearly as many names as there are instances of its application. Such an approach involves a three-stage process:

- The English court determines the *lex causae* in the usual way. In the example of the Englishman domiciled in Italy, the English court, applying the dual domicile test, would refer his marital capacity to Italian law, his *lex domicilii.*

- The English court then applies the conflict rules of the *lex causae.* In the example it would find that an Italian court dealing with the matter would refer to English law as *lex patriae.*

- As English conflict law refers to Italian law, we are back where we started. To avoid any further toing and froing the English court looks to Italian law to see whether an Italian court would accept or reject the remission. If an Italian court would accept the reference back the English court would apply Italian domestic law to the question of marital capacity. If, as is the case, an Italian court would not accept the remission, the English court would apply English domestic law to the substantive issue.

Despite palpable disadvantages, there is something to be said for *renvoi*   **8-08** in limited circumstances. Firstly, like other devices which can be resorted to in an attempt to produce a benevolent result, *renvoi* can be used to extricate the court from a result which the normal rules dictate. For example, it has been used to render formally valid testamentary dispositions which otherwise would have been void[10] and to recognise the legitimation of a child which would not otherwise have been possible.[11] But the defence of an anomaly on the basis that it sometimes

---

[9] [1926] 2 Ch 692.
[10] See *Collier v. Rivaz* (1841) 2 Curt 855.
[11] See *Re Askew* [1930] 2 Ch 259.

does good is not very convincing and counter examples can equally be found in the refusal of permission to marry in England[12] or the essential invalidity of a will.[13]

Secondly, *renvoi* in the English sense, can produce uniformity of result, in terms of the governing law at least, in cases where the English choice rules put a premium on this i.e. where the *lex situs* is applied on the basis of effectiveness. In such cases not to conform the decision to that which a court of the situs would produce defeats the purpose of the original reference. Suppose the English court is faced with a case involving intestate succession and some of the immovable estate is situated in Italy. If the reference to Italian law as *lex situs* is confined to the domestic law of Italy, the result will be that the deceased's immovables will be distributed as would those of his Italian neighbours. But such a course of succession would not be ordered by an Italian court, as Italian conflict law would refer the matter to the deceased's *lex patriae*. If the deceased would be regarded as having British nationality, and would be linked with English law by an Italian court, then an Italian court would refer to English law and find that English conflict law would refer the matter back to Italian law. Italian law would not accept the reference back so an English court, adopting total *renvoi,* would emulate that approach, apply English law and, thereby, achieve a legally consistent result. It needs to be remembered, however, that *renvoi* neither alters the original classification nor alters the distinction between substance and procedure.

Against this, however, it must be said that the foreign court theory can be applied only by one system, if the *lex causae* were also to apply it, there would be no way out of the revolving door.

Two arguments against *renvoi* which are often put but which have little weight should perhaps be mentioned. There certainly may be difficulties in discovering what the attitude of the courts of the *lex causae* to *renvoi* actually is. Wynn-Parry J. was faced by this dilemma in *Re Duke of Wellington*[14] but there is nothing more to this than any other case where there is difficulty in ascertaining foreign law and the argument can be directed with equal force at the whole conflict enterprise. The second is that it can produce silly results. In *Re O' Keefe*[15] on an issue of intestate succession to movables, *renvoi* took the English court, via the reference to the Italian *lex domicilii*, to the law of the south of Ireland with which the deceased had no connection and which had no separate existence for

---

[12] See *R. v. Brentwood Superintendant Registrar of Marriages Ex p. Arias* [1968] 2 QB 956, [1968] 3 All ER 279.

[13] *Re Annesley* [1926] 2 Ch 692 but the decision would have been the same without *renvoi.*

[14] [1947] Ch 506.

[15] [1940] Ch 124.

most of her life. But this is a compelling argument against the use of nationality as a connecting factor not against *renvoi* as such.

It has also been suggested that *renvoi* can defeat the expectations of the parties, so it can. But there is no more reason to suppose that a British national domiciled in Italy, who dies intestate, decided against making a will because he was happy with the domestic Italian intestacy rules than that he believed that his intestacy would be governed by his national law.

When is *Renvoi* Used?

Renvoi has been used in cases concerning the formal validity of wills,[16] a matter now covered by legislation which confines the enquiry to the internal law;[17] and to legitimate an adulterine child which would not have been possible under English law at the time.[18] More significantly, it has been used in cases of both testate[19] and intestate[20] succession.

8-09

References to the *lex situs* concerning succession to immovables have been taken to include *renvoi* on several occasions,[21] and there is a case for applying *renvoi* in all cases involving the *lex situs* including title to movables.[22] It has been suggested that the doctrine might apply to the formal validity of marriage[23] and, indeed, to essential validity also.[24] It has never been applied by English courts in torts or contracts and there is no good reason why it should be. In the case of contracts *renvoi* is now excluded by the Rome Convention.[25]

2 CLASSIFICATION

All legal systems work on the basis of categories in their common need to structure human relations into legally manageable units. But this common need is not mirrored in common categories or, if the categories are common, their contents are not.

8-10

---

[16] *Collier v. Rivaz* (1841) 2 Curt 855; *Re Fuld's Estate (No 3)* [1968] P 675, [1965] 3 All ER 776.

[17] Wills Act 1963 s.6(1) and 2(1)(b).

[18] *Re Askew* [1930] 2 Ch 259.

[19] *Re Annesley* [1926] 2 Ch 692.

[20] *Re O'Keefe* [1940] Ch 124.

[21] *Re Ross* [1930] 1 Ch 377; *Re Duke of Wellington* [1947] Ch 506.

[22] Suggested in *Winkworth v. Christie Manson & Woods* [1980] Ch 496, [1980] 1 All ER 1121.

[23] In *Taczanowska v. Taczanowski* [1957] P 301, [1956] 3 All ER 457.

[24] Law Com Working Paper No 89 but not in Report No 165 (1987); *R. v Brentwood Superintendant Registrar of Marriages Ex p. Arias* [1968] 2 QB 956, [1968] 3 All ER 279.

[25] Article 15.

8-11   English conflict law works on broad conceptual categories based on
the domestic law. In order to start the choice of law process, the case has
to be put into one of the legal categories upon which the system operates.
Often this will be done without consideration of the nature of the
exercise, as the issue will obviously be one of a contract, or tort, the
formal validity of a marriage or intestate succession to movables or some
other established category into which, and only into which, it can
possibly be fitted. But just as the development of the domestic law has
been advanced by the presentation of common relationships in
uncommon legal forms, so the conflict of laws can be advanced by the
ingenuity of the presentation of the case.

The mechanical approach which English law seeks to adopt –
category – choice of law rule – connection – legal system e.g. succession
to movables – personal law – domicile – *lex domicilii* – is not the only way
to operate a conflict system. Apart from a rule-selecting alternative to the
jurisdiction-selecting approach, the operational categories can be general
or specific. For marriage validity, for example, English law has two
classifications, formal validity which is governed by the *lex loci celebrationis*
and everything else which is governed by the personal law. In tort cases
there has been an insistence on a single category for all cases despite the
heterogeneity of the subject matter. It would be equally possible to have a
larger number of narrower categories, say, for non-age or prohibited
degrees or for libel or negligence.

Given for the moment the standard categories used by English law, it
will be apparent that some cases do not fit easily into any single one of
them, either because they can be accommodated in more than one, or
because they don't fit into any. Examples of the first type are ones which
would give trouble in domestic law if anything turned upon the matter
e.g. the relationship between employer and employee (contract or tort),
bailment (ditto), matrimonial property (marriage or property), sale of
goods (contract or property). Examples of the second type include the
duty under Greek law for a father to provide a dowry for his daughter,[26]
and the French status of prodigality.[27]

8-12   A classic problem of characterisation came before the Appeal Court in
Algiers in *Anton v. Bartola*.[28] The husband and wife were domiciled in
Malta at the time of their marriage. Subsequently they settled in France
and the husband bought land there. On his death the wife claimed a life
interest in the French land. French and Maltese law had the same choice
of law rules – succession to immovables was governed by the *lex situs*,

---

[26] *Phrantes v. Argenti* [1960] 2 QB 19, [1960] 1 All ER 778.

[27] See *Worms v. de Valdor* (1880) 49 LJ Ch 261; *Re Selot's Trusts* [1902] Ch 488.

[28] (1891) Clunet 1171.

while matrimonial property rights were matters for the *lex domicilii* at the time of marriage. However, French law classified the issue as one of succession whereas Maltese law saw it as matrimonial property. In the event the court applied Maltese law.[29]

While such cases show the importance of classification to the end result, and demonstrate how manipulation of the classification process can orient the decision, they do not demonstrate how the process of classification should be conducted.

The Initial Classification

The general practice is certainly that the initial classification is made by the *lex fori* on the basis of its own categories. This does not mean that the concepts of the domestic law should be applied uncritically, for the exercise is about choice of law and that presupposes that the case has international connections. So, for example, the concept of marriage extends to polygamy; contract to a relationship which, by reason of lack of consideration, would not be a contract under domestic law,[30] and property interests are initially classified into movables and immovables.[31] But this degree of extroversion neither ensures consistent classification among legal systems nor that a foreign contact is given the weighting which its legal context justifies. An obvious example is *Ogden v. Ogden*,[32] where the English court classified parental consent to marry as a formal requirement; whereas French law, which imposed the requirement, clearly regarded it as a matter of capacity. A similar situation, though not one which evokes the same concern, is the classification of the Maltese requirement that marriages take place according to the rites of the Roman Catholic church, a formal matter by English law, an essential one by the law of Malta.[33]

8-13

Can this mismatch be avoided? Suggestions that the classifications be made by the *lex causae* rather than by the *lex fori* present the obvious difficulty that the *lex causae* is only identified once the forum has applied its rules for the choice of law. As conflict problems are approached by English courts in a jurisdiction-selecting way, the broad categories employed for the initial classification preclude the narrowing adjustment which a more refined process requires. Nor is it practical to suggest that the court explores all the connected laws to see how they regard the issue in dispute,

8-14

---

29 See also *de Nicols v. Curlier* [1900] AC 21 above para 4-85.

30 *Re Bonacina* [1912] 2 Ch 314.

31 *Re Hoyles* [1911] 1 Ch 179.

32 [1900] P 46 see above para 6-48.

33 See *Chapelle v. Chapelle* [1950] P 134, [1950] 1 All ER 236; *Formosa v. Formosa* [1963] P 259, [1962] 3 All ER 419; *Lepre v. Lepre* [1965] P 52, [1963] 2 All ER 49, and above para 6-52.

because what the court explores is what the litigants present and the time and expense involved in canvassing the possibilities is not attractive to them. On the other hand, if the issue in dispute can be sufficiently narrowed, as it can in cases like *Ogden*, the conflict presents itself in a simple way. If the petitioner's sole contention is that the marriage is invalid because the requirements of French law have not been followed, then the court can, without departing from its categories of form and capacity, examine the French law in its context. If that examination leads to the conclusion that the requirement of parental consent is a formal matter by French law, the court can simply ignore French law and look to the *lex loci celebrationis*. If, however, it is satisfied that, by French law, a matter of capacity is involved, it can then decide whether to accept it or not on the basis of its ordinary rule on capacity i.e. by reference to the effect of the defect by the law which imposes it. Even if French law would render the marriage invalid, English public policy would still vet the result. If, for example, English public policy regards the restriction as an unacceptable limitation of individual freedom, English law could refuse to recognise it. Public policy would certainly refuse recognition to the Maltese religious incapacity in the Maltese marriage cases.

Not so easy are the cases where the connected foreign law would view the case as falling within a different legal category altogether – one for which the forum has a different choice of law rule. Examples of this might be where one system viewed the issue as contractual while the other saw it as tortious, or one as succession and the other as matrimonial property.

8-15   Rabel's[34] solution was to suggest that courts, in making the initial classification, should have regard to the findings of analytical jurisprudence and comparative law, but such a search for universals is likely to be fruitless in the very hour of need. For, while it is possible to establish broad categories, like marriage or contract, they come shorn of all the details which make the operation of a legal system possible. They certainly cannot answer questions such as whether the claim of a worker injured in the course of his employment is a contractual or tortious matter, or whether the power of parents to forbid the marriage of a minor child should be taken seriously or not.

Falconbridge[35] suggested that, while the initial classification must be made by the *lex fori*, the foreign rule which the process discloses must be viewed in the light of its legal context. This makes sense, but it cannot be used in the most difficult cases where the foreign law would start from an entirely different classification and, therefore, arrive at an entirely different governing law.

---

[34] *The Conflict of Laws: A Comparative Study* (1964).

[35] *Selected Essays on the Conflict of Laws* (1954).

It would appear that the best which can be done here is for the forum   **8-16**
to apply its basic categories with the maximum of flexibility

Statutes may make provision for classification. The Wills Act 1963
provides[36] that certain requirements imposed on testators of a particular
class, or qualities which a witness to a will must possess, are to be treated
as formal, whatever the view of the legal system which imposes them.

For the classification of rules as substantive or procedural see the
earlier discussion.[37]

3   THE INCIDENTAL QUESTION AND DÉPEÇAGE

Just as a conflict issue can crop up in what appears to be a purely   **8-17**
domestic case, so an incidental question can arise in any form of litigation.
In a purely domestic case, of course, the incidental question will be subject
to the same law as the main issue so, for example, in a wrongful death case
we may have a claim for damages for bereavement[38] from a "wife" and we
may have to ask questions, some easy, some not so, about what that means.
Does the right to claim extend to a divorced wife, and, if not, whether a
decree nisi or only a decree absolute will do; a wife living apart from her
husband, and whether or not under the terms of a judicial separation;
whether a wife of a void but putative marriage has a claim; whether
cohabitees can be treated as husband and wife for this purpose and whether
the several wives of a valid polygamous marriage are excluded, can claim
jointly and share the fixed sum, or can claim separately. These are all issues
which are incidental to the main claim which is the defendant's liability for
the death. Of course each of these issues is capable of arising as the sole
question if the defendant's negligence is admitted, no issue of contribution
arises, and all the other aspects of damage assessment are agreed. Some of
these matters, like the validity of a marriage, could raise conflict issues and,
if they did, it would be English conflict of laws, not the domestic law of
tort, which would be looked to for the answer.

Similar issues can arise in litigation which is undoubtedly conflictual.   **8-18**
Suppose the intestate succession is entirely governed by a foreign *lex
successionis* and the intestacy rules of that system identify the surviving
spouse as the main beneficiary. We can now import some of the issues
which were raised in the wrongful death example about who is a wife
and what that concept means, with the addition here that we have at least
three laws which might have an interest in answering the question and,
most importantly, might answer it in different ways.

---

36   S.3.
37   See above para 7-15.
38   Fatal Accidents Act 1976 s.1A (added by Administration of Justice Act 1982, s.3).

Suppose the problem is the initial validity of the marriage, a question quite clearly capable of a separate existence from the succession issue, and which could stand alone in, for example, a petition for nullity.

Clearly the starting point must be the *lex successionis*, for our conflict rules have allocated to that system the main issue - the identification of those entitled to succeed on intestacy. If the "wife" is clearly included in the succession whether or not her marriage to the deceased is valid, if for example the foreign law has expressly included long term cohabitees in its definition of surviving spouses, then the problem ceases to exist by definition. If, however, the intestacy rules of the *lex successionis* merely say "surviving spouse", we are left with a problem. Obviously, the *lex successionis* will have an answer to the question, or at least will have a means of providing one, but other systems have interests too.

The *lex fori* has an interest to the extent that if the same question arose on its own, or in a different context, a different solution to that provided by the *lex successionis* might be reached. This would be particularly significant where a different solution had already been reached e.g. a marriage legally identical to the one in question had been held to be void. Perhaps even the actual marriage in question had been declared void in nullity proceedings or found so in a different context.

The personal law of the "wife" has an interest too. She has a status under that law and her *lex domicilii*, may also have determined, directly or indirectly, the validity of the marriage.

Now although we may have a majority view on the matter, say English law would regard the marriage as void, the *lex successionis* and the personal law would regard it as valid, the majority vote method of conflict adjudication is neither sound in principle nor realistic in practice. To which legal system should an English court refer this question?

8-19   In those cases where the problem of the incidental question has been acknowledged, English courts have generally applied the *lex causae* of the main issue. So in *Padolecchia v. Padolecchia*[39] the main issue was the husband's petition for a decree of nullity on the ground of his own bigamy. While domiciled in Italy he had obtained a divorce from his first wife from a court in Mexico following which he had married his second wife, a Danish domiciliary, in Denmark. The incidental question, the validity of the Mexican divorce, was referred to Italian law - the law which governed the husband's marital capacity under the dual domicile test. In *R v. Brentwood Superintendent Registrar of Marriages Ex p. Arias*[40] a similar approach led to one of the rare applications in English conflict law of the doctrine of single *renvoi*. The main question was whether a

---

[39] [1968] P 314, [1967] 3 All ER 863.
[40] [1968] 2 QB 956, [1968] 3 All ER 279.

marriage should be allowed to take place in England. The proposed husband, an Italian national domiciled in Switzerland, had been divorced from his first wife by a Swiss court. The incidental question was the effect of this divorce. By English law the divorce was entitled to recognition but the question of the effect of the divorce was referred to the antenuptial domiciliary law and was referred in turn by that law to the husband's *lex patriae*. In contrast, in two other cases, one involving a foreign divorce[41] and the other a foreign nullity decree,[42] the incidental question of the validity of the decree was treated as if it were the sole question and was not referred to the *lex causae* of the main question, the law governing capacity to marry.

In *Schwebel v. Unger*[43] the Canadian court referred the incidental question – the validity of the *gett* – to the *lex causae* of the main question – the law governing capacity to marry, thereby accepting the recognition of the divorce by a subsequently acquired domiciliary law.

Under current English conflict rules the main issue, of capacity to marry, and the incidental question, of the validity of a prior divorce or annulment, have effectively been reversed. The recognition of the divorce or annulment enables the parties to marry irrespective of their personal laws' attitude to it.[44]   **8-20**

The *lex causae* of the main issue has been allowed to determine the incidental question in cases involving succession. In *Re Johnson*[45] the question of the deceased's legitimation was referred to Maltese law, the *lex successionis*. An Australian court in *Hague v. Hague*[46] applied the Italian *lex successionis* to the issue of a beneficiary's legitimation.

Dépeçage

Dépeçage, a French abbatoirial term for the process of chopping up or dismembering, (what English butchers would describe as jointing and, maintaining the perversity of language, perhaps accomplish by the use of a cleaver) suggests that separate parts of a conflict problem may be severed from the whole and referred to different systems of law.   **8-21**

The starting point, as with the incidental question, is what is seen as the problem as a whole. In some cases *dépeçage* simply recognises existing conflict practices e.g. if the whole issue is seen to be the validity of a   **8-22**

---

41 *Lawrence v. Lawrence* [1985] Fam 106, [1985] 1 All ER 506.
42 *Perrini v. Perrini* [1979] Fam 84, [1979] 2 All ER 323.
43 [1963] 42 DLR 2d 622. See above para 6-37.
44 Family Law Act 1986 s.50.
45 [1903] 1 Ch 821.
46 (1962) 108 CLR 230.

marriage then existing conflict rules would draw a distinction between formal validity, which is referable to the *lex loci celebrationis* and capacity or essential validity which is referred to the personal law. Similarly, testate succession may be referred to one law for the formal validity of the will, another for interpretation, while the essential validity of the dispositions is referable to the *lex domicilii* at death for movables and to the *lex situs* for immovables.

It can be seen from these examples that *dépeçage* is a real issue or an invented one depending on the way the question is posed. If we ask, not, "is this marriage valid?", but "is this marriage formally valid?" then there is no problem with *dépeçage* as we have converted the complex issue into a single one. But take, for example, a contract. We may accept that capacity and formal validity raise issues distinct from essential or material validity, but can different aspects of essential validity be hived off from the whole and referred to different systems of law? The Rome Convention supposes so.[47]

Dépeçage can be seen either as a variant of the incidental question or as a matter of classification. Suppose H injured W by careless driving in country X to which neither of them belong. Their common domicile is in country Y where there is a prohibition on interspousal suits. Suppose W sues H in the country of injury, X, which allows interspousal actions. Now, although the place of injury may be a perfectly reasonable place in which to litigate, it is likely in the present case that W is suing there in order to avoid the interspousal ban she would meet in the country of her, and her husband's, domicile.

What is a court of country X to do?. It could, if it was free to, refuse jurisdiction, on the basis that country Y is the *forum conveniens*, but this would be a harsh decision as the place of injury is not a contrived jurisdiction. If it classifies the ban on interspousal actions as tortious, then it chooses to apply its own rule rather than that of the domicile (assuming the *lex causae* of the tort action is the *lex loci delicti* and not, say, the *lex domicilii*), equally if it classifies the interspousal action ban as procedural it thereby rules out the possibility of applying any law other than its own.

It is possible, then, for the question "can W recover from H?" (actually his insurers) to be seen to be raising two questions:

i) Can W sue H? This first issue of interspousal immunity could be seen as a procedural matter for the *lex fori,* a status matter for the *lex domicilii*[48] or a tortious matter for the *lex causae* of the tort claim;

---

[47] Articles 3(1), 4(1).

[48] As it was in the case of *Haumschild v. Continental Casualty Co.* (1959) 7 Wis 2d 130.

ii)   Is H liable to W? Which involves two questions: is H guilty of
       the negligence or other default which caused the injury (clearly a
       tortious matter) and is he liable to her? Whatever reasons there
       may be for interspousal immunity it can hardly be justified on the
       basis that W has no right not to be injured by H. This would
       argue for the separation of the issue from tort and its reference to
       the law governing status.

As conflict rules become codified it may be expected that attention
will increasingly turn towards the separation of issues with the object of
taking severable issues outside the scope of the codified rules. It may be
expected that issues of *dépeçage* will become more common.

4 THE TIME FACTOR

Foreign law is a question of fact in English courts but, because it is   **8-23**
law it is not a constant. Other facts change, of course, and where they do
the issue is dealt with by stipulating the time when the fact is to be
determined. Some conflict rules are, similarly, time fixed e.g. the date of
the marriage, the time the contract was concluded, others are not. The
lex successionis for movable property is identified by reference to the *lex
domicilii* at the date of death, the *lex loci delicti* is fixed by the commission
of the tortious act; but that does not mean that the content of the legal
system so indicated should be regarded as chrystalised at that date.

Suppose an international contract - there must be an applicable law at
the time the contract is made, whether that law is chosen by the parties or
determined by reference to the rules of the Convention applicable in
default of choice; although the parties are free to change it later. Once
identified, the applicable law must be seen as a developing system and its
rules applied as they exist at the time of the dispute, not as they existed at
the time the contract was made.

The same applies to the law applicable to torts and trusts and it must
apply whenever reference is made to the *lex situs*, at least to the extent
that the *lex situs* would apply itself as a living body of law.

So, in short, if the connection with the *lex causae* is a single event -
the celebration of the marriage or the formal entry into the contract - it
would be expected that the *lex loci celebrationis* or the *lex loci contractus*, if
that is the governing law, would be applied as it stood at the operative
date,[49] and the same would apply to the parties' capacity to marry. The
applicable law of a contract or trust or the governing law of a tort should

---

[49]   But note the exception in the case of the formal validity of wills, above para 5-50.

be applied as a developing system. This must, of course, depend on the *lex causae*, for it would be simply officious to apply a rule of the *lex causae* which the courts of that system would not regard as applicable to a domestic case with the same operative contact because, for example, the legal changes were prospective only.

8-24   Some of the cases which have presented the time issue directly in the English courts have been cases of retrospective legislation in the *lex causae*. In some of them legislation specifically directed at the case in hand. So, in *Phillips v. Eyre*[50] the court recognised the Jamaican law which indemnified Governor Eyre from liability for the violation of civil rights in the quelling of a rebellion; in *Starkowski v. A-G*[51] retrospective Austrian legislation validating formally invalid marriages was recognised.

More conventionally, the invalidation of gold clauses,[52] the imposition of a moratorium on the payment of debts to exchange foreigners,[53] and the permission to repay a loan, originally due in gold, in devaluated paper money[54] – all changes brought about by the contracts' governing laws after the contracts had been made – were accepted by English courts.

Changes in the *lex causae* were not recognised in a couple of cases but both were exceptional and both concerned property in England. One[55] involved what was essentially the confiscation by a foreign state of property in England and public policy would have been a better basis for the refusal of recognition[56] than the insistence that the *lex successionis* was not only identified but chrystalised at the time of death. The other[57] involved not merely a change in the rules of the *lex causae* but of the legal system itself as Italian law replaced Austrian law in Padua.

5 FORUM SHOPPING

8-25   The possibility of forum shopping arises when a plaintiff has a cause of action which is justiciable in more than one country and has the ability to invoke more than one jurisdiction. Whenever this occurs he must make a decision about where to sue and that decision will depend on a number of considerations. Some of these can be described as practical, others as legal.

---

50   (1870) LR 6 QB 1. See above para 4-108.
51   [1954] AC 155.
52   *R. v. International Trustee for the Protection of Bondholders A/G* [1937] AC 500.
53   *Re Helbert Wagg* [1956] Ch 323.
54   *Re Chesterman's Trusts* [1923] Ch 466.
55   *Lynch v. Provisional Government of Paraguay* [1871] LR 2 P&D 268.
56   See e.g. *Banco de Vizcaya v. Don Alfonso de Borbon y Austria* [1935] 1 KB 140.
57   *Re Aganoor's Trusts* (1895) 64 LJ Ch 521; c/f *Nelson v. Bridport* (1845) 8 Beav 527.

Among the practical considerations are the availability of legal advice and representation, of evidence, of funds to fight the case and of assets against which judgment may be enforced, as well as more general matters of convenience, cost, and the time the whole business will take.

Legal considerations include the law which will be applied by the court, its procedural rules and its rules of evidence, its mechanisms of enforcement and any limitation periods it might apply. A particular consideration in some cases, especially personal injury litigation, will be the level of damage awards.

There can certainly be no objection to the plaintiff selecting the **8-26** forum which is most convenient to him in the conduct of his litigation unless his choice unwarrantably makes things more difficult for the defendant in the conduct of his case. Forum shopping becomes objectionable if the plaintiff's choice of forum has the effect of imposing financial burdens on the defendant which are out of all proportion to any possible benefit to the plaintiff, as where proceedings are taken in some distant location where the defendant will not be able to afford to fight. It is even more objectionable where the plaintiff gets the benefit of being able to found a cause of action which would not be available to him in a more obviously appropriate forum.

In *Machado v. Fontes*[58] action was successfully brought in England for a libel circulated wholly in Brazil, although no civil liability existed under Brazilian law. *Boys v. Chaplin*,[59] by contrast, though a case where the damages available in the place of injury were restricted, is a case where the plaintiff's choice of an English forum, rather than a Maltese one, was a reasonable exercise of choice as both parties were domiciled in England and, in the event, English law was applied, arguably as *lex causae*.

The divergence in the choice of law rules of different countries is not **8-27** the only, indeed it is not the major, reason for forum shopping. Substantial differences in the quantum of awards is a strong inducement to the plaintiff to seek an alternative forum. The levels of personal injury awards reflect the affluence or poverty of the society where they are made and they may also be influenced by other factors, like limiting legislation, the mechanism of assessment, or the way attorneys are paid. The retention of the jury in the U.S. has certainly been a major influence in escalating damage awards and has made suit in the U.S. an attractive possibility for those who can invoke state or federal jurisdiction.

In *Castanho v. Brown & Root (UK) Ltd.*[60] the plaintiff had begun proceedings in England, and had even obtained an interim award, when

---

[58] [1897] 2 QB 231. See above para 4-110.
[59] [1971] AC 356, [1969] 2 All ER 1085. See above para 4-113.
[60] [1981] 1 All ER 143.

the prospect of far more generous compensation in the U.S.A. was made known to him. He sought to discontinue his action in England and to pursue proceedings in the U.S.A.instead. The court gave leave for him to discontinue the English proceedings but in the Court of Appeal Denning M.R., dissenting, made his own views clear:

> "A Texas-style claim is big business. That is how the newspapers put it. The managers of the business are two attorneys of Houston, Texas. They keep a look-out for men injured on the North Sea oil rigs. The worse a man is injured the better for business. Especially when he has been rendered a quadriplegic and his employers have no answer to his claim. Their look-out man tells the Texan attorneys. They come across to   England. They see the injured man and say to him: "Do not bring your action in England or Scotland. You will only get £150,000 there. Let us bring it in Texas. We can get you £2,500,000 in Texas." If he agrees they get him to sign a power of attorney which provides for their reward. Under it the attorneys are to get 40% of any damages recovered. That is £1,200,000 for themselves. Big business indeed."[61]

The spectacle of the lawyers, from both sides, trying to sign up the wretched victims of the Bhopal chemical factory explosion in India was equally unedifying.

Victims of the Piper Alpha oil platform disaster in the North Sea settled for a compromise between the damages they might have obtained from a Scottish court and those which might have been obtained by suit in the U.S.A. - mid-Atlantic damages as they are known.

8-28   While some forms of forum shopping are generally deplored there is no easy solution to the problem of wildly discrepant damage awards. Quantification of damage is a matter for the *lex fori* and it would be difficult to imagine how the personal laws of the parties could be incorporated into the process.Suppose parties with different personal laws were injured to the same extent in the same accident. It would be highly objectionable to give the impression that one person's suffering was more worthy than another's even where the effect of equal treatment will result in substantial inequality back home. The English award may well be substantially less than a Californian might have received at home, while a Bangladeshi may become rich. The virtual impossibility of personalising non pecuniary losses makes this form of forum shopping in genuine international cases almost inevitable.

When forum shopping is seen as a bad thing how can it be controlled? There are a number of ways of tackling the problem and some of them can be considered briefly, here.

---

[61]   [1980] 3 All ER 72 at 76.

Domestic Jurisdiction Rules

English courts have an inherent power to control their own **8-29** proceedings and where proceedings are seen as oppressive, vexatious or an abuse of the courts process, they may be stayed. English courts are much readier than they used to be to exercise control by invoking the doctrine of *forum non-conveniens*.[62] This policy could certainly be used to prevent future cases like *Machado v. Fontes*. More generally, there may well be a case for the reconsideration of the flimsy connection of personal service in England which currently confers jurisdiction in common law actions.

Jurisdiction Conventions

The Brussels and Lugano Conventions,[63] by allocating jurisdiction **8-30** among the Contracting States, achieve two objectives in the control of forum shopping. By replacing the ordinary and "exorbitant" jurisdictional rules of national courts with a scheme of jurisdiction founded on more substantial connections, they seek to ensure a real nexus between the defendant or the dispute, or both, and the competent forums. By providing at least one available forum for each case they remove the best argument for the open forum – that a plaintiff has nowhere else to go. The territorial application of the Conventions is, however, limited and there is little prospect of wider agreement.

Applicable Law Conventions

Where the motive for forum shopping is the different choice of law **8-31** rules which available forums would apply, agreement on choice of law rules is an obvious deterrent. The uniform rules of the Rome Convention are the most prominent attempt to harmonise judgments among the Contracting States. It will be some time before the exercise can be evaluated, even in the central area of choice of law, as different interpretations of the Convention's rules and different exercises of the discretions which the rules embody are bound to occur. Moreover, the Convention deals only with choice of law, so the other practical and legal considerations will continue to apply wherever the plaintiff has a choice of forum.

---

[62] See above para 3-08.

[63] See above para 3-16.

6 INFLUENCES ON THE ENGLISH CONFLICT OF LAWS

8-32   In the Introductory chapter[64] I gave, as the reason for the existence of the conflict of laws, the simple statement that it would be wrong for the forum to apply its own law to every case involving foreign contacts as to do so would deny rights which individuals had under other legal systems or create rights which did not exist under the legal system connected with the issue. The basic principle of justice – that like cases be treated alike and different cases differently – was the only reason advanced for the conflict enterprise. This bare statement was not given because there has been a lack of theory in the conflict of laws but because the pragmatic approach of the common law needed no other. Once the principle, that cases with significant foreign contacts were special, was accepted by the common lawyers their response was to work out practical ways of dealing with them, but not in pursuit of any overall plan which would provide the key to conflict adjudication.

No Overall Philosophy

8-33   The conflict of laws is not engaged in, nor can it be used for, particular social, economic or political purposes, as choice of law rules cannot control the content of the particular foreign laws which the conflict process turns up. The forum can only restrict the application of foreign legal rules in individual cases in limited circumstances. This does not mean that jurisdictional rules, rules for the choice of law or the controls that the forum can exercise in individual cases cannot incorporate values, or that the exercise itself is value free. However, the identification of a controlling jurisdiction – the contract's applicable law, the *lex situs* of the property, the *lex domicilii* etc.– on the basis that its rules are the most proper to govern the matter, whatever the theoretical basis, leaves the content of those laws untouched; so that unless the ultimate dispositive rule can be manipulated, or ruled out by public policy, the forum is stuck with it.

Like procedural rules, which can also be value laden, the conflict of laws is equally indifferent to the actual outcome of a particular dispute. Two otherwise identical contractual disputes, two marriages suffering from the same alleged defect, can have different governing laws which produce opposite results by identical conflict processes. This is to say no more than that different legal systems approach the same problem in different ways; that the conflict of laws exists precisely because this is so, and that the proper reflection of these differences is all that a conflict system can aspire to achieve.

---

[64] See above para 1-04.

Particular Issues

The Dutch jurist Huber[65] set the agenda for many later debates by his recognition of the territorial power of a sovereign within his own country and the control he possessed over all those within the country, whether residents or visitors, with the concomitant limitation that a territorial power, however strong within, has no authority without. Yet the rights already vested by such an exercise of power in one State should, he argued, as far as possible, be respected in another, and the basis for that respect was comity.

8-34

Sovereignty

The authority of the sovereign State manifests itself in two ways - the territorial power of laws and the total, if local, powers of courts.

8-35

Outside of international agreements, laws are territorially limited; the laws of one national legal system have no operation in another. A foreign law which purports to apply to people in England will have no effect at all unless it is recognised and accepted here by the domestic legal authority. By the same token English laws are deemed not to have extra-territorial effect unless they say so, and, even if they do, it means no more than that courts and officials of the domestic system treat them so; it doesn't give them any actual effect in the foreign territory.

But sovereignty is not lost by the recognition of rights which have been vested under a foreign law and no civilised system of law could ignore the claim for their recognition.

Comity

The comity of nations involves one sovereign State respecting the acts of another, at least to the extent that the cost is minimal and that no interests of the recognising State are significantly infringed. The American jurist Story[66] was a strong advocate of this principle and it certainly provides for sovereign concession. It explains why a vested right can be upheld in a foreign court and also why the absence of a right can also be respected i.e. why an arrangement or transaction valid by the forum law is invalidated by the recognition of the foreign legal rule e.g. why a foreign marriage, say, which the parties want to be valid, may be declared not to be so by the application of a conflict rule of the forum which leads to the application of a foreign invalidating law. It can explain why English courts

8-36

---

[65] *De Conflictu Legum* (1689).
[66] *Conflict of Laws* (1883).

are increasingly prepared to decline jurisdiction or order a stay of proceedings *forum non conveniens*.

What it can't do is to explain why some foreign laws and not others are to be applied in a particular case. Suppose a case with genuine multi-state contacts where the forum has to choose, not between the application of the forum's own law or a foreign law, but between two foreign laws which are, on their own terms, equally applicable. Does the choice of one foreign State's law over another indicate more comitous relations with one State than another? Clearly not. Nor does the idea of comity apply to refuse recognition to the laws of a State which, the boot being on the other foot, would not recognise ours.

While comity can be used to underpin a decision, say, not to enforce a contract the performance of which would involve the breach of another country's criminal laws or interfere with its international policies, it cannot inform the choice of law process.

Vested Rights

8-37   While the theory of vested rights has some very distinguished academic and judicial supporters[67] and is immediately attractive, it is fatally flawed as a guide to the choice of law as it puts the cart before the horse. Where the case is wholly connected with a single legal system but merely happens to be litigated elsewhere, the recognition by the forum of the legal position arrived at by the foreign law gives full effect to vested rights and to the parties expectations. Where, however, the case is truly international, the search for vested rights can be the object of, but not the means to, the search for the applicable law.

Certainly an individual can *claim* that he has a right under a particular legal system but that does not solve the choice of law question. X can say, truthfully, that under Italian law, his *lex patriae*, he has a right to Y but unless the forum refers to the *lex patriae* on the issue in question, the claim is of no avail. So a claim to a status under the national law will cut no ice in an English court because the English conflict of laws refers status matters to the *lex domicilii*. Similarly both the defrauded owner and the innocent current holder of the goods can claim vested rights in them and support their claims by reference to valid laws, but they can't both be right. So while the vested rights idea provides a good reason for engaging in the conflicts process and stands as a valid argument against the application of the forum's domestic law, it does not provide any assistance in how the accommodation of foreign law is to be made.

---

[67] See Dicey: *Conflict of Laws* 5th ed. (1932); Beale: *Conflict of Laws* (1935); Holmes, and Cardozo among the American judiciary, see above para 7-05.

Modifications on the vested rights idea, based on the fulfilment of the parties' legitimate expectations, or on the local law of a particular set of relations, share many of its attractions and have, doubtless, been influential in individual decisions, but again, offer little help when expectations are in conflict or where the identity of the legal system which is at the centre of the relationship is in contention.

FURTHER READING

Texts

The leading authority on the English Conflict of Laws is:

Dicey & Morris: *The Conflict of Laws*
12th ed. (1993) Sweet & Maxwell

There are two other major texts:

Cheshire & North: *Private International Law*
12th ed. (1992) Butterworths

Morris: *The Conflict of Laws*
4th ed. (1993) Sweet & Maxwell

And two, fairly recent, Introductions:

Collier: *Conflict of Laws*
(1987) Cambridge

Jaffey: *Introduction to the Conflict of Laws*
(1988) Butterworths

And a casebook:

Morris & North: *Cases and Materials on Private International Law*
(1984) Butterworths

Among the texts on specific areas are:

Collins: *The Civil Jurisdiction and Judgments Act 1982*
(1983) Butterworths

Hartley: *Civil Jurisdiction and Judgments*
(1984) Sweet & Maxwell

Kaye: *Civil Jurisdiction and Enforcement of Foreign Judgments*
(1987) Dartmouth

Lasok & Stone: *Conflict of Laws in the European Community*
(1987) Professional Books

McClean: *Recognition of Foreign Judgments in the Commonwealth*
(1983) Butterworths

Some recent articles:

Berkovtis: *Transnational Divorces - The Fatima Decision*
(1988) 104 LQR 60

Briggs: *Which Foreign Judgments Should We Recognise Today?*
(1989) 36 ICLQ 240

Carter: *Choice of Law in Tort and Delict*
(1991)107 LQR 405

Carter: *The Role of Public Policy in English Private International Law*
(1993) 42 ICLQ 1

Carter: *Transnational Recognition and Enforcement of Foreign Public Laws*
[1989] CLJ 417

Carter; Domicile: *The Case for Radical Reform in the United Kingdom*
(1987) 36 ICLQ 713

Fawcett: *Evasion of Law and Mandatory Rules in Private International Law*
[1990] CLJ 44

Fentiman: *Domicile Revisited*
[1990] 50 CLJ 445

Fentiman: *Foreign Law in English Courts*
(1992) 108 LQR 143

Fentiman: *The Validity of Marriage and the Proper Law*
[1985] CLJ 256

Hall: *Common Law Marriages*
[1987] CLJ 106

Jaffey: *The Essential Validity of Marriage in the English Conflict of Laws*
(1978) 41 MLR 48

Marasinghe: *The Modern Law of Sovereign Immunity*
(1991) 54 MLR 664

Morse: *Consumer Contracts, Employment Contracts and the Rome Convention*
(1992) 41 ICLQ 1

Moshinsky: *The Assignment of Debts in the Conflict of Laws*
(1992) 108 LQR 591

Pilkington: *Transnational Divorces Under The Family Law Act 1986*
(1988) 37 ICLQ 131

Robertson: *Forum Non Conveniens in America and England; "A rather Fantastic Fiction"*
(1987) 103 LQR 398

Rogerson: *The Situs of Debts in the Conflict of Laws - Illogical, Unnecessary and Misleading*
[1990] CLJ 441

Slater: *Forum Non Conveniens: A View From The Shop Floor*
(1988) 104 LQR 554

Smith & Cromack: *International Employment Contracts: The Applicable Law*
(1993) 22 ILJ 1

INDEX